D0835436

SURPRISE ATTACK

Lightning Strikes of the World's Elite Forces

SURPRISE ATTACK

Lightning Strikes of the World's Elite Forces

PETER DARMAN

BLITZ EDITIONS

First published in Great Britain in 1993 by
Brown Books, 255-257 Liverpool Road, London N1 1LX

This Edition published in 1994 by:
Blitz Editions
an imprint of Bookmart Limited
Registered Number 2372865
Trading as Bookmart Limited
Desford Road
Enderby
Leicester LE9 5AD

ISBN 1-85605-228-1

Printed by Vincenzo Bona, Torino, Italy

Pages 2-3: *A US Navy SEAL. All SEALs are highly trained in clandestine operational techniques*

CONTENTS

INTRODUCTION

The arrival on the battlefield of the explosive shell, machine gun and the breech-loading rifle in the nineteenth century appeared to herald the end of elite units. World War I, with its trench warfare, seemed to confirm this. In fact, however, this conflict saw the reintroduction of elite units. The German Army found that small groups of highly trained men – stormtroopers – were very effective in the spearhead role; indeed, they held the key to breaking through enemy trench systems. Since then, such elites have grown in importance.

World War II witnessed an acceleration in the growth of specialist units, paradoxically aided by the advances in military technology: rapid-firing small arms, troop-carrying aircraft, submarines and light, fast vehicles. Indeed, some units, such as the German 7th Panzer Division, were elites because they were masters of the new technological tools of warfare, and all the major combatants employed airborne troops during the war – although in the United States and the Soviet Union there was initial distrust of the idea of elites.

In 1945, experts believed that the atomic bomb had placed technology totally in control of warfare, but in its shadow there developed many small-scale conflicts which assumed the nature of guerrilla warfare. Elite units were formed or re-formed by the West to fight them: for example the SAS was called back into being to fight in Malaya. Even the US Army came to recognise the importance of special forces, especially in Vietnam. Finally, elite forces the world over also adopted the roles of counter-terrorism and hostage-rescue to fight the growth in international terrorism. This book is a celebration of the most famous battles fought by the world's elite units since 1939, from the invasion of Poland to the 1991 Gulf War, bringing them to life with a stunning series of maps.

LEFT: *US Marines engage Japanese troops in the Pacific theatre during World War II.*

BELOW: *An American SEAL team member waits to ambush Viet Cong troops during the Vietnam War.*

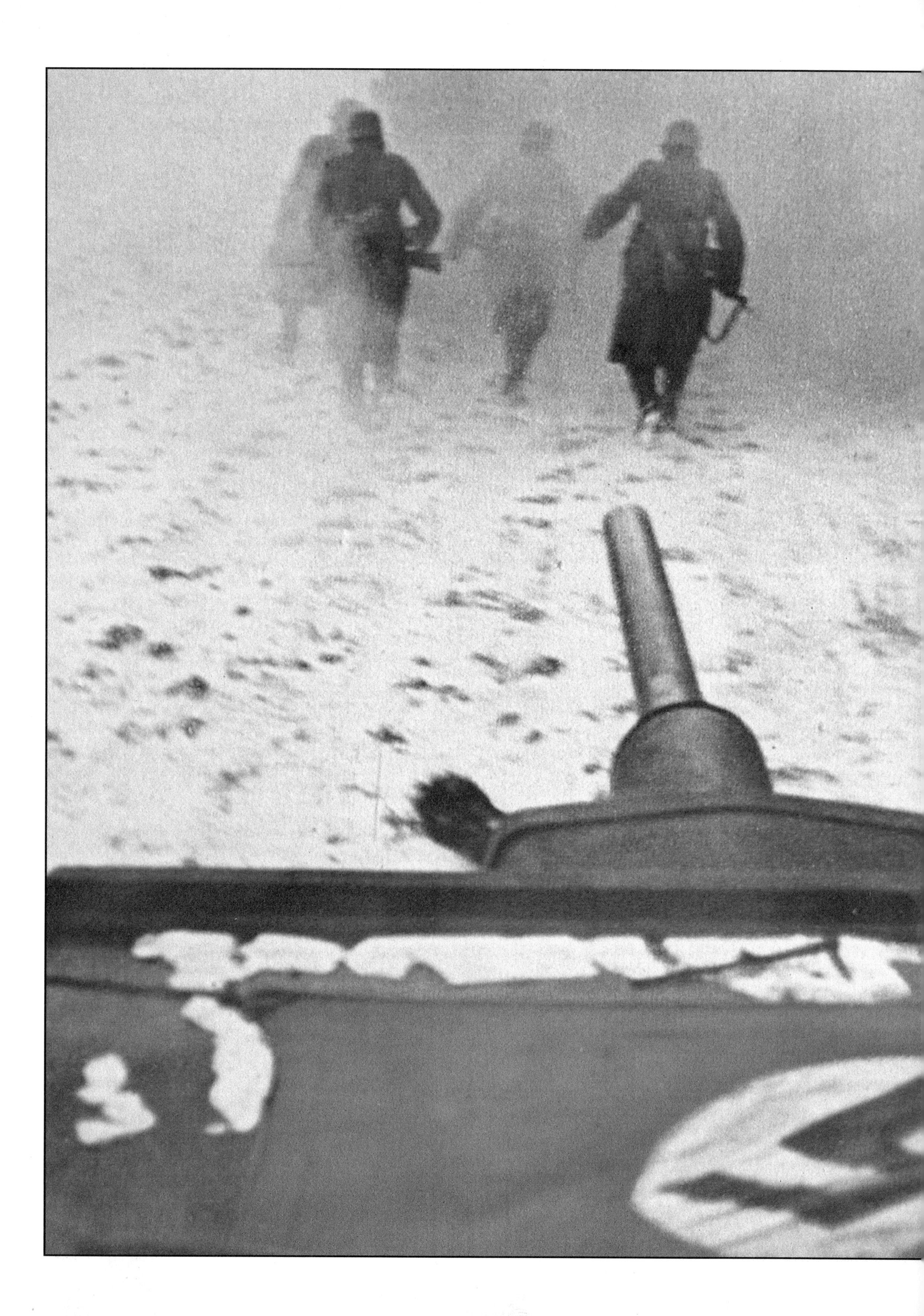

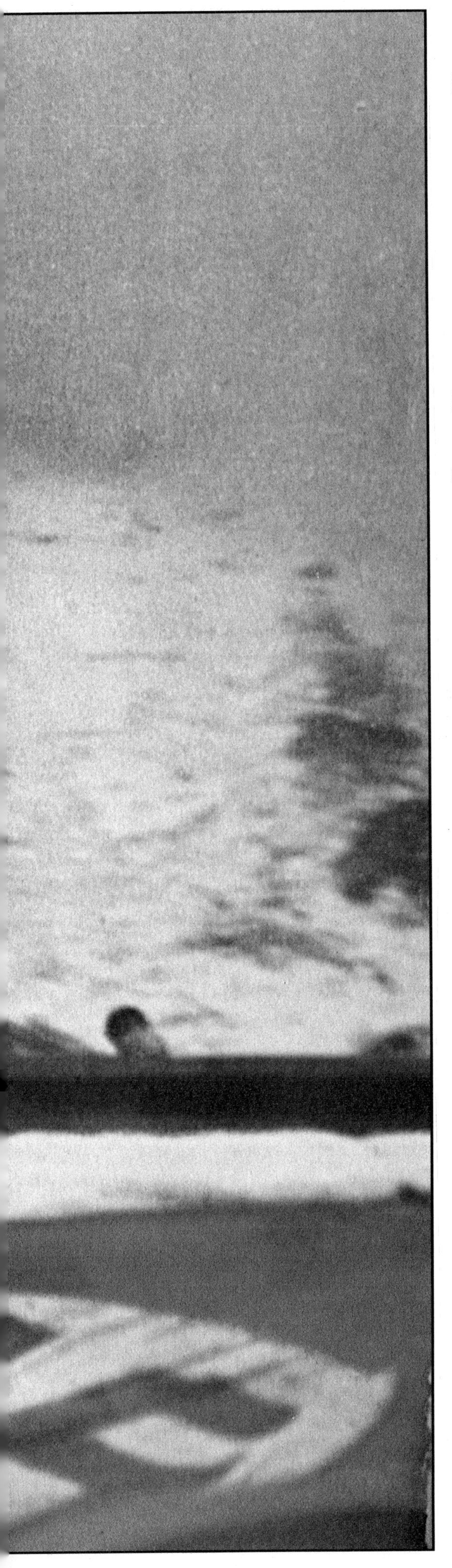

CHAPTER 1

WORLD WAR II

The conflict that engulfed the world between 1939 and 1945 was the most destructive war mankind had ever seen, involving as it did millions of people and many countries all over the globe. It was also a new kind of conflict. Though World War I had been cataclysmic, especially the horrors of trench warfare and the millions of casualties suffered by both sides in fruitless frontal assaults, the destruction was largely confined to the actual battlefields. World War II was different: the highly mobile armoured *Blitzkrieg* columns smashed their way through static defences and engulfed entire countries. Overhead, long-range bombers and ground-attack aircraft unleashed destruction on refugee columns and urban populations alike.

Yet, though the mechanics of war had changed, becoming total in every way and affecting every person who lived in the warring nations, on the battlefield certain things remained the same. Despite the advances in technology in such things as communications, aircraft, armoured vehicles, weaponry and so on, battles were invariably still decided by the courage, steadfastness and tenacity of individual units and soldiers; indeed, World War II witnessed a rapid expansion in the number of elite units as commanders came to appreciate the flexibility that these units provided. This was especially true of special forces operations. Units such as the German Brandenburgers, British Special Air Service and Royal Marine Commandos often depended on the courage of individual soldiers, rather than sophisticated equipment. But courage of the highest kind was not monopolised by elite units. Often, many 'ordinary' formations performed feats of heroism on the battlefield. The German 7th Panzer Division, for example, was dismissed by the German High Command as being rather second-rate, but it performed admirably during the 1940 invasion of France, not least because it was led by a superlative commander: Erwin Rommel.

Self-sacrifice was another quality that was displayed by many units during World War II. The most notable example is The Parachute Regiment at Arnhem in 1944, but there are others. The Soviet guards units at Stalingrad and Kursk, for example, displayed a doggedness that dumbfounded their German adversaries. Similarly, the men of the British Royal Horse Artillery displayed heroic self-sacrifice when they faced Rommel's *Afrika Korps* in November 1941, while the men of the Waffen SS often displayed courage and an irresistible fighting spirit against overwhelming odds.

The reader will find many American units featured in this chapter. This should not be surprising. US fighting formations fought with great distinction and courage in North Africa, in Europe and in the Far East. Indeed, American soldiers in World War II were involved in some of the most famous battles in history: the US Marines at Guadalcanal and Iwo Jima, the Rangers at D-Day and the 101st Airborne Division at Bastogne. This is not to detract from the other units described in this chapter. They are all examples of units and men rising above the ordinary to become elites.

German panzers and infantry on the Eastern Front. The Wehrmacht *and Waffen SS fought some of their most heroic actions in the Soviet Union.*

GERMANY

4TH PANZER DIVISION, POLAND, SEPTEMBER 1939

The German 4th Panzer Division, part of XVI Army Corps (Army Group South), was part of the encircling force which had been so successful in the attack on Poland in the first few days of September 1939. By 8 September, the division, led by Georg-Hans Reinhardt, was advancing towards Warsaw, confident that the Polish capital would be captured easily. However, the 4th would have to fight hard to achieve victory, and over the next few days, surrounded and assaulted by fanatical Polish formations, it would prove itself rock steady under fire and the epitome of German military professionalism.

On 9 September, the division received news that Polish forces were advancing towards Warsaw from the direction of Sochaczev. In fact, unknown to the 4th Panzer Division, it was the mighty Poznan Army, and the only thing between it and the Polish capital was the German unit. Undeterred, Reinhardt, one of the leading exponents of *Blitzkrieg*, deployed the 4th so it faced east and west. If he could withstand the attack, his unit could advance the end of the entire campaign. He then sent out calls to XVI Corps for help. The division needed it.

The German invasion of Poland was launched on 1 September 1939. Nine armoured divisions – including the 4th Panzer Division – swept through Poland in just eighteen days, putting the armoured vehicles, and the tactics that became 'blitzkrieg', to the test for the first time.

Polish counterattacks

The Poznan Army in the west swept aside the 7th Reconnaissance Battalion and crashed into a composite force made up of the SS regiment Leibstandarte Adolf Hitler (which had been sent by corps), the 2nd Battalion of the 103rd Artillery Regiment and what was left of the reconnaissance battalion. In the east the Warsaw garrison started to bombard the 4th Panzer Division. Reinhardt ordered his artillery to reply, and his guns started to fire both east and west at the enemy. He also launched an SS infantry attack on the western sector and a panzer assault to cut the Modlin-Warsaw road.

However, the Poles swiftly counter-attacked and forced the Germans onto the defensive. Polish infantry attacks crashed into the Germans throughout the 11th, the panzers being used as artillery support in an effort to repel the attacks. During the early hours of 12 September, the Poles launched an assault at Mokotov which forced the Germans back, and in the west the Poznan Army drove the SS from their positions, forcing Reinhardt to commit his last reserves. Battles raged throughout the day and into the night before the fighting waned, both sides utterly exhausted.

By the afternoon of the 14th, the 4th Panzer Division had regained contact with units to the south. Reinhardt therefore launched an attack to clear the western flank. The panzers raced north with SS men clinging to their sides. Corps HQ now ordered the division to gain the line of the Bzura and comb the woods that lay on the southern bank of the Vistula. Once they reached it the Germans prepared for the inevitable Polish counterattacks. They were not long in coming.

Wave after wave of cavalry and infantry smashed into the German line; but it held. Then Army Group South ordered a general advance and, on the 16th, Reinhardt led his tired command in an attack on Ruszki. Again the Poles launched a series of desperate attacks, trying to break through to Warsaw. These battles, which took place on the 18th and 19th, were ferocious, but they were the death throes of the Poznan Army. Its dead littered the banks of the Bzura, while the 4th Division, exhausted and shaken by the scale of its losses, continued the conquest of Poland.

Though the 4th had been hard pressed by the enemy, what it had done was to break the back of the Poznan Army and prevent it from reaching Warsaw, which had hastened the Polish defeat. Under the steady and competent leadership of Reinhardt, the 4th Panzer Division had proved itself to be an exceptional unit, repelling all enemy attacks and illustrating its mastery of *Blitzkrieg*-style warfare, particularly the interaction between artillery, tanks and infantry.

3RD MOUNTAIN DIVISION, NARVIK, JUNE 1940

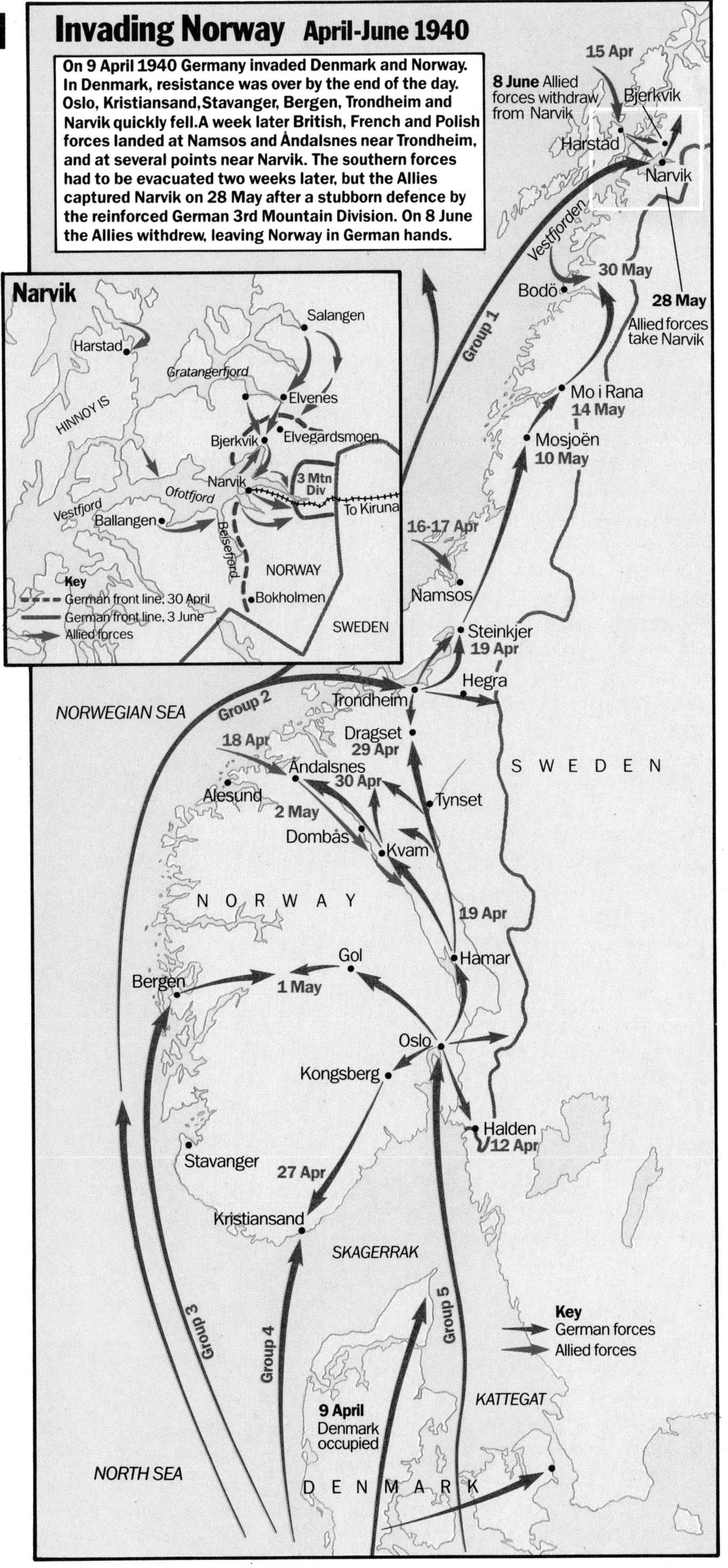

On the morning of 9 April 1940, German ships landed the 139th Mountain Infantry Regiment and the headquarters of the 3rd *Gebirgsjäger* (Mountain) Division at the Norwegian port of Narvik. It was the beginning of an operation that was to be a fine example of German initiative and daring, combined with Allied ineptitude. Resistance at Narvik was light, and soon the German leader, Major-General Eduard Dietl, had accepted his opponent's surrender.

Dietl was ordered to hold the port and secure the iron-ore railway to neutral Sweden. However, he was more concerned with consolidating his position, as his men were separated from other German forces and they had no heavy weapons. Dietl's position was extremely exposed: the Royal Navy blockaded the coast, the Allies could land troops and, because of bad weather, the *Luftwaffe* could not fly in supplies.

On 16 April, units of the 3rd Mountain Division attacked along the railway, dispersed the Norwegian troops and reached the Swedish border, which enabled the Germans to bring in supplies via Sweden.

By 14 April a large Allied force had landed off Narvik under Major-General Mackesy. On 24 April British ships shelled the town and Dietl prepared to withdraw eastwards. Until then, he would bluff it out, though he knew he was outnumbered. The Allies, overestimating German strength, were too cautious: it was only in mid-May that they began to advance.

Dietl had resolved to abandon the town and enter Sweden if he did not receive reinforcements. The condition of his men was appalling: they were running short of clothing and food. On 27 May the final Allied assault went in. Narvik was taken and by 1 June Dietl was being attacked from the north and south. He realised that troops advancing from the south would not reach him in time and so he planned the move into Sweden. However, the Allies had already begun to pull out of Narvik because their troops were in a desperate state, evacuating the port by 8 June. The surprised Germans retook it; Dietl's bluff had paid off.

7TH AIRBORNE DIVISION, EBEN EMAEL, 10 MAY 1940

In the early hours of 10 May 1940, 11 German DFS 230 gliders were being towed towards the Belgian border. They held the two officers and 83 men of Assault Section 'Granite', which was detailed to capture the supposedly impregnable fortress of Eben Emael. The latter protected the most important section of the Albert Canal and contained 64 concrete strongpoints housing a variety of artillery pieces such as cannon, anti-tank and anti-aircraft guns. The fort was also surrounded by minefields and stretches of barbed wire. Its garrison, believed by the Germans to number 1200 men, was commanded by Major Jottrand. The Belgians believed that the fortress was impregnable to all but the heaviest artillery bombardments and that any enemy wishing to take it would have to engage in a long siege. However, they had not reckoned on the men of the German 7th Airborne Division.

'Granite' was part of the larger Assault Group 'Koch', a group ordered to capture key bridges to aid the main invasion force. 'Granite's' men each carried a personal weapon and special explosives, the most important of which were hollow charges designed to blast open the fort's strongpoints. Because of difficulties with the towing aircraft only nine gliders landed on the Eben Emael plateau at 0520 hours, not including the one carrying the unit's commander, Rudolf Witzig.

The Germans storm the fort

The garrison, reduced to 700 men because of leave and dispersions, was initially surprised by the gliders and only directed sporadic fire at the attackers. In the first crucial 20 minutes the Germans, led by Oberfeldwebel Helmut Wenzel, started placing their charges and blowing open the fort's supposedly impregnable steel cupolas. Jottrand ordered Belgian artillery fire to be directed on the fortress in a last, desperate attempt to dislodge the attackers; but too late.

At 0830 hours a lone glider flew through the heavy flak and landed in one piece on Eben Emael. It contained Witzig, who ordered the remaining areas held by the enemy to be destroyed. Though the latter managed one infantry counterattack, by the afternoon Stukas had silenced most pockets of resistance. When nightfall came most of the Belgians had retreated into the fort's interior. Witzig, fearing a counterattack, concentrated his men and ordered the destruction of more strongpoints. However, it never came, and the next morning German infantry were entering the fort. Jottrand surrendered later that morning. Witzig had lost six killed and 20 wounded in an operation which was superbly planned and executed – it was probably the most daring airborne operation of World War II.

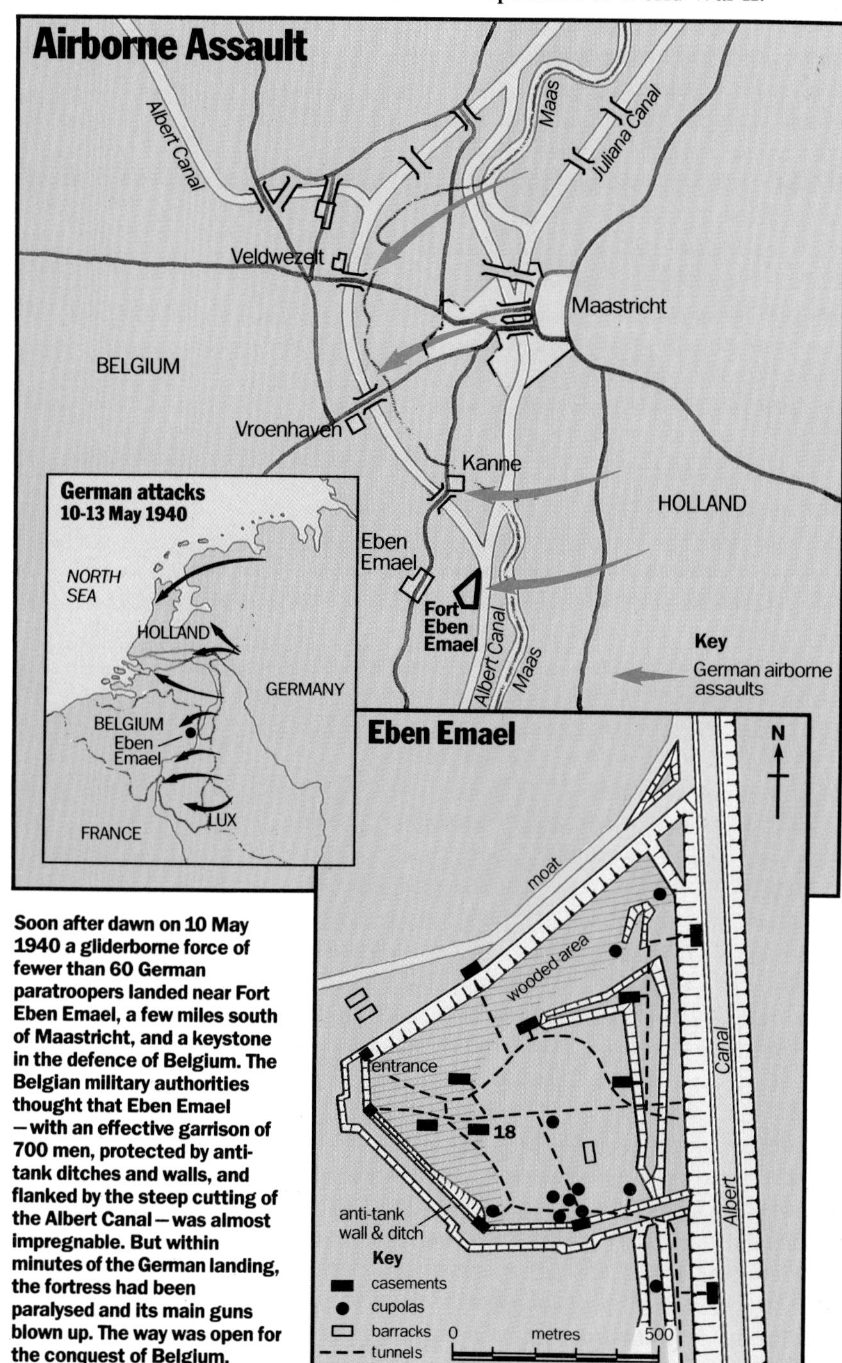

Soon after dawn on 10 May 1940 a gliderborne force of fewer than 60 German paratroopers landed near Fort Eben Emael, a few miles south of Maastricht, and a keystone in the defence of Belgium. The Belgian military authorities thought that Eben Emael – with an effective garrison of 700 men, protected by anti-tank ditches and walls, and flanked by the steep cutting of the Albert Canal – was almost impregnable. But within minutes of the German landing, the fortress had been paralysed and its main guns blown up. The way was open for the conquest of Belgium.

BRANDENBURG REGIMENT, FRANCE, MAY 1940

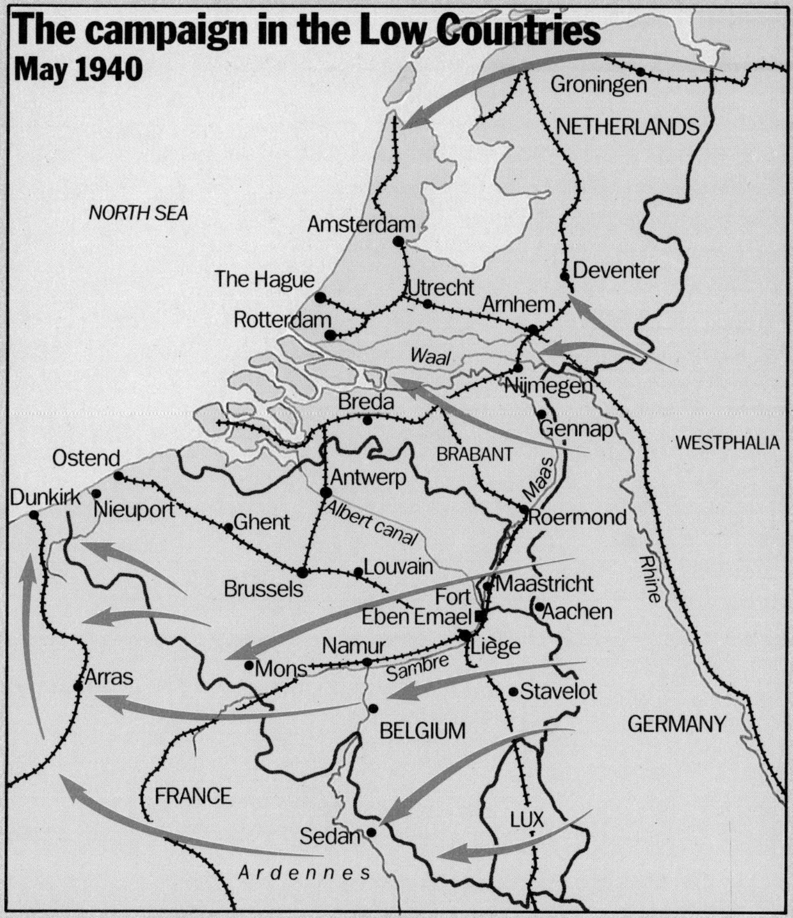

The *Abwehr*, the German intelligence and counter-intelligence organisation led by Admiral Wilhelm Canaris, had, by 1939, established a special forces unit under the command of Captain von Hippel. This formation, known as the Brandenburger Regiment, was composed of German volunteers who had lived abroad or came from those German communities around the country's borders (they were thus well versed in the languages and customs of other states).

The Brandenburg Regiment played a key part in the *Blitzkrieg* strategy: seizing vital rail junctions, crossroads, tunnels and bridges. Highly trained commandos would seize these locations and hold them until the armour arrived. Playing a vital part in the invasion of Poland in 1939, Canaris's men were thoroughly trained for their next campaign: the invasion of the Low Countries.

The campaign in the Low Countries
May 1940

Only hours before the German offensive in the Low Countries was due to begin, on the night of 9/10 May 1940, German special forces were deployed to secure the invasion routes by seizing bridges and holding them until the arrival of the main invading army. They took the key bridges at Stavelot, Roermond and Gennap; and as the German armoured divisions drove on to the North Sea the clandestine work of the 'Brandenburgers' continued.

The ruse is successful

The Netherlands presented a number of challenges to the commandos, due to the vast and crucial number of bridges over the Dutch rivers and canals. The German offensive began on 10 May 1940, but the Brandenburgers went in on the night of 9/10 May. Second Lieutenant Walther was ordered to seize the major railway bridge at Gennap, on the Meuse, in neutral Holland. The Brandenburgers put in motion a subtle plan: they would wear German uniforms but would act as prisoners, being escorted by Dutch Nazis dressed in the uniforms of the Royal Dutch gendarmerie. The prisoners would also be carrying concealed weapons.

Seven 'prisoners' and two 'guards' appeared on the bridge 10 minutes before the German attack. Walther gave a signal and the 'prisoners' attacked one of the two guardposts, knocking it out. However, the other post at the far end of the bridge remained in Dutch hands. In the firefight three Brandenburgers were wounded. The Dutch guards, seeing the men in their own uniforms advancing towards them, were undecided as to what action to take. Their indecision allowed Walther to lob a grenade into the second guardpost and take control of the detonator set up to blow the bridge. At this moment the first panzers raced onto the bridge and began to roll across.

Another successful Brandenburger mission prevented the opening of the sluice gates at Nieuport and thus the flooding of the Yser plain, which would have blocked the German advance, as it had in World War I. The important pump houses were situated on the south bank of the Yser River, next to the Ostend-Nieuport road bridge. On 27 May, the German Army was close to Ostend and Belgium was near to capitulation. The Brandenburgers had captured a Belgian Army bus and, wearing Belgian uniforms, Second Lieutenant Grabert drove his men into the morass of civilians and soldiers around Ostend and approached the bridge.

The south bank was held by British troops and the bridge had been mined with demolition charges. As the bus approached the bridge, the British opened fire. Grabert's men got off and took cover. When night came Grabert and an NCO crawled across the bridge and cut the wires to the demolition charges. Reaching the other side they opened fire, the signal for a general attack. The Brandenburgers raced across the bridge, raking the defenders with submachine gun-fire. Soon they had control of the pump houses and bridge. It had been another Brandenburger success.

GROSSDEUTSCHLAND REGIMENT, FRANCE, MAY 1940

In May 1940, the Grossdeutschland Regiment stood ready to take part in the campaign against France. The regiment had only been in existence since April 1939, and had missed out on the conquest of Poland because it was being organised and equipped. It was, therefore, untried in battle. However, the first two weeks in May would see the regiment transform itself from a raw unit into an elite, its men infused with the spirit of *Blitzkrieg* tactics which enabled them to win a key action at the Meuse.

The regiment was allotted specific tasks for the attack on France: the 3rd Battalion was given the job of destroying the frontier position at Bodange, near Martelange. Commanded by Major Eugen Garski, the 3rd Battalion was transported to the area in 100 Fieseler Fi 156 aircraft. Armed with only grenades and light weapons, the battalion attack went in at 0520 hours on 10 May, the aircraft crossing the Belgian border and landing without a shot being fired. Garski's grenadiers fought with some success throughout the day, but in the evening were hard pressed by a French tank attack. However, the Germans held off the armour with their grenades and small arms. At midday on 11 May, the grenadiers were relieved by tanks of the 1st Panzer Division. In the face of heavy pressure the 3rd Battalion had held its vital objective, an accomplishment which won Garski the Knight's Cross.

As the 3rd Battalion was fighting heroically at Bodange, the main elements of the Grossdeutschland were racing

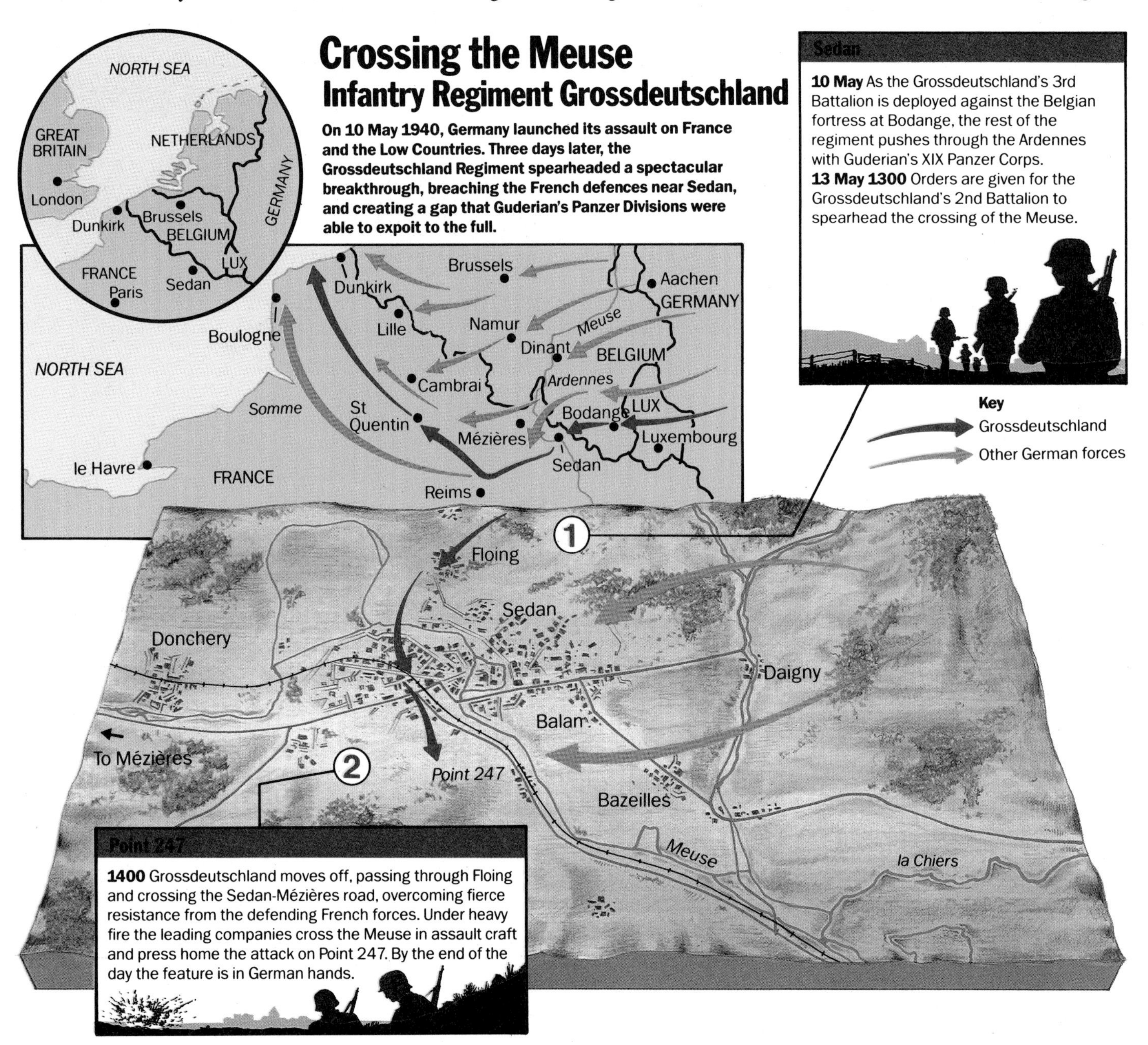

towards the River Meuse. They reached the river on 12 May, where they were joined by the 3rd Battalion. The regiment was part of Guderian's panzer divisions which were striving to break through the French line at Sedan by crossing the River Meuse. Though river crossings in wartime can be extremely risky, the Germans were aided by the fact that the French had placed second-rate units at Sedan. Their High Command was also distracted by the speed and extent of the German advance. Finally, the Luftwaffe had complete mastery of the skies, having destroyed most of the French Air Force on the ground, and was able to bomb the French defences.

Halting several kilometres from the river, the men of the Grossdeutschland rested as the engineers prepared the assault boats. The order to commence the crossing was given at 1300 hours, and the next two hours were spent reaching the river while Stukas pulverised the French positions. As they reached the river bank, the grenadiers came under fire from pillboxes on the opposite bank. The fire was so intense that 88mm guns had to be brought up to silence them. The men of the 2nd Battalion then rushed forward to the boats and began to cross. Several were hit by gunfire, their occupants being cut to pieces in the water. However, within a few minutes lead elements were on the west bank of the Meuse.

The drive to the Channel

The 2nd Battalion's objective was Point 247, located four kilometres from the river. Using small arms, the grenadiers pressed forward in the face of heavy French infantry and artillery fire, finally taking their objective. As the 2nd Battalion was seizing Point 247, the rest of the regiment had been holding off French armoured counterattacks.

The Grossdeutschland had played a small but important part in Guderian's plan, which resulted in a wedge being driven between the French Second and Ninth Armies and allowed the panzers to drive west towards the Channel. The Grossdeutschland was then ordered south to protect Guderian's exposed left flank, and for two days, aided by the 10th Panzer Division, engaged French forces in a vicious battle around Stonne. The French, desperate to re-establish contact between their armies, threw in wave after wave of infantry and armour, but the Grossdeutschland held the town until relieved by the 29th Division in mid-May. The regiment, after some rest and reorganisation, then took part in the drive to the Channel. Swinging south after Dunkirk, the Grossdeutschland Regiment entered Lyons on 19 June.

For a unit that had only been in existence for under a year, the Grossdeutschland had performed remarkably well. Its men had proved they had grasped the essentials of the *Blitzkrieg*, in particular the need for junior officers to seize the initiative in battle.

ABOVE: *German panzers in France, May 1940. The breakthrough of German armour at Sedan was greatly aided by the Grossdeutschland Regiment, which breached the defences of the River Meuse in the face of determined resistance.*

7TH PANZER DIVISION, FRANCE, MAY-JUNE 1940

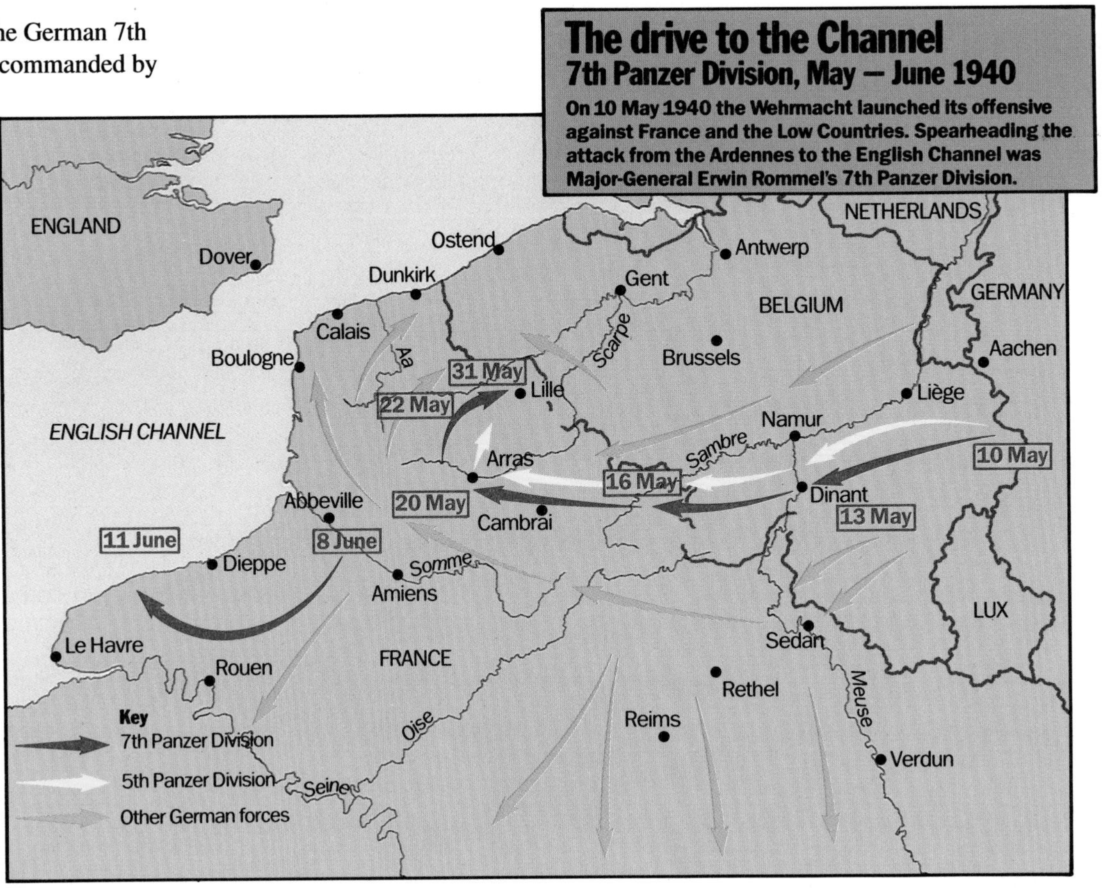

The campaign of the German 7th Panzer Division, commanded by Major-General Erwin Rommel, in France in May 1940 is an excellent example of how an ordinary line unit can win key actions if led dynamically. In Rommel the 7th had just such a commander. Though he had only been in command of the division for three months, he quickly trained it to a high level and imbued it with the essentials of panzer warfare.

The drive to the Channel
7th Panzer Division, May – June 1940
On 10 May 1940 the Wehrmacht launched its offensive against France and the Low Countries. Spearheading the attack from the Ardennes to the English Channel was Major-General Erwin Rommel's 7th Panzer Division.

The division began its campaign in the West at 0532 hours on 10 May 1940, storming across the Belgian frontier south of Liège. It was part of General Hoth's Panzer Corps, which had as its objective the seizure of the Meuse river crossings between Givet and Namur.

Rommel always led from the front, and his dynamic style of command had immediate effects. On 13 May, for example, his lead elements arrived at Dinant on the Meuse and came under heavy French artillery fire which prevented the river crossing. Rommel ordered a number of abandoned houses to be set alight to provide a smoke screen, allowing infantry to cross using rubber dinghies. He then took part in a tank battle during a French counterattack, and by 15 May had established the German bridgehead over the Meuse. The French Ninth Army began to fall back, quickly pursued by the 7th Panzer Division.

On 16 May Rommel was ordered to drive west towards Avesnes and punch a hole through French defences in that sector. He penetrated the enemy's field fortifications by ordering his tank crews to wave white flags from their tanks. This surprised the French so much that the Germans were through to the bunkers before a shot had been fired. The bunkers were destroyed by a combination of grenades and flame-throwers, and by the morning of 17 May the division had broken through Avesnes and reached Landrecies.

The British counterattack

Despite being exposed to French attacks, and with ammunition and supplies running low, Rommel pushed on, capturing Cambrai on 18 May. Two days later the division attacked south of Arras, though French tanks and infantry nearly turned back the advance before the Germans threw infantry and artillery against them and broke up the attack. On 21 May the division, supported by the SS Totenkopf Division, was on the move again, moving southwest of Arras. It then ran straight into a British counterattack which smashed the 6th Infantry Regiment and threatened the entire division. The Germans were particularly demoralised by the failure of their anti-tank shells to penetrate the armour of the Matilda tanks. Rommel, ordering concentrated fire, managed to stop the British attack – but it had been a close thing.

The 7th Panzer Division, after a two-day halt, reached the area west of Lille and had trapped half of the French First Army. With the arrival of some infantry reinforcements, the 7th was withdrawn for a few days' rest. It had been a spectacular campaign: Rommel's command had taken 6849 prisoners, captured 48 light tanks and knocked out 18 heavy and 295 light tanks. Though the division would take part in mopping-up operations in June, it was the exploits against the British and French in May that had marked it out as an elite formation, or at least one commanded by a great and imaginative leader.

7TH ARMOURED DIVISION, NORTH AFRICA, DECEMBER 1940-FEBRUARY 1941

Since early December 1940, the British 7th Armoured Division, as part of Lieutenant-General Sir Richard O'Connor's British Western Desert Force, had been fighting Marshal Rodolfo Graziani's Italian Tenth Army in an effort to dislodge it from the Egyptian border. The operation, codenamed 'Compass', was a success, and by early 1941 the Italians were retreating westwards. General Archibald Wavell then ordered O'Connor to mount a raid against Benghazi, the main town in Cyrenaica, which he hoped would trap the retreating Italians between O'Connor's units.

In late January 1941, O'Connor ordered the 6th Australian Division to take the town of Derna and the 7th Armoured to concentrate on Mechili. The latter division would then drive through the desert to intercept any Italian forces retreating along the coast road. The tanks required at least six days for repairs and re-supply before they could move; they were given two hours!

On 4 February, the 7th's advance guard, called 'Combeforce' after its commander, John Combe, began to move forward. It consisted of A and C Squadrons of the 11th Hussars and a troop of the King's Dragoon Guards (KDGs). Following this force were 50 A9/A10 cruiser and 40 Mark VIB light tanks of the 4th Armoured Brigade. Each vehicle carried two days' supply of water, petrol and as much ammunition as they could carry. A composite force of field and anti-tank guns followed them

As the British vehicles picked their way through the terrain, the armoured cars began to get too far ahead. It was decided to support them and so the artillery and The Rifle Brigade were sent forward. The 11th Hussars were pushing hard. They cleared an Italian garrison from Msus on the afternoon of the first day and then headed towards Antelat. On the morning of 5 February, the tanks arrived at Msus, thus allowing the KDGs and infantry (which had arrived before them but after the 11th Hussars) to push on to Antelat. Their orders were to block the Benghazi road, and by 1400 hours a company of The Rifle Brigade, the 11th Hussars and several guns were in position to await the Italian attack.

The leading elements of the Italian Tenth Army came into view within half an hour of the British taking up their positions. By 1700 hours so many Italian troops had arrived that their front covered the area from the foothills to the coast. The armoured cars of the 11th Hussars attacked the column and were then joined by light tanks of the 7th Hussars. These, together with more tanks of the 2nd Royal Tank Regiment which had also just arrived, caused such panic that the Italians started to surrender in droves.

That night the men of the 7th Armoured waited anxiously for the morning. Though they had halted the enemy, they knew they were heavily outnumbered. The Italian commander, General Bergonzoli, was determined to smash through the British cordon.

On the morning of 6 February, those tanks of the 4th Armoured Brigade that had survived the journey from Msus arrived, but even so the British had difficulty in stemming the Italian attack. The next day the Italians resumed the action, but The Rifle Brigade and the artillery managed to destroy most of the Italian tanks, which demoralised the rest of the army. Soon thousands of Italians had surrendered, signalling the end of the Italian Tenth Army. It was a remarkable achievement for a British division whose tanks and trucks were falling apart.

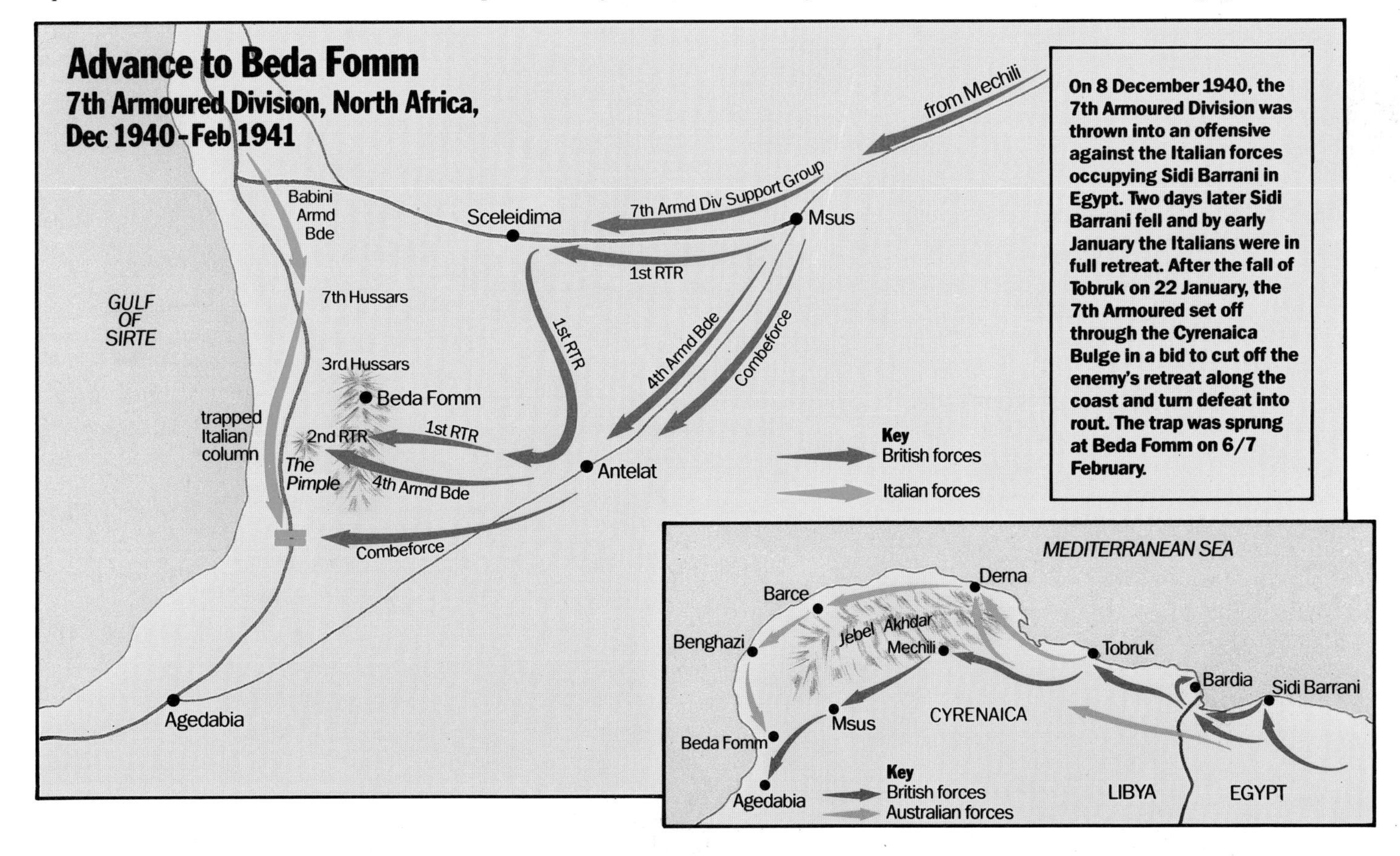

On 8 December 1940, the 7th Armoured Division was thrown into an offensive against the Italian forces occupying Sidi Barrani in Egypt. Two days later Sidi Barrani fell and by early January the Italians were in full retreat. After the fall of Tobruk on 22 January, the 7th Armoured set off through the Cyrenaica Bulge in a bid to cut off the enemy's retreat along the coast and turn defeat into rout. The trap was sprung at Beda Fomm on 6/7 February.

2ND SS PANZER DIVISION DAS REICH, YUGOSLAVIA, APRIL 1941

In April 1941, the men of 2nd SS Panzer Division Das Reich, commanded by SS Obergruppenführer Paul Hausser, were stationed on the border of Romania, ready to invade Yugoslavia. They formed part of General Georg-Hans Reinhardt's XLI Army Corps, and eagerly awaited the order to attack Yugoslavia. However, their zeal for the coming fight was not just ideological fervour; it was also to do with rivalry with the Grossdeutschland Regiment which was also part of XLI Corps. Indeed, Hausser had issued orders that the Das Reich Division must be the first German unit to enter Belgrade, ahead of the rest of the army and the Grossdeutschland in particular. The latter accepted the challenge and the race to Belgrade was on.

An armed forces coup in the Slav state in March 1941 had removed the weak Prince Paul from power. In place of the agreement the latter had signed admitting Yugoslavia into the Axis, the new leaders in Belgrade had offered Germany a non-aggression treaty. Denied permission to base his troops on Yugoslav soil, Hitler had flown into a rage and ordered the planning of the invasion of Yugoslavia. The conquest was organised in record time – the conquest of Russia, planned for the summer, could not wait – and by 10 April the units involved were at or near their marshalling areas. For the 2nd SS Division the route to Belgrade was far from easy, passing as it did through marshes and roads that had been turned into quagmires by heavy rain and sleet. Because of the conditions, the division would have to go into battle without most of its heavy artillery.

The race to Belgrade begins

The division began the attack at 0905 hours on 11 April. The SS men took many local objectives but were forced to abandon dozens of vehicles in the mud. Always in their minds was the desire to beat their rivals in the Grossdeutschland to Belgrade. General Reinhardt told General-leutnant Walter Hoerlein, commander of the Grossdeutschland, 'SS Division Reich is battling on foot under even greater, more unimaginable difficulties...in places through flooded "paddy fields". The gunners go barefoot since their boots get stuck in the mud.' However, Das Reich did have one stroke of luck. Aerial reconnaissance had discovered a bridge intact over a canal which was subsequently taken by an SS motorcycle battalion. As a result, it was Das Reich soldiers, and not those from Grossdeutschland, who first entered the pivotal town of Alibunar.

Brushing aside light resistance in the town, a motorcycle reconnaissance battalion, led by Hauptsturmführer Fritz Klingenberg, was instructed to push on to

BELOW: *Two SS soldiers cover the advance of their comrades during the German invasion of Yugoslavia. As usual, the SS fought with great courage.*

SS-Division Reich

The Race to Belgrade April 1941

In the months immediately following the outbreak of World War II, the Balkan region of Europe remained at peace. The countries in the area had been intimidated by the German occupation of Czechoslovakia, and by the signing of the German-Soviet pact in 1939. However, when Greece repelled an Italian invasion in 1940, the situation began to change. On 27 March 1941 a coup d'état overthrew the Yugoslav government, bringing into power a regime less sympathetic to the Germans. Adolf Hitler, alarmed by the appearance of a Greek-Yugoslav bloc, planned an immediate invasion. The assault included the men of SS-Division 'Reich', who moved up to the Yugoslav border from their positions around the town of Denta in Romania. As part of the XLI Corps, the division was given the objective of capturing Belgrade, the Yugoslav capital.

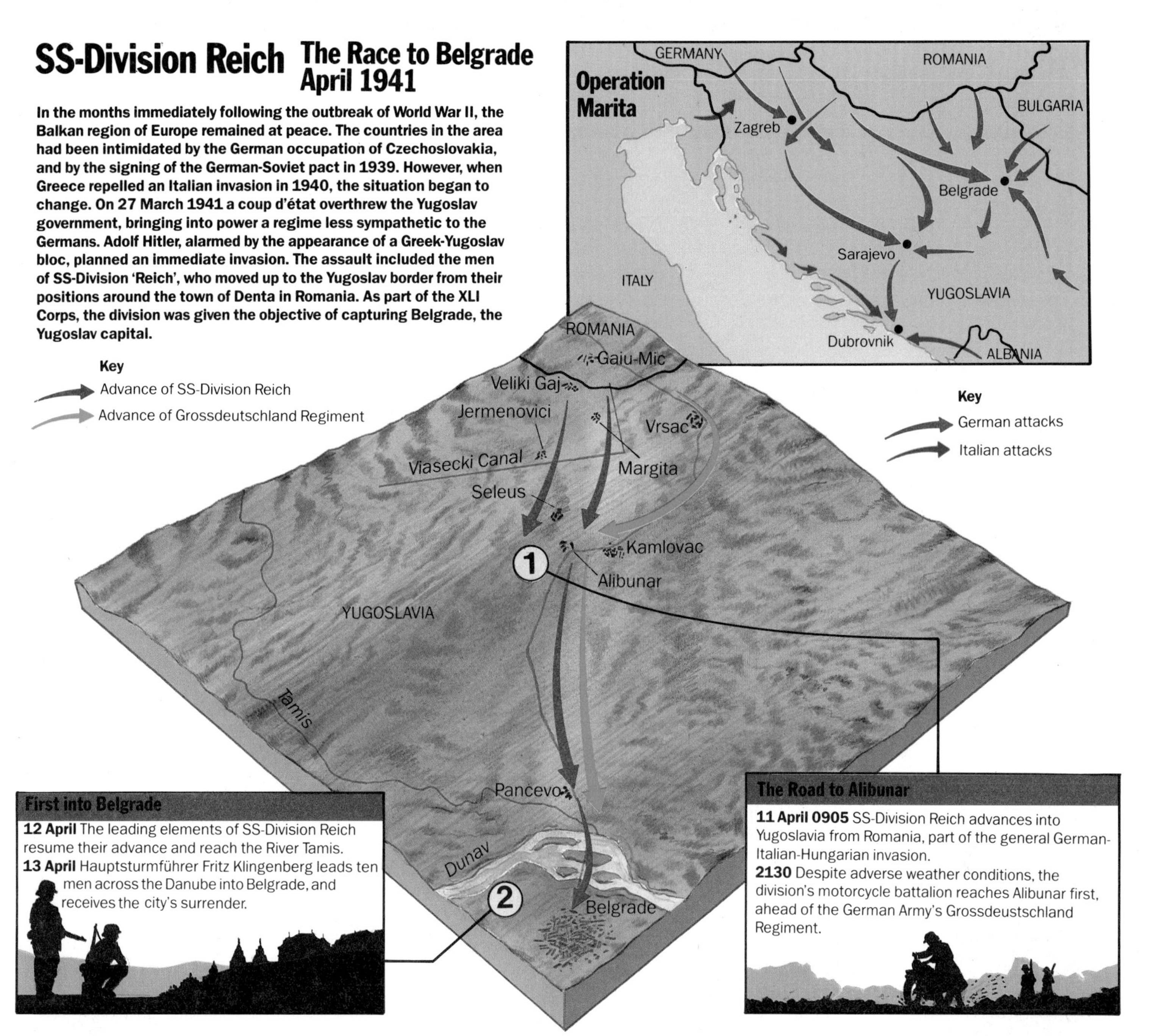

Pancevo, 20km south. Though they reached the town, Hausser, seeing the exhausted state of his men, ordered them to secure local objectives and prepare for further action the next day. However, the high command believed that the Das Reich could make little headway under such conditions and had given priority to the Grossdeutschland. Despite this, the SS pushed on, and on the morning of 12 April were ready to move again, aware that during the night the Grossdeutschland had overtaken the main SS force and made contact with Klingenberg's men.

General Reinhardt then ordered both SS and Army units to halt until trailing elements of both formations could catch up. However, Klingenberg had already surveyed the south bank of the River Danube and the approaches to Belgrade and discovered they were only lightly guarded. Finding a broken-down motor boat, he took 10 men, crossed the river and entered the city.

As the SS soldiers wandered around the near-deserted streets, they came across an elderly German gentleman who informed them of the German Mission being attacked by a large crowd. Arriving at the building, Klingenberg summoned the Mayor of Belgrade and demanded he surrender his charge or face a massive Stuka attack. Not knowing it was a bluff, the mayor surrendered and the city of Belgrade fell to Klingenberg at 1845 hours on 12 April 1941.

A message did not reach Hausser's HQ until 0600 hours on 13 April, though when it did the recipients were stunned. It read: 'SS Hauptsturmführer Klingenberg occupied Belgrade at 1645 on 12 April with 10 men. The appearance of the battle group caused the Mayor...to hand over the city.' Despite the easier route to the city enjoyed by the Grossdeutschland Regiment, Das Reich had been the first unit to enter the city, thus winning the race to Belgrade.

9TH AUSTRALIAN DIVISION, TOBRUK, APRIL-MAY 1941

In early April 1941 the 9th Australian Division was an untried and relatively unknown unit. However, its heroic and stubborn defence of Tobruk earmarked it as an elite unit.

In that month Rommel's *Afrika Korps* attacked British positions near Beda Fomm, North Africa, and threw them back towards Egypt in some confusion, capturing their commander, Lieutenant-General Sir Richard O'Connor, in the process. The British knew that if the Germans were to be stopped, the port of Tobruk must be held. They therefore despatched the 20th, 24th and 26th Brigades of the 9th Australian Division, commanded by Major-General Leslie Morshead, and the 18th Brigade of the 7th Australian Division, some 15,000 soldiers in total, to Tobruk to hold it against the *Afrika Korps*.

The port's defences were strong: it was surrounded on three sides by an outer anti-tank ditch supported by a line of barbed wire and trenches; an inner line of platoon strongpoints; a minefield between the two lines, and, nearer the town, artillery positions and self-contained forts.

The German attack started early, Rommel ordering General Heinrich von Prittwitz und Gaffron to lead his 8th and 605th Battalions against the Australians. At 0900 hours on 10 April, German units hit the port's western perimeter. However, the Australians, nicknamed the Diggers, held off the enemy with artillery and infantry fire, and the Germans broke off the attack at 1030 hours, von Prittwitz having been killed by an anti-tank shell.

The Italians and *Afrika Korps*, undeterred, probed the Australian defences, which had been strengthened with 200 guns – the 'bush artillery' – cannibalised from captured Italian artillery pieces, for weak points. From the west came the Italian 'Brescia' Division, from the southeast the armoured units of the German 5th light Division. The Diggers beat off the attack with artillery and infantry fire, forcing the enemy to retreat.

Two days later the Germans were back, the 8th Battalion under Oberst Ponath going in just west of the El Adem road. Supported by assault engineers, artillery and aircraft, the Germans crossed the anti-tank ditch but were then halted by the Diggers' ferocious defensive fire. On 14 April, supplemented by armoured units of the 5th Light Division and the Italian armoured division 'Ariete', Ponath began to make steady gains, only to be flung back when the Australians threw in their reserves. After heavy fighting and Italian losses, Ariete fled towards Derna and Mechili, and the 8th Battalion would have been surrounded and destroyed by the Australians had not Rommel sent some relief.

Undeterred, Rommel launched two Italian divisions, Trento and Ariete, against the

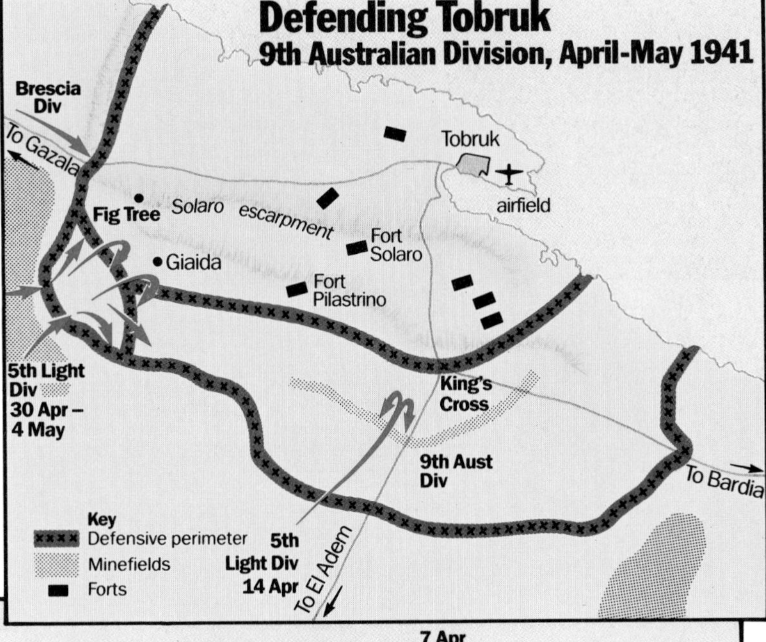

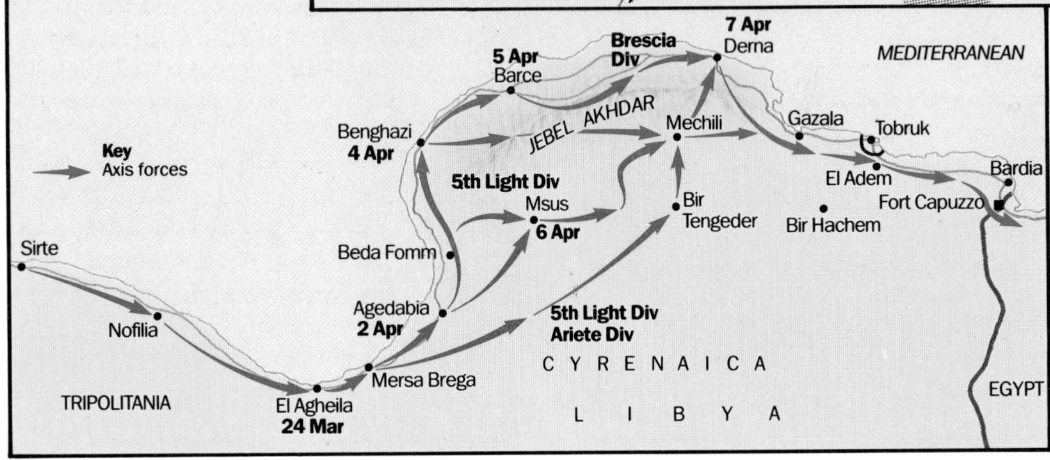

In the winter of 1940-1941, the British forces in North Africa advanced deep into Italian-held Libya, reaching El Agheila by early February. On 24 March, the newly arrived Afrika Korps under General Erwin Rommel launched its first offensive and by 2 April the British were in full retreat. The 9th Australian Division fell back on Tobruk. Leading elements of the German 5th Light Division reached Tobruk by 11 April and a full-scale attack began three days later. The Australians held on steadfastly, and the siege of Tobruk, which was to last for more than a year, was under way.

ABOVE: *Digger 'bush artillery' opens up against Axis positions during the siege of Tobruk. The Australians employed aggressive tactics in their defence of the port, and it was often the besiegers who were forced onto the defensive.*

defences on the 16th and 17th. However, their efforts proved abortive: 90 out of Ariete's 100 M-13 and L-3 tankettes were lost and many Italian soldiers gave themselves up to the Australians. The next Axis attack came on the 24th and was directed against Fort Pilastrino. The *Afrika Korps* managed to penetrate the line but was then hurled back by Australian counterattacks. The battle for the Ras el Madauer salient was bitter and savage, with each side launching attacks, suffering casualties and engaging in vicious hand-to-hand fighting. The result was stalemate.

The Diggers strike back

The conditions in Tobruk were grim: heat, flies and the constant bombardment. To keep up the Diggers' sagging morale, Morshead implemented a programme of hard work, hard fighting and recreation. Though Rommel had deployed three Italian divisions – 'Brescia', 'Bologna' and 'Pavia' – plus German units that included the 115th Regiment and the 361st 'Afrika' Regiment to grind down the defences, it was often Axis forces that were forced onto the defensive due to the Australians' aggressive tactics. German and Italian artillery was a favourite target because of the bombardment, and the Australians proved to be particularly adept at sniping, which made life thoroughly miserable for the besiegers. In addition, the Diggers launched a series of trench raids that demoralised the enemy. Casualties on both sides were heaviest in the Ras el Madauer salient.

The siege continued throughout May to October 1941, the Diggers remaining steadfast. However, the Australian government was pressing hard for the British to form all the divisions into an Australian corps. London agreed and began pulling out the Diggers and replacing them with British troops. The Australians were transported to Egypt, where they were welcomed as 'The Rats of Tobruk'. Though the defence of the port was perhaps the finest achievement of the 9th Division, the Australians went on to perform brilliantly at the Battle of El Alamein and then in the Pacific theatre against the Japanese.

GERMANY

7TH AIRBORNE DIVISION, CRETE, MAY 1941

The capture of Crete by German paratroopers in May 1941 is an excellent example of the fighting qualities displayed by small groups of lightly equipped airborne soldiers when up against heavily armed, well-entrenched opposition. The assault on Crete was the brainchild of General Student, who had convinced an unenthusiastic Hitler that an aerial attack on Crete could succeed. Student's plan, codenamed 'Mercury', entailed using his XI Air Corps, consisting of the 7th Air Division with nine battalions; the Parachute Assault Regiment of four battalions; and Lieutenant-General Ringel's 5th Mountain Division (it was felt mountain troops would be useful because they were trained to fight with light equipment and in rugged terrain). To lift this force Student had at his disposal 500 Junkers 52 transport aircraft and 80 DFS 230 gliders. In support were a considerable number of *Luftwaffe* fighters and bombers.

The initial assault

The operational plan was to conduct an initial assault with the 8000 paras of the 7th Air Division and the Parachute Assault Regiment in two air lifts (Lift Two to take place eight hours after Lift One), because there were insufficient transport aircraft. Lift One would consist of a Western Group made up of the Parachute Assault Regiment whose objective was Maleme airfield. The Centre Group consisted of the 3rd Parachute Regiment, divisional anti-aircraft and engineer battalions, and two companies from the Parachute Assault Regiment. Its objectives were the areas around Canea and Suda Bay. Lift Two consisted of the remaining element of the Centre Group, two battalions of the 2nd Parachute Regiment which would land at Retimo, and the Eastern Group. The latter consisted of the 1st Parachute Regiment and one additional battalion. It was tasked with capturing Heraklion airfield to allow the 5th Mountain Division to land.

The attack on Crete began at 0700 hours on 20 May 1941, when German paras and gliders began to land on the island. However, their intelligence had underestimated the strength of Allied troops on the island, and the paras jumped straight into a blood bath. At Maleme, men of the 1st Parachute Battalion landed by glider and headed inland towards the important objective Hill 107. The area was defended by New Zealanders and the paras suffered 50 per cent casualties. The 3rd Parachute Battalion of the Assault Regiment, dropped east of Maleme, also ran into the New Zealanders and suffered heavy casualties. To the west and south of the airfield, the 2nd and 4th Parachute Battalions of the Assault Regiment dropped without much opposition.

Farther to the west, at Canea, the paras also met heavy resistance from the Welch Regiment and the Northumberland Hussars. The 2nd and 3rd Parachute Battalions dropped around the village of Galatas but were unable to act as cohesive military units because of the New Zealand presence. By mid-morning on 20 May, Lift One had met unexpectedly heavy resistance and had suffered accordingly. The garrison of Crete – 27,500 British and Dominion, and 14,000 Greek troops under Major-General Bernard Freyberg – was still very much a force to be reckoned with.

The paras run into difficulties

Lift Two got under way and immediately ran into severe problems: the paras dropped at Heraklion were shot by soldiers of the Black Watch as they descended to the ground, and any survivors were then gunned down on the ground. The 2nd Battalion of the 1st Parachute Regiment suffered over 400 casualties alone. Though the 3rd Battalion of the 1st Paras and the 2nd Battalion of the 2nd Regiment met less opposition, they too were involved in heavy fighting when they hit the ground. The Germans still could not secure Heraklion airfield. The 2nd Parachute Regiment dropped around Retimo and fought Greek and Australian troops in a series of savage battles.

By early evening Student in Athens realised things were going wrong, but what he didn't know was that the Allied commanders were taking decisions that would assure a German victory. Because he lacked proper communications, Freyberg did not control the battle from his HQ. Initiative therefore rested with local commanders. During the night few counterattacks were made, and at Maleme Allied troops withdrew. In the morning the paras were able to push towards Canea, and by early evening the 5th Mountain Division was being flown into Maleme and began deploying to the east. They began to 'roll up' the Allied positions, so much so that by 24 May Freyberg had given up all hope of holding Crete, giving the order to evacuate three days later.

Victory - but at a price

The Germans had suffered 4000 men killed and 2400 wounded, as well as losing 170 JU 52s and 40 combat aircraft. Casualties were particularly heavy among the men of Lift One, with many senior officers being killed or wounded. Hitler was disturbed by the losses, so much so that he decided the paras would never be used in a large airborne operation again.

The paras had performed magnificently, the men having to fight in blazing weather wearing heavy uniforms (due to a logistical failure the paras were wearing clothing designed for them to use in the Norwegian campaign of 1940), and often without heavy weapons as these were lost in the special containers. In the final analysis, the operation on Crete proves that daring alone cannot guarantee the success of an airborne assault (as Arnhem was to prove later); indeed, without the overwhelming superiority of the Luftwaffe, plus the enemy providing him with an opportunity to reinforce Maleme, Student's men would have probably been defeated.

Assault on Crete
German XI Air Corps, May 1941

After the German conquest of Greece, Crete was the next target. The British had naval control of the area, but air cover was weak and the Germans decided on a massive airborne assault. The invasion began soon after dawn on 20 May with landings at Maleme, Galatas, Retimo and Heraklion. Heavy resistance was encountered at first but by next day the airfield at Maleme was captured. Within ten days the Allied forces were confined to a bridgehead around Sfakia, and on 31 May the conquest of Crete was complete.

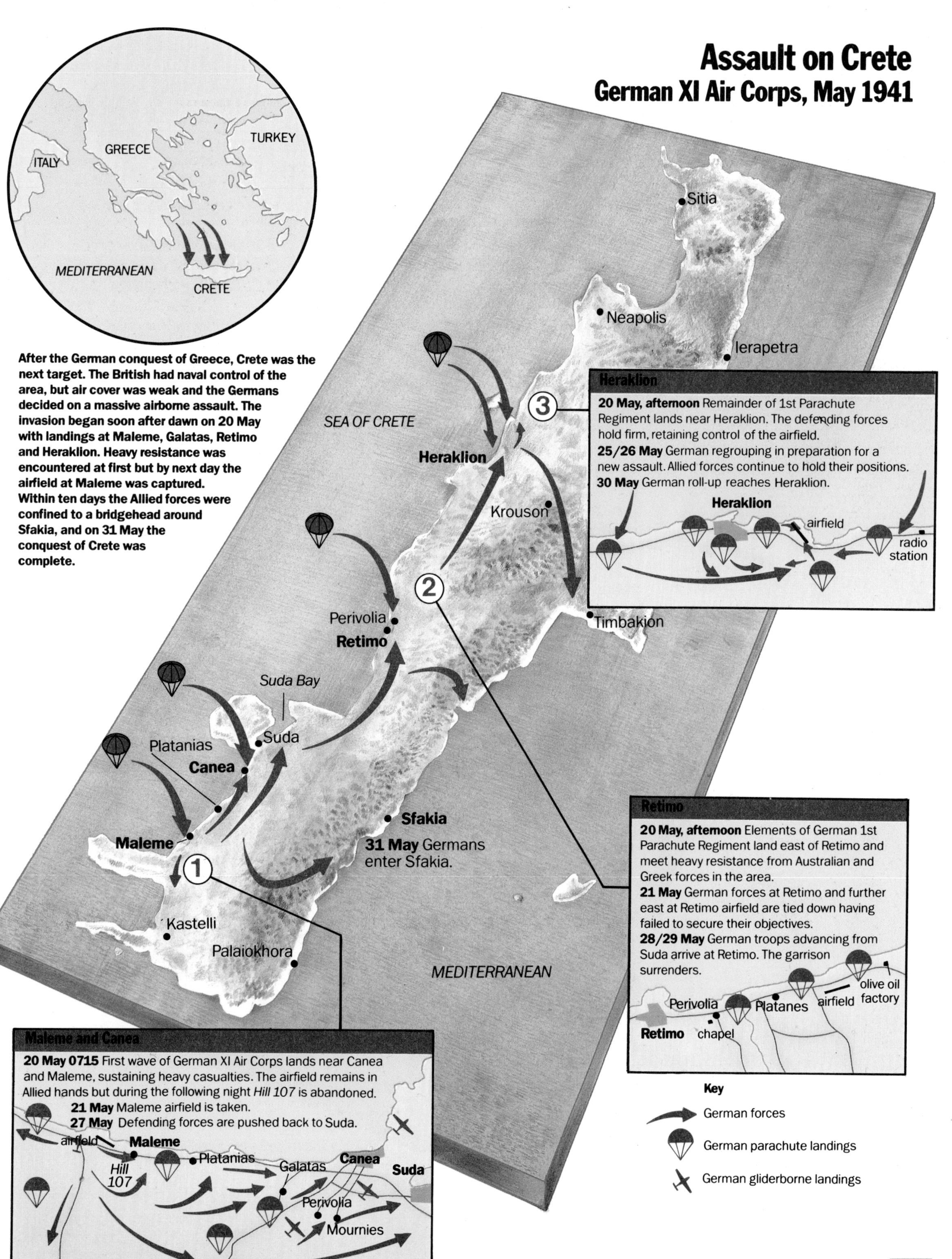

15TH PANZER DIVISION, NORTH AFRICA, JUNE 1941

Early in 1941 the Axis war effort in North Africa was near to collapse. General Wavell had effectively destroyed the Italian Army in Libya and what remained of it had no morale. At this point arrived a man who would change the situation: Erwin Rommel.

In May 1940, German forces had begun to arrive at Tripoli, the spearhead of what would become the *Deutsches Afrika Korps*. In April 1941, Rommel had attacked the British in Cyrenaica and pushed them back into Egypt. Then, at the end of the month the 15th Panzer Division's armoured spearhead, the 8th Regiment, arrived at Tripoli.

Wavell, aware of its arrival, put into effect his own offensive, codenamed 'Battleaxe', and on 12 May was reinforced with 238 Matilda and Crusader tanks. Rommel deployed his units in and around the Halfaya Pass. The Pass and Points 206 and 208 were fortified with 88mm anti-tank guns, and behind these positions were 200 tanks. The 15th Division lay behind Fort Capuzzo.

At dawn on 15 June, British tanks rumbled towards Rommel's trap. The German gunners waited for the tanks to get bogged down in the minefield. The British attack ground to a halt as tank tracks were blown off their vehicles. Then the 88s opened up, blowing both tanks and their crews to pieces; it was a slaughter.

The German attack came on 16 June, when Rommel despatched the 8th Panzer Regiment in a frontal assault against Fort Capuzzo, with the 5th Light Division making a diversionary attack south at Hafid Ridge. The advance began at 0500 hours, the panzer crews confident of success. For the next six hours the panzers attacked in an effort to break the British line, but in vain.

Rommel regrouped the 8th Regiment and 5th Light Division and ordered them to make a wide, sweeping thrust to outflank the British at Fort Capuzzo and Hafid, and then to relieve the garrison at Halfaya. At 0900 hours on 17 June, the tanks of the 15th Division advanced. The British were caught off guard, and panzers and Matildas slugged it out in the desert. For six hours the battle raged, but by the evening of the 17th Rommel had won a significant victory and stopped Operation 'Battleaxe'. The British had lost over 100 tanks.

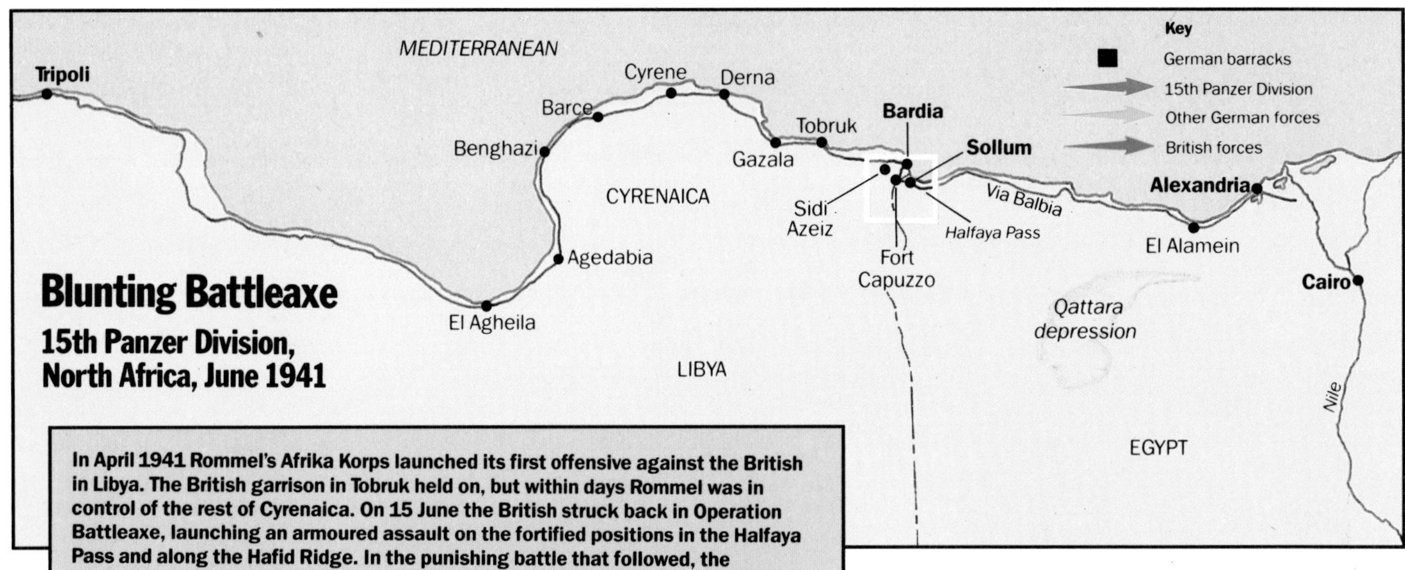

Blunting Battleaxe

15th Panzer Division, North Africa, June 1941

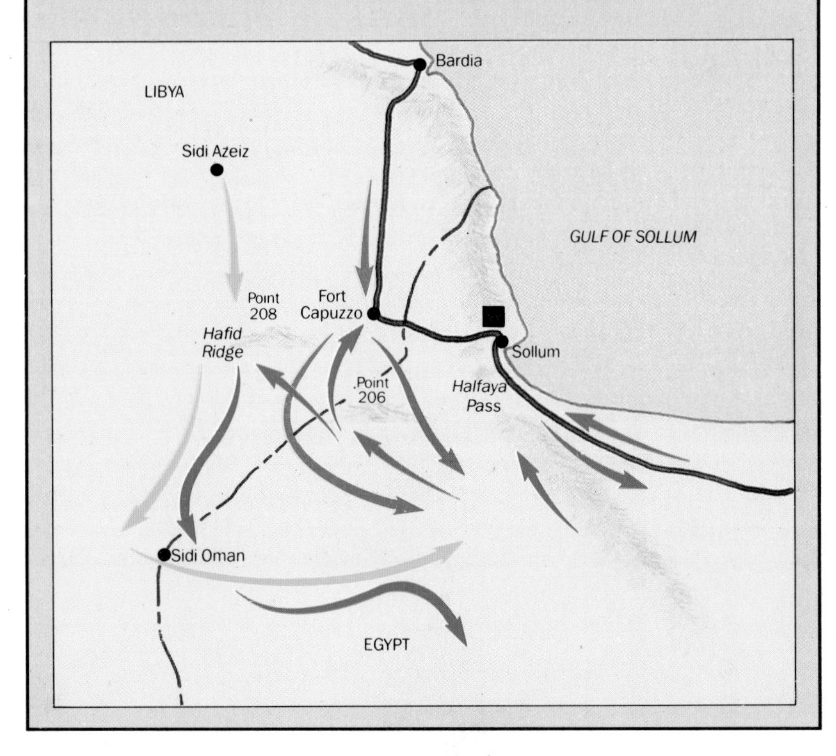

In April 1941 Rommel's Afrika Korps launched its first offensive against the British in Libya. The British garrison in Tobruk held on, but within days Rommel was in control of the rest of Cyrenaica. On 15 June the British struck back in Operation Battleaxe, launching an armoured assault on the fortified positions in the Halfaya Pass and along the Hafid Ridge. In the punishing battle that followed, the newly-arrived 15th Panzer Division suffered heavy casualties. But on 17 June, after regrouping, the division began an outflanking manoeuvre to the south, engaging its opponents south of Fort Capuzzo and forcing them to withdraw.

SAS, NORTH AFRICAN CAMPAIGN, 1941-1943

The SAS was born in July 1941, its name, L Detachment, Special Air Service Brigade, was a deception to convince the enemy that the British had a complete airborne brigade. In fact, the new unit totalled seven officers and 60 men, based at Kabrit in the Suez Canal Zone. The men were rigorously trained, and any man not up to scratch was immediately returned to his unit (RTU'd). David Stirling, the creator of the SAS, had hit upon the idea of his unit operating in four-man teams, with each member having a speciality: navigation, explosives, signals or weapons. Their role was to attack Rommel's supply lines in North Africa, and especially to attack airfields.

Blowing up aircraft on the ground required the right sort of explosive device, and so one of the original members of the SAS, 'Jock' Lewes, devised the Lewes bomb: a small, light incendiary bomb made of plastic, oil and thermite. After a successful trial run, which involved planting dummy bombs on some RAF aircraft following a 150km march through the desert, L Detachment was ready for its first operation.

Unfortunately, the SAS's first raid, against two enemy airfields in support of General Sir Claude Auchinleck's Operation 'Crusader' in November 1941, was a total disaster. The men, dropped by parachute from five RAF aircraft, were widely scattered across the desert and their equipment containers were lost. Only 22 men made it back to the rendezvous with the Long Range Desert Group (LRDG). Undeterred, Stirling, following discussions with David Lloyd Owen of the LRDG, decided that the latter could provide the transport to and from the targets in the future. The SAS was back in business.

Over the following weeks the SAS hit a number of enemy airfields, 'Paddy' Mayne destroyed 24 aircraft at Tamet in December, while Bill Fraser put a further 37 out of action at Agedabia. Two weeks later, Mayne went back to Tamet and destroyed 27 more aircraft. The relationship between the SAS and LRDG was bearing fruit. Aircraft were not the only targets, however. Ports, depots, railway lines and vehicles were also vulnerable to attack. Between January and May 1942, for example, the SAS attempted, albeit unsuccessfully, to destroy shipping in the harbours of Bouerat and Benghazi, and did destroy a number of supply dumps and vehicles.

In mid-1942 the SAS was given a new weapon: the Willys jeep. Armed with Vickers and Browning machine guns, the jeeps were put to devastating use at Sidi Haneish airfield in July: 40 aircraft were destroyed by the jeeps' machine-gun fire. The SAS was proving that a small-sized unit, operating behind the lines, could cause damage out of all proportion to its size.

Following the Eighth Army's victory at El Alamein in November 1942, the SAS was tasked with helping speed up the end of the war in Africa: assisting the Eighth Army in the capture of Tripoli, reconnoitring the Mareth Line and harassing supply lines. This work was not as fruitful as its earlier action; as the enemy's supply lines shortened, there was more risk of SAS patrols being intercepted. In one such incident David Stirling himself was captured, a particular blow to the SAS because he had kept his plans concerning the future of the unit to himself. Nevertheless, his men continued to campaign and by the end of the African war there were two SAS regiments.

By any measure the SAS, which had started life under 100 strong, had proved its worth in North Africa. It had destroyed around 400 aircraft on the ground, Rommel's railway line bringing up petrol and ammunition was cut on several occasions, and nearly 50 separate attacks were made on key German locations. All this activity caused the enemy to divert air and ground forces away from the main battle areas.

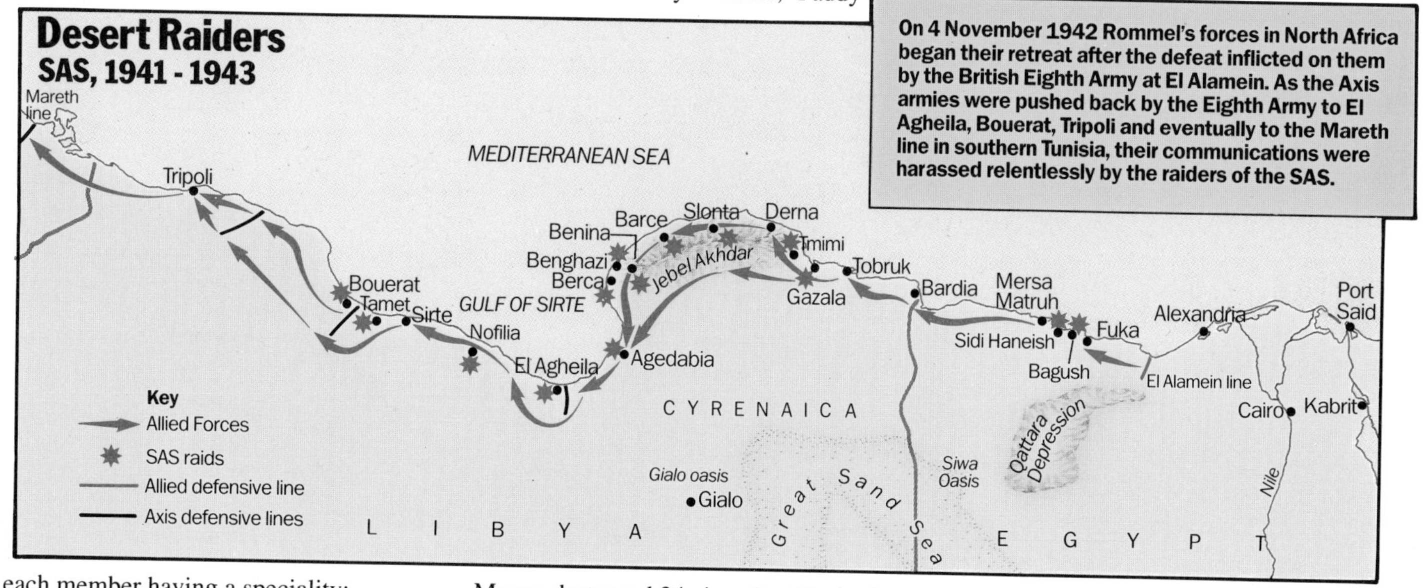

Desert Raiders
SAS, 1941 - 1943

On 4 November 1942 Rommel's forces in North Africa began their retreat after the defeat inflicted on them by the British Eighth Army at El Alamein. As the Axis armies were pushed back by the Eighth Army to El Agheila, Bouerat, Tripoli and eventually to the Mareth line in southern Tunisia, their communications were harassed relentlessly by the raiders of the SAS.

Key
Allied Forces
SAS raids
Allied defensive line
Axis defensive lines

BRANDENBURG REGIMENT, SOVIET UNION, JUNE-JULY 1941

By the summer of 1941, Admiral Canaris's Brandenburg Regiment comprised three battalions and several autonomous companies. These special forces soldiers were poised to take part in Operation 'Barbarossa', the German invasion of Russia, scheduled to begin on 22 June. Their task was much the same as that performed in the West the year before: operating ahead of the main forces and seizing vital points to ease the invasion.

Typical of the kind of daring possessed by the Brandenburgers was the seizure of a crucial bridge in the Pripet marshes on 27 June. The marshes presented many problems for tanks, and so any road bridges became very important to the offensive. Panzers had initially been entrusted to seize the bridge, but it was realised their approach would merely result in it being demolished. Therefore, Brandenburgers disguised as Soviet soldiers would approach the bridge which the Russians were planning to blow up, capture it and cut the wires to the demolition charges, thus allowing the tanks lying in wait nearby to roll across.

The Brandenburgers approached their target in the evening, the men being carried in two captured Red Army trucks. The leader of the commandos leapt from the lead truck and located the Russian officer responsible for blowing the bridge. Trying to persuade him not to detonate the charges until the second, 'broken down', truck was off the bridge (part of the plan), the other Brandenburgers searched for the wires. The leader of the commandos then tore off his Soviet uniform and revealed his true identity, signalling the start of the battle.

On the bridge the Brandenburgers held off the Russians with machine-gun fire, although the panzers were delayed because the lead tank had broken down on a forest road. At the bridge the Brandenburgers were saved only by the timely work of a Stuka unit that pounded the Soviet positions. Eventually the tanks arrived. The Brandenburgers had secured another vital objective.

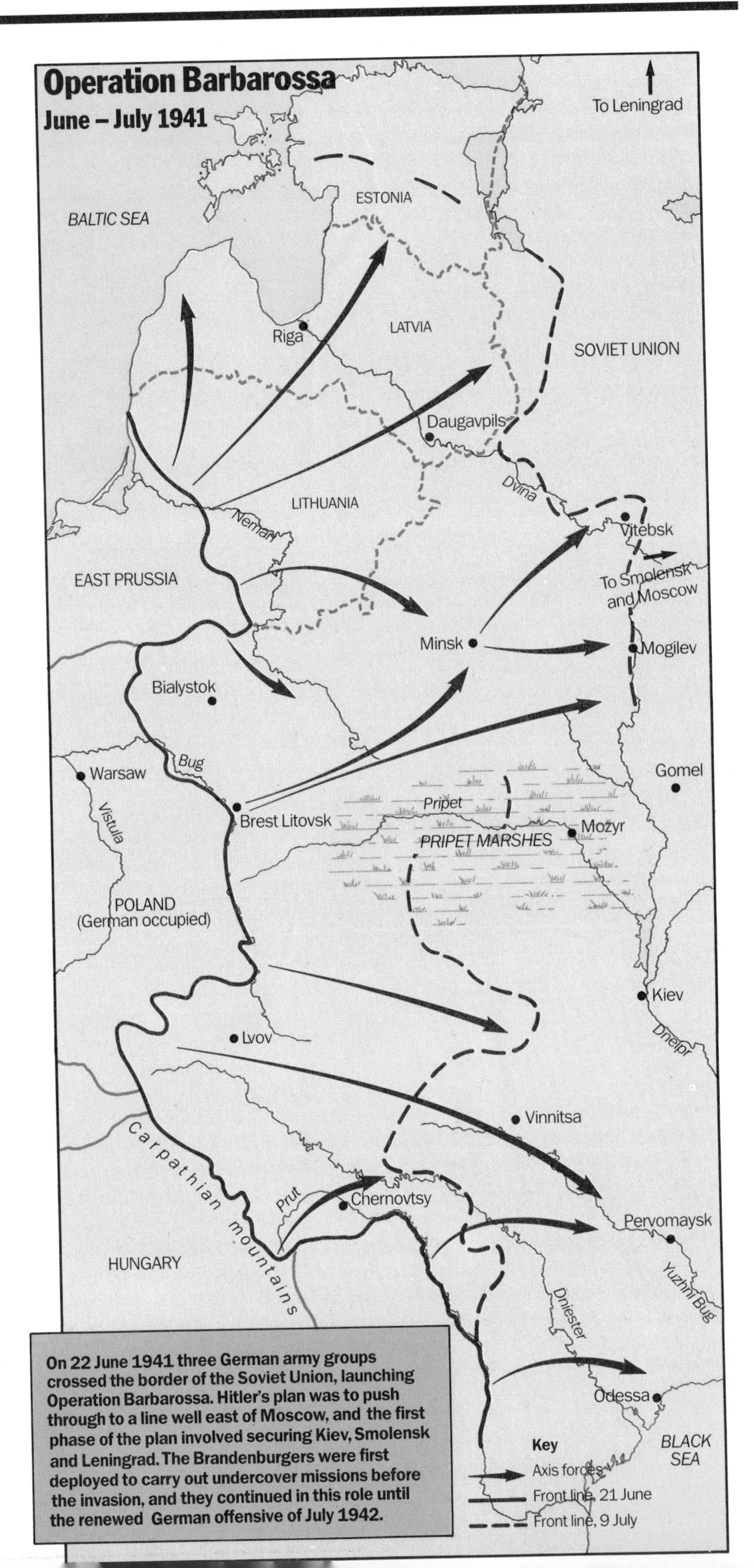

On 22 June 1941 three German army groups crossed the border of the Soviet Union, launching Operation Barbarossa. Hitler's plan was to push through to a line well east of Moscow, and the first phase of the plan involved securing Kiev, Smolensk and Leningrad. The Brandenburgers were first deployed to carry out undercover missions before the invasion, and they continued in this role until the renewed German offensive of July 1942.

ROYAL HORSE ARTILLERY, OPERATION 'CRUSADER', NOVEMBER 1941

In the autumn of 1941, the British Eighth Army came into existence: it comprised the New Zealand Division, the 4th Indian Division, the 1st Army Tank Brigade, the 4th Armoured Brigade, the 1st South African Division, the 22nd Guards (Motor) Brigade and the 2nd South African Division. In Tobruk, waiting to break out, were the 70th Division, the 32nd Army Tank Brigade and the Polish 1st Carpathian Infantry Brigade Group.

With this force at his disposal, General Sir Claude Auchinleck, Commander-in-Chief Middle East, was determined to drive the Germans out of Cyrenaica. The operation, codenamed 'Crusader', began on the night of 17 November 1941: Allied and Axis armoured units clashed in the vicinity of Sidi Rezegh.

The 3rd Regiment, Royal Horse Artillery (RHA), provided the mobile anti-tank force for the 7th Armoured Brigade and consisted of three batteries of 2-pounder guns mounted on portees (special trucks). The unit was defending a raised plateau with the enemy to the south and north, and was commanded by Major Bernard Pinney.

Though 'Crusader' initially caught Rommel off guard, by 20 November he had recovered and organised a counterattack, launching the 15th and 21st Panzer Divisions against the Sidi Rezegh positions. In the early hours of 21 November, the Panzer Mark IIIs and IVs moved forward. Major Pinney's troops were ready. 'A' Troop, commanded by Second-Lieutenant Ward Gunn, was to provide anti-tank fire for the support company of the 2nd Battalion, The Rifle Brigade, on the southeast of the escarpment.

The advancing panzers crashed into the 7th Hussars and, despite grim resistance, soon what was left of the Hussars' force was retreating northeast. The 2nd Royal Tank Regiment, positioned on the enemy's left flank, was unable to provide any support because it was pinned down by anti-tank fire. The panzers rolled on, stopping at Abiar en Nbeidat to be re-supplied with fuel and ammunition. A small force then pushed on to recce the Sidi Rezegh positions, and ran straight into the British artillery.

Ward Gunn's pieces knocked out four enemy tanks before the Germans retreated, though he had also lost two of his 2-pounders. Following a lull, 150 tanks of the two German divisions rolled towards Sidi Rezegh. The British soldiers brought every gun to bear in an effort to battle the whirlwind that was about to hit them: the 25-pounders of the 4th Regiment, RHA, and the 60th Field Regiment, and the four 2-pounders under Ward Gunn.

The 7th Armoured Brigade sent in its mobile reserve of five Crusader tanks, but they were soon ablaze on the battlefield. The panzer advance continued. The British gunners had to endure a hail of machine-gun, tank, mortar and artillery fire, and from the air came Stuka dive-bombers to pound them. Eventually only one of Ward Gunn's 2-pounders remained in action – and then its crew were all killed or wounded by enemy fire. Ward Gunn and Major Pinney, seeing this, raced over to man the remaining 2-pounder. The German tanks were only 500m away, but Ward Gunn, by keeping cool, managed to aim and fire several times, destroying two German tanks and disabling a number more.

Perhaps inevitably, Ward Gunn was hit by enemy fire. He was killed and the portee was soon engulfed in flames. Pinney, however, managed to escape to another troop and carry on the fight. The 7th Armoured Brigade, despite heavy casualties, had thwarted Rommel's plans. Ward Gunn was awarded a posthumous VC for his bravery at Sidi Rezegh.

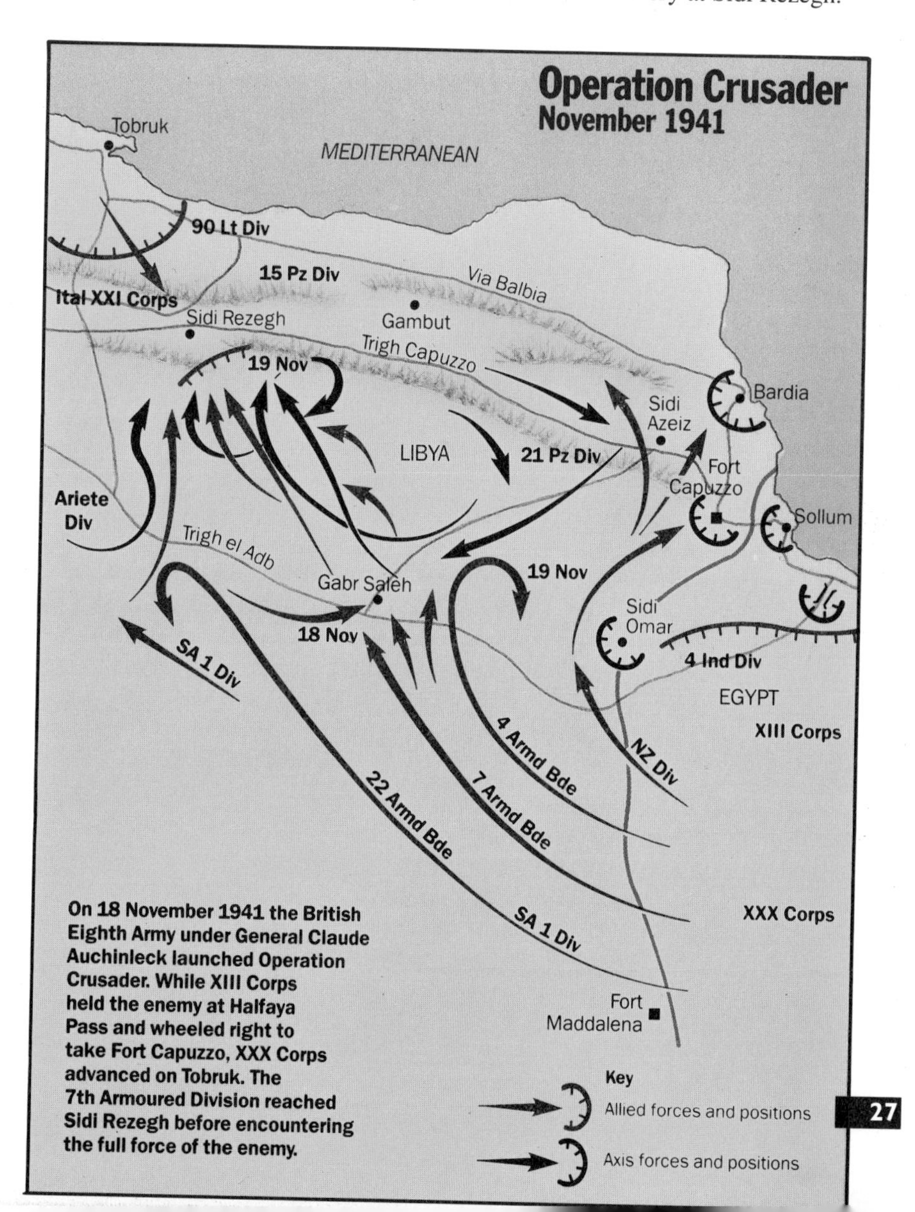

On 18 November 1941 the British Eighth Army under General Claude Auchinleck launched Operation Crusader. While XIII Corps held the enemy at Halfaya Pass and wheeled right to take Fort Capuzzo, XXX Corps advanced on Tobruk. The 7th Armoured Division reached Sidi Rezegh before encountering the full force of the enemy.

1st Air Fleet, Pearl Harbor, 7 December 1941

By mid-1941 it was clear to the Japanese military that any further expansion of their overseas empire would bring them into direct conflict with the British, Americans and Dutch. In the Pacific itself, the greatest threat to the Japanese came from the US Navy. To neutralise the danger posed by the American surface fleet, the Japanese planned a pre-emptive strike against Pearl Harbor in the Hawaiian Islands, the major US naval yard in the Pacific. Carrier-based aircraft would be used in the attack.

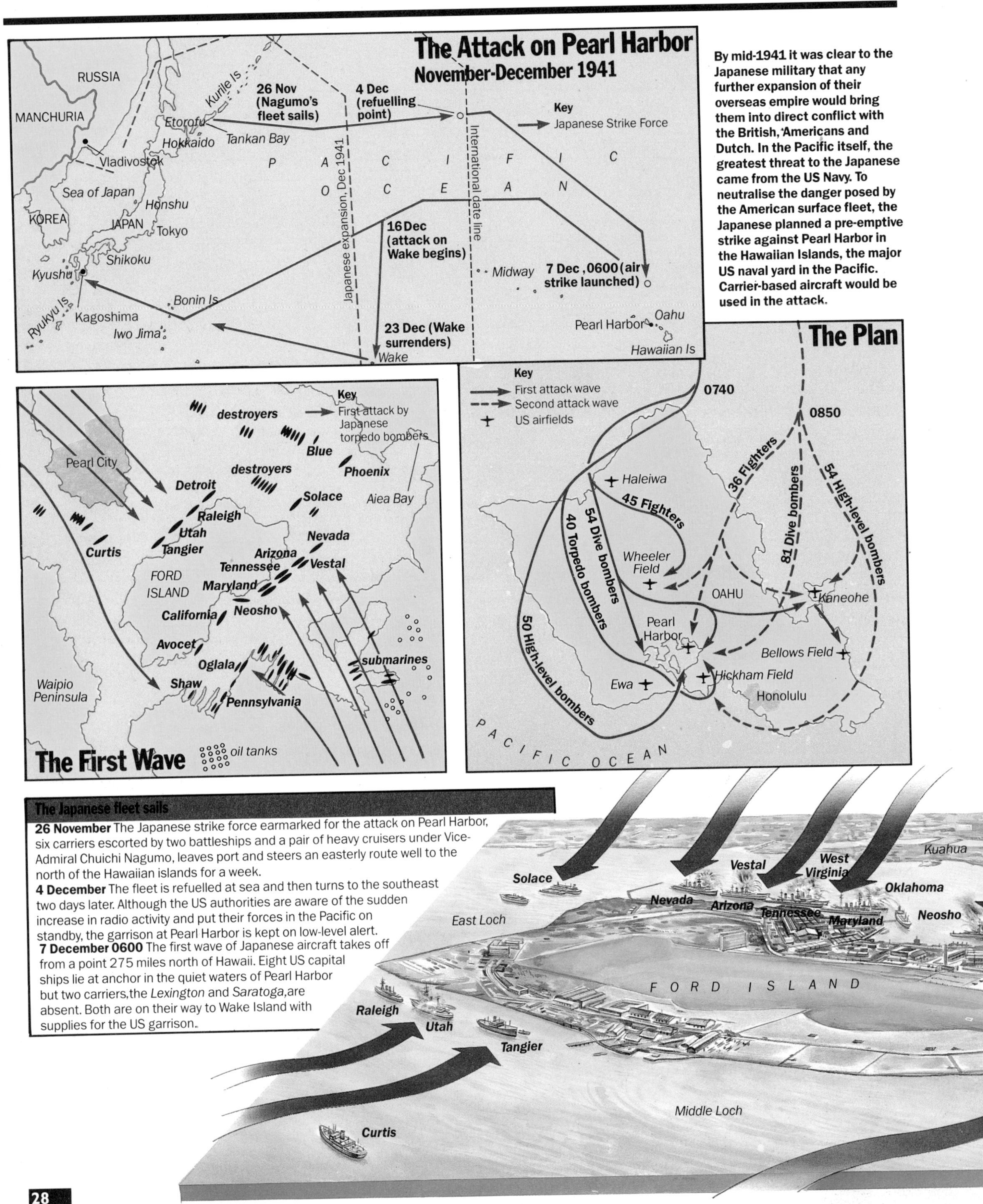

The Japanese fleet sails

26 November The Japanese strike force earmarked for the attack on Pearl Harbor, six carriers escorted by two battleships and a pair of heavy cruisers under Vice-Admiral Chuichi Nagumo, leaves port and steers an easterly route well to the north of the Hawaiian islands for a week.

4 December The fleet is refuelled at sea and then turns to the southeast two days later. Although the US authorities are aware of the sudden increase in radio activity and put their forces in the Pacific on standby, the garrison at Pearl Harbor is kept on low-level alert.

7 December 0600 The first wave of Japanese aircraft takes off from a point 275 miles north of Hawaii. Eight US capital ships lie at anchor in the quiet waters of Pearl Harbor but two carriers, the *Lexington* and *Saratoga*, are absent. Both are on their way to Wake Island with supplies for the US garrison.

Six aircraft carriers, the Imperial Japanese Navy's First Air Fleet, set out from the Tankan Bay in the Kuriles on 26 November 1941. Their objective was the US Pacific Fleet's base at Pearl Harbor, on the Hawaiian island of Oahu. Great care had been taken to ensure the secrecy of the fleet's approach: the carriers and their escorts had left in groups of two and three to avoid any suspicion of hostile activity, and their voyage across the Pacific went through areas that were rarely frequented by merchant shipping. The plan had been devised by the brilliant Commander-in-Chief of the Combined Fleet, Admiral Isoruku Yamamoto, though the fleet was commanded by Vice-Admiral Chuichi Nagumo, based on the carrier *Akagi*.

The Japanese naval air arm

In late 1941 the Japanese naval air arm was a force to be reckoned with, and the First Air Fleet contained the cream of naval pilots. All Japanese carrier forces were grouped into carrier divisions, each having two carriers, each with its own air group. Division 1 comprised *Akagi* and *Kaga*, Division 2 *Hiryu* and *Soryu*, and Division 5 *Zuikaku* and *Shokaku*. As the latter's aircrews were not trained to the same high standard as those of the other two divisions, they were detailed to attack airfields. Each carrier's air group usually comprised 21 A6M Zero fighters, 18 D3A Val dive-bombers and 27 B5N Kate torpedo bombers.

On the evening of 6 December, the First Air Fleet had reached a position 800km to the north of Pearl Harbor. The ships then altered course and headed southwards to enable the aircraft to be launched early the following morning. Each aircrew had a map detailing the location of the US Navy's warships in the harbour (intelligence had been supplied by a Japanese agent on the island), and, to confirm these maps, several reconnaissance aircraft were launched from the fleet ahead of the main attack group.

The first wave hits Pearl Harbor

At 0600 hours on 7 December, the 213 aircraft of the first wave took off and headed towards their target. In the first echelon were the 89 Kates detailed to attack the US warships, 40 armed with torpedoes and the rest carrying armour-piercing bombs. Both weapons had been specially adapted for the Pearl Harbor mission, the torpedoes by the addition of a wooden 'air tail', the bombs by fitting a 14in shell with stabilising fins. The modifications to the torpedoes meant they could be dropped in the shallow waters of the harbour, since their initial plunge after release took them only slightly below their standard running depth, while the bombs could be delivered from level flight against stationary ships.

Fighter escorts for the Kates consisted of 43 heavily armed A6M Zeroes, which were ordered to strafe US airfields if no fighter opposition was encountered. One hour after the first wave had left the carriers, the second wave was launched: 50 Kates, 40 Zeroes and 80 D3A Vals. Meanwhile, the first wave was approaching the target. Two plans had been devised for the actual attack. First, if total surprise was achieved the torpedo-bombers would spearhead the attack on the warships, closely followed by the bomb-armed Kates. The Val dive-bombers would attack the naval air base on Ford Island. Second, if the aircraft had been detected, the suppression of the air defences would become a priority (the Japanese aircraft were in fact detected, but were mistaken for a squadron of B-17 Flying Fortresses that were due to arrive from California).

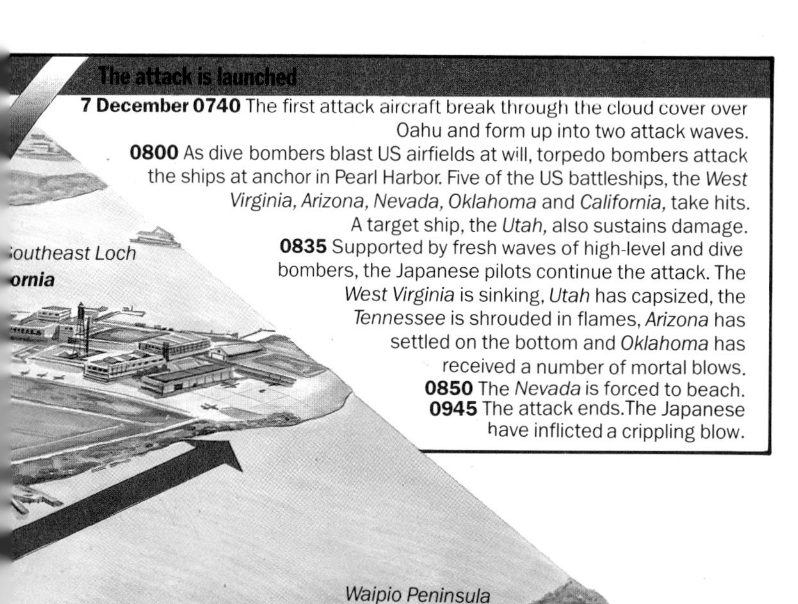

As the aircraft swooped in to attack, the radio message 'Tora, Tore, Tora' was transmitted to the fleet, signalling total surprise had been achieved. As no US aircraft carriers were in the harbour, the battleships became the focus of the action. Very soon five US battleships had taken hits: the *West Virginia*, *Arizona*, *Nevada*, *Oklahoma* and *California*. A target ship, the *Utah*, was also hit. The *Nevada* began to steam out of the harbour, despite having been hit by a bomb and a torpedo. The other four battleships and the *Utah* began to sink. In addition, the battleship *Pennsylvania* in dry dock was badly damaged.

The *Nevada* is beached

The Japanese aircraft detailed to strike airfields caused great damage. Of the 143 serviceable United States Army Air Force (USAAF) aircraft on Oahu, less than one third survived the attack. At 0850 hours the second wave of aircraft filled the skies over the harbour. The *Nevada*, steaming towards the open sea became a prime target, and very soon she had been hit at least three times. Rather than block the main channel, her captain reluctantly beached her.

By 1000 hours the aircraft were returning to their carriers, having completed their mission. The last aircraft to leave the area was a section of A6M Zeroes responsible for assessing the damage. Their pilots were able to report that the Japanese attack had resulted in four battleships sunk and at least four more damaged. Other ships had been destroyed, together with many American aircraft and several installations onshore. Of the Japanese aircraft, only 29, most from the second wave which ran into the American defences, had failed to return. By 1330 hours the First Air Fleet had recovered its aircraft and set course for Japan. It had been an excellent day for Japan's naval air arm, and a fine example of a well-planned military raid.

3 COMMANDO, VAAGSO, 27 DECEMBER 1941

The raid on the Norwegian port of Vaagso was the first action undertaken by the newly formed Commandos, elite light infantry that could operate from landing craft. The characteristics of such units were high mobility, thorough training in the use of small arms and explosives, and high levels of physical fitness. The Boer War had seen well-organised units of horsemen, the Boer commandos, inflict serious damage on the British, and in World War I Germany had formed elite shock troops (*stosstruppen*) to attack heavily defended positions on the Western Front. Thus there were clearly great opportunities for similar methods at the outbreak of World War II.

The Commandos were tasked with raiding enemy coasts. At first they got very little action, but in October 1941 Lord Louis Mountbatten became Director of Combined Operations. Full of energy and determination, Mountbatten's first operation was against Vaagso.

The force assembles in Scapa Flow

No 3 Commando, reinforced by 100 men from No 2, formed the raiding force. The British contingent comprised the light cruiser HMS *Kenya*, the destroyers HMS *Chiddingford*, *Offa*, *Onslow* and *Oribi*, the submarine HMS *Tuna*, and the infantry assault ships HMS *Prince Charles* and *Prince Leopold*. Joint force commanders were Rear-Admiral H M Burrough and Brigadier J C Haydon, both of whom were based on *Kenya*. In addition, the Royal Air Force provided some fighter and bomber support.

The force assembled in Scapa Flow, where the final exercises took place. The men were thoroughly briefed with maps and models until everyone completely understood the plan. The force sailed for Sollum Voe in the Shetlands on Christmas Eve. There was a westerly gale, force eight, blowing in from the Atlantic and the assault ships, with their top hamper of landing craft, pitched and rolled in the heavy seas. As a result of the battering the ships took, the raid was postponed for a further 24 hours in order to repair the considerable damage that had been sustained.

The German defences

German forces in and around Vaagso comprised 150 infantry and one tank, 100 men of the German Labour Corps, two coastal defence batteries, four guns on the islet of Maaloy, two heavy guns on Rugsundo Island, a battery of guns at the northern entrance to Ulvesund, and one or two armed trawlers. In addition, there were *Luftwaffe* airfields at Herdla, Stavanger and Trondheim, from where Messerschmitt Bf109 fighters could easily reach Vaagso.

The attack on Vaagso

At 1600 hours on 26 December 1941, the British force left the Shetlands and headed for Norway. At 0842 hours on 27 December, the flotilla entered the fjord and the landing craft were lowered into the water. The ships had not gone unnoticed. The lookout on Husevaago island spotted the flotilla and tried to alert the battery on Maaloy. Fortunately, the battery commander's servant was polishing the officer's boots, and did not even bother to pick up the phone. The lookout then tried the harbour master's office in South Vaagso. This time he succeeded in getting through, and he told a clerk that he had seen seven blacked-out destroyers entering the fjord. The clerk suggested that he was drunk! Undeterred, the lookout then signalled the signal station on Maaloy. By this time the first Commandos (who were split into three Groups for the operation) had landed and Group 1 had quickly taken out the German post near Hollevik. At 0848 hours the Royal Navy ships opened fire, sending a barrage of high-explosive shells crashing into the town. The Maaloy battery itself was quickly blown to pieces, and the sky was illuminated by a host of red Verey lights to allow RAF Hampden aircraft to drop smoke bombs on the Commandos' landing sights.

The Battle of South Vaagso

0858 Group 2 lands near South Vaagso and mee stiff resistance from the German garrison.
1000 Elements of Group 2 reach the north end o South Vaagso but fighting continues.
1020 Group 4, the floating reserve, is committed north of South Vaagso.
1035 Captain Peter Young and his men fight their way along the steamship wharf.
1230 Resistance in South Vaagso is virtually over and the demolition of key installations is in progre
1250 The order to re-embark is given.

VAAGS
Halnoesvik
VAAGSO ISLAND
South Vaagso
VAAGSFJORD

During the next four hours the Commandos were engaged in house-to-house fighting, using Tommy guns, Brens, rifles and grenades. The action was short, vicious and confused. On Maaloy, 5 and 6 Troops stepped ashore without firing a shot, and secured the islet in eight minutes. Taking South Vaagso was not so easy. Group 2 got ashore, but not before a Hampden had accidentally dropped a phosphorus

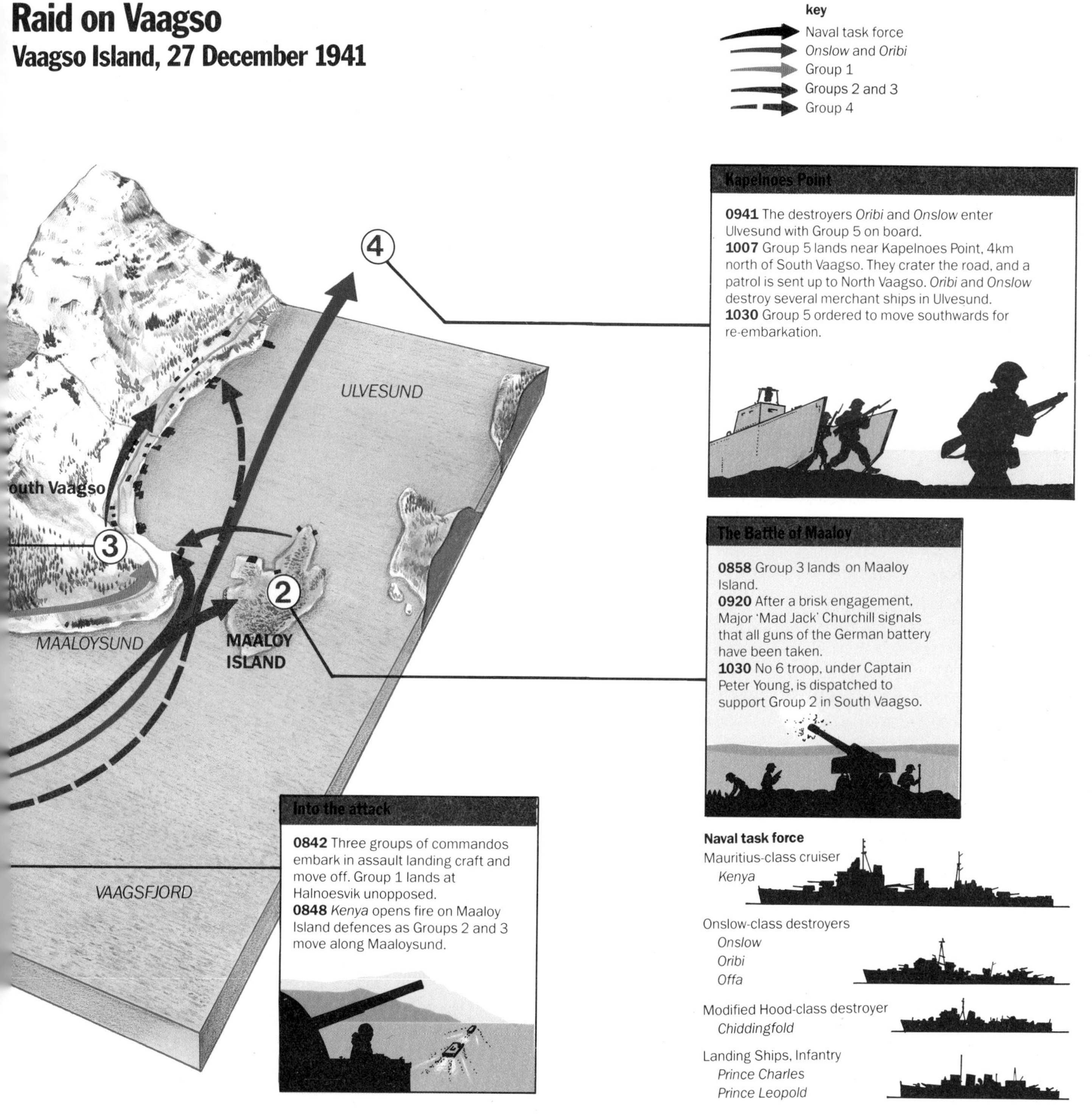

smoke bomb into one of the landing craft, burning or killing half of 4 Troop. The Commandos raced into the town, clearing buildings and factories as they went. However, the Germans put up a stiff fight, and both 3 and 4 Troops ground to a halt in the face of enemy fire and mounting casualties. Reinforcements arrived and were deployed along the waterfront, but still the Germans continued to fight. By 1445 hours, having completed all the demolition tasks, the Commandos withdrew.

The raid had given the Germans a bloody nose, but at a price: 20 Commandos killed, 57 wounded, eight RAF aircraft lost and the *Kenya* hit. On the other hand, the garrison of Maaloy had been captured or killed, 16,000 tonnes of enemy shipping had been sunk, and in Vaagso the defenders had lost 11 killed, seven wounded and 16 missing. Perhaps more important, the raid had been the first land attack on German positions in northern Europe since Dunkirk (it had also brought back more prisoners than the British Expeditionary Force had taken during the whole of the 1940 campaign in France). In addition, the Christmas raid on Vaagso had proved that Britain's new Commandos meant business, and that the coast of enemy-occupied Europe was vulnerable.

5TH (SAMURAI) DIVISION, MALAYA, DECEMBER 1941-JANUARY 1942

In the early hours of 9 December 1941, 14 vessels approached the Thai port of Singora. Four were destroyers, while the rest were transport vessels carrying two regiments of the Japanese Army's 5th Infantry Division, tasked with the seizure of the port and airfields at Singora. After this, they were to march south into British Malaya and capture Singapore, quite a feat considering the Japanese troops were heavily outnumbered.

In heavy seas the Japanese soldiers transferred themselves from the ships into the small boats that would take them ashore. The journey to the beach took one hour, the soldiers leaping through the surf once they had left the boats. On land, the first unit to organise itself was a battalion of the 41st Infantry Regiment, commanded by Major Kobayashi. He was sent forward to the nearest military barracks (housing Thai police) to arrange an agreement with the local authorities. His column was ambushed, however, and so, at 1200 hours, artillery fire was directed at the Thais, which ended their resistance. More importantly, the Japanese had secured the airfield and their aircraft now began to land on it.

The 5th Division strikes south

The 5th's Reconnaissance Battalion then headed south into Malaya. They were briefly held up by a small force at the Thai village of Ban Sadao, but an outflanking movement forced the British to retire. On 10 December, Japanese forces were at Changlin, their engineers repairing a bridge that had been blown up by the British. Two events now conspired to wreck British plans: Japanese attacks and a torrential downpour, which together forced the defenders of Changlin to retreat. As the British troops were preparing to fall back, they were overrun by the Japanese Reconnaissance Battalion. Worse, a battery of anti-tank guns was captured as the gunners were sheltering from the rain.

Moving at speed, the battalion had reached Jitra by 11 December, and though outnumbered, the Japanese continued to harass British positions. At 0600 hours on 12 December, after enduring a counterattack, the Reconnaissance Battalion ruptured the enemy line and gained possession of the main roadblock. By this time, reinforcements from the 41st and 11th Infantry Regiments were pouring in and were directed against the British right flank. Japanese artillery started to pound the British positions. The British, fearing their position had been compromised, pulled back to a better defensive position, and then the High Command ordered a further withdrawal to Gurun.

More British setbacks

A further threat began to materialise in the shape of the Japanese 42nd Infantry Regiment, which had landed at Patani and then marched south. Its advance would take it into the rear of any enemy forces in northern Malaya, and so the British withdrew into central Malaya. The fighting over the next few weeks was characterised by speed and surprise. The Japanese moved as quickly as possible to keep up the momentum. The British made determined efforts to stop them, but were defeated either by frontal infantry assaults or threats to their flanks. A major British disaster occurred at the Slim River Bridge when a group of Japanese light tanks smashed their way through four British battalions in less than two and a half hours. The bridge was captured and the Japanese triumphantly entered the city of Kuala Lumpur on 11 January 1942.

Resting for two days, the men of the 5th Division then prepared for their greatest challenge: the capture of Singapore. On the night of 8/9 February, 440 guns of the Twenty-Fifth Army began a heavy barrage of Singapore, and at midnight the first wave of the 5th Division crossed the straits. As the division made its way through mangrove swamps and wire entanglements, the Australian troops manning the defences were prevented from using their machine guns effectively because of Japanese artillery fire. Japanese forces began to pour across the straits, and by 11 February they were overlooking the city itself. The fighting continued, but the capture of the last reservoir from the British on 13 February signalled the end. Two days later the defenders requested a ceasefire to secure surrender terms. At 1810 hours on 15 February, the instrument of surrender was signed. It was 30 days ahead of schedule. The Japanese 5th Division had, by a combination of speed and skill at arms, achieved a remarkable victory, one that stunned the Commonwealth defenders of Malaya.

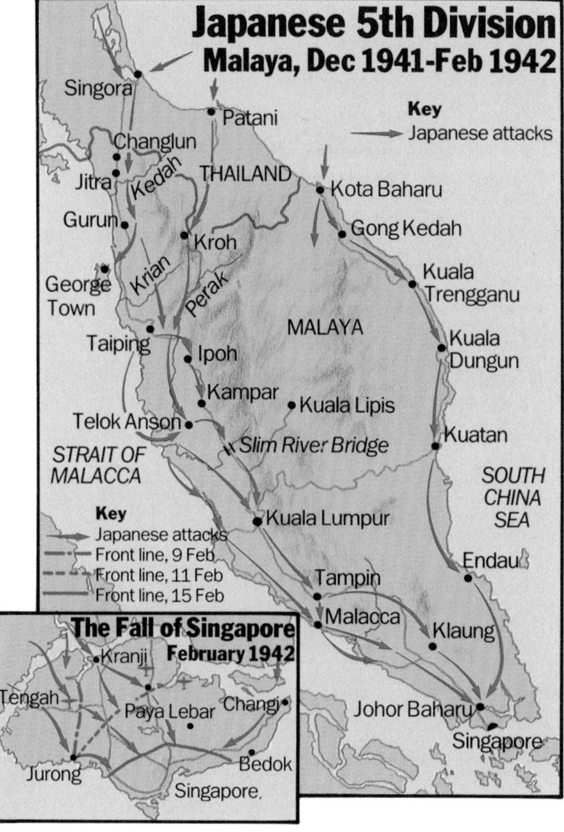

3RD SS PANZER DIVISION TOTENKOPF, THE DEMYANSK POCKET, JANUARY 1942

The 3rd SS Division Totenkopf fought with distinction during Operation 'Barbarossa', the invasion of Russia in June 1941. When the offensive ground to a halt in the first week of November, the division, as part of the Sixteenth Army, had dug in on a line between Lakes Ilmen and Seliger. Over the next two months the SS men had to face not only savage attacks from the Red Army, but also appalling weather conditions.

The Soviet High Command was planning a big new attack; and within 24 hours of the opening of the offensive of January 1942, the Russians had penetrated the front to a depth of 30km either side of the Sixteenth Army, threatening to surround it and cut it off. Its commander, General Ernst Busch, looked to the Totenkopf to avoid a disaster. The latter's commander, General Theodor Eicke, was dismayed to see his men being split up to secure various sectors: five battalions to hold the road and rail junction of Staraya Russa, two more sent southeast to Demyansk.

As Hitler forbade any withdrawal, very soon the Sixteenth Army was split in two, with the bulk of the Totenkopf and II and X Corps encircled by 8 February. In this pocket were 95,000 men and 20,000 horses, surrounded by over 15 Soviet divisions. The Totenkopf was split into two regimental battle groups: one under Eicke, the other under SS Standartenführer Max Simon, who was deployed to the northeast to block the Soviet Thirty-Fourth Army. Eicke was deployed to the west to prevent any widening of the gap between the German frontline across the River Polist and the encircled units.

Fighting in deep snow and freezing conditions, the SS men held off wave after wave of Soviet infantry, the Germans unwilling to yield an inch of ground. The fighting was savage, and by the third week of February Eicke's group had been reduced to 36 officers, 191 NCOs and 1233 soldiers. By the end of the month the Soviets had split the SS units into small groups and Eicke reckoned the end was near. However, the Soviets were also in a desperate situation, trying to destroy the enemy before the milder weather turned the ground into a quagmire, thus preventing any armoured thrusts. In fact, the exhausted Soviets had ceased their attacks by the end of March.

It was not until 22 April that the German Army managed to link up with the pocket and end 73 days of isolation. The Totenkopf's performance in the Demyansk Pocket had been outstanding, and in recognition of this Hitler awarded 11 Iron Crosses to men of the division. However, such fighting prowess did not come cheap. By the end of May 1942 the division was down to 6700 men out of an establishment of 17,000. In addition, the survivors were exhausted, shell-shocked and malnourished. But Hitler refused to allow the Totenkopf to withdraw, keeping it in what had been the Demyansk Pocket until August.

ABOVE: *Soldiers of the Totenkopf Division, trapped in the Demyansk Pocket, await the next Soviet onslaught. Note the captured Russian weapons.*

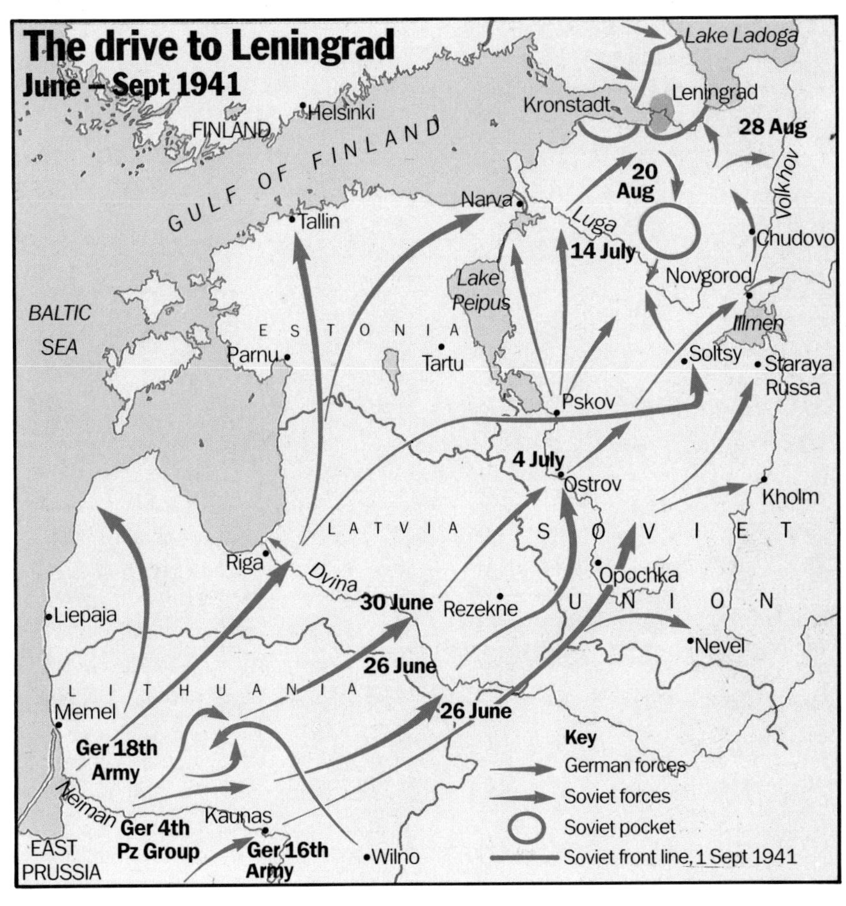

THE PARACHUTE REGIMENT, BRUNEVAL, 28 FEBRUARY 1942

On 28 February 1942, 120 men of the British Parachute Regiment were crammed into the fuselages of converted Whitley bombers, heading for France. Their objective was the German villa and radar station at Bruneval. They were to capture the installation, dismantle the essential parts and take them back to England.

The enemy were in three main bodies. First, the signallers and guards on duty at the radar station itself, thought to number 30 men in all. Second, reserve signallers and coast defence troops who were based at 'La Presbytère', buildings 400m north of the villa which contained the radar equipment, 100 men in all. Third, there was a garrison in the village of Bruneval itself, 40 men who manned the pillboxes and earthworks that covered the beach.

The Paras dropped in three parties in the early hours of the 28th. 'Nelson', 40 men led by Lieutenants John Ross and Euen Charteris, was tasked with capturing the beach defences so the party could evacuate by sea safely. 'Drake', led by Major John Frost, was to capture the villa and radar station and dismantle the parts. Finally, 'Rodney', under John Timothy, was placed between the radar station and any likely enemy approach.

The success of the mission depended upon complete surprise; and this was achieved as the men silently parachuted to earth on a bitterly cold, moonlit night, though the 'Nelson' party was dropped short and had to fight a small battle with a German patrol en route.

Gathering his men at the rendezvous, Frost gave the order to move out, and soon the Paras had surrounded the villa. Frost walked towards the door and blew his whistle, the signal for the attack to begin. His men rushed into the building – resistance was very light and soon they had secured the area. Now, however, the Germans at 'La Presbytère' began to

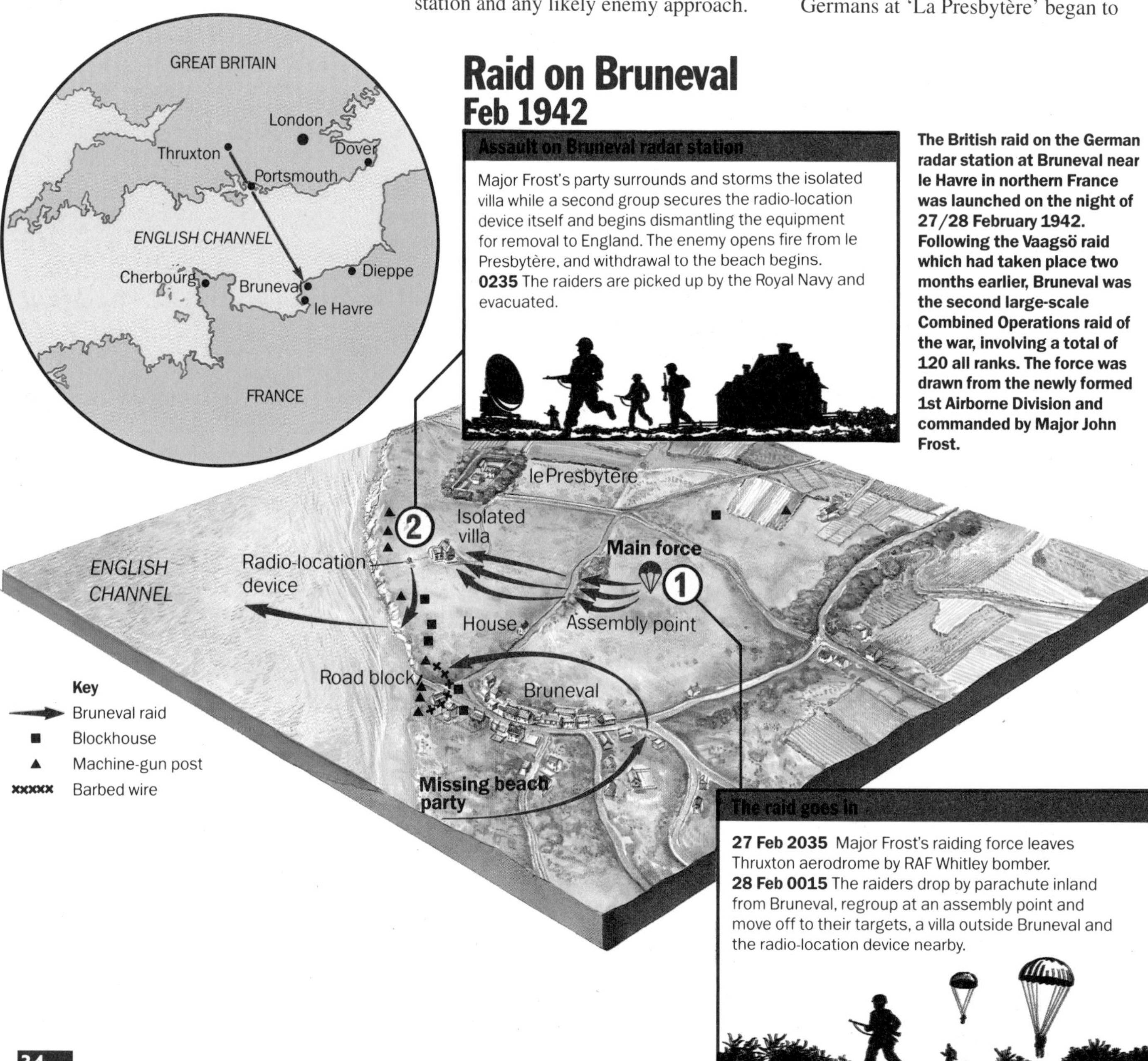

The British raid on the German radar station at Bruneval near le Havre in northern France was launched on the night of 27/28 February 1942. Following the Vaagsö raid which had taken place two months earlier, Bruneval was the second large-scale Combined Operations raid of the war, involving a total of 120 all ranks. The force was drawn from the newly formed 1st Airborne Division and commanded by Major John Frost.

open fire on the villa as the Paras frantically dismantled the radar.

Then Frost's men noticed vehicles moving towards the villa. Frost, realising that if his men were caught they would be badly cut up, gave the order to pull out. Putting the equipment they had dismantled into canvas trolleys, the Paras moved off towards the beach. As they approached the beach, a machine gun opened up on them from a pillbox, inflicting some casualties. The Paras were now in some difficulty, because word then reached them that the Germans had reoccupied the villa and were advancing towards them from that direction. As they were only armed with Sten guns and grenades, the Paras were very vulnerable. However, the Germans were in some confusion as to who they were up against and, luckily for the Paras, did not press home their attack.

The pillbox was dealt with by the 'Nelson' party and the beach was secured. With the object of the raid achieved, Frost was anxious to get his men off the beach. He therefore ordered the Royal Navy to be told to send the boats. However, no radio contact could be established with them. A red Verey light was therefore fired several times, but there was still no sign of the boats. In fact, the Royal Navy had encountered a few problems itself. As the six boats were lying motionless offshore, a German destroyer and two E-boats had passed nearby. Fortunately they did not spot the boats, but they had to maintain radio silence and so could not answer Frost's calls. Frost himself, somewhat downcast, prepared his men for a defence of the beach. At that moment, however, several boats appeared out of the darkness; the navy had arrived.

In some confusion the men were loaded onto the boats, though not before the Germans had fired at them. Nevertheless, in the end all had gone well and the men of the Parachute Regiment had carried out a very audacious raid, one that would enter Para folklore.

ABOVE: *The heroes come home: soldiers of The Parachute Regiment photographed after their participation in the Bruneval raid. Their CO, Major John Frost, is on the bridge, second from left.*

ARMY COMMANDOS, ST NAZAIRE, 28 MARCH 1942

By early 1942 the Allies were suffering heavy losses in the Atlantic. German U-boats were sinking many thousands of tonnes of shipping every month, and enemy warships stood ready to strike out into the Atlantic and attack Britain's weak lifeline. The dry-dock at the French port of St Nazaire was the largest in the world and could accommodate these mighty German ships.

Lord Louis Mountbatten, head of Combined Operations, was ordered to prepare an attack on the port from the sea. He put together a scratch force: an old destroyer, HMS *Campbeltown*, 16 motor launches (MLs), one motor gun boat, and a fast torpedo boat. The MLs were each armed with 20mm Oerlikon cannon and heavy machine guns, and four had torpedo tubes mounted on their bows. The Commando assault force comprised 200 men from No 2 Commando, and special demolition teams from Nos 1,2,3,4,5,6,9 and 12 Commandos, totalling 90 men.

St Nazaire
March 1942

In the early morning of 28 March 1942 HMS *Campbeltown*, accompanied by a small force of motor launches, a gun boat and a torpedo boat, sailed into the Loire estuary towards the German-held port of St Nazaire. Their task was to destroy dock installations that could have made a crucial difference to the war in the Atlantic.

The flotilla rendezvoused with the submarine HMS *Sturgeon* late on 27 March off the French coast near the estuary of the Loire. At 2330 RAF bombers flew over St Nazaire in a decoy raid. The naval force remained unchallenged for some two hours, until German searchlights illuminated the leading vessel at around 0122.

At 0134 *Campbeltown* crashed into the dock gates and her commandos went into action. The 'greatest raid of all' was under way.

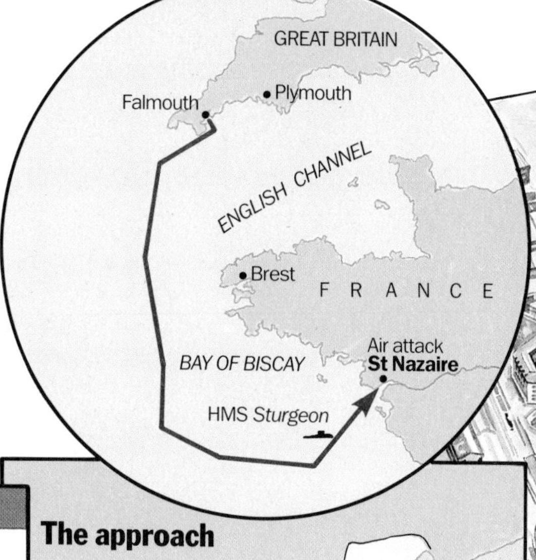

① Falmouth to St Nazaire

26 Mar 1400 The Operation Chariot naval force, with the commando assault and demolition teams on board, leaves Falmouth accompanied by the escort destroyers *Athelstone* and *Tynedale* and a lone RAF Hurricane.
27 Mar 0705 The flotilla adopts daylight anti-submarine sweep formation after an uneventful night, and turns eastwards towards the French coast. Soon afterwards, *Tynedale* investigates a vessel on the horizon. The vessel is a U-boat – *Tynedale* attacks and drives the submarine off.
2215 The flotilla reaches the rendezvous with HMS *Sturgeon*.
28 Mar 0122 German searchlights detect the leading vessel. A few minutes later, enemy coastal defences open fire.

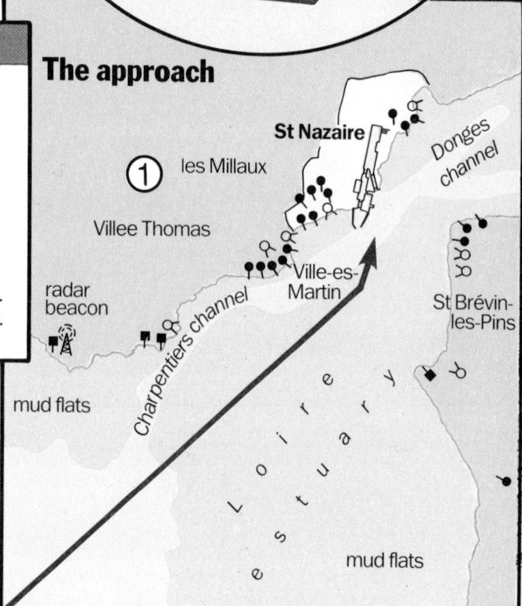

The *Campbeltown* is hit

Operation 'Chariot' began at 1400 hours on 26 March 1942, when the naval force left Falmouth in England. By 0100 hours on the 28th, the force was approaching St Nazaire undetected. The RAF had laid on a decoy in the shape of 60 bombers, which alerted the port's 90 heavy and medium guns. Flying German flags and sending messages to shore that they were friendly vessels, the British force edged ever closer. Unconvinced, the shore batteries began to open fire; the raiders then struck their flags and hoisted White Ensigns, firing as they did so. *Campbeltown* was hit several times and set on fire. Nevertheless, she steamed on, and at 0134 hours smashed into the gate of the Normandie dock.

The demolition teams and Commandos left the ship. The pumphouse was rigged with explosives and blown up, as was No 2 winding station and the gate at the other end of the dry-dock. However, the Commandos had suffered many casualties and the MLs had also sustained heavy damage. Firing at point-blank range, the German guns tore into the flimsy hulls of the vessels. Many sailors and Commandos were killed, others were drowned in the waters of the Loire, which were covered by blazing petrol from ruptured fuel tanks. The MLs made for the docks, especially the Old Mole, their surviving occupants joining up with those who had landed from the *Campbeltown*. Most were killed or captured as the morning wore on.

At 1100 hours, with Germans swarming over the docks area, the *Campbeltown* blew up (over four tonnes of booby-trapped blasting powder had been hidden below her decks), killing 60 enemy officers and 340 soldiers who were on her at the time, bits of the bodies being strewn over nearby buildings. Only seven MLs and the motor torpedo boat escaped from the Loire, and the British lost 159 killed and 200 captured. However, the dry-dock had been destroyed and no German capital ship ever ventured into the Atlantic again. The raid was marked by courage of the highest kind, with no less than five VCs being awarded. It was another glorious episode in the history of British naval history.

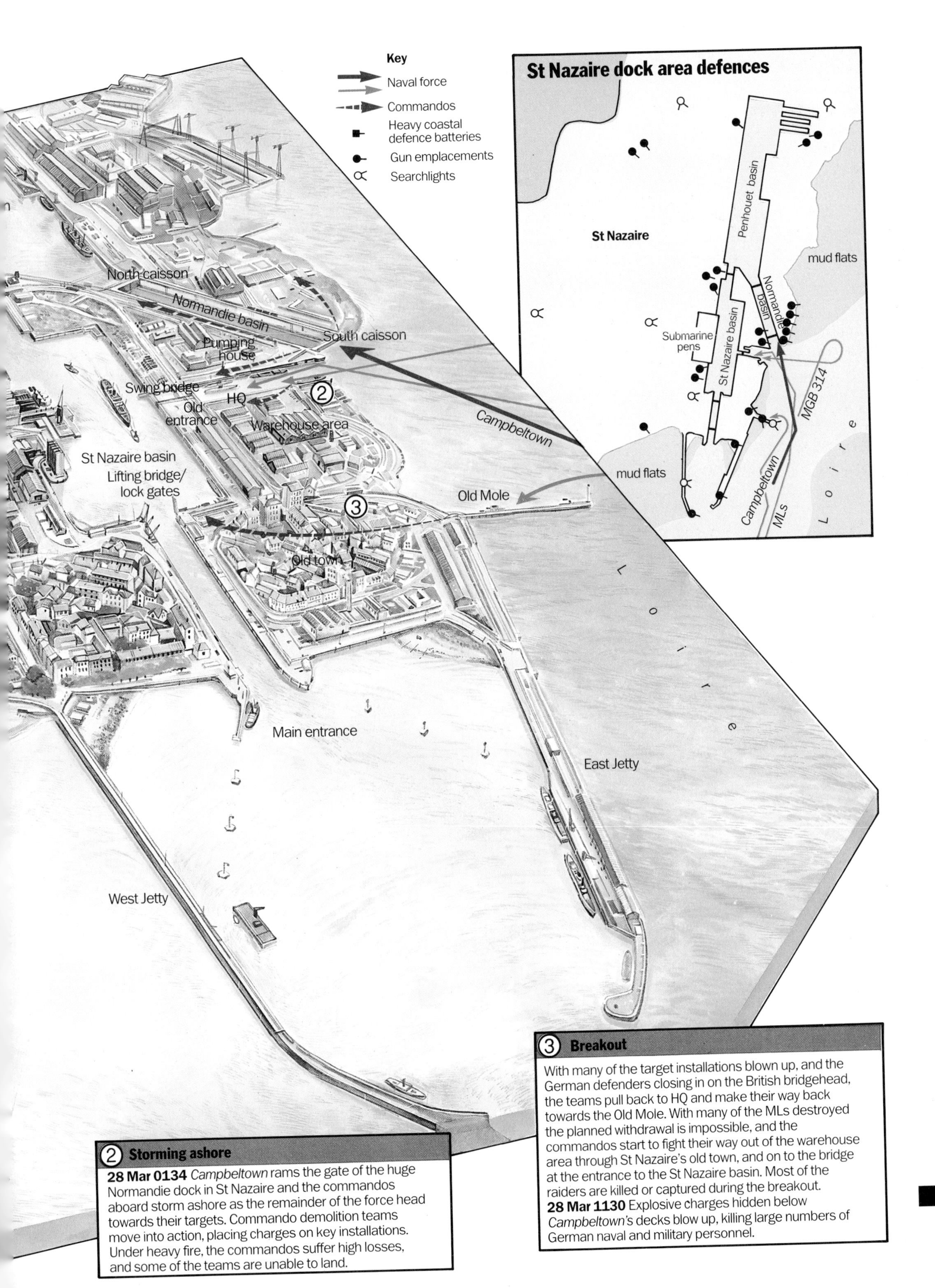

③ Breakout

With many of the target installations blown up, and the German defenders closing in on the British bridgehead, the teams pull back to HQ and make their way back towards the Old Mole. With many of the MLs destroyed the planned withdrawal is impossible, and the commandos start to fight their way out of the warehouse area through St Nazaire's old town, and on to the bridge at the entrance to the St Nazaire basin. Most of the raiders are killed or captured during the breakout.
28 Mar 1130 Explosive charges hidden below *Campbeltown's* decks blow up, killing large numbers of German naval and military personnel.

② Storming ashore

28 Mar 0134 *Campbeltown* rams the gate of the huge Normandie dock in St Nazaire and the commandos aboard storm ashore as the remainder of the force head towards their targets. Commando demolition teams move into action, placing charges on key installations. Under heavy fire, the commandos suffer high losses, and some of the teams are unable to land.

90TH LIGHT DIVISION, BATTLE OF GAZALA, MAY-JUNE 1942

Made up of three motorised infantry regiments, the *Afrika Korps*' 90th Light Division first saw action in November 1941, when it helped blunt the British Operation 'Crusader'. The division had performed extremely well in that campaign, not least because many of its men were tough ex-French Foreign Legionnaires and so were used to desert warfare. By January 1942, the division was equipped with a large number of captured British vehicles and other materiel, heeding General Erwin Rommel's advice that 'if you are short of anything, go across and take it from the enemy. He has plenty.'

From February to mid-May 1942, there was a lull in the North African war as both sides re-equipped and prepared for the coming offensive. Rommel was determined to push the British out of Cyrenaica, while Churchill wanted his commander in the area, General Claude Auchinleck, to resume the offensive and destroy the reputation of the 'Desert Fox'. The British had constructed a defensive line between Gazala on the coast and Bir Hacheim 64km south. A number of heavily defended 'boxes' (strongpoints) had been built to cover possible German attack routes. Each 'box' was held by a brigade-strength force and had substantial artillery support. There was also an unfinished line running from Sidi Muftah to El Adem. When Rommel launched his offensive, Auchinleck had a force of 100,000 men, 849 tanks and 200 aircraft to hold his position.

The 'Desert Fox' had only 90,000 men and 560 tanks to combat this force, but his 500 aircraft guaranteed him air superiority. In addition, 109 of his tanks were of the latest design, being Mk IVs. On 27 May the *Afrika Korps* launched Operation 'Theseus', the drive against Gazala. The 90th was deployed to protect the flank of the Axis armoured forces and to collect information concerning the whereabouts of British armour.

The men of the 90th fought in small, tightly knit, heavily armed groups. Rommel ordered them to drive on relentlessly, taking the offensive to the enemy without halting. The divisional objective was El Adem, and three German battlegroups raced confidently forward. Resistance was stiff, however: they often underwent a ferocious barrage of British artillery and tank fire.

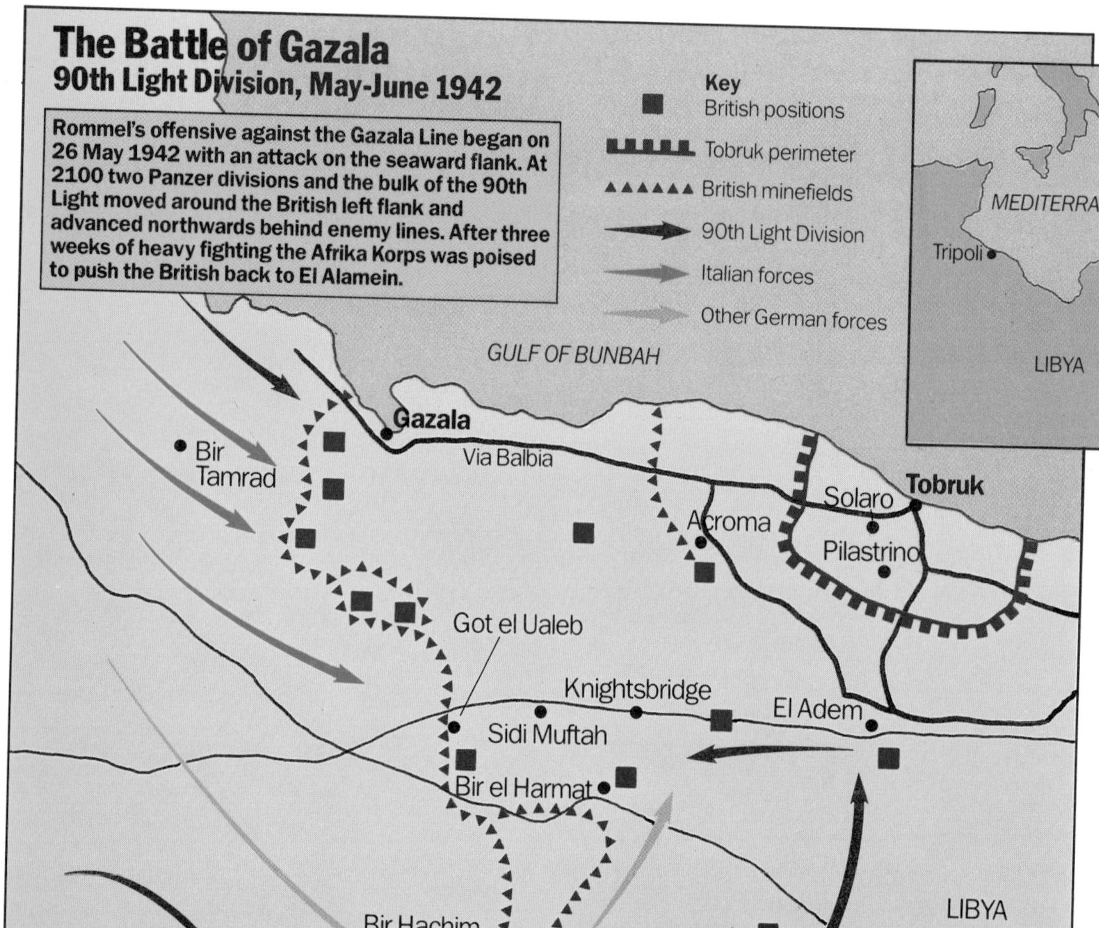

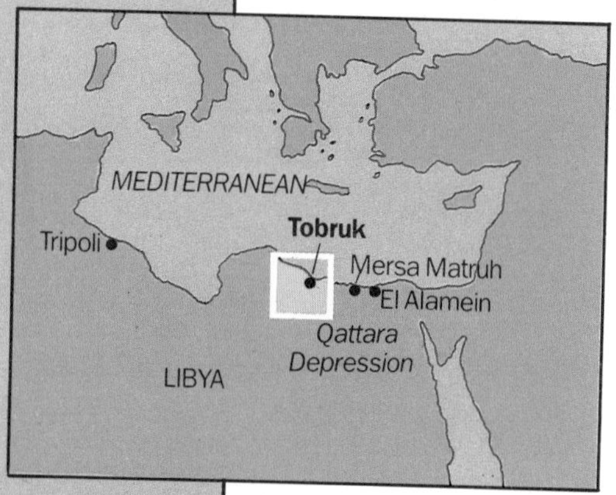

The Battle of Gazala
90th Light Division, May-June 1942

Rommel's offensive against the Gazala Line began on 26 May 1942 with an attack on the seaward flank. At 2100 two Panzer divisions and the bulk of the 90th Light moved around the British left flank and advanced northwards behind enemy lines. After three weeks of heavy fighting the Afrika Korps was poised to push the British back to El Alamein.

ABOVE: *German artillery pounds British positions during Operation 'Theseus', which drove the British back to the Egyptian border.*

The 90th dispersed, losing contact with the rest of the *Afrika Korps*. Its Headquarters Group moved forward towards the objective, having some success against the enemy before being surrounded by British tanks.

All seemed lost, but during the morning of the 28th the battle groups reported in, as did the divisional artillery. The advance was resumed, to be halted when a minefield was encountered. Sending forward sappers, a narrow channel was cleared. The vehicles edged slowly forward, but it took some time to get the densely packed trucks through. Then there was another halt; a second minefield had been discovered. While the sappers cleared a path through this one, a lone RAF bomber swooped over the column and dropped a cluster of bombs. Panic ensued as the trucks were driven into the minefield to escape the aircraft. Within minutes 40 trucks had been blown up, though order was soon restored.

The next day the *Afrika Korps* fared better. It had breached the British minefields and could bring up supplies. During the day it beat off a number of enemy armoured brigades, and the 90th was ordered south to capture the Bir Hacheim 'box'. The 90th suffered fearful casualties before the position was taken on 11 June. It had suffered an attrition rate of 50 per cent of its officers and 25 per cent of its rank and file.

The capture of Mersa Matruh

The division's next objective was the British 29th Indian Brigade 'box' at El Adem, and it was only with the support of the 21st Panzer Division that the infantry were able to make any gains. The fighting was savage: the 90th lost one man in two. However, the bloodshed paid off on 17 June, when the 'box' fell. The 200th and 361st Regiments of the division were then ordered to spearhead the attack on Tobruk, while what was left of the division was marched through the desert to Mersa Matruh to cut the British off as they retreated towards the Nile. Mersa Matruh fell on 29 June.

Still there was no rest for the 90th. Major Briel of the 606th Flak Battalion was given the best fighting elements of the division and told to head for the Nile as the spearhead of the *Afrika Korps*. Although exhausted, the men responded superbly, allowing Briel to advance rapidly, and by 30 June he was only 100km away from Alexandria. On 1 July, however, he was ordered to wait for the rest of the 90th to come up, and was then told his group would be reorganised into a battlegroup.

At first light on 1 July, the *Afrika Korps* launched an offensive to try to break the so-called Alamein Line. The 90th attacked a position at Deir el Shein in a day-long engagement. Though it was taken, the division lost its whole artillery strength,: 105mm field howitzers and 88m anti-aircraft/anti-tank guns. The assault was continued the next day, but the *Afrika Korps* was by now too weak to make any gains. The 90th was subjected to a ferocious bombardment, and with-drew under the cover of a sandstorm. It had been reduced to 58 officers, 247 NCOs and 1023 men. It had fought superbly, but in the end too much had been asked of it.

FREE FRENCH FOREIGN LEGION

13TH DEMI-BRIGADE, BIR HACHEIM, 27 MAY-11 JUNE 1942

Bir Hacheim was at the end of an Allied defensive line that had been constructed during the February-May 1942 stalemate in North Africa. It was garrisoned by the First Free French Brigade: 3700 men under the command of the experienced General Marie-Pierre Koenig. The 2nd and 3rd Battalions (2 BLE and 3 BLE), of the Foreign Legion's 13th Demi-Brigade (13 DBLE) comprised the heart of the garrison. Led by Lieutenant-Colonel Amilakvari, the unit had distinguished itself earlier in the war in both Africa and Syria.

For four months, the action around Bir Hacheim consisted of nothing more than a series of skirmishes. Koenig undertook a building programme that included constructing underground shelters and digging deep slit trenches. Vehicles were half-buried to protect them against explosions, and a minefield around the perimeter was devised to channel any enemy armour into preselected killing grounds.

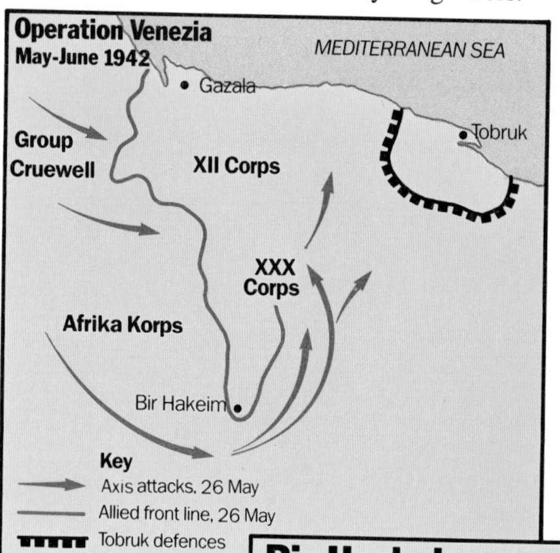

The Italians receive a bloody nose

At 1600 hours on 26 May 1942, a French patrol made contact with a large enemy force that was approaching Bir Hacheim. By nightfall it was clear that the main German offensive had begun, and Rommel was attempting to outflank the Allied position from the south. The following day two Italian units, the 102nd 'Ariete' Armoured Division and the 101st 'Trieste' Motorised Division, with a combined total of 220 light and 50 medium tanks, approached Koenig's command. The Italians directed their attack against the eastern side of the 'box', the tanks firing their guns as they charged towards the French. The latter waited and then, as the tanks drew near, opened fire with a furious barrage from their 54 75mm anti-tank guns. The Italian armour faltered as many tanks were blown to pieces at short range. Others were immobilised by mines and stood helpless in the sand, to be picked off at leisure by the gunners.

Six Italian tanks did manage to break through the line and into the heart of the French position, but, unsupported by infantry, their crews were killed by Legionnaires who jumped onto the vehicles and fired through the sight slits. The Italians withdrew, having received a very bloody nose and losing 32 tanks. It was clear that Bir Hacheim was not going to sell itself cheaply.

The next four days were quiet for Koenig and his men; indeed, on 1 June he was ordered to go onto the offensive to support Eighth Army operations to the northeast. He sent a motorised column westwards to seize a position known as Rotunda Segnali. However, on the same day Rommel ordered that Bir Hacheim's capture be carried out as a matter of urgency. This time the garrison was to be subjected to a furious air and artillery bombardment to force its surrender. The German 90th Light Division and the

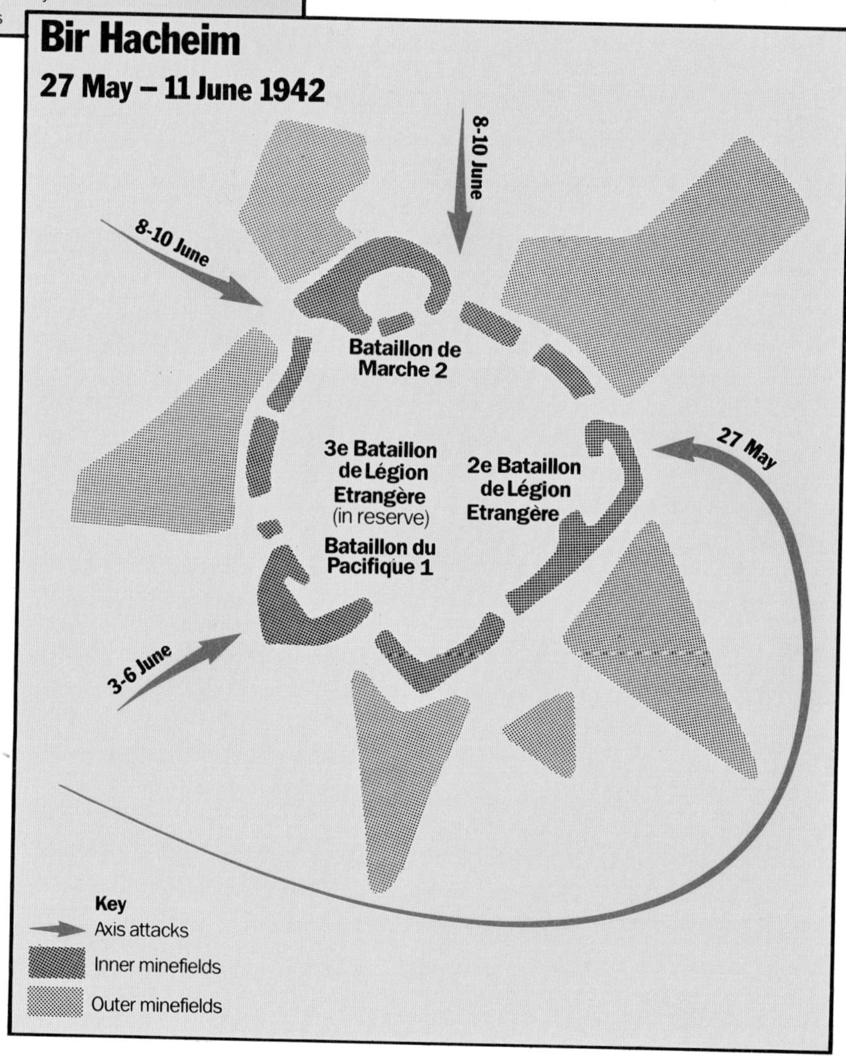

Italian 101st Division set off for Bir Hacheim, and Stuka dive-bombers began their relentless attacks.

On the morning of 2 June, the 1000 vehicles of the enemy column were spotted advancing from the northeast. Refusing a call to surrender, the garrison was then shelled heavily. The bombardment began again on the 3rd, the *Luftwaffe* adding to the misery of the defenders (although the latter were cheered by the arrival of aircraft of the Desert Air Force, which chased off the Stukas). For two more days Axis artillery and aircraft battered the defenders, to no avail. Supplies were still getting through to the French, transported at night by lorries, and the underground shelters kept casualties to a minimum.

An Axis infantry assault was launched on 6 June. But against the strong defences, and without cover, the men were mown down before they reached their objectives. A second assault later that day fared no better. Nevertheless, the enemy was drawing an ever-tighter noose around Bir Hacheim. The last convoy got through on the night of 7/8 June, and strict water rationing came into effect from then on.

Overhead swarms of enemy aircraft – 60 or 80 at a time – clashed with Allied Spitfires and Hurricanes, and wave after wave of infantry, supported by the tanks of the 15th Panzer Division, were hurled at the defences. On 9 June the enemy almost broke through in the north, with hand-to-hand fighting taking place in many places. The situation was only saved when Koenig despatched a group of Bren gun carriers to mount a counterattack. Though the French had performed miracles, it was only a matter of time before enemy strength told.

ABOVE: *The colour of the 13th Demi-Brigade. The unit's epic defence of Bir Hacheim entered Legion folklore.*

During the night of 10 June the order was given for the French to break out. Sappers cleared a path through the minefield and the trucks began to leave in single file. The column was spotted, however, and chaos reigned for a time as trucks were hit, blown up by mines, or got stuck in the sand. Koenig, desperate, ordered his Bren carriers to form up and charge the enemy lines, followed by the trucks. The gamble paid off, and all through the night men and vehicles made their way to a rendezvous with the British. In all, 2600 soldiers escaped from Bir Hacheim after a heroic resistance.

7TH DIVISION, NEW GUINEA, JULY 1942-JANUARY 1943

In late 1941 and early 1942, Japanese forces had secured a number of decisive victories that had brought them to within striking distance of the Australian mainland. Now the Japanese General Headquarters issued orders to take New Guinea.

At the same time as Japanese bombers attacked Darwin, the first phase of the conquest of New Guinea began. Troops were landed on the northern coast and headed inland, clashing with units of the Australian Imperial Force (AIF) and the New Guinea Volunteer Rifles. Though the Japanese had planned to launch an amphibious assault on Port Moresby, their defeats at the Battle of the Coral Sea and Midway forced them to concentrate on the Kokoda Trail, a native supply route that ran from Buna in the north to Port Moresby in the south.

The 39th Battalion holds the line

On the night of 21/22 July, a 2000-strong Japanese force landed at Buna and began to advance down the trail towards Kokoda. They ran into the understrength and untried Australian 39th Battalion, and vicious fighting began. Unit cohesion was soon lost in the hilly and heavily wooded terrain, with small groups fighting at close quarters with guns and grenades. In such conditions men were lost in the jungle and casualties were left behind, never to be seen again. But the rapid Japanese advance had been slowed.

The Australian counterattack

The determined Australians acquitted themselves well, yielding ground slowly and inflicting substantial casualties on the advancing Japanese. The 39th pulled back to Deniki, its ranks thinned by death, injury and disease. However, reinforcements were on the way in the shape of the 53rd Battalion, which arrived in the nick of time.

Both sides now began to build up their forces. The Japanese regional commander, Lieutenant-General Harukichi Hyakutake, sent 13,000 men to the island, all of them veterans. The AIF's 7th Division, under Major-General 'Tubby' Allen, moved north from Uberi. The Japanese were pushing hard, achieving some gains but also extending their vulnerable lines of communication. Two of the 7th's units, the Second Australian Imperial Force's 14th and 16th Battalions, relieved their exhausted comrades on the Kokoda Trail. At the end of August, despite some hard fighting, the Australians had been pushed back to Templeton's Crossing, and then to Ioribaiwa in early September, unable to stop the Japanese momentum. Here they were determined to make a stand. From this place there would be no more retreats.

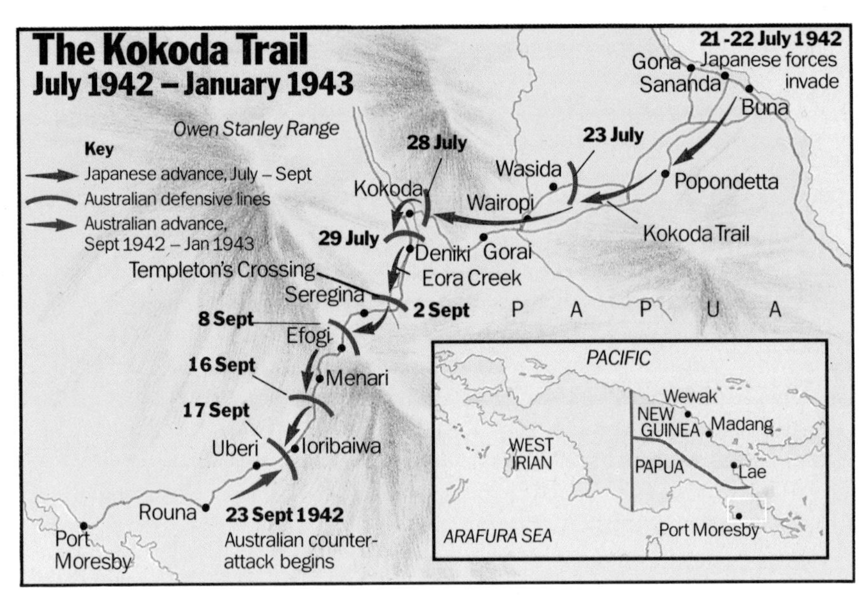

Along the Imita Ridge the Australians dug trenches and strongpoints, and the 7th's 25th Brigade was moved up to the ridge. The Japanese also pushed up 1000 reinforcements. Between 17 and 26 September, the Japanese tried to cut through the Australian line. Savage fights broke out between small groups of men for a few metres of sodden ground. The Japanese were ferocious in their attacks, but they were losing three times as many casualties as the Australians. Above all, they could not shift the stubborn Diggers, and on 26 September began to pull back from the ridge.

The Japanese had been stopped by a sound defensive position, shortage of supplies, growing Allied air superiority and, above all, the indomitable fighting spirit of the ordinary Australian soldier. The Japanese advance on Port Moresby had been stopped in its tracks, and now the enemy began to recoil from the ridge. The Diggers' turn had come.

The Australians' counterattack was launched soon after. By the first week of October they had reached Templeton's Crossing. On 16 October the 25th Brigade was relieved by the veteran 16th Brigade, and the advance continued. The Japanese proved adept at defensive warfare, particularly concealment and ambushing. The grim attritional warfare continued, though by now the Japanese were at the end of their tether. The Australians entered Kokoda on 1 November, its fall marking a turning point in the war in the southwest Pacific. A grim campaign had been won by the heroism of a few thousand Australian soldiers. Though the fight for New Guinea was far from over and it would be many months before the Japanese were evicted from their enclaves on the northern coast, Port Moresby and Australia were safe from the Japanese. The Diggers had saved their homeland from the Rising Sun.

LONG RANGE DESERT GROUP, RAID ON BARCE, 13 SEPTEMBER 1942

In September 1942, a column of vehicles from the Long Range Desert Group (LRDG), the intelligence-gathering and raiding unit, was heading across the North African Desert towards the Axis-held port of Barce. Its task, codenamed 'Caravan', was a raid that would be part of a large combined operation by the LRDG against enemy supply lines and airfields. The leader of the column was Captain Jake Easonsmith and it comprised three patrols: S2, commanded by Captain John Olivey; T2, under Captain Nick Wilder; and G1, led by Sergeant Jack Dennis and accompanied by Major Vladimir 'Popski' Peniakoff and two Arab agents.

The plan was for S2 to divert towards Benghazi and support the Special Air Service raid on that port. T2 and G1 were to proceed directly to Barce. The column left Fayoum in the Nile Delta on 2 September. The distance to be covered amounted to 1600km over difficult terrain, and the mission was fraught with danger. Travelling across the desert could be extremely tedious – vehicles broke down, taking evasive detours took a great deal of time, and approaches to supply dumps and rendezvous points had to be concealed by laying false trails. Enemy aircraft also posed a threat.

By 12 September the column had reached the foothills of the Libyan Jebel Akhdar mountain range. Easonsmith left a truck filled with rations, water and petrol as an emergency rallying point at Bir el-Gerrari, 96km from the target. The column reached the vicinity of Barce in the late morning of 13 September, the vehicles being camouflaged among olive groves while Easonsmith and Peniakoff reconnoitred the enemy positions.

The party hits the port

When darkness fell the men checked their weapons and time bombs and started the vehicles. Easonsmith led the way with his jeep, which was armed with two Vickers 'K' machine guns. Behind him were 11 trucks and another jeep. The column approached and shot up a police post at Sidi Raui, but during this action two trucks collided, damaging them both. Leaving them behind, the column pressed on. When they reached the town the party split up, Dennis driving towards the main Italian barracks and Wilder heading off to the airfield. The three trucks and one jeep led by Dennis began to shoot up and throw grenades into the barracks, its occupants caught totally by surprise by the raiders. Wilder's party was equally successful at the airfield, destroying 20 aircraft and damaging 12 others, in addition to the buildings that were destroyed. Having achieved their aims, all the raiders had to do was withdraw safely.

Though the LRDG encountered some opposition while leaving the port, it was Italian aircraft that did the most damage. Forty kilometres from Barce, enemy aircraft caught the column in the open and began to strafe it. Though the men found shelter in the rocks, their vehicles were sitting ducks and by dusk only two jeeps and one truck remained intact. With these three vehicles 33 men, six of them wounded, had to travel nearly 1300km to safety. The column was split into two: one with the wounded was to take the truck and a jeep to LG 125, a temporary airstrip, while the other would head for the spare truck at Bir el-Gerrari. Both parties made it back to friendly lines. Despite the loss of 10 men (all POWs) and most of the vehicles, the LRDG's raid had been a success, not least because of the damage it did to Italian morale.

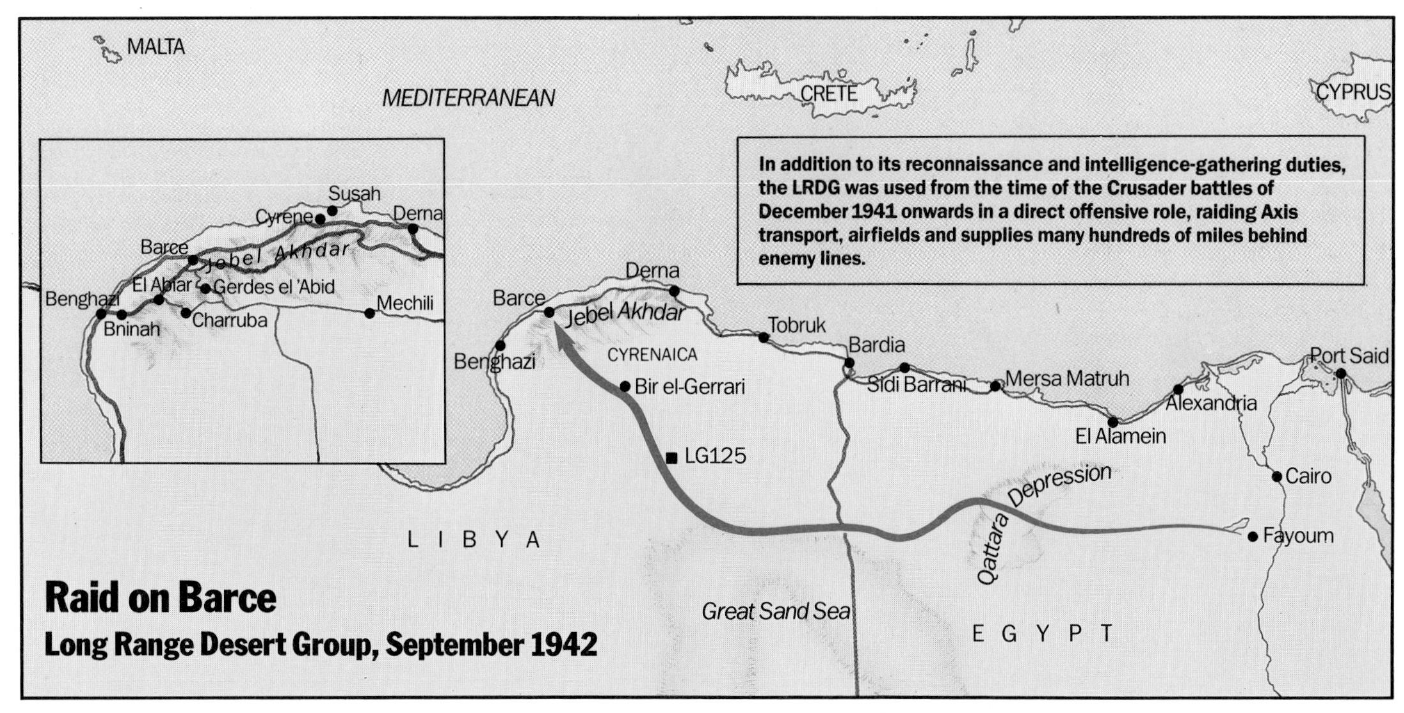

Raid on Barce
Long Range Desert Group, September 1942

13TH GUARDS DIVISION, STALINGRAD, SEPTEMBER 1942

During September 1942, the Soviet 13th Guards Division suffered appalling losses as it tried to stem the German advance in the central sector of the city of Stalingrad. The division had been attached to the Stalingrad Front from the Soviet Army's central reserve on 9 September, two-and-a-half weeks after the battle had begun. On 23 August, the 8th German Air Corps had subjected the city to a furious bombardment, and that evening the 79th Panzer Grenadier Regiment reached the suburb of Spartanovka. The following day the tractor plant in the northern suburbs came under heavy fire.

General Paulus, commander of the German Sixth Army, was ordered to launch an all-out offensive to take the city on 15 September, while on the Russian side General Zhukov and Colonel-General Vasilevsky were ordered to prepare for a Soviet counteroffensive. Stalin ordered the 10,000-strong 13th Guards Division, commanded by Major-General Alexander Ilyich Rodimtsev, to cross the Volga and hold Stalingrad at all costs.

On the night of 14/15 September, the guards crossed the Volga under heavy German fire. Once on the other side, they advanced straight into the battle that was being fought for the narrow strip of the city still held by the Red Army. The guards relieved an NKVD force about to launch a counterattack on a German strongpoint in the State Bank building. The 13th managed to establish a bridgehead but could not set up sound defensive positions, and on 15 September German air attacks prevented any further guards units crossing the river. Nevertheless, the formations already in position, the 34th and 39th Regiments and the 1st Battalion, 42nd Regiment, prepared to clear the German 71st Infantry Division and the 295th Infantry Division from the central railway station and the heights of Mamayev Kurgan respectively.

The guards took the heights but the Germans launched a fierce counterattack, and the battle for this position was to last throughout the winter. The Russian tactic was to occupy buildings and turn them into 'breakwaters' to blunt German attacks. The 13th bore the full weight of the Sixth Army's push to the Volga between 15 and 26 September, and also the attack to cut the Soviet sector in two on 1 October. In one incident on the 2nd, 300 German troops of the 295th Infantry Division infiltrated the rear of the 34th Guards Regiment through a storm drain – but the guards wiped them out.

On 19 November, the Soviet counteroffensive began, smashing into the weak flanks of the German Sixth Army, and on 26 January 1943, tanks of the Soviet Sixty-fifth Army linked up with Russian forces in the city. German resistance ended on 2 February.

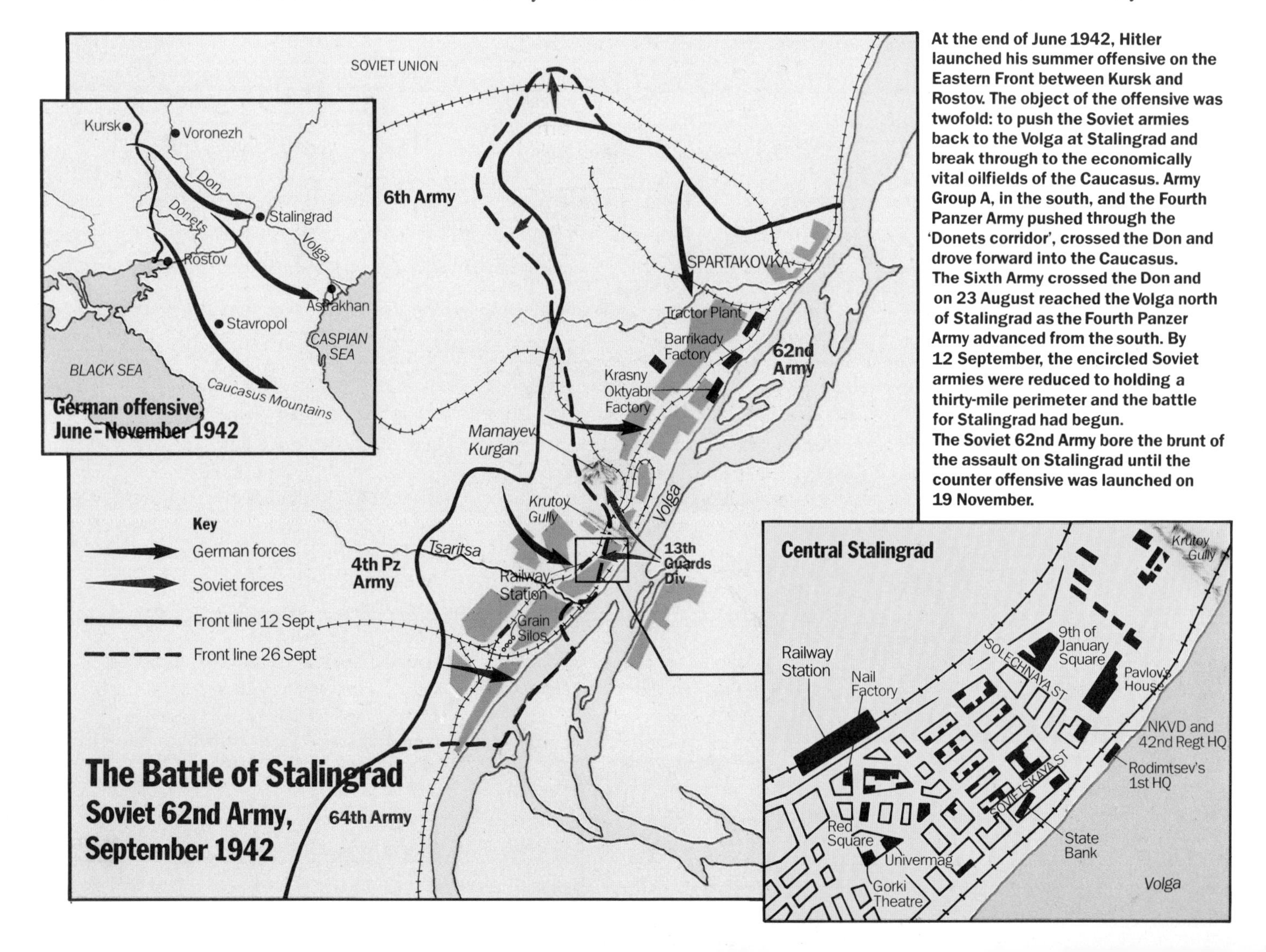

At the end of June 1942, Hitler launched his summer offensive on the Eastern Front between Kursk and Rostov. The object of the offensive was twofold: to push the Soviet armies back to the Volga at Stalingrad and break through to the economically vital oilfields of the Caucasus. Army Group A, in the south, and the Fourth Panzer Army pushed through the 'Donets corridor', crossed the Don and drove forward into the Caucasus. The Sixth Army crossed the Don and on 23 August reached the Volga north of Stalingrad as the Fourth Panzer Army advanced from the south. By 12 September, the encircled Soviet armies were reduced to holding a thirty-mile perimeter and the battle for Stalingrad had begun. The Soviet 62nd Army bore the brunt of the assault on Stalingrad until the counter offensive was launched on 19 November.

THE RIFLE BRIGADE, 'SNIPE', 27 OCTOBER 1942

The Battle of El Alamein opened on 23 October 1942. But during the evening of the 24th, it became apparent that although the infantry of XXX Corps had reached their main objective – the Oxalic Line – the armour of X Corps was making little progress because of enemy anti-tank defences. Major-General R Briggs, commander of the 1st Armoured Division, sought to rectify this by sending forward two rifle battalions to take positions that would allow them to dominate enemy anti-tank positions to the west, and thus create a passage through which the British armour could pass.

The advance party of the 2nd Battalion, The Rifle Brigade, led by Lieutenant-Colonel Victor Turner, headed towards the location codenamed 'Snipe'. By 0345 hours on 27 October, 19 6-pounder anti-tank guns were in position for an all-round defence. Turner had 300 men under his command, and they watched in astonishment as enemy tanks rolled past their position just after dawn. The Germans were unaware of the British anti-tank guns, which had a field day. After 30 minutes the Germans withdrew, leaving behind six German and eight Italian tanks destroyed, as well as two self-propelled guns. The British had lost three anti-tank guns.

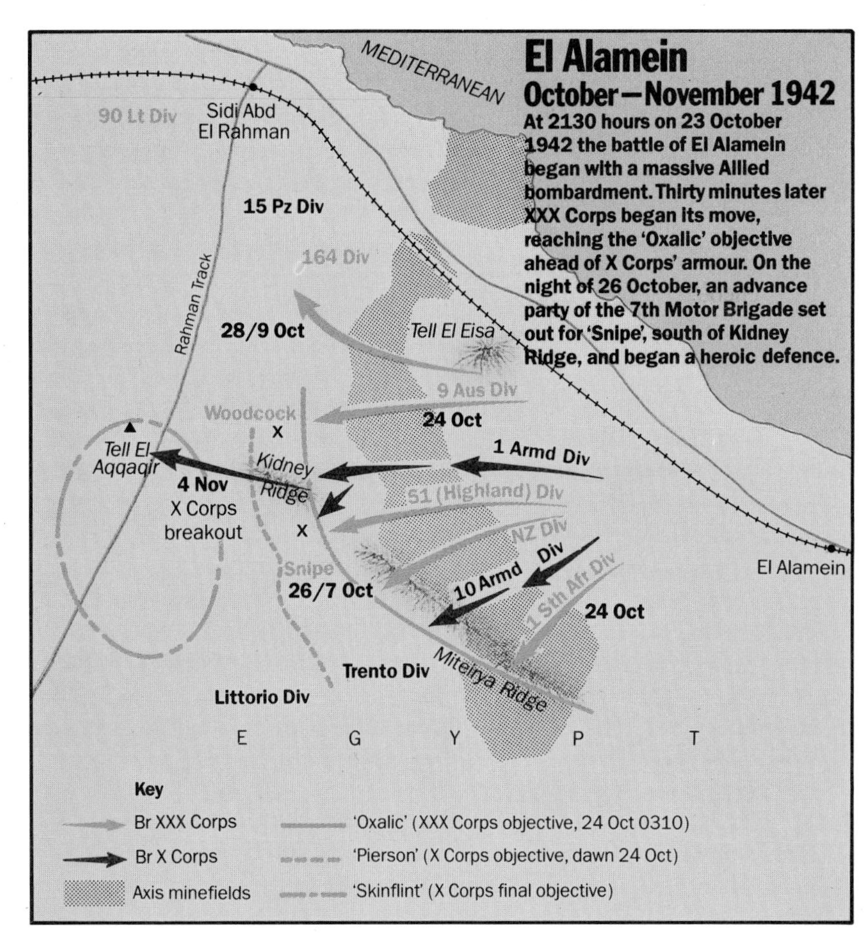

A group of Sherman tanks of the 24th Armoured Brigade then moved up to support the 'Snipe' position, but withdrew when seven of them were destroyed by German 88mm guns. The riflemen were once again on their own. At 1000 hours Italian infantry were spotted massing to the west, whereupon Turner ordered the Bren carrier platoon to disperse them. The latter charged straight at the infantry, causing them to retreat. Then 13 Italian tanks rumbled towards 'Snipe', but they were dealt with by the 6-pounders, which destroyed four before the rest retreated. The British gunners were enjoying great success.

The next assault came from a group of panzers to the south, but these were cut to pieces by a combination of fire from the 6-pounders and the Shermans of the 24th Armoured Brigade. However, 'Snipe' had by this time attracted much attention, and Axis artillery started to inflict casualties on the riflemen. Six Bren gun carriers were hit in a barrage just after noon on the 27th, and after 1300 hours enemy shelling and machine-gun fire increased in intensity. Then, to the southwest appeared eight Italian tanks and one self-propelled gun, heading for the sector of the defences where only one 6-pounder remained in operation. However, unfortunately for the enemy, the gun was manned by Sergeant Callistan. In a remarkable demonstration of coolness and gunnery, Callistan, assisted by Turner and Lieutenant Toms, destroyed all eight tanks and the self-propelled gun.

The riflemen in 'Snipe' were now in a precarious position, having only a few guns and running short of ammunition. The Germans sent 15 panzers forward to finish them off, confident that they would at last destroy these troublesome Englishmen. Making good use of cover, the German tanks crept forward and swept each gun position with machine-gun fire. However, one gun knocked out the leading tank and then a second tank was destroyed by anti-tank fire, the shell passing through the hull and hitting another tank. The panzers then drew off, somewhat shocked by the determined resistance. As darkness fell it was decided to abandon the 'Snipe' position. By 2230 hours the riflemen were gone.

The defence of 'Snipe' by the men of The Rifle Brigade had been outstanding. For the loss of 100 men, they had destroyed 34 tanks or self-propelled guns and had brought the German attack to a halt. Turner won a Victoria Cross for his actions, and Callistan a Distinguished Conduct Medal.

2ND MARINE RAIDER BATTALION, GUADALCANAL, NOVEMBER 1942

The 1st US Marine Division had been on the Pacific island of Guadalcanal since August 1942, battling against the stubborn Japanese defenders. On 4 November they were reinforced by Carlson's Raiders, the 2nd Marine Raider Battalion, which landed on Guadalcanal. Moving inland, the Raiders encountered enemy small-arms fire but pressed on, reaching the village of Kema on 9 November and the Metapona river the next day. To the north of the Metapona river, Japanese forces were engaging the 7th Marines and the 164th Infantry.

Very soon the lead elements were reporting that they had run into a battalion-sized Japanese force armed with machine guns and mortars. Though they had surprised the enemy, killing a number of Japanese, the Raiders had taken casualties themselves, and so were ordered south to a rendezvous point north of the village of Asamana. The Raiders remained in the area until 19 November when, under orders from the 1st Marine Division, they established a base on the Tenaru river and then patrolled around that area and the Lunga river.

The unit, minus two companies that were left behind, started out for the upper Tenaru and established a camp a few kilometres south of Henderson field, being joined a few days later by the two detached companies. Patrols were constantly being sent out, and on 29 November two Raider companies clashed with a Japanese force, killing 75 enemy soldiers.

In early December the Raiders were on the move again – down the Lunga trail into the division's main perimeter. Again there were numerous skirmishes with the Japanese, the Americans often catching the enemy unawares and inflicting many casualties with small-arms fire. By 5 December the Raiders had reached the beach, where the transports waited to take them back to Espiritu Santo. The Raiders had spent a tiring month on Guadalcanal and had conducted a 240km trek through the jungle. They had fought over a dozen actions against the Japanese, killing over 500 and driving the rest into the interior. In addition, although the battle for Guadalcanal was to last until 9 February 1943, by which time the Japanese had suffered a total of 25,000 dead, the Raiders' operations had undermined the enemy's belief in final victory. It had been a superb hit-and-run operation.

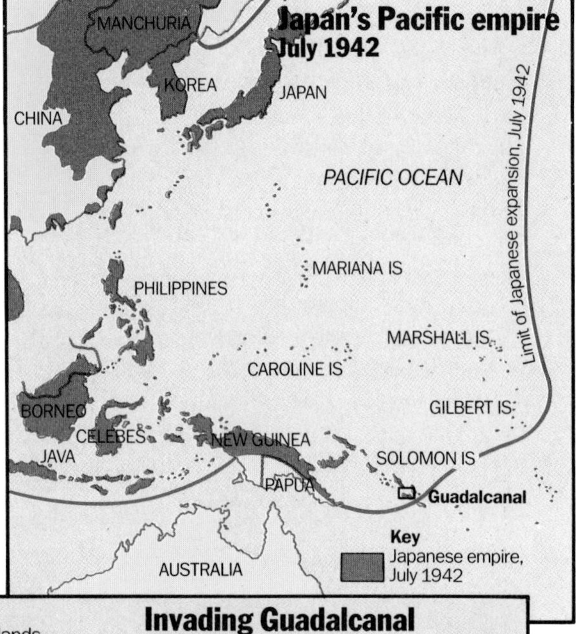

Guadalcanal

The US 1st Marine Division landed on Guadalcanal on 7 August 1942. Two days later it had established a perimeter near Lunga Point, but throughout the following three months the Japanese received heavy reinforcements and the marines had to repulse a series of determined assaults.

On 4 November, the 2nd Marine Raider Battalion landed at Aola Bay, some 40 miles from American lines, and began an epic march through enemy-held territory.

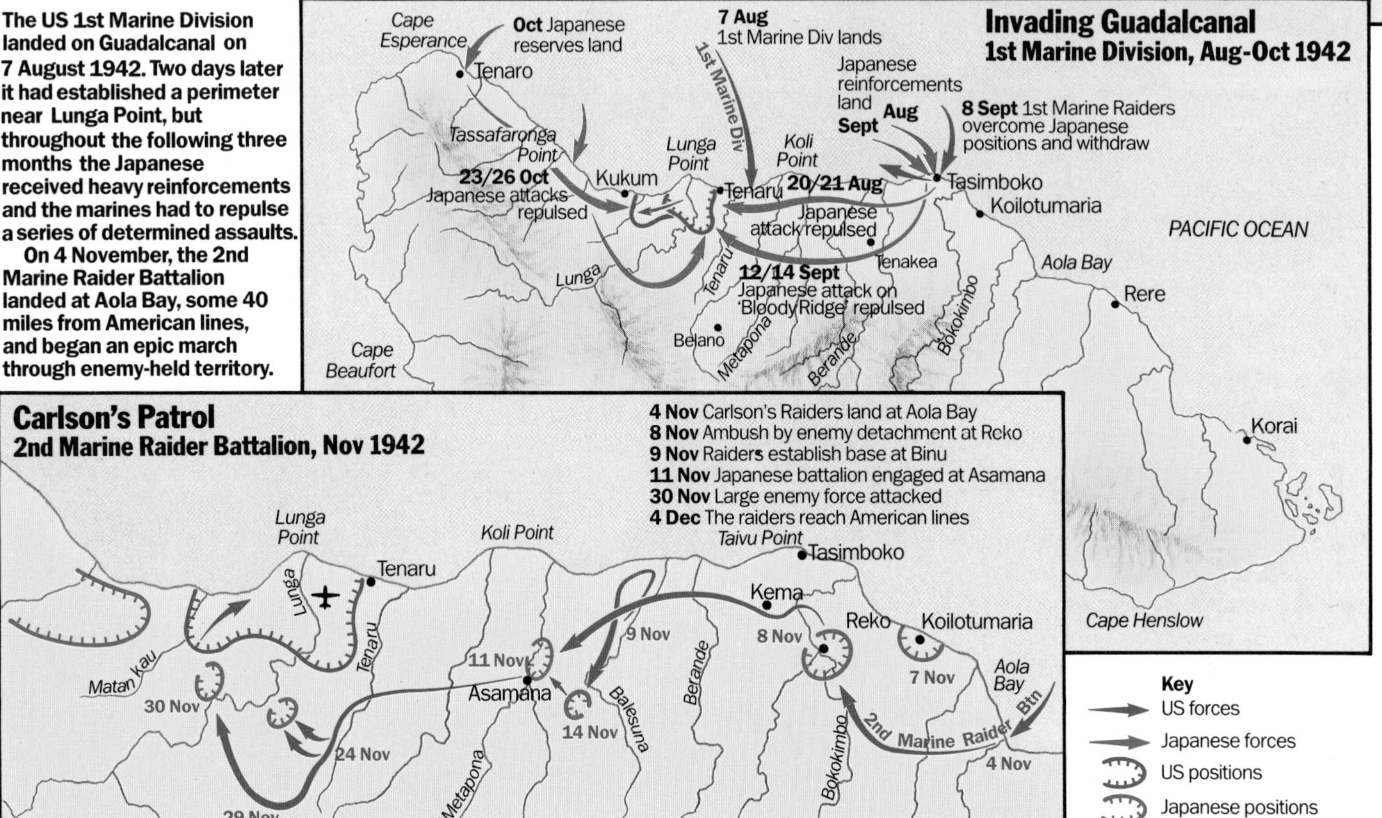

ROYAL MARINE BOOM PATROL DETACHMENT, BORDEAUX, DECEMBER 1942

Operation 'Frankton' was designed to cripple as many Axis merchant ships as possible operating out of the French port of Bordeaux. The men of the Royal Marine Boom Patrol Detachment, formed in July 1942 and specialising in deployment from submarines in canoes, were detailed to carry out the mission. Comprising 12 men and six canoes and led by Major H G Hasler, the party boarded the submarine *Tuna* on the morning of 30 November.

The unit was split into two groups: A Division under Hasler and B Division under Lieutenant J W Mackinnon. There were estimated to be around 12 Axis ships in Bordeaux, and the Marines were to place two limpet mines on each ship below the waterline and then escape overland with the help of the French Resistance. On the evening of 7 December, the Marines left the submarine and began to paddle inland. One canoe had been damaged as it was being launched and its crew had to re-board the ship. The five remaining vessels approached their first hazard, a tide-race, where one of the canoes, *Coalfish*, was lost. The other four carried on, passing the lighthouse at the Pointe de Grave. However, another tide-race was encountered and another canoe, *Conger*, capsized.

The main party pushed on, pausing to rest when daylight came at 0630 hours on 8 December. However, yet another canoe, *Cuttlefish*, had been lost and the mission was in danger of failing. The rest of the party waited for night and then continued, the men chilled to the bone. Lying up during the day, the party then paddled through the night of 9/10 December. Because of tides and narrow channels, the Marines did not make the progress they had on the two previous nights. The two canoes continued, however, and came across the first Axis ships on the river.

Hasler decided to drift through the docks on the last flood tide of the day and then turn on the ebb to lay mines on the ships. The two canoes split: Hasler would deal with the ships on the Bordeaux side of the river, while the other canoe, commanded by Corporal Laver, would attack the vessels on the eastern bank at Bassens South. They were far away from Bordeaux when the first explosions took place – two ships were sunk and three damaged.

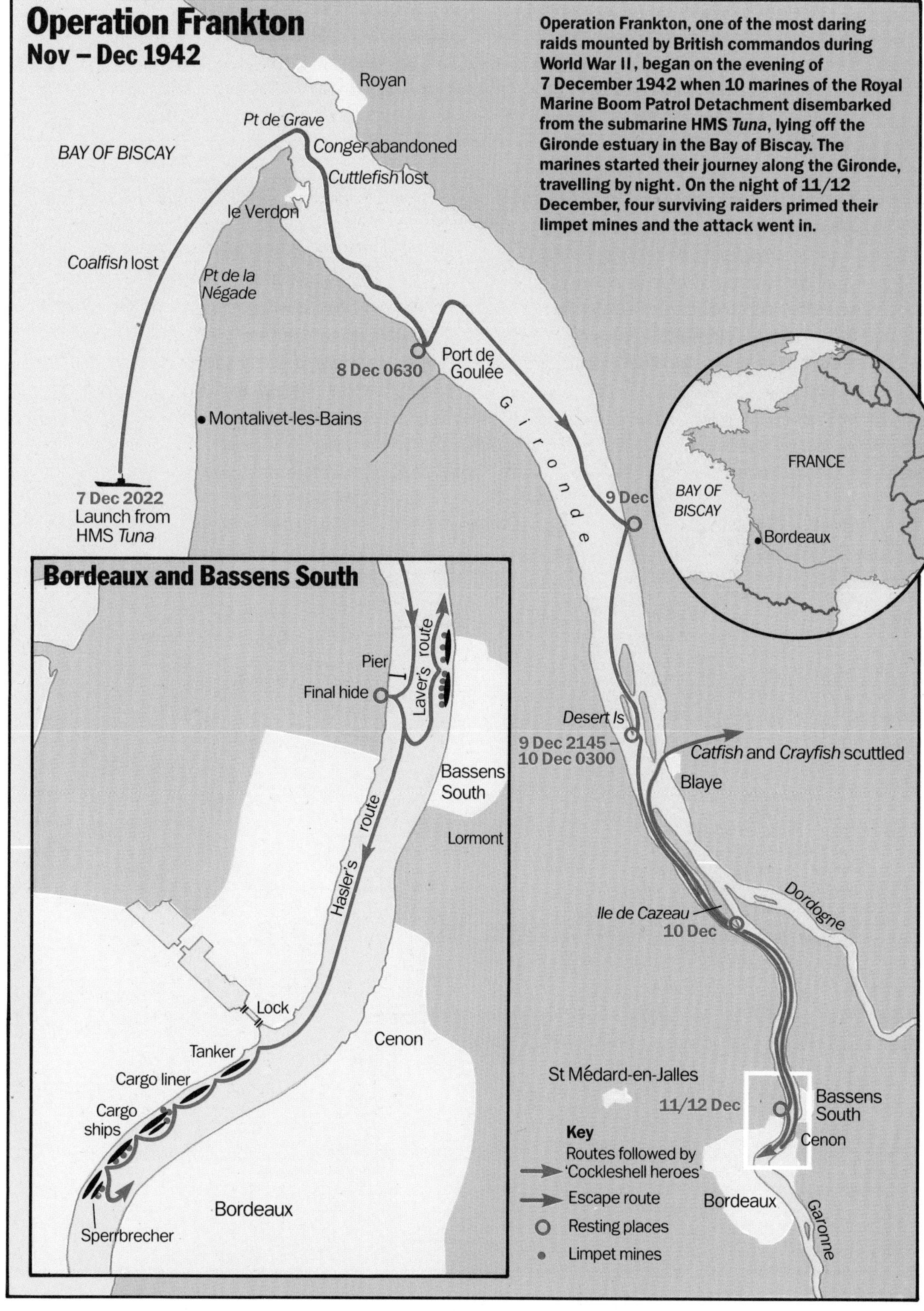

2ND BATTALION, THE PARACHUTE REGIMENT, OUDNA, NOVEMBER 1942

On 12 November 1942, the 2nd Battalion, The Parachute Regiment, led by Lieutenant-Colonel John Frost, landed at Algiers as part of the eastward thrust of the British First Army, commanded by Lieutenant-General Sir Kenneth Anderson. The British Eighth Army, led by General Montgomery, had defeated Axis forces at the second Battle of El Alamein, and on 8 November Allied forces landed in northwest Africa as part of Operation 'Torch'. The capture of Tunis and Bizerta would cut off Axis supply lines and consolidate Allied positions in Tunisia before the winter rains came. The Allied advance was being hampered by enemy aircraft operating from airfields to the west of Tunis and so, on 28 November, Frost was ordered to parachute his men onto a German airstrip at Pont du Fahs in Tunisia and destroy any aircraft he could find. The battalion would then move on to the airstrips at Depienne and Oudna and perform the same task. Finally, the battalion would link up with the First Army at St Cyprien. At the last minute intelligence revealed that there were no aircraft at Pont du Fahs or Depienne – so the drop zone was changed to Depienne, from where the Paras would advance straight to Oudna.

The drop was successful, and by 1100 hours on 30 November the Paras were overlooking Oudna. Leaving one company to keep watch on the high ground, Frost took the rest of the battalion towards its objective. Just as they neared the airstrip, the Paras came

BELOW: *A pensive look on the face of this British Para as he anticipates the drop near Oudna. Once on the ground, the Paras fought with skill and valour.*

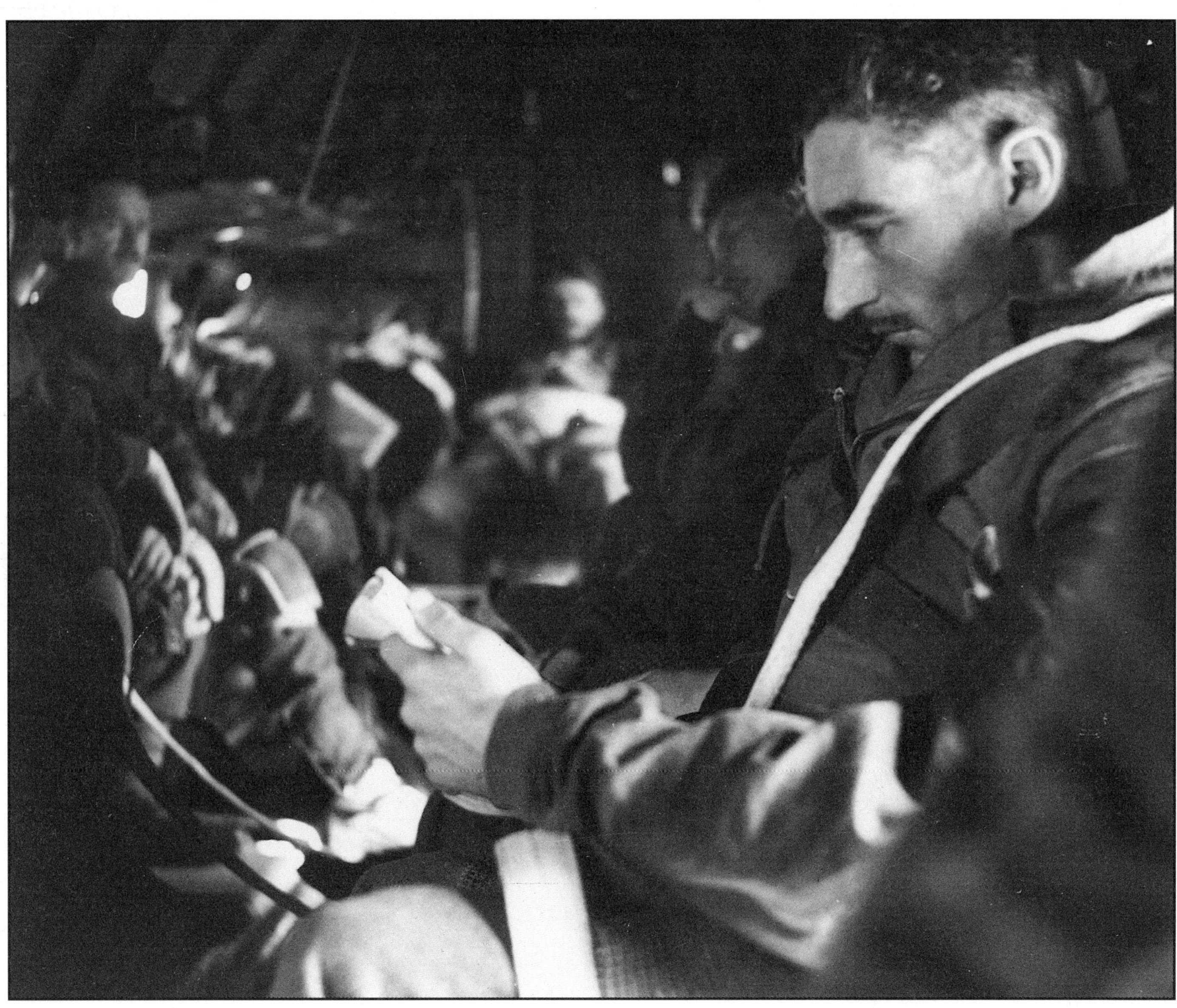

The advance on Tunisia
Nov 1942 – Jan 1943

On 8 November 1942 the Allies launched Operation Torch. Three task forces landed in Morocco and Algeria and began an eastward drive along the North African coast towards the vital ports and airfields of Tunisia. Axis forces moved into Tunisia in strength, establishing a defensive line including Tunis and Bizerta by 10 November. In late November, an Allied offensive reached as far as Tebourba, and 2 Para dropped near Oudna with orders to seize the airfield and link up with the advancing Allies at St Cyprien.

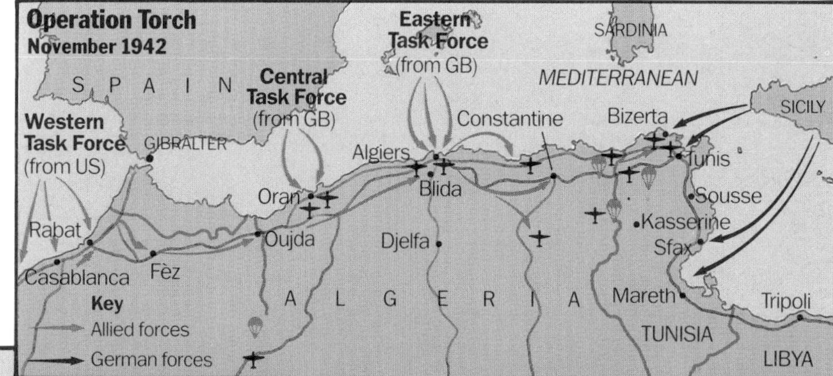

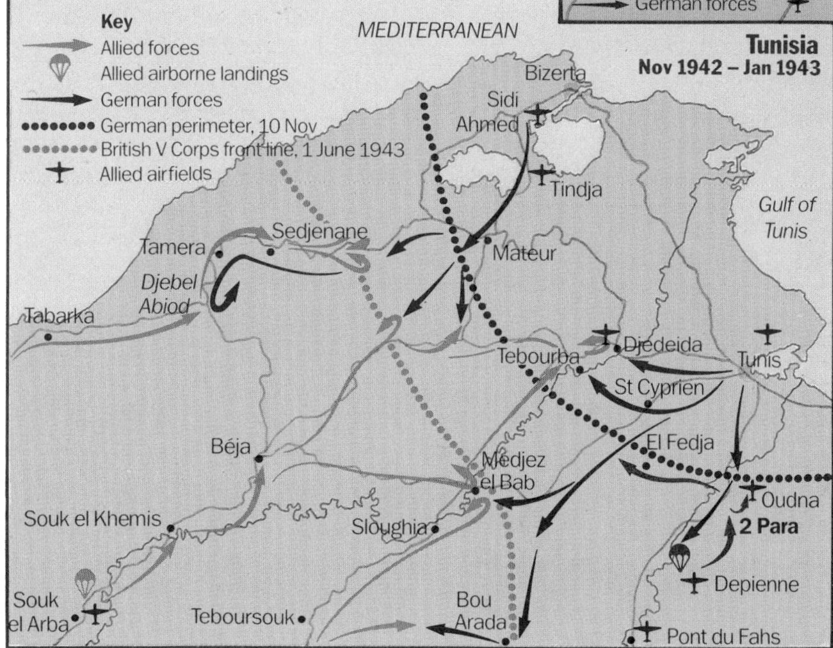

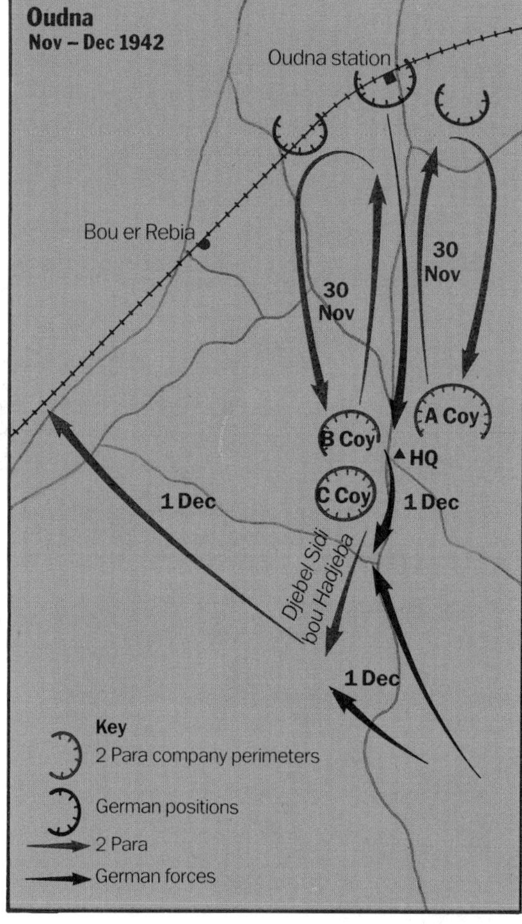

under intense machine-gun and mortar fire. Forging on, they managed to reach some buildings inside the perimeter of the airfield. However, the Paras now faced two deadly threats. First, a column of German tanks attacked the British in an effort to throw them back from the airstrip. A charge by the Paras to destroy the tanks with grenades failed, many men being cut down in a hail of fire. Second, Messerschmitt Bf 109 fighters began to strafe Frost's men mercilessly, with scrub the Paras' only cover.

German artillery opens up

The tank and aircraft fire subsided as the evening wore on, and the Paras started to withdraw to the high ground at Prise de l'Eau. Frost was now in a very precarious position: his men had taken casualties and they were running short of ammunition. No enemy aircraft had been found at Oudna, so Frost decided to make for the forward elements of the First Army. However, at 1000 hours on 1 December, an enemy column left Oudna and approached the Paras' position. Brushing aside Frost's ambush party, the Germans shelled the British. Replying with mortars, the Paras scored a direct hit on a vehicle and the column withdrew. Relief was at hand for the Paras, however. Soon after this incident tanks and armoured cars of the First Army made contact with the battalion.

The Paras are hit by Stukas

The frontlines were still fluid, however: Frost led his men to a hill known as Sidi Bou Hadjeba. But they were still vulnerable to attack, and at 1500 hours German infantry and tanks made an assault on the hill. The Paras clung on grimly, making good use of the reverse slope of the hill to rake the enemy infantry with machine-gun fire. The Germans replied with artillery and tank fire, and very soon the Paras were under an intense barrage. To add to their misery, Stuka dive-bombers joined in the attack, until the German aircraft mistakenly bombed their own troops, whereupon they were hastily recalled. This gave the Paras a much-needed breathing space, allowing them to withdraw as darkness fell. Though they hadn't destroyed any aircraft, they could feel justly proud for remaining unshaken in the face of tank and aerial attack.

1ST SS PANZER DIVISION, BATTLE OF KHARKOV, JANUARY-MARCH 1943

Following the disaster at Stalingrad in January 1943, the Germans in the south of the Soviet Union were reeling under the onslaught of Soviet counteroffensives. Hitler forbade any withdrawal, much to the frustration of the commander in the area, Field Marshal Erich von Manstein. However, the Führer did send I SS Panzer Corps, comprising 1st SS Panzergrenadier Division Leibstandarte SS Adolf Hitler, 2nd SS Panzergrenadier Division Das Reich and 3rd SS Panzergrenadier Division Totenkopf, as reinforcements. The Leibstandarte contained a panzer battalion which was armed with the latest 'Tiger' tanks under the command of Sturmbannführer Joachim Peiper. The divisional commander was General Josef 'Sepp' Dietrich, and the formation contained many battle-hardened veterans.

In January 1943, Hitler ordered I SS Panzer Corps to make a counterattack to stabilise the situation around Kharkov. The Leibstandarte held a bridgehead at Chuguyev in a divisional front of over 100km and in appalling weather conditions: severe temperatures and snow storms. As expected, the Leibstandarte held, fighting a number of Soviet attacks in early February. But other army units, notably the 320th Infantry Division, gave way, opening up a gap of 60km. As a result, I SS Panzer Corps was in danger of being cut off. Between 11 and 16 February, the Leibstandarte fought a series of battles in an effort to re-establish a continuous frontline. Dietrich formed a *kampfgruppe* (battlegroup) which stopped the Soviet advance after a counterattack.

In vicious hand-to-hand fighting, the Das Reich, Leibstandarte and Totenkopf were decimated, but they did not budge. Elan, daring and a willingness to withstand heavy fire stemmed the Soviet onslaught. Leibstandarte rescued the isolated 320th Infantry Division on 13 February; the 1st Battalion of the panzer regiment rescued the divisional reconnaissance battalion around the village of Bereka.

General Paul Hausser, commander of I SS Panzer Corps, abandoned Kharkov to the enemy. However, this was only the start of a German counteroffensive, and on 22 February Leibstandarte attacked and linked up with elements of Army Group Centre, trapping an entire Soviet armoured corps and destroying it. The Tigers and armoured personnel carriers roamed over the steppe at will, inflicting heavy casualties on the Soviets.

By 9 March, I SS Panzer Corps was deployed to the north and west of Kharkov. Hausser gave the order to attack the city, and Leibstandarte raced in. However, the Soviets fought tenaciously. Bitter house-to-house fighting ensued and the division's heavy armour was reduced to 14 tanks by 12 March. Nevertheless, by 15 March Soviet resistance came to an end. Leibstandarte had proved itself to be an elite.

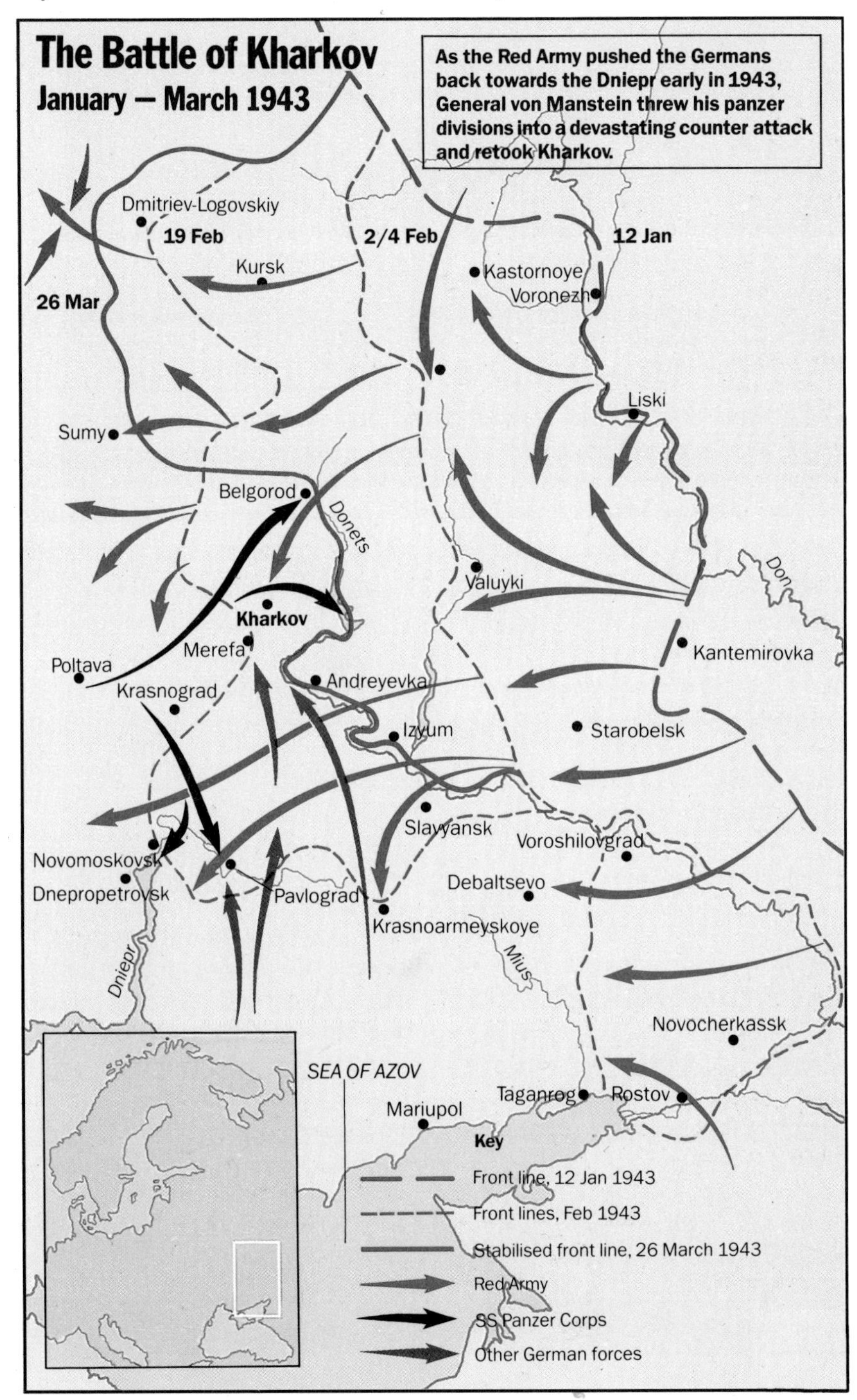

1ST RANGER BATTALION, SENED PASS, 10 FEBRUARY 1943

The first action the 1st Ranger Battalion had tasted was the seizure of the port of Arzew, North Africa, in early November 1942. Since that time they had spent their days in endless training – and had engaged in more than their fare share of bar-room brawls. The Rangers' commander, Lieutenant-Colonel William Darby, knew he must face a more constructive outlet for the energies of his men.

Following the invasion of North Africa, Allied forces had pushed eastwards into Tunisia. However, in February they ran into stiff resistance, especially at the Sened Pass, where Italian troops were dug in and supported by German armour. Darby was ordered to lead his men in a lightning raid against this position to inflict the maximum amount of damage.

By November 1942, the Rangers had matured into a commando-style unit of excellent quality, but they yearned for action. The Sened Pass gave them the chance to show their abilities. On 7 February they were flown to II Corps' headquarters at Tebessa, Tunisia, and then transported by truck to Gafsa, the southernmost tip of the Allied line. The raid was carried out by three of the battalion's seven companies: A, E and F. They were to advance through the barren desert on the night of 9 February, lie up during the following day and then attack at night. Once they had hit the Italian positions, the Rangers would make a speedy withdrawal and try to make it back to friendly lines.

The Rangers achieve total surprise

At 2130 hours on 10 February, the men boarded trucks and set out. Each man was equipped with a ration pack, a water canteen, and a groundsheet. When the trucks stopped the men jumped off and headed to the target on foot: 180 men led by Darby, who set a ferocious pace. The route passed through arduous mountain ravines and mountain passes, but still the men forged on, covering over 20km by daybreak. As dawn broke they reached the first objective: a large depression between two mountain peaks. Camouflaging themselves among the rocks, the Rangers spent the day trying to get some well-earned sleep. Their target, the Sened Pass, was only 10km away.

When night fell the Rangers went forward, their faces blacked and strict silence being observed. The surprise was total until the Rangers were within 100m of the Italian line, then the Americans were spotted and the enemy opened up with a hail of machine-gun and cannon fire. Hitting the earth, the Rangers crawled to a rise in the ground just before the first Italian line. Then grenades were hurled into the enemy positions and the Rangers charged forward. Firing Thompson submachine guns from the hip, they cut down the Italian machine gunners and raced on, supported by mortars. In close-quarter fighting with bayonet, knife and grenade, the Americans killed without pity until all resistance had ended. Explosive charges were placed on Italian support weapons and then Darby gave the order to withdraw.

An exemplary victory

Taking their wounded with them, the Rangers had to cover some 32km before dawn. Pushing themselves to the limit, Darby and his men marched through the night and had covered 22km by daybreak. They pushed on despite the conditions, the weeks of training paying off as the pace was maintained. Then they encountered a British armoured car column which had been sent to cover the final stages of their withdrawal. It had been a stunning success: for the loss of one man killed and 18 wounded, the Rangers had killed 100 Italians, destroyed six cannon and 12 machine guns, and taken 11 prisoners in a superb hit-and-run action.

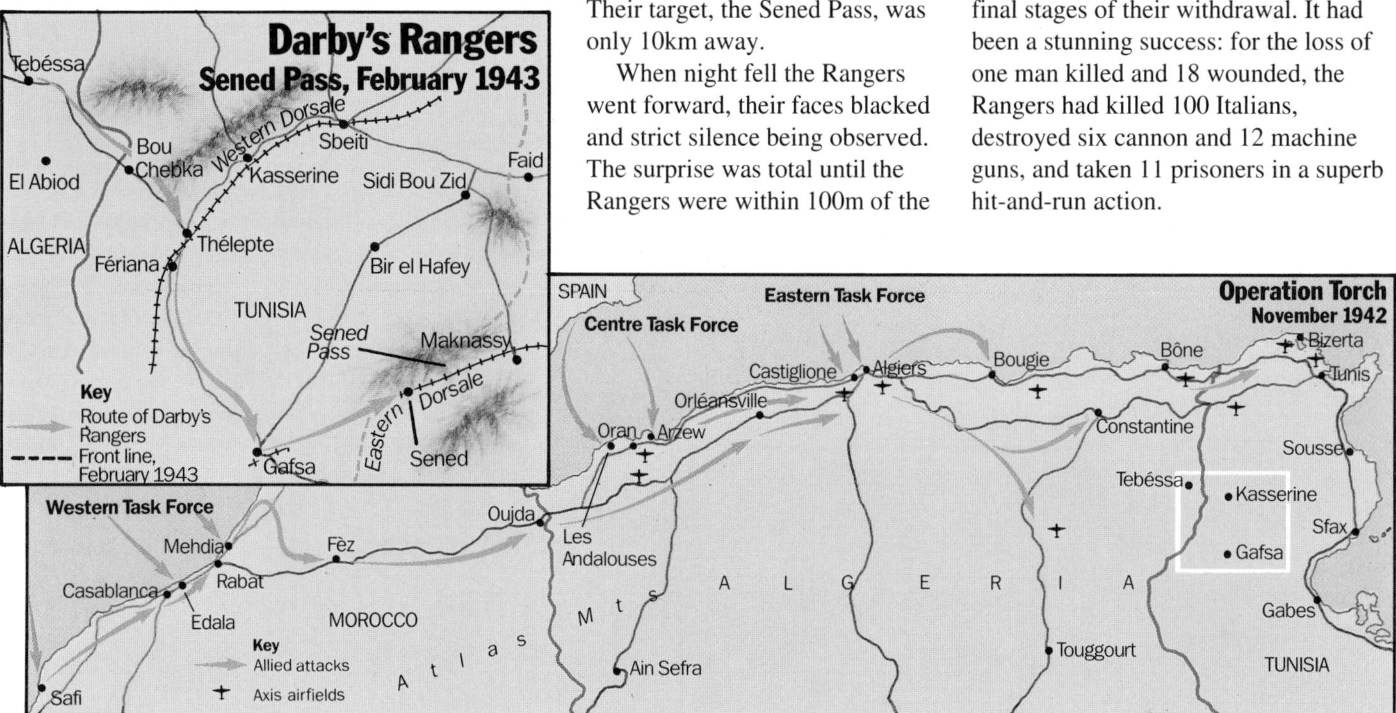

77 INDEPENDENT BRIGADE (CHINDITS), BURMA, FEBRUARY-MARCH 1943

As part of the proposed attack on Japanese forces in northern Burma in 1943, the British commander in Southeast Asia, General Sir Archibald Wavell, instructed Brigadier Orde Wingate's 77th Indian Infantry Brigade, the Chindits, to strike at the Mandalay-Myityina railway.

The Chindits were a mixed force of 3000 British, Gurkha and Burmese troops who were skilled in jungle fighting. They were divided into 300-strong 'columns', each one a self-contained force with its own mule train, heavy weapons and a signals detachment. With the aid of aerial re-supply, the Chindits could operate for long periods behind enemy lines.

On 5 January 1943, Wavell met Wingate and informed him that the operation was cancelled. Wingate, incensed at this and his men thirsting for action, managed to convince his superior that his Chindits deserved a crack at the enemy. Wavell relented, but told Wingate that he would be operating independently, and not as a part of a major offensive.

As a preparation, Wingate put his men through a strict training routine, and to prepare for the mission he had a vast sand table built which showed rivers, trails, mountains, and suspected enemy positions. By 8 February the men were ready. Each man was equipped with a rifle, bayonet, ammunition, hand grenades, a water bottle, plus clothing and rations – the whole lot weighed 35kg.

Wingate's plan was to leave the British forward position at Imphal and cross the Chindwin river at two points, move eastwards through the jungle and then strike at the railway between Bongyaung and Kyaikthin. The Chindits were split into two groups, the northern one consisting of 2200 men and 850 mules, led by Lieutenant-Colonel S Cooke, and the southern group made up of 1000 men and 250 mules, commanded by Lieutenant-Colonel H T Alexander. The latter would head for Mongmit, while the northern group would strike at the railroad between Bongyaung and Nankan.

The two groups began their missions on the night of 14/15 February. Wingate pushed his men hard, believing that marching prevented malaria, and he even stage-managed a few mock ambushes to keep the men on their toes. Despite his

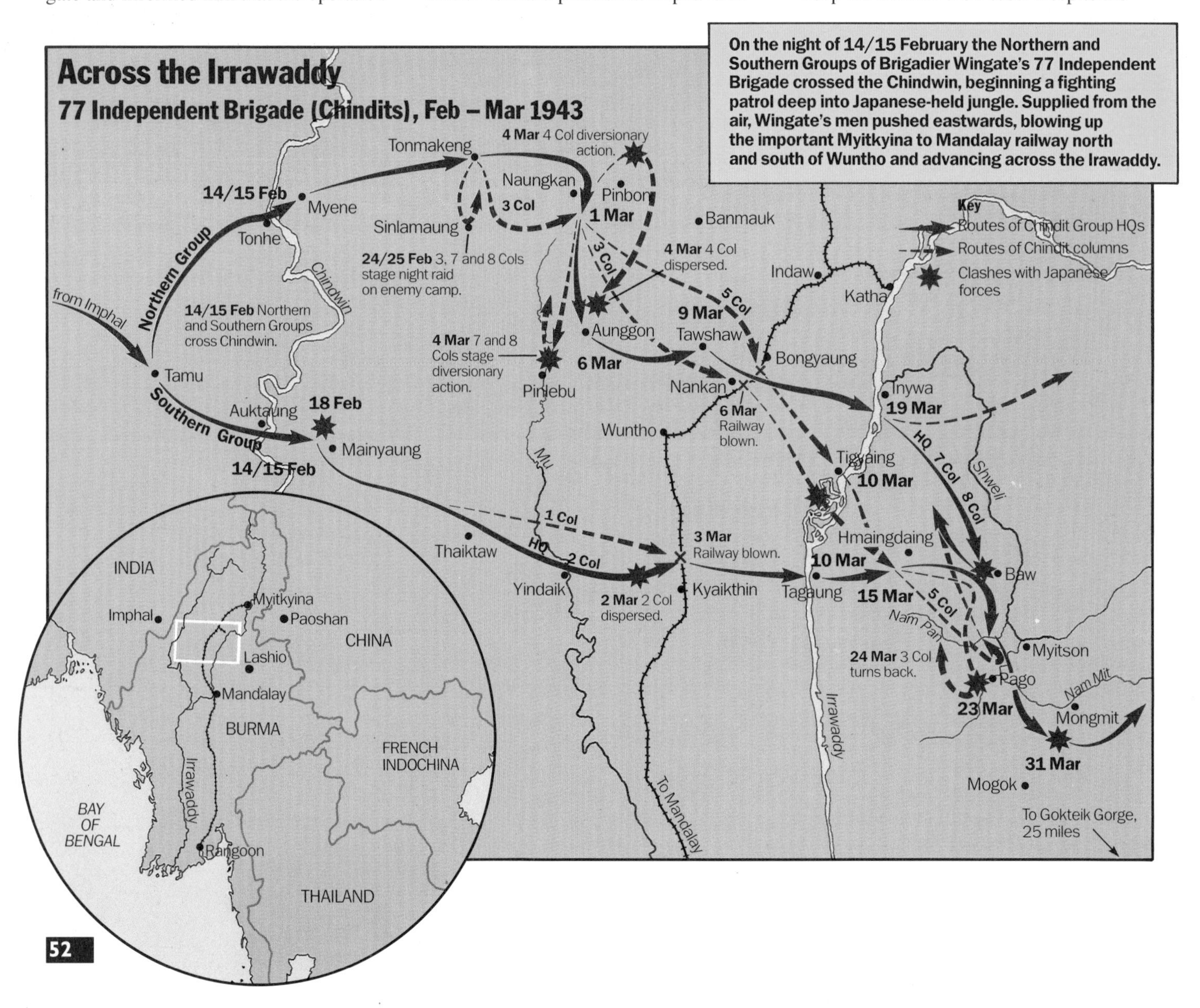

On the night of 14/15 February the Northern and Southern Groups of Brigadier Wingate's 77 Independent Brigade crossed the Chindwin, beginning a fighting patrol deep into Japanese-held jungle. Supplied from the air, Wingate's men pushed eastwards, blowing up the important Myitkyina to Mandalay railway north and south of Wuntho and advancing across the Irawaddy.

efforts, progress was slow in the jungle. The northern group reached Pinbon on 1 March, where the force was split into five 300-strong columns. However, disaster struck one of the columns when it was hit by a Japanese force near Pinlebu and scattered. The other columns forged on and located some railway bridges near Bongyaung, which were blown up.

Such activity was bound to attract attention, and the enemy commander in the area, Lieutenant-Colonel Renya Mutaguchi, deployed his 18th and 33rd Divisions to track and destroy the Chindits. However, he at first made the mistake of blocking the crossing points of the Chindwin, not knowing Wingate's men were being supplied from the air. But by mid-March three Japanese battalions were heading for Tagaung, the Irrawaddy, and the area north of the Shweli river. If Wingate continued his advance, he would run into these units.

The southern group hit the railway line at Kyaikthin, but was also ambushed. Wingate, believing they had crossed the river at Tagaung, decided to take the northern column deeper into enemy territory (he also believed that to turn back would jeopardise the Chindits' future). On 19 March he crossed the Irrawaddy just south of Inywa. His objective was the confluence of the Irrawaddy and Shweli rivers. However, the area was unsuited to guerrilla operations, being arid jungle and crossed by roads heavily patrolled by the Japanese. The commander of the British IV Corps, Lieutenant-General G A P Scoones, on hearing that the Japanese had confiscated all the boats on the Irrawaddy, ordered the Chindits to return.

Wingate split his men into small parties to avoid detection, the southern group heading east to China and the northern one aiming for the east bank of the Irrawaddy. The men eventually crossed the river, but they were malnourished and in poor condition, having to avoid enemy forces rather than stand and fight. Of the 3000 men who had crossed the Chindwin, only 2200 returned, and many of those were so crippled through illness and malnutrition that they would never fight again. The balance sheet of Chindit operations has always been controversial: they had severed the railway line in 75 places, but the track was soon repaired. The raid had, however, proved that the initiative in the war in Burma could be wrested from the Japanese Army.

ABOVE: *A column of Chindits operating behind the lines in Burma. Though Wingate's men inflicted much damage on Japanese supply lines, the jungle and enemy forces often exacted a heavy toll, destroying the health of many men.*

GREAT BRITAIN

6TH BATTALION, GRENADIER GUARDS, BATTLE OF THE HORSESHOE, 16-17 MARCH 1943

The 6th Battalion, Grenadier Guards, commanded by Lieutenant-Colonel A F L Clive, was part of the 201st Guards Brigade in March 1943 in General Bernard Montgomery's Eighth Army. The Eighth was about to attack Axis positions around the so-called Mareth Line, a barrier of tank traps, pillboxes and bunkers 100km inside Tunisia.

The 201st Guards Brigade was tasked with securing an area of ground shaped like a horseshoe which straddled the Gabes to Medinine road. However, the Germans had captured plans for the British attack before it began, and their 90th Light Division was deployed in strength to stop the brigade's advance. The brigade moved forward at 1930 hours on 16 March, with the Grenadier Guards on the right and the 3rd Battalion, Coldstream Guards, on the left.

The guardsmen meet problems

Clive designated three assault companies to attack the right, centre and left of the Horseshoe. These were No 3, No 1 and No 4 respectively. No 2 group was armed with machine guns, mortars and vehicles and was tasked with warding off any counterattacks. The preliminary artillery barrage began at 2045 hours on 16 March, and the battalion left its start position and advanced towards the objective. The German troops held their fire as the British crossed the Wadi Zess and approached them. Then they opened up and caught the guardsmen in a hail of machine-gun and mortar fire. Casualties quickly mounted, but the guardsmen pressed on.

One hour after moving off, the assault companies got through the first minefield – only to hit another. Still the advance continued. At 2230 hours, No 3 Company took Hill 139; by 2320 hours the other two companies had cleared the Germans from their trenches, many of the defenders being bayoneted by the British soldiers. As silence descended over the battlefield, the guardsmen assessed the damage. No 4 Company had suffered 70 per cent casualties, No 1 had been reduced from 120 to 35 men, and No 3 had been similarly devastated.

However, the battle was far from over. The Germans launched a counterattack which threatened to isolate then destroy the companies. Enemy fire from Point 117 was particularly heavy. The sappers below, aware that the guardsmen were cut off, began to work frantically to clear a passage through the minefields to allow Bren gun carriers to come up. The Germans increased the ferocity of their attack. Clive realised that the consolidation company had to find a way through or his other companies would have to withdraw. The Bren gun carriers of the company therefore advanced through the minefield and came across a track which led between the positions of Nos 1 and 4 Companies. Despite many casualties, the consolidation group started to retrieve survivors from the battlefield.

At 0525 hours, just before dawn, Brigadier Gascoigne ordered a withdrawal to the southern side of the wadi. The artillery started to drop smoke to cover the retreat. However, No 1 Company had lost its radio communications and did not hear the order. Surrounded and under fire, the unit, commanded by Major Evelyn, was in grave danger. The major had decided to withdraw anyway, but looking at his men he knew that such an order would crush their morale. He therefore decided to assault Point 117! At that moment four Bren gun carriers crested the ridge to take the company to safety. Though one was hit by enemy fire, the other three made it back to safety.

The Battle of the Horseshoe was over when Clive returned to the southern side of the Wadi Zess at 1000 hours. The 6th Battalion had lost 77 men killed, 93 wounded and 109 taken prisoner, but had captured and held its objectives until ordered to withdraw. The Grenadier Guards had displayed great courage in the face of devastating enemy fire.

BELOW: *Exhausted British infantry take a well-earned rest during the advance against German positions in Tunisia.*

The Battle of the Horseshoe
6th Battalion, Grenadier Guards, 16-17 March 1943

After the decisive defeat inflicted on the Afrika Korps at El Alamein in late 1942, the Eighth Army began a headlong drive to the gates of Tunisia that was finally brought to a halt by a series of Axis defences known as the Mareth Line. Although Operation Torch, the Allied landings in Algeria and Morocco during early November 1942, had forced the Axis forces to fight on two fronts, the Allies were still looking for a decisive battle. After a pause to regroup and re-organise, the Eighth Army began operations against the Mareth Line in March 1943. To test the quality of the German defences, a number of probing attacks were organised. On 16 March, the 6th Battalion, Grenadier Guards, was launched against the Horseshoe.

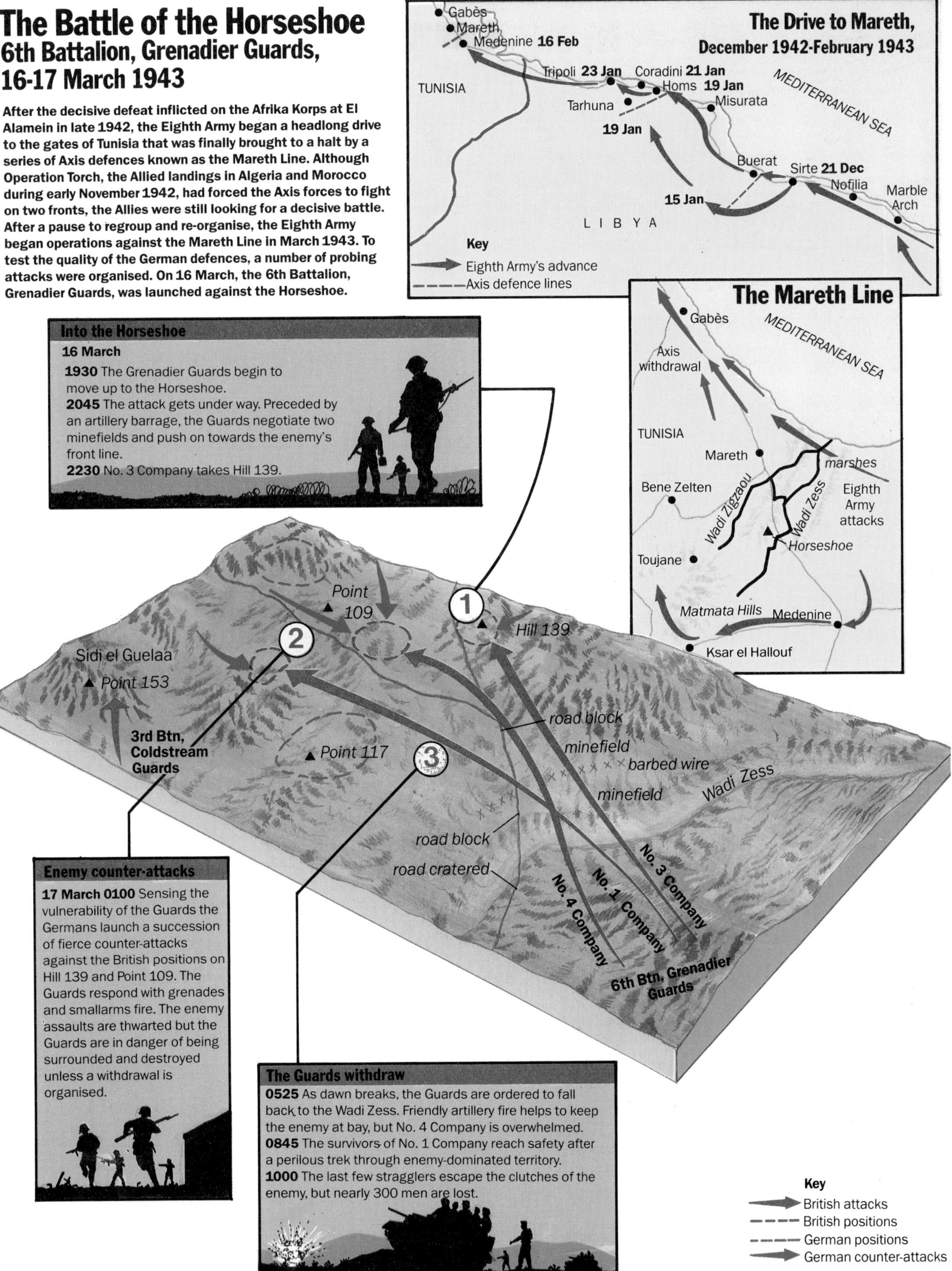

Into the Horseshoe

16 March

1930 The Grenadier Guards begin to move up to the Horseshoe.
2045 The attack gets under way. Preceded by an artillery barrage, the Guards negotiate two minefields and push on towards the enemy's front line.
2230 No. 3 Company takes Hill 139.

Enemy counter-attacks

17 March 0100 Sensing the vulnerability of the Guards the Germans launch a succession of fierce counter-attacks against the British positions on Hill 139 and Point 109. The Guards respond with grenades and smallarms fire. The enemy assaults are thwarted but the Guards are in danger of being surrounded and destroyed unless a withdrawal is organised.

The Guards withdraw

0525 As dawn breaks, the Guards are ordered to fall back to the Wadi Zess. Friendly artillery fire helps to keep the enemy at bay, but No. 4 Company is overwhelmed.
0845 The survivors of No. 1 Company reach safety after a perilous trek through enemy-dominated territory.
1000 The last few stragglers escape the clutches of the enemy, but nearly 300 men are lost.

GROSSDEUTSCHLAND DIVISION, BATTLE OF KURSK, JULY 1943

In July 1943, the panzergrenadier Grossdeutschland Division was poised to take part in Operation 'Zitadelle', Hitler's plan for the destruction of the Soviet salient at Kursk. The plan was for the Fourth Panzer Army in the north and the Ninth Army in the south to cut through the Soviet defences and link up a few kilometres to the east of Kursk. The Grossdeutschland Division formed part of the XLVIII Panzer Corps, in the Fourth Panzer Army.

The division, led by Generalleutnant Walter 'Papa' Hoernlein, was battle-hardened and ready for action, but the Soviets had prepared well – mutual attrition would decide the encounter. 'Zitadelle' began at 1500 hours on 4 July, when the 11th Panzer Division and the Grossdeutschland attacked a commanding height to the north of the German frontline. Though the position was taken, Soviet resistance was heavy, a foretaste of things to come. The division pressed on, launching another attack at 0500 hours on 5 July. However, the attack was soon halted, the division's Panther tanks becoming bogged down in the mud and a minefield. The tanks were sitting ducks for anti-tank guns, so the engineers had to rush forward under heavy fire and remove the mines, clearing a path for the Panthers.

By the late evening of 5 July, the division had taken Point 237, but progress had been slow. The pace did not quicken on the 6th, but on the 7th and 8th the Grossdeutschland did manage to force the Soviets back to a line based on the villages of Gremutsky and Ssyzewo, inflicting heavy casualties on Red Army units. The Soviets were then forced to retreat behind the Pena river, but although the division began an outflanking attack against Beresowka, it again ran into stout Soviet resistance.

The entire operation had become bogged down by this stage: the men of the Grossdeutschland had suffered heavy losses and were exhausted. However, they were given no respite. On 10 July they were ordered south to destroy Soviet forces operating on the left flank of XLVIII Panzer Corps. A battlegroup went to assist the 3rd Panzer Division, and, with the aid of Stuka dive-bombers, eliminated a Soviet armoured column. The next day the division continued its advance northwards.

On 12 July the Grossdeutschland was spectator to a massive tank battle, as the Soviets launched a counterattack against II SS Panzer Corps. Around 850 Red Army tanks and self-propelled guns clashed with 700 German tanks and assault guns in one of the biggest tank battle in history. Both sides lost approximately 300 tanks, but the offensive capability of II SS Panzer Corps had been effectively broken.

On 13 July the Grossdeutschland was ordered west to help the 3rd Panzer Division, which was being hammered by Soviet attacks. Fighting through stiff Soviet artillery and tank fire, the division eventually linked up with the 3rd Panzer Division at the village of Beresowka, stabilising the vulnerable left flank of XLVIII Panzer Corps. However, by this stage the division had lost all its Panthers and half its men were casualties. It was withdrawn from the area on 18 July and sent to reinforce Army Group Centre. 'Zitadelle' had by this time been cancelled by Hitler. The experience of the Grossdeutschland Division at Kursk is an excellent example of an age-old military truth: that troops, no matter how well trained and eager, cannot break through in-depth, well-prepared fortifications manned by determined soldiers. The division had been literally ground down by the Soviet defences in a savage battle of attrition.

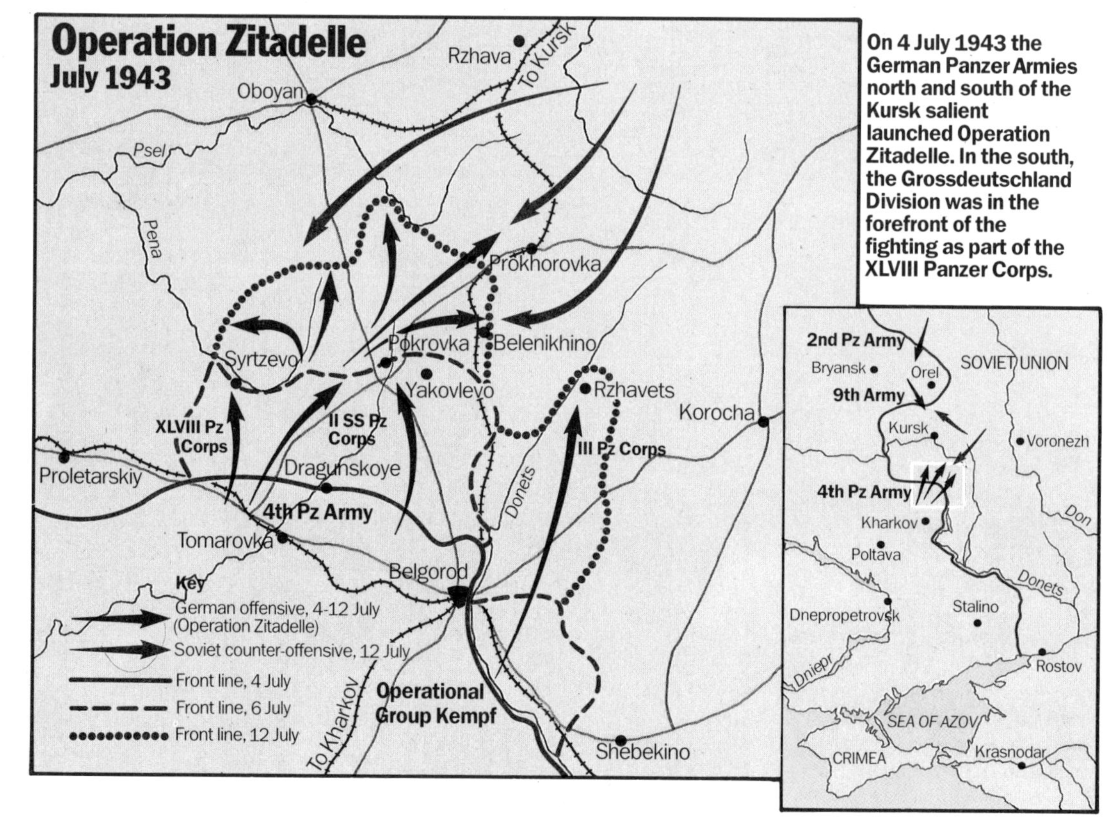

On 4 July 1943 the German Panzer Armies north and south of the Kursk salient launched Operation Zitadelle. In the south, the Grossdeutschland Division was in the forefront of the fighting as part of the XLVIII Panzer Corps.

82ND AIRBORNE DIVISION, SICILY, JULY-AUGUST 1943

The 82nd Airborne Division's orders for Operation 'Husky' were simple: seize key terrain and bridges to stop enemy forces dislodging the amphibious troops. The airborne assault would be led by the British 1st Air Landing Brigade, with the 'All American' 82nd landing on Sicily's south coast. A few hours later, three divisions of General Patton's US Seventh Army would land on the beaches.

The 505th Parachute Infantry Regiment was selected for the night drop. Made up of over 3000 paratroopers, the force, called the 505th Combat Team, was led by Colonel James Gavin.

The wind blew the transport aircraft carrying the men off course, with the result that the paras were dropped in small groups over the entire southeast and southern coasts. Some of Gavin's men dropped near the east coast, where they aided the British landings. Most of the 1st Battalion, 505th Parachute Infantry Regiment, were strung out in small groups to the east of Gela.

The 2nd Battalion landed and assembled east of the Gela drop zone, and then stormed the heights overlooking the beaches. By noon on 11 July, it had captured the Sicilian towns of Santa Croce, Camerina and Vittoria. Many of Gavin's men were engaged in heavy fighting: a group from the 1st Battalion stormed 16 pillboxes east of Gela on 10 July and held them until the lead units of the 1st Infantry Division arrived.

A second parachute drop had taken place on the morning of 11 July, when two strengthened battalions of the division were airlanded and dropped onto Farello airstrip. By 18 August, Axis forces had escaped across the Straits of Messina. By preventing Axis mobile reserves, especially the Hermann Göring Division, from reaching the beachheads, the 82nd Airborne had played a crucial role in the success of Operation 'Husky'.

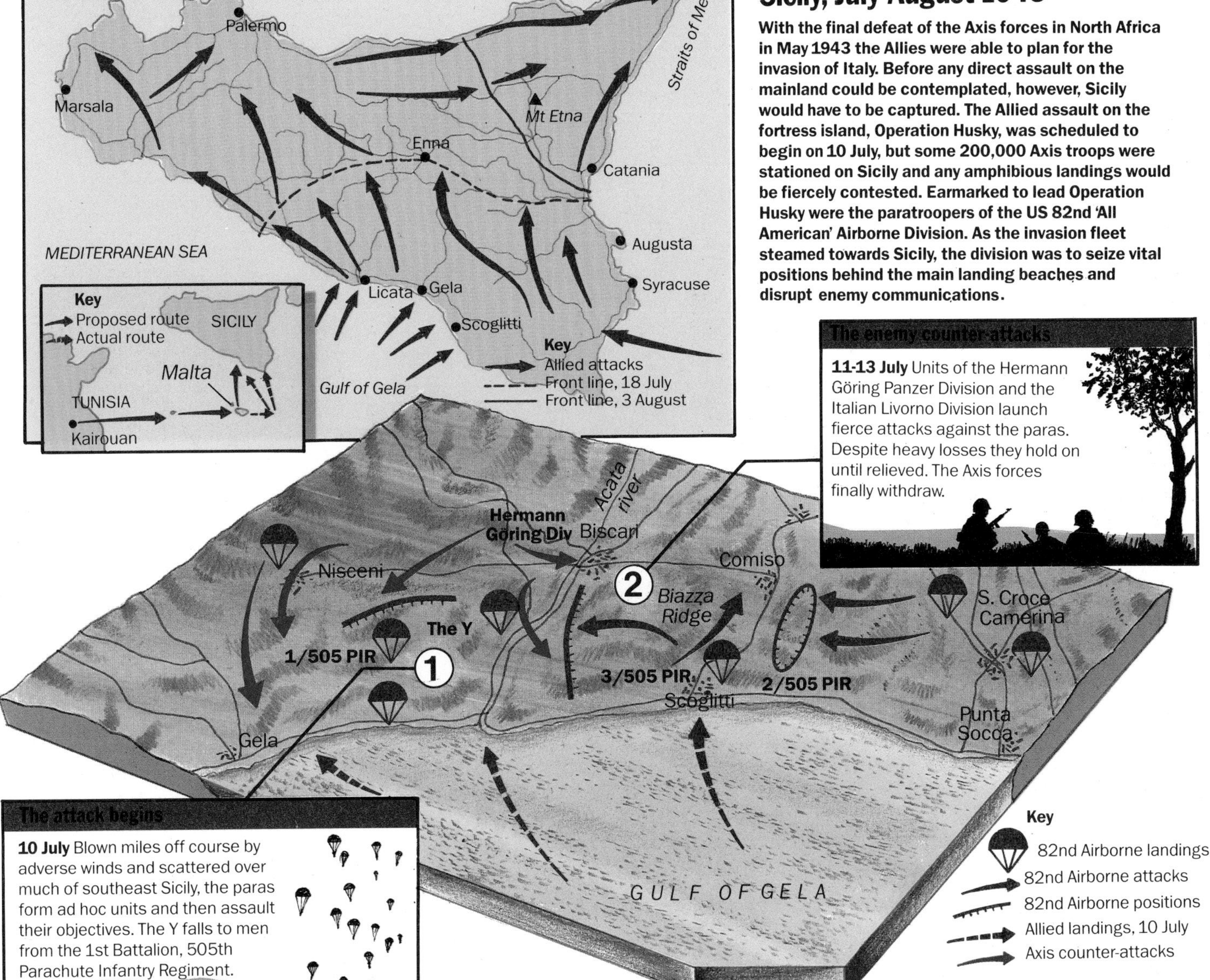

5TH GUARDS TANK ARMY, BATTLE OF KURSK, JULY 1943

The Battle of Kursk erupted in early July 1943, when German forces made a series of ferocious attacks to destroy the Russian salient during Operation 'Zitadelle'. By 8 July, German gains in the south had worried the Soviet commander of the Voronezh Front, Lieutenant-General N F Vatutin, so much that he had sent a message to Moscow requesting aid. The 5th Guards Tank Army, commanded by Lieutenant-General Rotmistrov, was despatched from the reserves to the front. The 5th comprised the 18th and 29th Tank Corps and the 5th Mechanised Corps, and contained over 500 T-34 tanks and SU-85 tank destroyers and 35 lend-lease Churchill tanks.

By 11 July the situation in the south was desperate: the Germans were across the Psel and in possession of Prokhorovka. Rotmistrov decided, therefore, to attack the next day. At 0830 hours on 12 July, the Voronezh Front's guns and mortars pounded the positions of the II SS Panzer Corps. The Soviet tanks rolled forward, and overhead, aircraft battled for supremacy of the skies.

Rotmistrov, at his headquarters overlooking Prokhorovka, started to receive reports that the Germans were advancing to meet his force: over 400 Tiger, Panther and Mark IV tanks. He knew that the German tanks had better armour and that their guns out-ranged the T-34's 76.2mm main weapon. He decided, therefore, that his tanks were to charge at full speed at the German armour! Racing forward, the T-43s were soon in the midst of the German panzers. It was every tank for itself as countless engagements erupted over the battlefield. The battle around Prokhorovka was extremely fluid, with villages and farms changing hands repeatedly. However, by midday on 12 July, it was obvious that the Germans had lost their offensive momentum.

Rotmistrov despatched the 2nd Tank Corps to attack the right flank of II SS Panzer Corps. Here there was a gap because other enemy forces had been unable to maintain the same momentum as the Fourth Panzer Army. Now it was the Germans' turn to launch counter-attacks to stem the Soviet armour. At 2100 hours the fighting ceased, both sides taking up defensive positions. Some 208 destroyed German tanks littered the fields around Prokhorovka, with another 100 around Rzavets in the south. However, the 5th Guards Tank Army had also lost no less than 420 tanks in the battle. Such was the price for stopping the German advance.

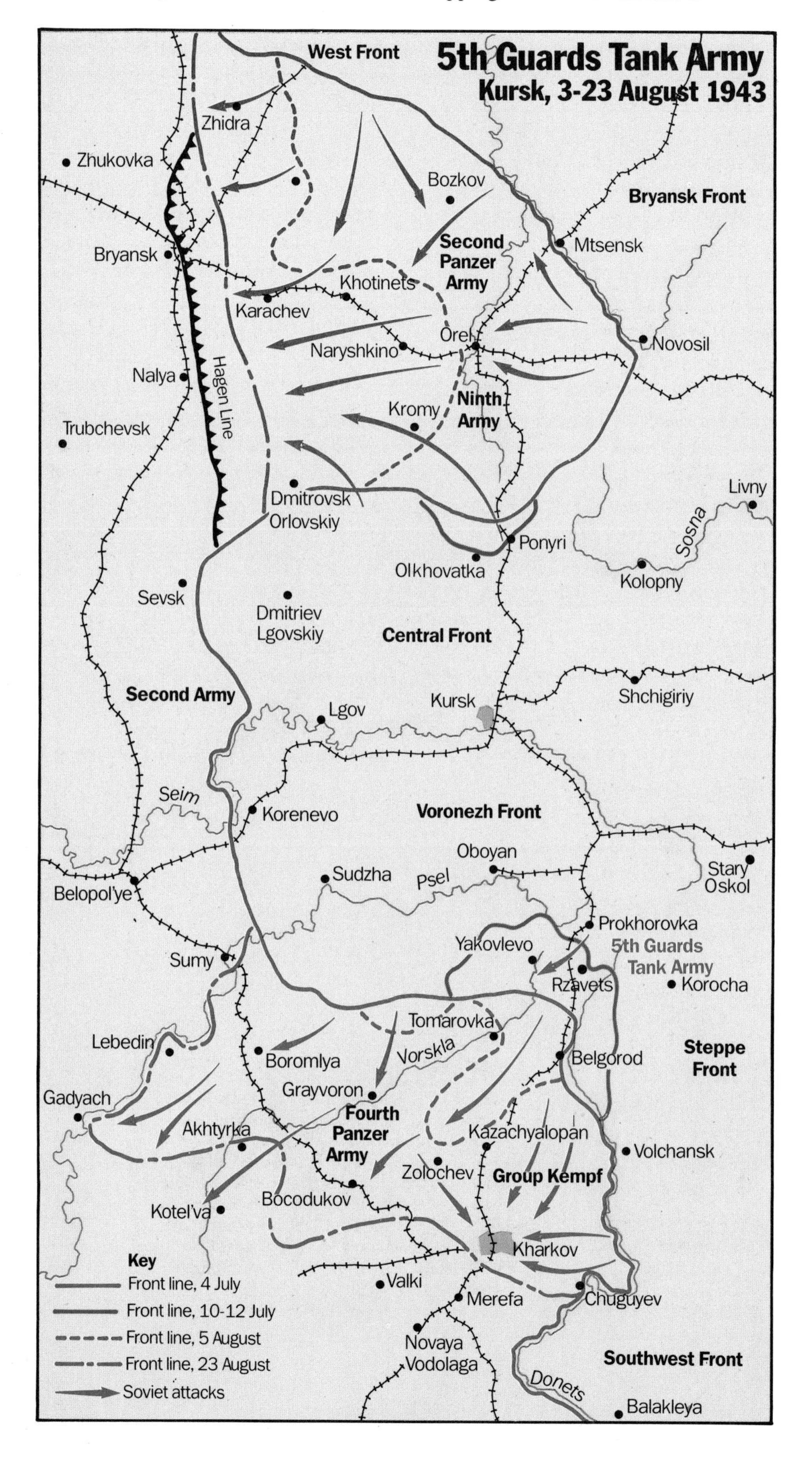

SOVIET GUARDS AIRBORNE BRIGADES, DNIEPR BEND, SEPTEMBER 1943

By autumn 1943, the *Wehrmacht* was totally on the defensive on the Eastern Front, but the Germans put up a tough resistance, and made good use of natural defensive features, such as the river systems of the Soviet Union. One such barrier was the River Dniepr. Here, the Soviets had detected a gap between the German Fourth Panzer Army in the north, based around Kiev, and the Eighth Army in the south, deployed between Kanev and Cherkassy, and decided to use their elite airborne forces to assist the crossing.

Soviet troops of the Third Army began to cross the Dniepr at Zarubentsy in late September, despite attempts by elements of the 19th Panzer Division to stop them. To support the troops crossing the river, the Soviet High Command decided to commit the 1st, 3rd and 5th Guards Airborne Brigades, which had moved south from Moscow. Comprised of battle-hardened veterans, each brigade had a strength of around 2500 men, divided into four 500-man battalions, a mortar section, an engineer section, an anti-aircraft section, an anti-tank section, and a medical section. Unfortunately, the drop was postponed until 1730 hours on 24 September because of a lack of transport aircraft.

The drop goes in

The drop was a shambles, the men being dropped in small parties because only older TB-3 aircraft were available. In addition, their equipment was either improperly loaded or left behind. As they dropped, the 5th Guards paras came under fire from the 19th Panzer Division below, with the result that many were killed before they hit the ground. The drops continued throughout the day and early evening, especially in the southwest. Around 300 paras from the 3rd Brigade were dropped at Shandra and another 400 from the same unit at Beresnyagi. However, like those dropped earlier, they were in scattered parties and were immediately engaged by the German 34th Infantry Division, which happened to be in the area.

Of all the units dropped, only the 1st Guards Airborne Brigade was able to land and operate as a cohesive force, clearing airstrips for the 2nd and 4th Guards Airlanding Brigades, which were to be brought in along with artillery and tanks. More paras were dropped throughout the night of 24/25 September, in addition to Soviet troops crossing the Dniepr near Zarubentsy.

Combined actions with partisans

Systematically, the Germans began to search for the remaining paras in their rear areas. As for the paras, they linked up with guerrilla units already operating in the area. They also undertook many separate actions, such as the attack by 150 paras on the German police headquarters in the village of Potok on the night of 29/30 September. This group later made its way south and, on 5 October, joined a larger group of paras acting as guerrillas under the command of Lieutenant-Colonel Sidorchuk, the commander of the 5th Guards Airborne Brigade. In fact, Sidorchuk's men were by far the best organised of the ad hoc units. In addition, they also had quite a bit of their equipment, and on 6 October they established radio contact with Fortieth Army HQ and were able to request resupply. This group continued to strike at enemy targets throughout October and into November. For his leadership, Sidorchuk was named a 'Hero of the Soviet Union'.

Overall, however, the Dniepr bend operation was poorly planned and executed and resulted in the loss of two-thirds of all the paras who took part. If the operation had been launched one or two days earlier, it would have stood a better chance of cutting off large numbers of German troops on the east side of the river. Similarly, if air transport had been properly allocated, then the mission would stood more chance. Despite the failures, the operation still resulted in large numbers of paras being a thorn in the enemy's side and then fighting with the partisans for many weeks.

In late August 1943 the Red Army launched its autumn offensive in the eastern Ukraine aimed at pushing the Germans back across the Dniepr. By the end of September the German army was in retreat and the Soviets had established bridgeheads west of the Dniepr. Despite stubborn defensive actions by the Germans, the Red Army was able to concentrate its strength at key points and maintain the momentum of the advance. By December, Germany's Eastern Rampart was in Soviet hands.

SKORZENY'S COMMANDOS, GRAN SASSO, 12 SEPTEMBER 1943

The Italian dictator Mussolini had been removed from Rome in July 1943. Following numerous journeys, he ended up at the Hotel Albergo-Rifugio on the Gran Sasso, a mountainous ridge northeast of Rome. In response, Hitler despatched Captain Otto Skorzeny, chief of Germany's special forces, to find and rescue him. Temporarily placed under the command of General Kurt Student, chief of airborne troops, Skorzeny eventually located Italy's ex-leader in September.

Personal research of the hotel revealed that it was located on a small plateau, a small triangle of clear ground with the top station of the cable-car on one side. The plan was for one group of paras and commandos to land near the hotel, another to seize the lower end of the cable-car, and for a third to rescue the wife and family of Mussolini from their house near Rocca della Cominata. The force would be transported in 12 DFS 230 gliders and D-Day was fixed for 12 September. Each glider could carry 10 men plus the pilot. Skorzeny also took along an Italian officer, General Soletti, to act as an interpreter.

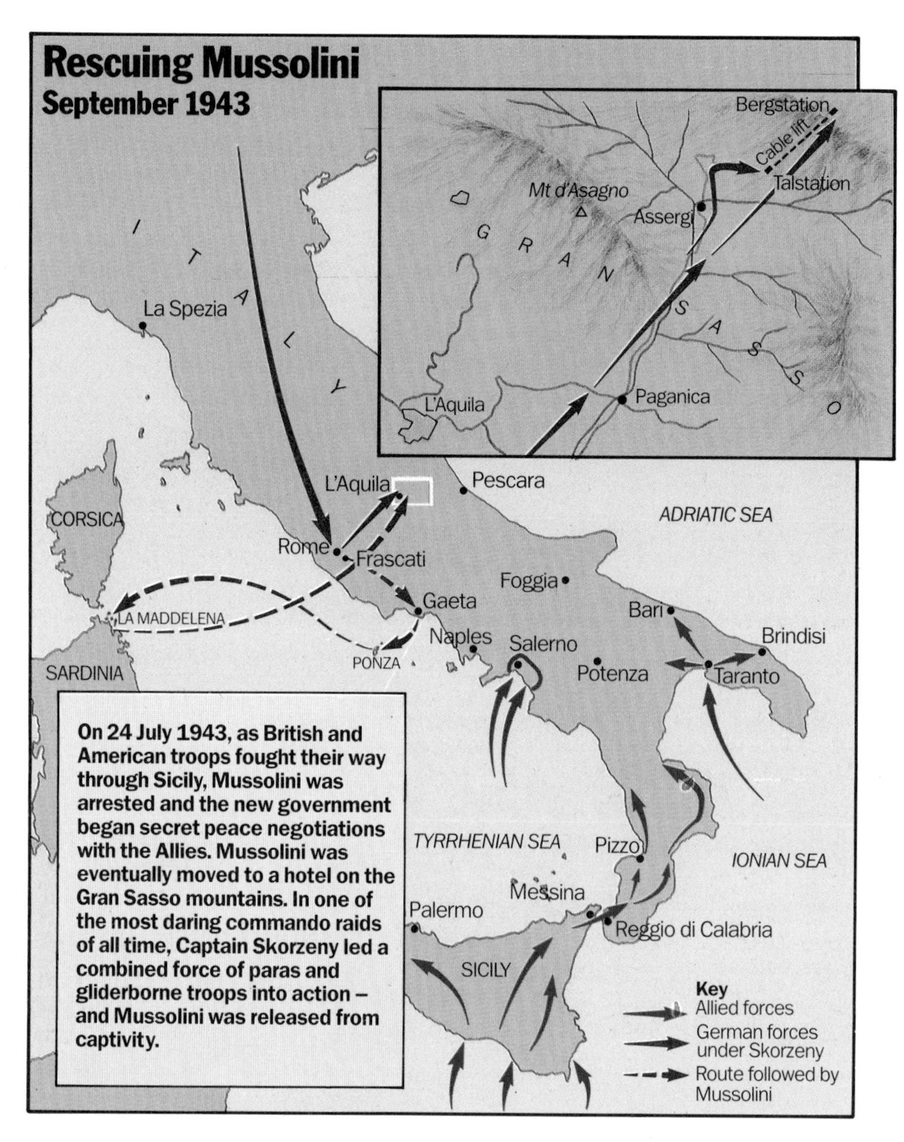

On 24 July 1943, as British and American troops fought their way through Sicily, Mussolini was arrested and the new government began secret peace negotiations with the Allies. Mussolini was eventually moved to a hotel on the Gran Sasso mountains. In one of the most daring commando raids of all time, Captain Skorzeny led a combined force of paras and gliderborne troops into action – and Mussolini was released from captivity.

The commandos capture the hotel

However, an Allied air raid took place at the departure airfield at 1230 hours, damaging the runway. Undeterred, Skorzeny ordered the aircraft to take off. Assembling above the clouds, Skorzeny's pilot told him two of the gliders had failed to take off because of the condition of the runway. Nevertheless, the operation pressed on.

Approaching the hotel, it became clear that the landing site was not flat but a steep slope. Skorzeny ordered the somewhat alarmed pilot to land, which he did, bringing the glider to a halt around 16m from the hotel. Skorzeny leapt from the aircraft and rushed towards the hotel, quickly followed by the rest of his squad. Bursting through an open door, they discovered a signaller desperately trying to send a warning. However, he was booted across the room and Skorzeny's rifle butt smashed the transmitter. As the Germans swept through the building, not a shot was fired by the Italian guards, who were totally shocked by the speed of the daring raid.

The commandos rushed up the main stairs, and found Mussolini and two officers in a room on the right: *Il Duce* was safe. Watching his remaining gliders coming in to land, Skorzeny was shocked to see the eighth caught by a warm thermal and smashed against the side of the mountain. Hearing gunfire, Skorzeny shouted for the senior Italian commander. He demanded the latter, a colonel, surrender the garrison. The Italian asked for time to consider. Skorzeny, his blood up, gave him one minute. The colonel left the room then quickly returned, and formally surrendered. As the first Germans reached the hotel by cable-car, a message was despatched to General Student informing him of the success of the mission.

Skorzeny and Mussolini flew to Rome and then on to Vienna. Just before midnight there was a knock at Skorzeny's door; it was the chief-of-staff of the Viennese garrison. Congratulating him on the success of his mission, he removed the Knight's Cross he was wearing and presented it to Skorzeny on Hitler's orders. Fortune had certainly favoured the brave.

2ND BATTALION, 1ST PARACHUTE REGIMENT, US MARINE CORPS, CHOISEUL, OCTOBER-NOVEMBER 1943

In October 1943, US forces were set to launch an attack on the Solomon Islands. As a diversion, the 2nd Battalion of the 1st Parachute Regiment, US Marine Corps, would land on Choiseul to fool the enemy on Bougainville into thinking it was the main objective.

The Marines landed at around 0100 hours on 28 October, and immediately set up a defensive perimeter around the village of Voza. Moving inland, and guided by bearers, the Marines ambushed a small enemy patrol on the 29th and then hit the village of Singigai on the 30th. The fighting in the latter place was grim, with the US troops having to flush the Japanese out of their hiding places one by one. At the end of the action, 70 Japanese were dead, together with four dead Marines and nine wounded. The pressure on the Japanese was kept up; on 2 November the Marines fought a successful action with an enemy unit at Choiseul Bay. The Marines were withdrawn on the 3rd. It had been a well-executed mission – in the true tradition of the Marine Corps.

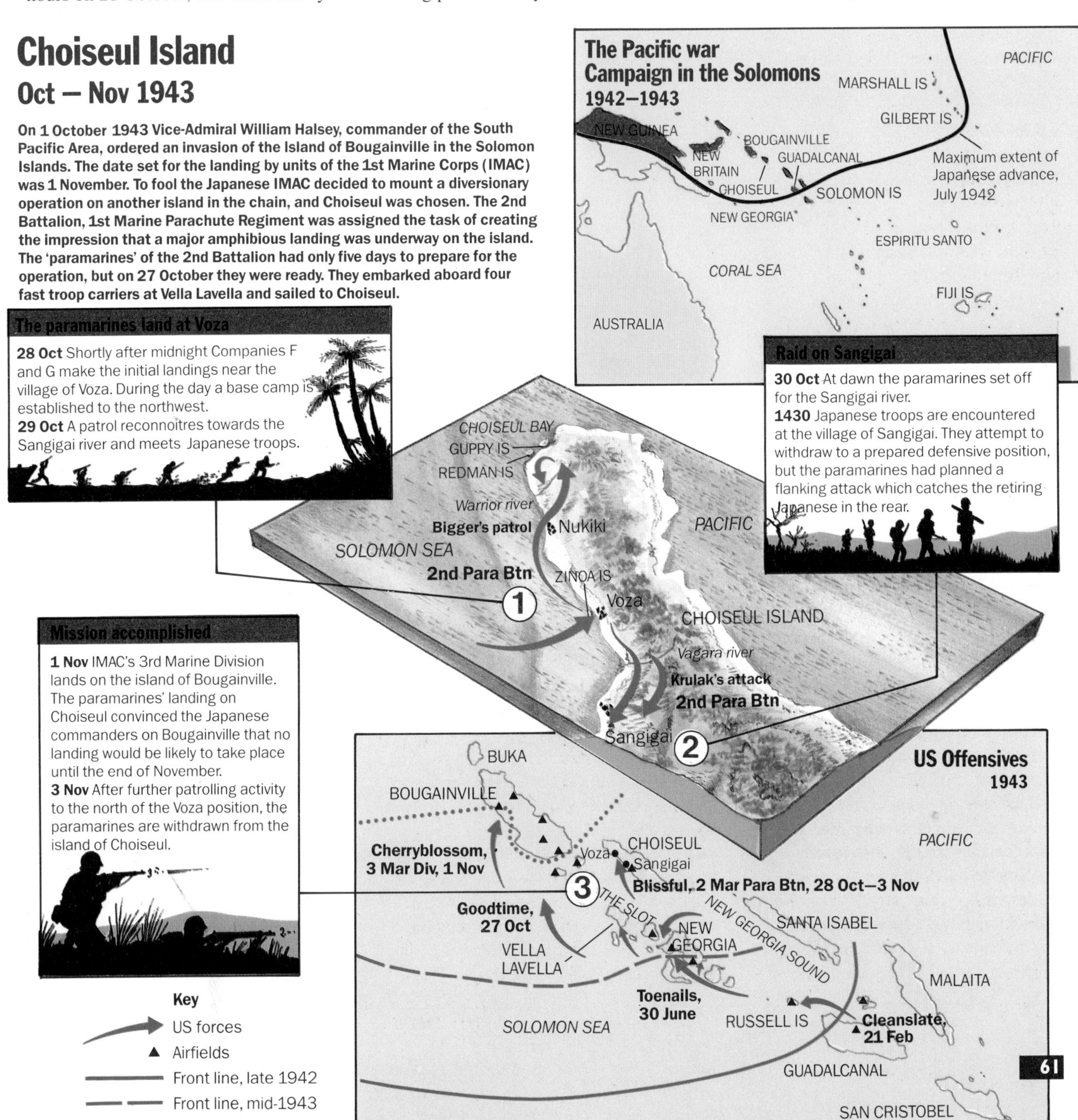

BRANDENBURG DIVISION, LEROS, NOVEMBER 1943

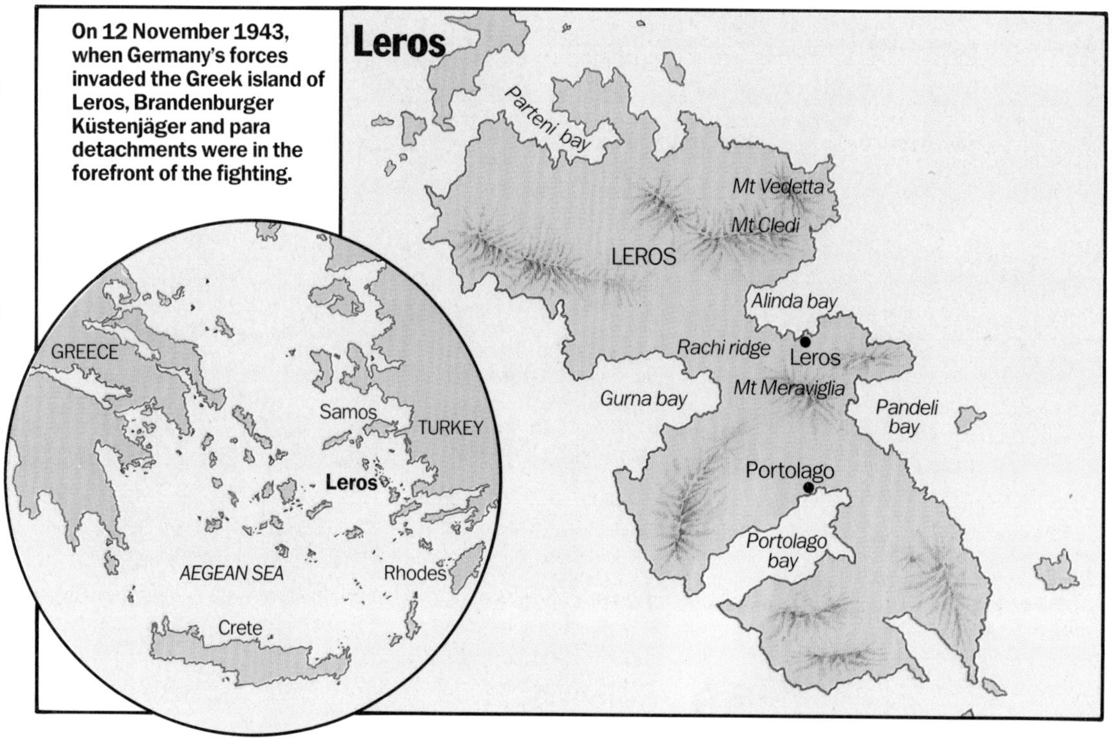

The attack on the Greek island of Leros in 1943 was the last effective German offensive of the war in the Mediterranean. The plan had four phases. First, neutralisation of the enemy's defences by bombers. Second, landings along the coast. Third, the individual groups would then link up. Finally, the groups would defeat the island's garrison. However, Operation 'Leopard', which was spearheaded by elements of the Brandenburg Regiment, proved to be more difficult to accomplish than originally thought. Phase one was launched, but though the *Luftwaffe* made over 1000 attacks on Leros, the island's guns were not knocked out. Phase two also encountered difficulties: D-Day was set for 12 November 1943, the first assault wave made up of men from the 1st Battalion of the 2nd Parachute Regiment and from the Brandenburgers' Para Company. However, when the aircraft were near the drop zone they were recalled. The seaborne group of the Western Task Force, which was also heading for Gurna Bay, had been driven back by gunfire from the coastal batteries. No landings would take place on the western side of the island until the progress of the Eastern Task Force was known.

On 12 November 1943, when Germany's forces invaded the Greek island of Leros, Brandenburger Küstenjäger and para detachments were in the forefront of the fighting.

In fact, the Eastern Task Force had been successful and had established two bridgeheads. The paras set off again, this time the slow-moving JU 52s running into a hail of flak. The drop zone chosen by Captain Kuhne, the commander of the airborne assault group, was a small strip of land between Gurna and Alinda Bays. What Kuhne didn't know, however, was that the area was defended by the 2nd Battalion, Royal Irish Fusiliers, one of the three battalions of British infantry that formed the island's garrison.

Dropping from a low height, the paras were on the ground before the British infantry could respond. The Germans had soon organised themselves and secured Rachi Ridge for future operations. Meanwhile, the Eastern Task Force was running into problems. The Brandenburgers' coastal raiders had landed at Pandeli Bay, with other troops landing at Alinda Bay. The men stormed ashore and scaled the vertical wall of rock, above which lay Mount Appetici, but only a small number made it to the summit.

Extension of the bridgeheads

The Germans requested air strikes, but the first wave mistakenly bombed their own men. However, the second wave was more successful, and soon the Brandenburgers were advancing towards the mountain. Their first assault was unsuccessful, and so they re-grouped and decided to attack an enemy battery on Castle Hill. In this they were successful, but during the night of 12/13 November they were shelled by British artillery, and failed to take Mount Appetici.

On other parts of the island the Germans had consolidated their positions and had entered phase three of the operation: extension of the bridgeheads. German reinforcements reached the island on the 13th, and British counterattacks on the 14th and 15th were smashed by Brandenburgers firing MG42 machine guns and 81mm mortars. However, the British did manage to link up in the centre of the island and attack the town of St Nicola. If they could take it, the Germans around Leros would be bottled up. In the little town some of the fiercest fighting of the operation took place; and the paras, in desperate hand-to-hand fighting, forced the British to withdraw.

Fearful that the operation was losing momentum, the German commanders requested reinforcements. Therefore, the 3rd Battalion of the Brandenburgers' 1st Regiment was landed on the island on the 16th. Phase four began. Going straight into action, they captured the heights to the south of the town. The 1st Battalion then made an assault on the British headquarters the next day; by 1500 hours Mount Meraviglia had been taken. The battle for Leros was over.

SPECIAL BOAT SQUADRON, SIMI, 20 NOVEMBER 1943

Following Italy's surrender in early September 1943, the Allies endeavoured to secure the Aegean islands that had been under Italian control before the Germans did the same. The units that were earmarked to perform this task were the Earl Jellicoe's Special Boat Squadron (SBS), the Special Raiding Squadron under 'Paddy' Mayne, and the Long Range Desert Group.

One SBS unit, Major J M 'Jock' Lapraik's M Squadron, reached Simi on 17 September. Once ashore, Lapraik negotiated the surrender of the 140 men of the garrison (nearly three times the size of his own force). In the following weeks his men made recces of Rhodes and the neighbouring islands. However, his plans were rudely interrupted on the morning of 7 October when German forces landed on Simi. Putting up a furious barrage of fire, particularly from their Bren guns, the SBS soldiers managed to repulse the invaders, killing over 50 Germans to M Squadron's one killed and two wounded. Despite this, the *Luftwaffe* began a systematic bombardment of the island that inflicted many SBS casualties. Reluctantly, Lapraik gave the order to withdraw.

The Germans had placed a garrison on Simi by November 1943 which consisted of a major, 18 Germans, two Italian officers, 60 men from the Italian Fascist Militia and numerous administrative staff. Posts were established at Malo Point, Panormiti and in the governor's house. These defences seemed perfectly adequate – but the Germans under-estimated M Squadron, SBS.

In late October, the Raiding Forces' staff at GHQ Middle East began planning a raid on Simi that would become a classic example of the use of seaborne forces for small raids. Recce teams were landed on the island to examine and report on the defences. On 20 November, the main force arrived off the island in two caiques and were put ashore. The men were armed with captured German submachine guns, Bren guns and explosive charges. Moving towards the island's HQ, the SBS men encountered some Germans but quickly dealt with them. However, the firing had alerted the garrison, and numerous machine gun posts began to open fire. Undeterred, Lapraik's men forged on and came to the boatyards. They planted bombs to disable the boats and then withdrew, having inflicted a great deal of damage and many casualties on the enemy.

Getting back to the caiques safely, Lapraik then raided the island of Nisiros, 40km to the west of Simi, destroying some caiques in the harbour and disabling the island's submarine telephone cable (by which the individual garrisons communicated with each other). The Island of Piscopi was the next target: here, a handful of Italians were disarmed. The SBS raids against the three islands had been so successful that the Germans suppressed any news of them, although they were forced to commit over 18,000 men to the defence of the islands in the Aegean, which meant they had fewer men for the Eastern Front. The Allies never deployed more than 3000 men in the Aegean, testimony to the effectiveness of units such as the SBS.

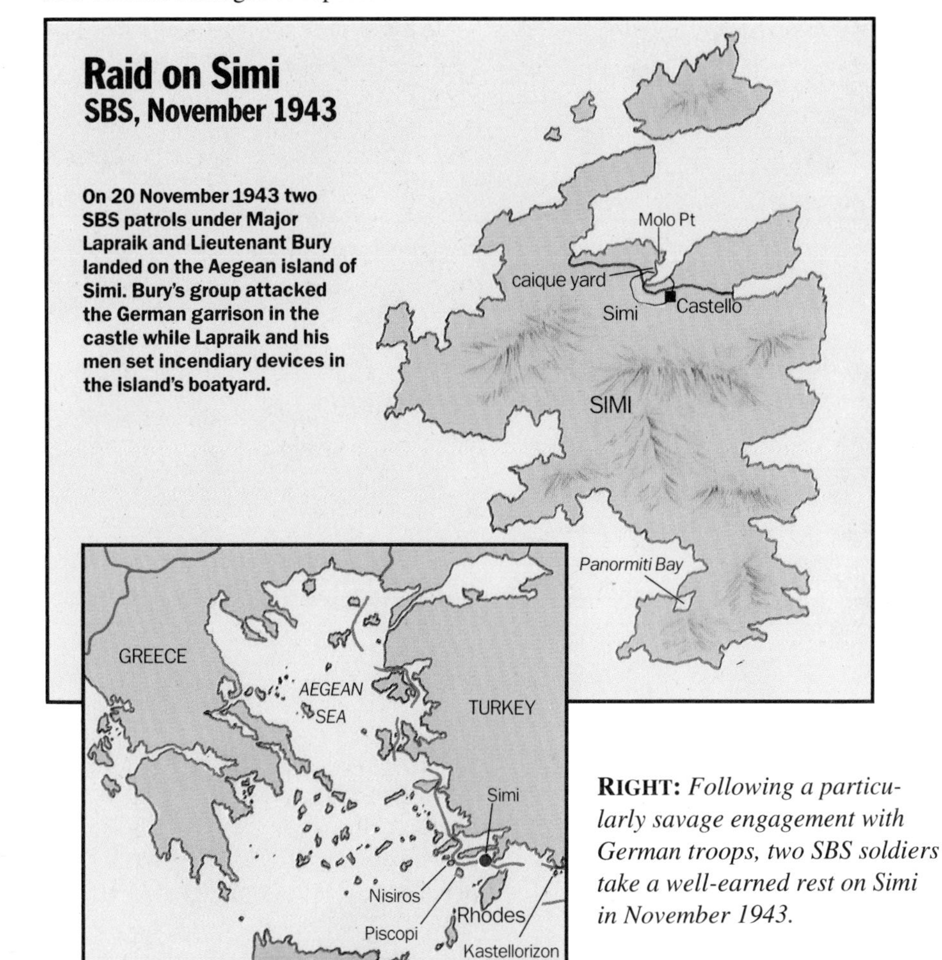

RIGHT: *Following a particularly savage engagement with German troops, two SBS soldiers take a well-earned rest on Simi in November 1943.*

2ND MARINE DIVISION, TARAWA, NOVEMBER 1943

On 20 November 1943, Major-General Julian Smith's 2nd Marine Division steamed towards Tarawa Atoll as part of Operation 'Galvanic', the attempt to seize the Gilbert Islands in the Pacific Ocean. Tarawa, a bracelet of tiny coral islands, was heavily defended by Japanese machine gun posts, batteries of artillery and some 4000 men under Rear-Admiral Meichi Shibasaki. However, the greatest obstacle for the Marines at Tarawa was the fortified island of Betio.

The attack was spearheaded by Colonel David Shoup's 2nd Marines and the 2nd Battalion, 8th Marine Regiment, with the remaining two battalions of the 8th Marines being held as a divisional reserve. The naval bombardment of the Japanese positions was nothing short of brutal, though rather ineffective. Other naval support included two minesweepers that cleared a channel in the lagoon for the landing craft.

Massacre on Red 2

The landing craft approached the shore at 0830 hours, the naval bombardment ceasing to allow them safe passage. Taking advantage of the lull, the defenders crept back into their positions and started firing on the landing craft with machine-gun fire and 75mm air-burst shells. At 0855 hours the first Marines, men of the 2nd Marine Regiment, reached the end of Betio's pier and stormed it. The first Marines hit the beaches at 0910 hours, and were almost immediately pinned down by heavy and accurate machine-gun fire. The fight was going to be long and bloody.

The situation in the water was worse than on the beach, with some landing craft blown apart and others unable to cross the lagoon. The subsequent waves of Marines had to walk ashore across several hundred metres of treacherous reef, all the time under heavy machine-gun, mortar and artillery fire.

Each battalion landing team was allocated a separate beach: Red 3 was the target of the 2nd Battalion, 8th Marines, Red 2 was the objective of the 2nd Battalion, 2nd Marines, and Red 1 was the target of the 3rd Battalion, 2nd Marines. The Marines on Red 3 managed to push inshore after beaching, but on the other two beaches the situation was less favourable. The Marines on Red 1, for example, were forced to withdraw, and those on Red 2 could only cling on grimly in the face of murderous fire. On the latter, the 1st Battalion of the 2nd Marines lost 200 men while attempting to land on the beach at 1200 hours.

That night, to the relief of the Marines, there was no counterattack. In the morning the 1st Battalion, 8th Marines, was brought ashore under heavy covering fire to reinforce Ryan's men. With air and naval gunfire support, his men began to advance against the Japanese positions. This time they were successful, and Green Beach was secured at 1200 hours. By the late afternoon, the 2nd Battalion, 6th Marines, was coming ashore on Green Beach, and the Marines in the centre also pushed forward.

ABOVE: *Into the meat grinder. Marines go into the attack on Tarawa.*

The Marines on Red 3 managed to organise themselves and launch an attack with the aid of a few medium tanks, which established a joint perimeter. One of the divisional reserve battalions, the 3rd Battalion, 8th Marines, was then brought ashore, despite receiving heavy flanking fire from Japanese positions. Meanwhile, at the western edge of Betio Island, Major Michael Ryan had assumed command of those elements of the 1st, 2nd and 3rd Battalions of the 2nd Marines that had been forced westwards by the ferocity of the Japanese defenders on Red 1. With the aid of two tanks, he launched an attack southwards along Green Beach. However, the tanks were knocked out and the Marines had to halt.

The long-awaited and feared Japanese counterattack came during the evening of 22 November, but it was too late. The advancing enemy troops were decimated by naval gunfire and artillery, and were cut to pieces at close quarters by the Marines. Despite this defeat the Japanese fought on, and Betio was not secured until 1312 hours on 23 November, and Tarawa by 28 November. The cost of this battle was high: some 4600 Japanese soldiers had been killed, together with 1000 Marines and a further 2000 more wounded. For the Marines, Tarawa was a hard-fought victory.

Tarawa
2nd Marine Division November 1943

On 20 November 1943 the American central Pacific campaign opened with Operation Galvanic – the retaking of the Japanese-held Gilbert Islands. The most difficult objective in the Gilberts was the heavily fortified island of Betio, part of a ring of coral islands known as Tarawa Atoll. The assault on Tarawa by marines of the 2nd Marine Division cost 1000 American lives, but by 28 November the atoll was secure.

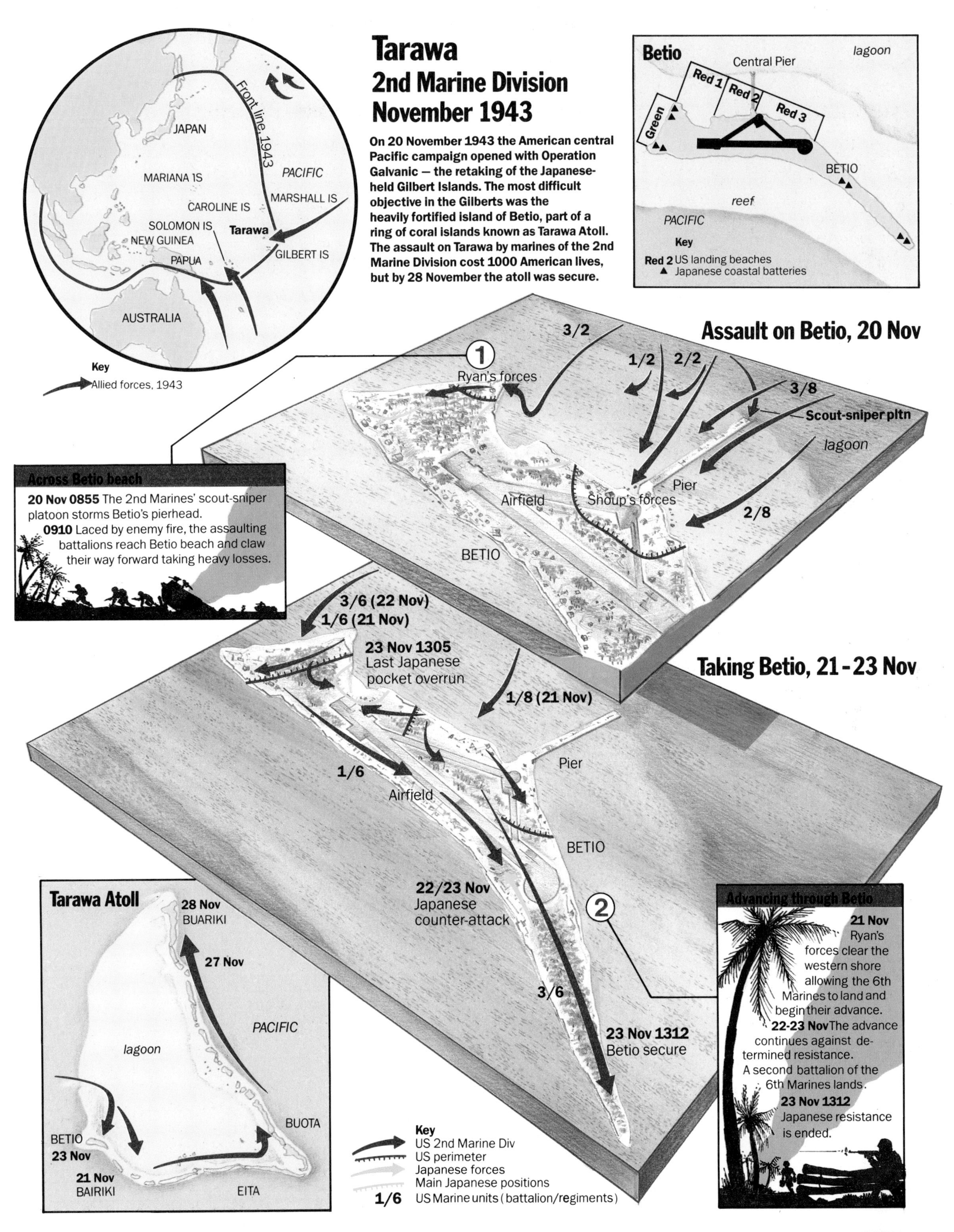

5TH SS PANZER DIVISION WIKING, CHERKASSY, JANUARY-FEBRUARY 1944

At dawn on 24 January 1944, the Soviet 2nd Ukrainian Front (equivalent to an army group) launched an attack on the vulnerable German salient at Korsun-Schevchenkovskiy. Holding the southeast sector of the German front was the 5th SS Panzer Division Wiking, containing many Dutch and Scandinavian volunteers, and the Wallonien Brigade. The Soviet offensive broke through German positions to the north and south, and by 28 January a total of 56,000 men, including four infantry divisions, two corps headquarters, assorted army troops and Division Wiking, had been encircled in what was called the Cherkassy Pocket, which stretched for a length of 40km and a depth of 30km.

The Soviets, having isolated the Pocket, surrounded it with an inner circle and an outer one to prevent German relief forces getting through. The Soviets arrayed 13 rifle divisions and three cavalry divisions, supported by 2000 guns and 138 tanks, and launched the first attacks to the south of Korsun to clear German units from the area. The Division Wiking was deployed to the east of Korsun. Most of the area was flat and marshy, and had become one vast lake of mud after the winter thaw. Many *Luftwaffe* supply aircraft were shot out of the sky, and those that got through found that the weather had destroyed the airstrips. This meant Division Wiking soon became short of ammunition and petrol. The Soviets even tried to persuade the SS men to surrender, guaranteeing safe conduct and good conditions, though these efforts failed.

During the night of 1/2 February, the Wallonien Brigade withdrew from the village of Losovok to concentrate on Moshny, and then follow Division Wiking in a general withdrawal to the west. The Soviets harried the withdrawal all the way, the men of the Wiking fighting desperate rearguard actions to stave off collapse. On 3 February, in an effort to save the division's vehicles and equipment, the decision was taken to withdraw two-thirds of the troops from combat. The rest were to hold the line.

By 5 February, the division held a defensive line from Storoselye to Derenkovez atop high hills which contained many trench systems. But the SS men were exhausted by the continuous fighting; and after holding up the Soviets for two days, the Wiking then withdrew to Korsun. By 13 February the division had withdrawn through the town and, two days later, the Pocket had been reduced to an area of 60 square kilometres containing 45,000 men. Wiking was the only unit in the Pocket that had any sort of cohesion and discipline.

Wiking begins the breakout

General Stemmermann, overall commander in the Pocket, was told that the III Panzer Corps in the southwest could not reach him, so he was ordered to organise an all-or-nothing breakout, to begin at 2300 hours on 16 February.

The attack began when three German regiments, using knives and bayonets, cut through the Soviet outposts and their main screen. However, Wiking was not so fortunate, being forced by enemy fire to turn south and cross the Gniloy Tikich river to reach Lysyanka. Hundreds drowned in the river as the division desperately tried to escape, the Soviets pouring machine-gun, mortar and artillery fire into the Pocket. Isolated tanks and sections of infantry heroically tried to stop the Russians, but by midday the division had disintegrated as the SS men tried to get across the river.

Some 30,000 men escaped from the Cherkassy Pocket, 6000 of them from the Division Wiking, but the latter had lost all its equipment and its men were in a poor state. The Wiking was formed into a battlegroup and thrown back into combat. Such was the quality of its men that it continued to perform as a fighting unit. There is no doubt that its presence in the Pocket helped stabilise the situation and prevented the affair becoming a disaster.

SAS, SICILY AND ITALY, 1943-1944

When the war in North Africa came to an end, the British Special Air Service (SAS) consisted of the Special Raiding Squadron (SRS), commanded by Lieutenant-Colonel 'Paddy' Mayne, and 2 SAS, led by Lieutenant-Colonel William Stirling. Both units would prove their worth in the Sicilian and Italian campaigns of 1943-44.

The SRS was involved in the Allied assault on Sicily on 10 July 1943, capturing an enemy gun battery on the Capo Murro di Porco. Reaching the shore by landing craft, the men threw themselves against the cliff and began to climb to the summit. The Italian garrison, around 700 strong, was still underground as the SRS men reached the battery. Within minutes the Italians had been made prisoners and the guns spiked. Fighting throughout the night, the SRS destroyed six heavy guns, killed 100 Italians and captured some 2-3000 more. Collecting his scattered teams, Mayne then pressed on towards Syracuse. Though the journey involved considerable fighting, the SRS reached the town on the 12th. There it was relieved by lead elements of the British 5th Division, and then departed for a well-earned rest.

The assault on Bagnara

The SRS's next objective, the port of Augusta, was a tougher nut to crack. It was held by the elite troops of the Hermann Göring Panzer Division, and the fighting for possession of Syracuse was a messy and bloody affair. Mayne's men cleared it using grenades and small-arms fire, and had taken it by late on the 12th.

The fighting now switched to mainland Italy, and the SRS was tasked with capturing the port of Bagnara, to the north of the British positions around Reggio. Reaching the shore by landing craft at 0400 hours on 12 September 1943, the SRS encountered fierce resistance, and was unable to clear the Germans from the hills around the town. Digging in, Mayne's men were then subjected to a number of counterattacks over the next two days, until they were relieved by British troops.

The SRS was then withdrawn to Sicily to rest and prepare for its next mission: the capture of Termoli. Landing with British Commandos on 4 October, the SRS advanced into the town and secured it. However, the Germans launched a fierce counterattack, during which 22 SRS men were blown to pieces in the back of a truck. Shaken, Mayne and his men hung on grimly. The fighting was bitter as the British held on for three days, before finally beating back the Germans.

Termoli was the final action for the SRS in Italy, because it was subsequently withdrawn to England to prepare for Operation 'Overlord', the Allied invasion of France. However, 2 SAS continued to fight in Italy, operating behind the lines and attacking German communications right up to the end of the war. Both it and the SRS lived up to the standards of excellence demanded by David Stirling, the Special Air Service's founder, in the North African war, and proved the SAS could operate in any theatre.

504TH PARACHUTE COMBAT TEAM, ANZIO, JANUARY-MARCH 1944

The US 504th Parachute Combat Team, comprising the 504th Parachute Infantry Regiment of the 82nd Airborne Division and the 509th Parachute Infantry Battalion, took part in the landings at Anzio on the Italian coast on 20 January 1944. The men were originally to be dropped by parachute behind the beachhead, as had been the case at Sicily and Salerno. However, the commander of the US VI Corps landing forces, Major-General John Lucas, feared the paras would be gunned down by friendly fire, and thus ordered them to be an element of the amphibious landings.

The 3000 men of the 504th Combat Team therefore approached the target area in landing craft, one being blown out of the water by enemy aircraft, with all on board killed. By mid-afternoon, after the landing, the paras had formed up and marched 3km inland. Had Lucas been more determined, the Allied landings would have been more successful. However, his dithering gave the Germans time to prepare a counterattack. Digging in, the paras endured a calm but windy night on the Italian mainland. It would be the last uneventful night for a few weeks.

The 504th is stopped by the SS

The German commander, Field Marshal Albert Kesselring, was about to launch his riposte. By 22 January he had around 11 divisions converging on Anzio, and although the British 1st Division and the US 3rd Division had moved out of the beachhead briskly, they soon encountered fierce resistance.

The paras of the 504th Infantry Parachute Regiment were placed on the right flank of VI Corps. They advanced and captured the village of Borgo Piave on 24 January, only to be promptly thrown out by an assault by SS tanks and artillery. Slowly the Germans forged a ring of steel around Anzio.

Lucas, urged on by his superiors, decided to make an ambitious and massive attack. The British 1st Division, reinforced by elements of the US 1st Armored Division and the 3rd Battalion of the 504th Infantry Parachute Regiment, would launch an assault towards Campoleone. Then, the 1st Armored would drive to the west and outflank German positions on the Alban Hills. Meanwhile, another attack would be mounted against Cisterna and Velletri using the US 3rd Infantry Division, Rangers and the 1st and 2nd Battalions of the 504th Parachute Infantry Regiment.

The attack was launched on 30 January and initially did well, before being stopped by dogged German resistance. The paras with the US 3rd Infantry Division made good progress and, in a hard-fought action, cut to pieces the Germans sent to stop them. They were having a good day and they sensed victory, but the supporting armour was unable to reach them and the initiative passed back to the Germans.

The Germans then launched a counterattack against the whole Allied line, forcing back both the British and Americans. The paras of the 3rd Battalion held on grimly, but were decimated by repeated tank and artillery attacks. The 509th Parachute Infantry Battalion held the ground near the centre of the beachhead in the face of heavy enemy attacks. But now the Germans were pounding Anzio with a massive and unrelenting barrage of artillery fire. The paras dug in and held on, their training and fighting spirit ensuring they held the line. For 63 days the battle continued, each side involved in deadly night-time trench warfare. The Germans nicknamed the men of the 504th Parachute Infantry Regiment 'devils in baggy pants' for their tenacity.

Two more major German attacks were launched against Anzio in February: on the 16th and 20th, with the main weight of the assault on the 20th falling on the men of the 509th. But still they held.

For its bravery and steadfastness, the battalion was awarded a Presidential Unit Citation. The enemy then moved up 210mm and 280mm railway guns and pounded the Allied positions. The 504th was withdrawn from Anzio to Naples after 63 days of continuous fighting, its strength reduced to half. The 509th was pulled out of the line shortly after, its strength reduced to 125 out of a normal complement of 700. Both units had performed superbly.

HERMANN GÖRING DIVISION, ANZIO, JANUARY-MAY 1944

When Allied forces landed at Anzio on 22 January 1944, Field Marshal Albert Kesselring, commander of all German forces in Italy, issued the codeword 'Richard' to all his units. This was the signal to those formations not immediately in the frontline, which included the Hermann Göring Panzer Division and two battalions from the 4th Parachute Division, to contain the landings. Kesselring was able to seal off Anzio quickly, not least due to the caution of the Allied commander: Major-General John Lucas.

The division digs in

An artillery detachment from the Hermann Göring Division was one of the first to arrive in the Alban Hills overlooking the Allied forces, and the gunners hurriedly dug in and awaited the onslaught. However, it seemed a long time coming, and soon numerous panzergrenadier and infantry divisions had arrived to stiffen the defence. Though continually strafed by Allied fighter-bombers, the Hermann Göring Division soon turned every barn and farmhouse into a machine-gun nest. The division was deployed in the south, to block any Allied attack on Cisterna and safeguard the rear of General Heinrich von Vietinghoff's Tenth Army which was deployed around Cassino.

By the time Lucas got around to launching a full-scale attack, the German troops defending the perimeter had grown from 20,000 to 70,000, under the overall command of General Eberhard von Mackensen. On 30 January, the US 1st and 3rd Ranger Battalions, with the 4th in reserve, moved forward and ran straight into the division. General Paul Conrath, the commander of the division, had laid his defences well: sniper, machine guns and mortars in well-concealed positions were supported by Mk III and IV tanks and Stug III self-propelled guns. Though the Rangers managed to knock out three tanks almost immediately, they were soon pinned down by enfilading fire. Despite some savage hand-to-hand fighting, the Rangers were soon surrounded. Of the 809 men in the two Ranger battalions, only six escaped.

Between 3 and 10 February, the Germans at Anzio launched their own assault, forcing the Allies back. Conrath's division retook the village of Ponte Rotto in a daring night attack. By mid-February, the Germans had established a numerical superiority of 125,000 to 100,000, and Mackensen, confident of success, was determined to attack the centre of the Allied line. However, Hitler overruled him and insisted on an assault towards Aprilla. The main assault was to be supported by the Hermann Göring Division, whose task was to pin down the US 3rd Division and prevent Allied reserves being transferred to the threatened sector.

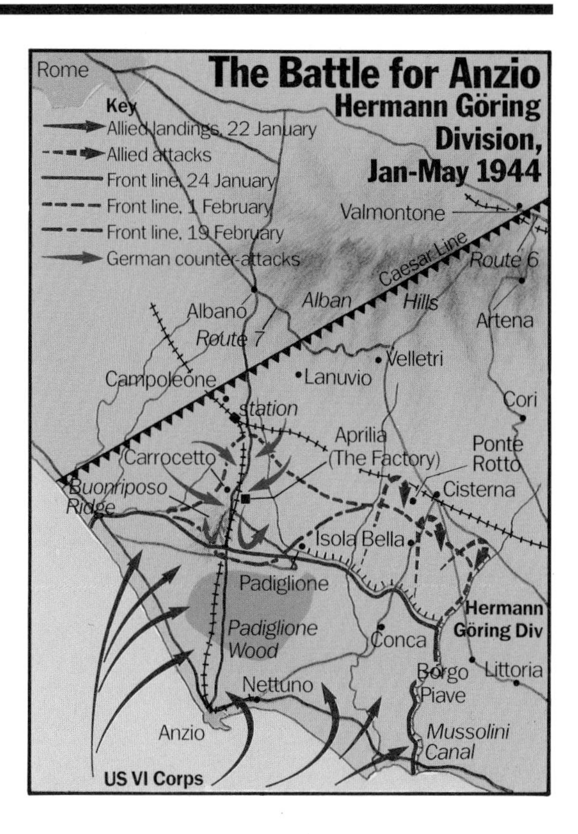

The German counterattack

The attack went in during the early hours of 16 February, the spearhead Infantry Lehr Regiment soon disintegrating when it came up against the Allied defences. Not so the hardened professionals of the Hermann Göring Division. With grim determination they pushed on, taking and inflicting heavy casualties. By the morning of 17 February the situation for the Allies was critical: the Germans, despite heavy losses, were attacking and making substantial gains. It seemed victory was within their grasp. However, it was not to be.

Though the battle was resumed on the 18th, the artillery of the 3rd Division stopped the Hermann Göring Division in its tracks, and the assault ground to a halt on the afternoon of the 19th. Mackensen resumed the attack on the 28th, this time against the Cisterna sector, using the Hermann Göring Division and the 26th and 362nd Divisions, but only limited headway was made against the minefields and entrenched positions of the 3rd Division. On 2 March Allied bombers pounded the German positions, forcing Mackensen to call off the attack. This was the last German offensive, and the Hermann Göring Division, battered and tired, was pulled out of the line.

The division returned to action in late May when the Allies launched a major offensive. Entrusted with the defence of Valmontone, the Hermann Göring Division, along with the badly mauled 362nd and 715th Divisions, held the road open long enough to allow the Tenth Army to escape from the Cassino battle. Once again, the division had displayed a high level of professionalism and doggedness. Its performance around Anzio and later at Valmontone is all the more remarkable given that the Allies had almost total aerial superiority over the battlefield, and were also superior in the quantity and quality of military materiel they could deploy.

1ST PARACHUTE DIVISION, MONTE CASSINO, FEBRUARY-MARCH 1944

In February 1944, German forces in Italy were manning the Gustav Line, a major defensive front across the whole country. Allied bombers had destroyed the abbey of Monte Cassino on 15 February in the mistaken belief that it was occupied by German forces. In fact, Field Marshal Kesselring, the German Commander-in-Chief South, had prohibited his troops from entering it. However, after its destruction the ruin was to become a fortress for the battle-hardened paras of Germany's 1st Parachute Division.

ABOVE: *A machine gunner of the German 1st Parachute Division searches for targets in the ruins of Monte Cassino. Note the stick grenades.*

Located on the slopes below the monastery was battlegroup *Schulz* (comprising the 1st Parachute Regiment, the 1st Parachute Machine Gun Battalion, and the 3rd Battalion of the 3rd Parachute Regiment). The battlegroup then received reinforcements from the 1st Parachute Division, commanded by Lieutenant-General Richard Heidrich, who deployed three regiments around the monastery: the 3rd covered the monastery itself and the town, the 4th the massif, and the 1st the area around Monte Castellone and the lower slopes of Monte Cairo.

As the monastery was still being shelled by Allied artillery, the defensive preparations had to be carried out at night. Though the division was under-strength and many of its men were suffering from malaria, the paras knew they were an elite force that had been given the job because other units were not up to it. They were determined to uphold their reputation. No longer used as airborne soldiers, the paras had been equipped with 75mm and 100mm anti-tank and field guns. Their morale was very high. In addition, their fighting spirit and physical toughness, combined with experience and training, resulted in a formidable body of soldiers.

The third battle of Cassino began at 0830 hours on 15 March 1944, when the town was subjected to a colossal bombardment. Some 500 American bombers dropped 1000 tonnes of bombs on the town, and then 746 Allied guns unleashed nearly 200,000 artillery shells. Before the bombardment, the 2nd Battalion had a strength of 300 men and five guns; afterwards it numbered 140 men and one gun. Other companies had taken a similar battering, though No 6 Company, sheltering in a rock cave, was untouched. Heidrich had lost contact with most of his men, and so the defence of Monte Cassino therefore rested with scattered groups of men that had managed to scramble out of the rubble after the bombardment.

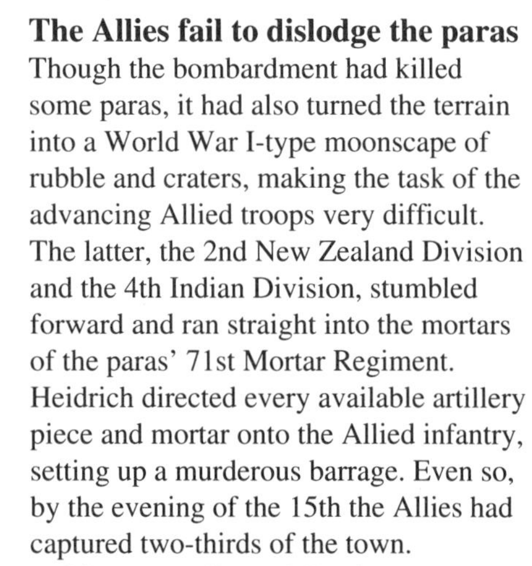

The Allies fail to dislodge the paras

Though the bombardment had killed some paras, it had also turned the terrain into a World War I-type moonscape of rubble and craters, making the task of the advancing Allied troops very difficult. The latter, the 2nd New Zealand Division and the 4th Indian Division, stumbled forward and ran straight into the mortars of the paras' 71st Mortar Regiment. Heidrich directed every available artillery piece and mortar onto the Allied infantry, setting up a murderous barrage. Even so, by the evening of the 15th the Allies had captured two-thirds of the town.

Lieutenant-General Freyberg, commander of the New Zealanders, decided to throw the 4th Indian Division against the monastery itself, but the assault made only limited gains, and for the next six days the Allies and paras slugged it out. Heidrich turned two positions, the Continental Hotel and the Hotel des Roses, into strongpoints. The battle raged on until 22 March, when the Allies called off their offensive. The 1st Parachute Division had lived up to expectations.

The formation was also engaged in the fourth battle of Cassino in May. Once again subjected to an intense bombardment, they were also heavily outnumbered and the troops of the Polish II Corps managed to throw the paras off the hill. Though it was eventually regained, the division was withdrawn north on 17 May because it was threatened with encirclement. It had fought tenaciously, and in the end was still undefeated in the town and on the surrounding hills.

Defending Cassino

German 1st Parachute Division, Feb-March 1944

The US Fifth Army reached the Gustav Line along the Garigliano and Rapido rivers early in 1943. The offensive against the section of the line at Cassino, which dominated the route to Rome, began late in January with an assault by the US VI Corps. The troops advanced to within 400 yards of the monastery but were repulsed. The 2nd New Zealand Division and 4th Indian Division attacked in mid-February without success. On 15 March they attacked again, and the Third Battle of Cassino began.

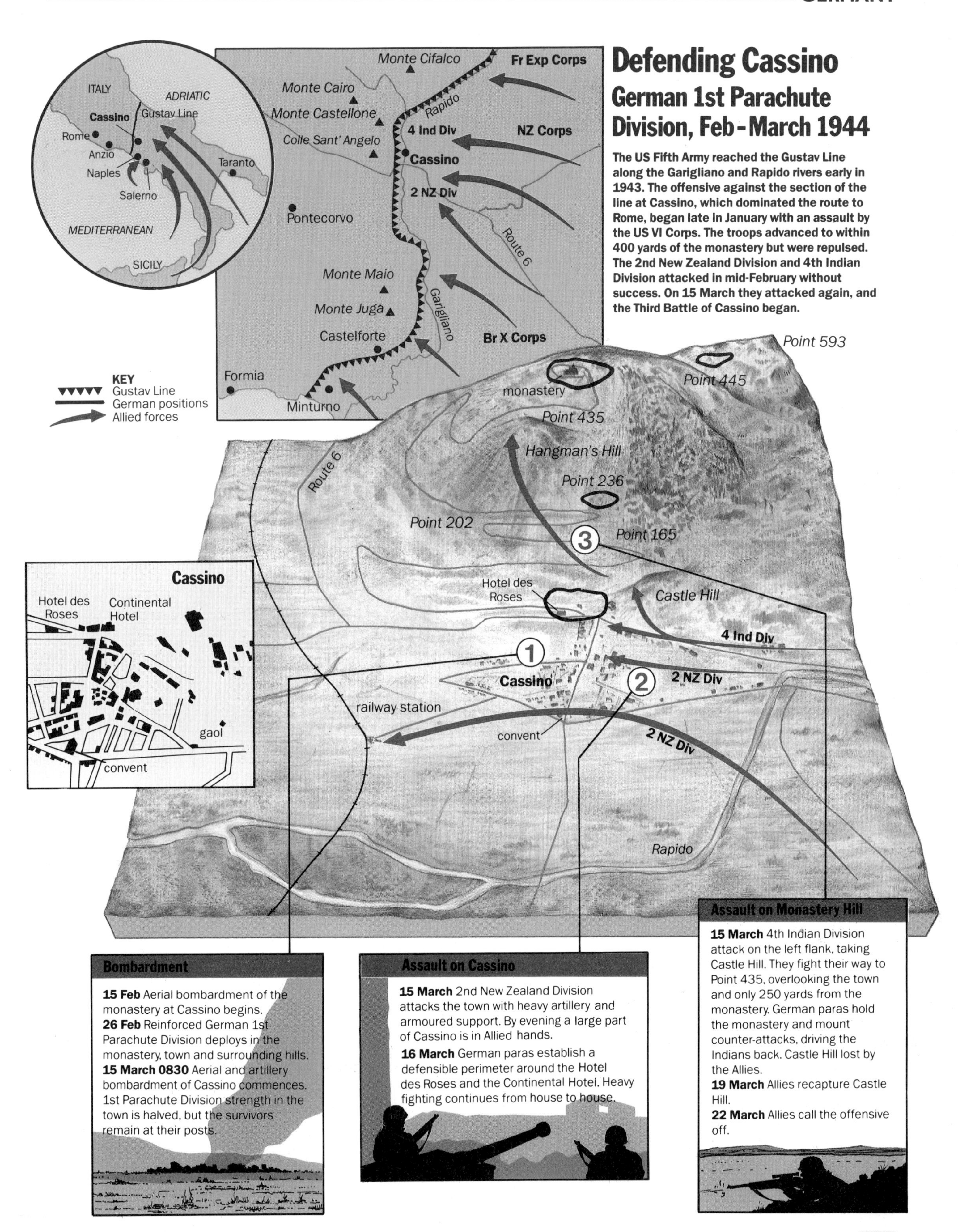

Bombardment

15 Feb Aerial bombardment of the monastery at Cassino begins.
26 Feb Reinforced German 1st Parachute Division deploys in the monastery, town and surrounding hills.
15 March 0830 Aerial and artillery bombardment of Cassino commences. 1st Parachute Division strength in the town is halved, but the survivors remain at their posts.

Assault on Cassino

15 March 2nd New Zealand Division attacks the town with heavy artillery and armoured support. By evening a large part of Cassino is in Allied hands.
16 March German paras establish a defensible perimeter around the Hotel des Roses and the Continental Hotel. Heavy fighting continues from house to house.

Assault on Monastery Hill

15 March 4th Indian Division attack on the left flank, taking Castle Hill. They fight their way to Point 435, overlooking the town and only 250 yards from the monastery. German paras hold the monastery and mount counter-attacks, driving the Indians back. Castle Hill lost by the Allies.
19 March Allies recapture Castle Hill.
22 March Allies call the offensive off.

5TH BATTALION, GRENADIER GUARDS, ANZIO, 7-9 FEBRUARY 1944

In January 1944, the 5th Battalion, Grenadier Guards, was part of the 24th Guards Brigade which had landed at Anzio on the Italian coast. There was only one road that ran northwards from Anzio into the hinterland, and a patrol of grenadiers was detailed to recce it to locate the main German defences. The patrol ran into the enemy near the town of Carroceto. Brigadier Murray, commander of the 24th Brigade, ordered his force forward the next day – 25 January – to clear the town.

Resistance was fierce, and fighting was particularly heavy around a group of buildings known as the 'Factory'. As the guardsmen advanced, high explosive and smoke shells were fired at them. Though the Factory was cleared, the 5th Battalion took 130 casualties. The Factory became the linchpin of the Allied drive into the hinterland, but intelligence revealed that at least five German divisions were deployed against the beachhead. By 4 February the attack had ground to a halt, the guardsmen then having to fight off a series of enemy counterattacks.

The German infantry, having overwhelmed one company on Buonriposo Ridge, set up their machine guns in readiness for their attack on the Gully (a depression that defended the road to Anzio itself). The Germans opened fire, their guns being answered by the guardsmen in the Gully. However, the enemy vanguard soon reached the entrance to the Gully. Showing superb fighting spirit, a small group of guardsmen led by Major William Sidney charged forward and held off the enemy with small arms and grenades. Eventually wounded in the head and legs, Sidney was forced to retire, but he had stopped the enemy's attack (for his bravery under fire, this officer was awarded the VC).

At 0300 hours on 8 February, the Germans launched their second attack. It was met by a hail of small-arms fire which cut down many men, as did the British artillery fire. By daylight there were 29 guardsmen and 45 Americans in the Gully. During the afternoon the Germans launched yet another assault, but this too was repulsed. The guardsmen held their ground until the early hours of 9 February. The 5th Battalion had distinguished itself in the face of the enemy.

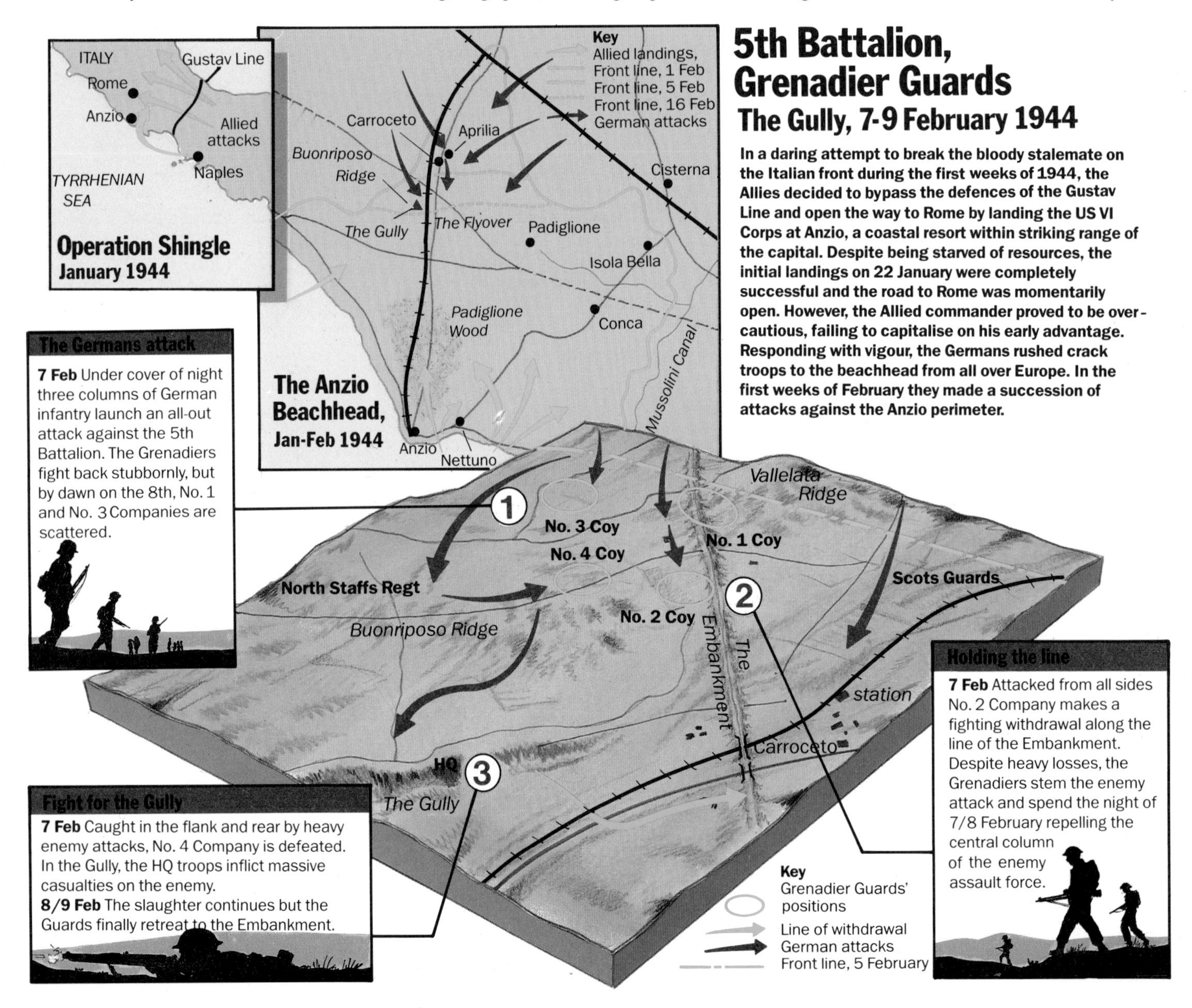

14, 16, 77 AND 111 CHINDIT BRIGADES, WHITE CITY, FEBRUARY-APRIL 1944

In March 1944, the Japanese 18th Division was advancing against the forces of US General 'Vinegar' Joe Stillwell in Burma. The Chindits, in response, began to block the road and railway running north-south through Mawlu, thus cutting the 18th's main line of communication.

The Chindits had soon erected a massive wire obstacle, supported by anti-tank and anti-personnel mines. The position, called White City, contained hardened bunkers, anti-aircraft and field guns. In addition, 13 Vickers machine guns were sited to fire along the wire and eight 3in mortars were positioned to bring fire onto enemy attacks.

The Japanese probe the defences

Such activity, particularly the constant air drops, was bound to attract attention, and on the night of 21/22 March the 3rd Battalion of the 114th Regiment of the Japanese 18th Division launched an attack from the north. At this time the garrison consisted of half a battalion of South Staffords, one column (half a battalion) of 3/6th Gurkhas, one column of 1st Lancashires, and a strong brigade defence company of 3/6th Gurkhas. With gunners, sappers and headquarters staff, the total was around 2000 fighting men. A mixed force of Gurkhas and South Staffords met the Japanese and threw them back, losing 34 men killed.

The commander of White City, Brigadier Mike Calvert, then decided to clear the railway town of Mawlu, which was achieved in a skilful attack conducted by the 3/6th Gurkhas and Lancashire Fusiliers. During the next few weeks the garrison cleared the Japanese off 80km of their mainline railway.

Major-General Yoshida Hyashi was tasked with destroying White City. Moving at speed, Hyashi began the siege on 31 March, launching an attack against the position after a heavy bombardment. The first assault was defeated easily, as were two subsequent attacks, while the Chindits' 25-pounders were proving very effective against the enemy's artillery. At dawn the next day, US Mustang and Mitchell aircraft bombed the Japanese in Mawlu. The Japanese also tried to use aircraft against White City, but the batteries of anti-aircraft guns proved their worth: in one incident nine enemy bombers were shot down.

Bangalore torpedoes and suicide attacks failed to breach the defences, and Japanese dead littered the wire. Hyashi continued the attack, however, until, on the night of 17/18 April, Brigadier Calvert formed a counterattack force and, aided by 36 USAAF Mustang fighter aircraft, threw back the Japanese. The enemy had been broken. Japanese soldiers began to stream back to Indaw in disarray; Hyashi was dead, along with 3000 of his men. The battle of White City was over. The position was abandoned on 10 May, though Calvert's men rigged it with a host of booby traps. The White City area still remains a hazardous zone.

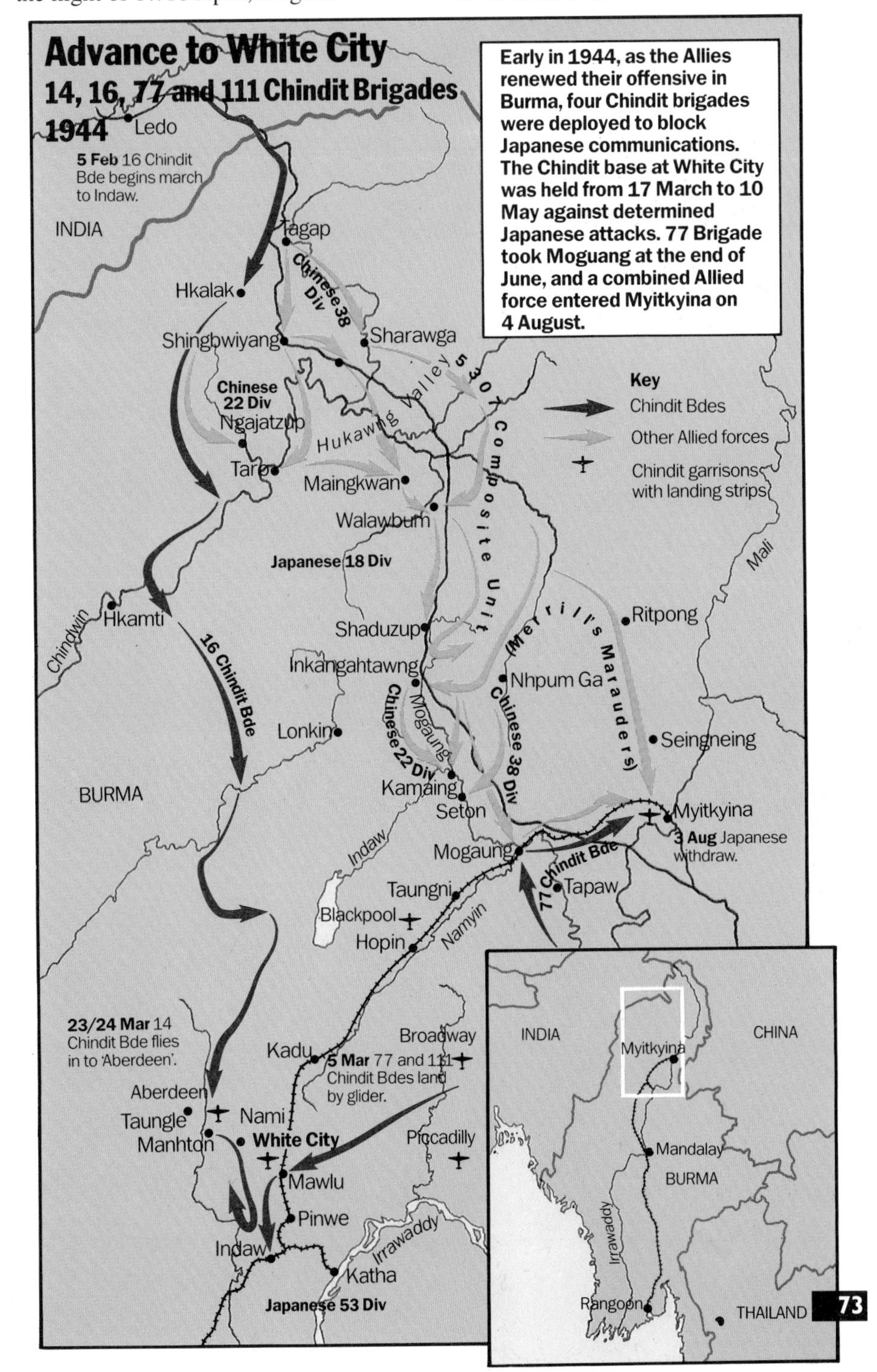

MERRILL'S MARAUDERS, NHPUM GA, MARCH-APRIL 1944

In early 1944, as part of the overall Allied strategy to reopen a supply route through northern Burma to China, Merrill's Marauders, the long-range penetration unit under the command of Brigadier-General Frank Merrill, was engaged on its first mission. On 28 March 1944, its 2nd Battalion Blue Combat Team was withdrawing from the Burmese village of Auche towards Nhpum Ga. Chopping their way through the jungle, the Americans ran into Japanese 75mm guns deployed at the village of Warong. The artillery inflicted a number of casualties, and threatened to turn the retreat into a rout.

The Marauders had been part of raids against Shaduzup and Inkangahtawang in March which had met heavy resistance; therefore the Americans had been forced to withdraw to the village of Hsamshingyang, hotly pursued by the enemy.

The 2nd Battalion reached Nhpum by 1030 hours on the 28th, and hastily started to prepare defensive positions in expectation of a Japanese attack. It was not long in coming, and very soon the enemy had severed communications between Nhpum and Hsamshingyang and the former was under siege. The Japanese brought up artillery which blasted the defences, and all day enemy snipers kept the Marauders' heads down.

Just before dawn on 31 March, the artillery opened up to signal a three-sided attack on the Americans. The Japanese succeeded in taking the Marauders' water supply, a grievous loss (more had to be flown in on 3 April).

Despite the fact that they were under constant artillery and infantry attack, the Marauders gave a good account of themselves and killed at least 200 Japanese soldiers. The bodies, together with the corpses of over 100 mules, lay rotting within the defences. The smell was unbearable. However, the Marauders fought on. One of them, Sergeant Roy Matsumoto, crept into the jungle every night to snipe and gather intelligence. He was awarded the Legion of Merit and the Bronze Star for his bravery and devotion to duty.

Meanwhile, the Marauders' 3rd Battalion at Hsamshingyang was trying to break through the Japanese positions. Supported by 75mm guns, the 3rd launched its attack on 3 April to reach Nhpum. Though the going was tough, by nightfall the leading elements of the 3rd Battalion were within 1000m of their comrades. The situation changed little over the next two days, and by 6 April the defenders in the village were too weak to resist further attacks. On the 7th, news reached them that the Marauders' 1st Battalion was only 500m from their position. Advancing slowly forward, the men of the 1st met little resistance, discovering only equipment scattered on the floor. The Japanese had given up.

The siege had lasted for 10 days. The 2nd Battalion had suffered only 25 men killed, but had inflicted over 400 fatalities on the Japanese.

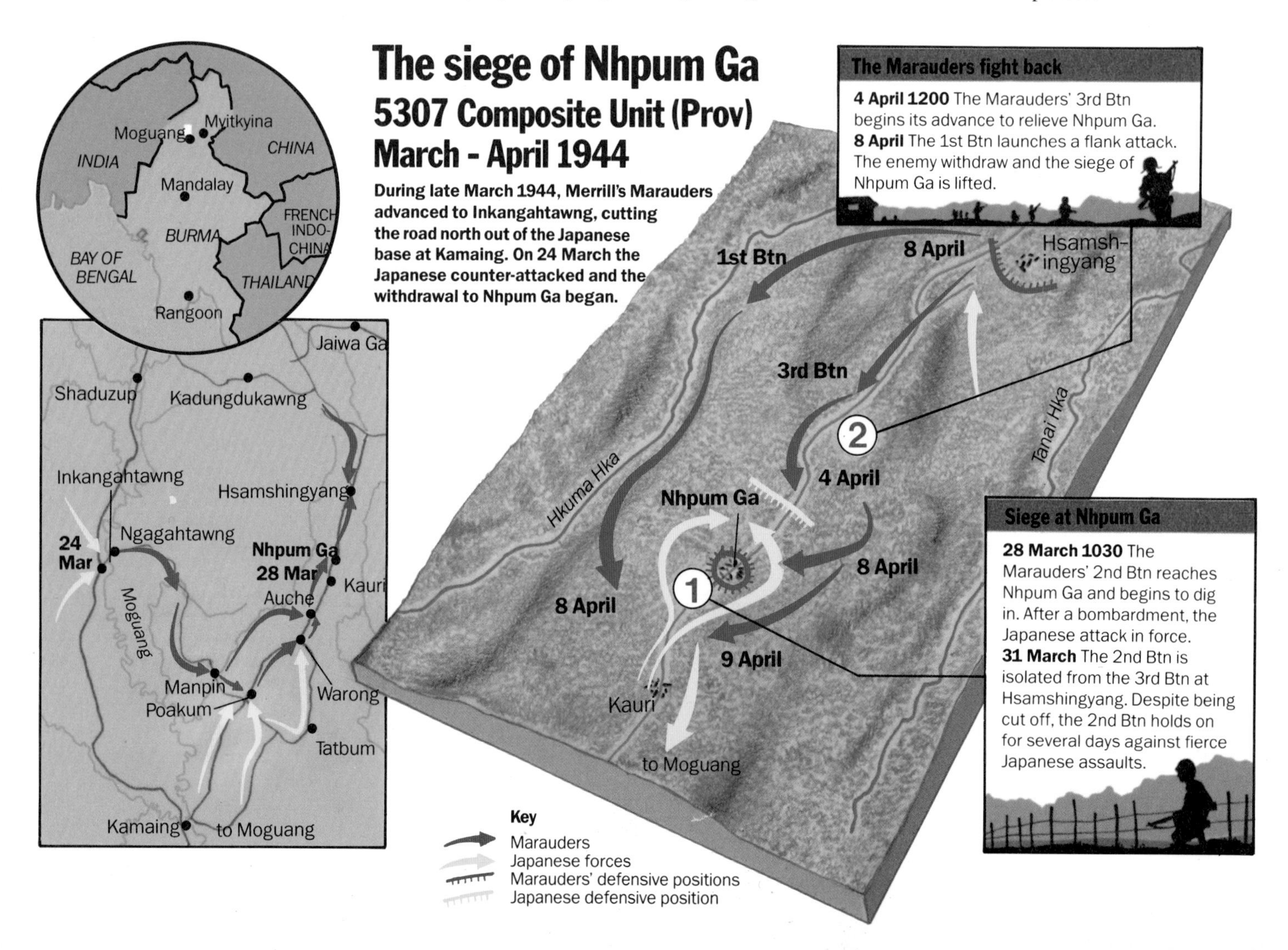

II Polish Corps, Monte Cassino, May 1944

In late April 1944, II Polish Corps, 50,000 strong, went into the line at Monte Cassino. Led by Lieutenant-General Wladyslaw Anders, it was eager to have a crack at the Germans.

The defences were extremely strong: strengthened bunkers and shelters which commanded broad arcs of fire across the maze of gullies, ridges and ravines. Anders decided to launch two attacks: one against Point 593 and the other against Phantom Ridge and Colle Sant'Angelo. After his men had taken Point 593, they would strike towards the German strongpoint at Albaneta Farm.

The Poles moved into their forward positions. In appalling conditions they waited. At 2300 hours on 11 May, 1600 Allied guns erupted into action, shelling the German lines. Then, at 0100 hours on the 12th, the Polish attack began.

The initial assault, led by the 2nd Battalion, 1 Carpathian Brigade, met with success: Point 593 was taken after 30 minutes. Those Poles approaching Phantom Ridge were not so lucky, however. As they picked their way across the terrain, artillery and mortar fire rained down on them, killing many before they had even reached the objective. Those that did reach the German bunkers could not drive off the enemy, and they were soon pinned down. The advance on Albaneta Farm met with a similar fate, the Polish tanks of the 2nd Armoured Brigade being stopped by mines and anti-tank guns. Meanwhile, those Poles who had taken Point 593 endeavoured to storm Point 569, but were stopped by a hail of fire. Point 593 then became a killing ground. By daylight the Poles were back at their start line.

The Poles were in action again on 17 May, taking Colle Sant'Angelo and Point 593. Though the Germans pummelled their positions with artillery, the Poles held on. During the night of 17/18 May, German forces started to withdraw. The next morning, a detachment of the 12th Podolski Lancers entered the monastery. They found it deserted. The Poles had taken Monte Cassino. It was a fitting tribute for the Polish Corps, which had lost 3799 dead in one week of fighting.

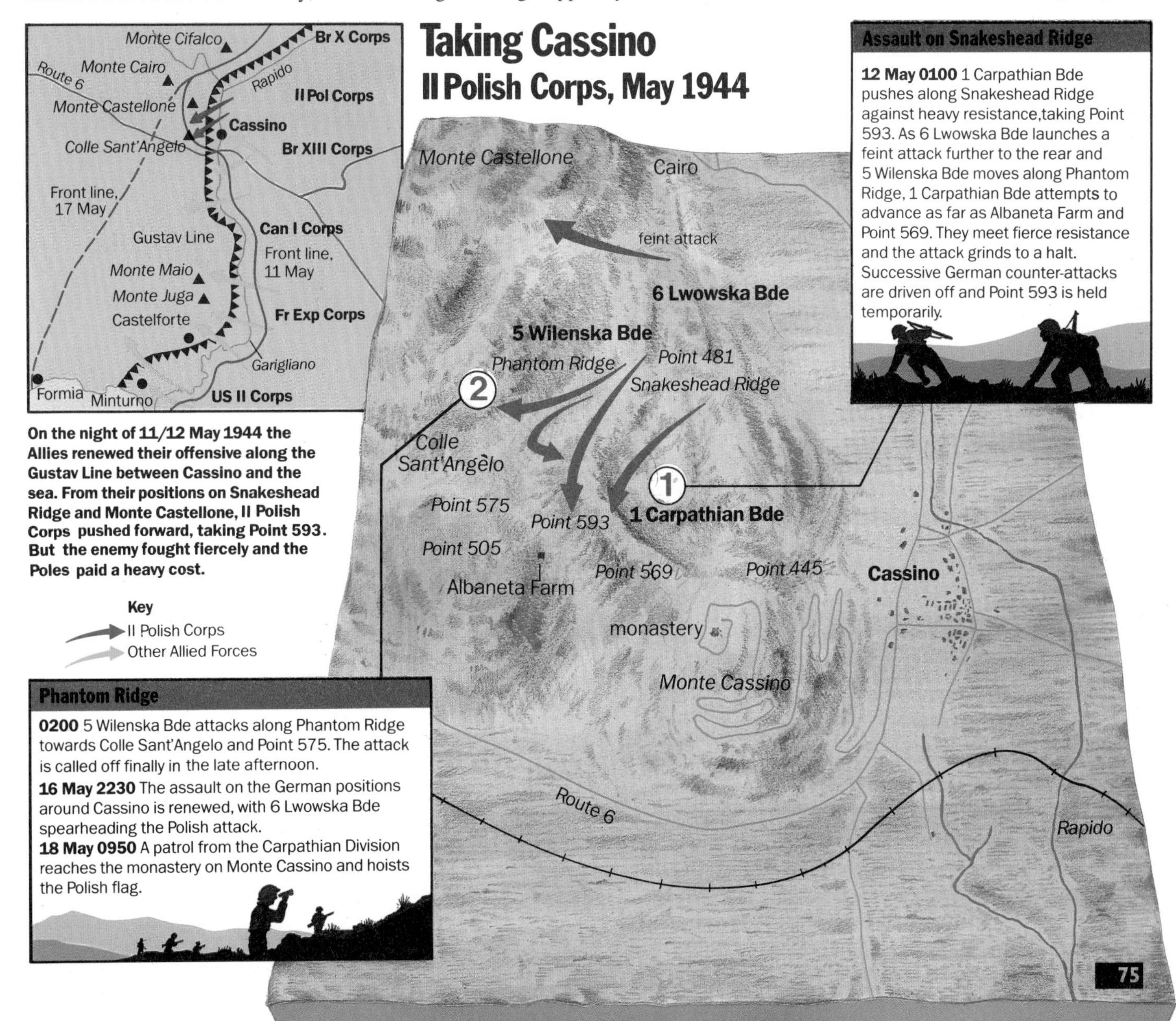

On the night of 11/12 May 1944 the Allies renewed their offensive along the Gustav Line between Cassino and the sea. From their positions on Snakeshead Ridge and Monte Castellone, II Polish Corps pushed forward, taking Point 593. But the enemy fought fiercely and the Poles paid a heavy cost.

RAF GLIDER PILOT REGIMENT, PEGASUS BRIDGE, 5-6 JUNE 1944

Operation 'Deadstick' was the codename for the attempt to seize the bridges over the Orne river and canal on D-Day, the Allied invasion of France, on 6 June 1944. Six Horsa gliders would take D Company, 2nd Battalion, Oxfordshire and Buckinghamshire Light Infantry, commanded by Major John Howard, to France and land them on two landing zones (LZs): X and Y. The gliders were piloted by men of the Glider Pilot Regiment, each aircraft having two aircrew. The men of the regiment were highly trained; not only could they fly gliders, they were also expert in using small arms, driving trucks and jeeps, firing field guns and using wireless sets.

When over the French coast, the gliders were released and headed for the bridges. The troops inside the fuselages linked arms and lifted their feet off the floor, bracing themselves for the crash. Howard's glider raced across a field and ground to a halt near Pegasus bridge, its cockpit having been smashed during the heavy landing.

His men jumped out and raced towards the bridge. There was no shooting, as his men had achieved total surprise and the glider had breached the bridge's wire defences. However, the calm was soon shattered by the explosion of a phosphorus grenade which lit the scene as the first platoon went into action against the pillbox near the bridge. Two other gliders made it down safely, but another landed at an angle and broke up on impact with the ground, killing one man and injuring several others. The other aircraft then came in. The pilots had done a magnificent job, landing five out of the six platoons on target and on time. The troops also performed superbly, capturing the bridges and securing them in the face of repeated German counter-attacks which continued into the night and throughout the following morning, and included an enemy patrol boat being sent down from Caen. By midday on 6 June, the men had been relieved by Lord Lovat's Commandos and the glider pilots were withdrawn to England.

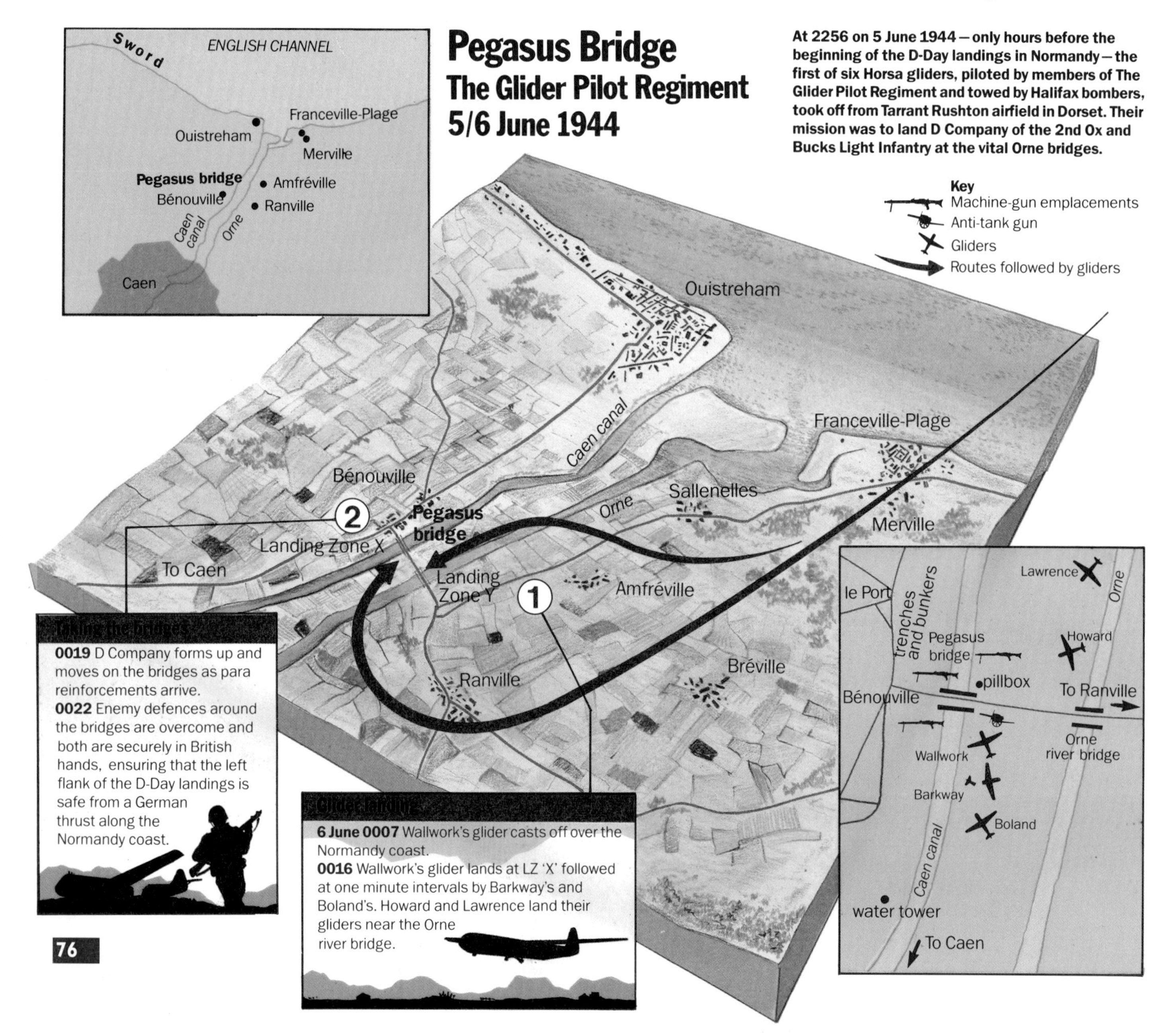

NO 3 COMMANDO, D-DAY, 6 JUNE 1944

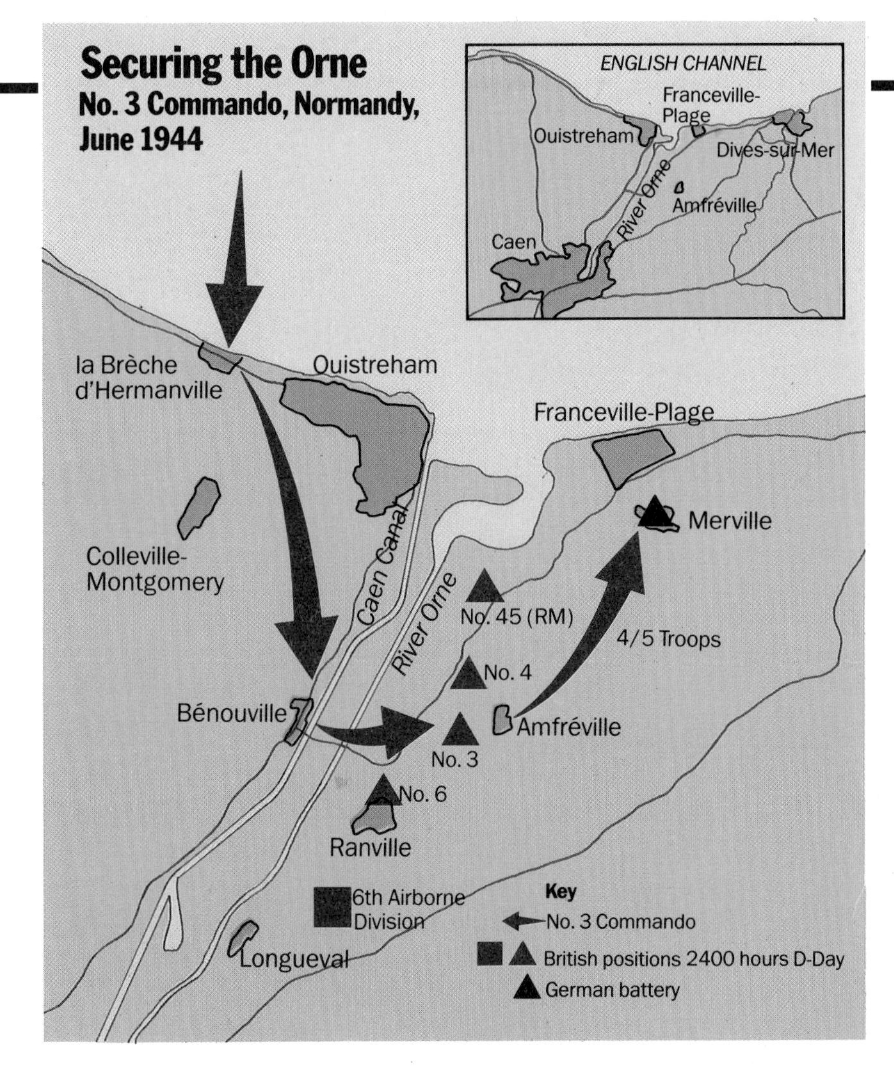

No 3 Commando, part of the 1st Special Service Brigade, was tasked on D-Day (6 June 1944) to seize and make secure the coastal strip on the eastern flank of the Allied landings. It would then push inland, capture bridges over the River Orne, and link up with 6th Airborne Division, which had landed to the northeast of Caen to establish a defensive screen.

Commanded by Colonel Peter Young, the 450-strong Commando landed on the beaches in the early hours of 6 June. Moving inland, his men secured the bridge over the Caen Canal at Benouville, and by mid-afternoon most of No 3 Commando was over the bridge and had taken up defensive positions in order to stave off any German counter-attacks. It soon became apparent that in order to strengthen the Allied defence along the Orne, the village of Amfreville would have to be taken. The village stood on a low ridge east of the Orne overlooking a large part of the Allied lodgement area. From there German artillery could direct heavy fire onto the vulnerable Allied beachhead around Ouistreham.

5 Troop encounters difficulties

Three Troop was ordered to advance into the village, only to be stopped by a hail of German machine-gun fire. Halting to reorganise their attack, the Commandos cleared some houses overlooking the village square and started to fire their 2in mortar at the Germans. After a while, convinced they had demoralised the garrison, they charged across the square to capture the village school, the main centre of resistance. In the assault the troop suffered no casualties, though they killed eight Germans and captured a further 20.

At 1300 hours on 7 June, two troops from No 3 Commando were ordered to support No 45 Commando's attack on Franceville-Plage by clearing the battery at Merville to the southeast. While 4 Troop gave covering fire, 5 Troop moved forward, and walked straight into a minefield. Miraculously, only three men were wounded; the rest pressed on and captured the battery. Colonel Young then ordered forward 4 Troop to assist in mopping-up operations.

Young conducts a fighting retreat

Positioned as they were far in front of the Allied lines, it was only a matter of time before the Germans counterattacked the exposed Commandos. Young realised this and reluctantly requested permission to withdraw. Brigade HQ agreed, but by the time permission came through the enemy had already closed in. Therefore, a fighting withdrawal had to be made. The enemy brought up two self-propelled artillery guns to support their attack, and these pieces, firing at close range, inflicted a number of casualties on the British Commandos. When the two troops finally reached Allied lines, they had been reduced to half strength.

While these troops rested, the rest of No 3 Commando waited at Amfreville for the German attack. It was not long in coming. On 8 June an enemy battalion approached the Commandos' position, to be met with a well-timed counterattack which threw them back. The Germans had lost 30 killed and 45 taken prisoner. Over the next few days the enemy launched more assaults, but these were also defeated by the Commandos. By 13 June the enemy had given up and dug in 1000m east of No 3 Commando's position. The battle now became one of sniping and patrolling. The Commandos maintained their position, and sent out patrols to harass the enemy until the latter began to fall back towards Falaise. Once again, the Commandos had proved themselves to be crack soldiers.

2ND RANGER BATTALION, POINTE DU HOC, 6 JUNE 1944

The 2nd Ranger Battalion, led by Colonel Jim Rudder, had a vital part in the D-Day landings: seizing the German battery on the cliffs of the Pointe du Hoc which overlooked the beach codenamed Omaha. The battery, if not taken, threatened to decimate those US troops coming ashore on Omaha. At 0415 hours on 6 June, the landing craft containing the Rangers and their equipment approached the shore. There were also four DUKW amphibious vehicles in the flotilla, two of which were modified to carry ladders that could be extended up the cliffs. The other two carried the Rangers' support weapons that would be used to hold the cliff-top position until reinforcements arrived.

As the flotilla approached the shore, two of the store-carriers were lost in heavy seas, a bitter blow as they contained explosives and reserves of food and ammunition. In addition, Rudder's ships were off-course, and although the mistake was realised and the direction amended, the Germans opened fire on the landing craft.

Hitting the beach, the Rangers fired their rocket lines, but the ropes only travelled 15m, being heavy with sea water. Several men then climbed up the rock face, enemy small-arms fire erupting all around them. Thirty minutes later there were 100 Americans on the top of the Pointe du Hoc. The Rangers worked their way forward to the battery. However, it didn't contain any guns – they had not been mounted!

Rudder established his HQ on the tip of the Pointe and sent patrols east and west, one of which found the 155mm pieces that were destined to serve as the Pointe du Hoc battery. These were spiked. But then the Germans counter-attacked and forced Rudder to withdraw his sections into a tighter perimeter.

Although he had received a few reinforcements from the 5th Rangers and some ammunition, Rudder was in a perilous position. However, he elected to take the fight to the enemy. When relieved on the morning of the 8th, there were only 50 of the original 200 Rangers of the 2nd left on the Pointe du Hoc.

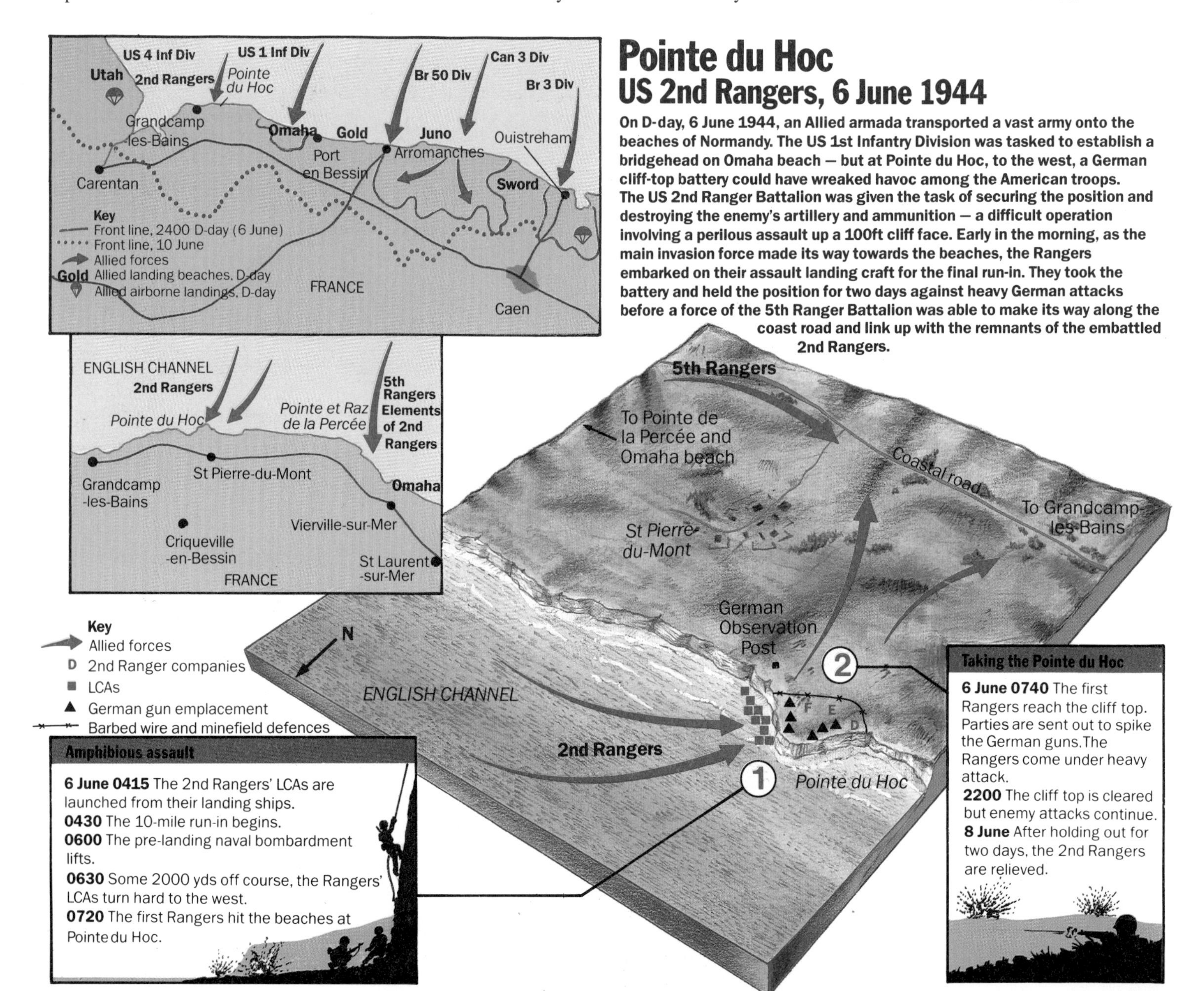

9TH BATTALION, THE PARACHUTE REGIMENT, D-DAY, 6 JUNE 1944

In the early hours of 6 June 1944, the men of the 9th Battalion, The Parachute Regiment, drifted down in gliders and by parachute to attack the German battery at Merville, which contained four 75mm guns protected by 3m of concrete. The battery posed a grave threat to the British landings on Sword, Juno and Gold beaches. The commander of 9 Para, Lieutenant-Colonel T B H Otway, was informed that the battery was garrisoned by 130 men armed with 20 machine guns and one 20mm dual-purpose gun. There was also a minefield 16m deep behind the cattle fence that encompassed the battery.

The battalion took off during the evening of 5 June. Though the flight was uneventful, problems arose when the aircraft reached the drop zone (DZ). The Germans had flooded the low-lying ground alongside the Dives and Orne rivers, making the identification of landmarks impossible. The flak started to erupt around them, and many men were dropped wide of the DZ. On landing, Otway found many of his men were missing. He collected 150 men, however, and decided to advance.

The gliders had arrived at the wrong Landing Zone (LZ). They too had failed to identify landmarks, and had landed well out of sight of the battalion. Denied the heavy equipment carried in the gliders, Otway improvised. B Company, divided into two teams, prepared to force a breach to allow A and C Companies to silence the guns. As a diversion, a seven-man team would carry out an attack at another part of the defences.

Otway gave the order to attack. One officer, in typical British fashion, sounded the charge on his hunting horn as the Paras rushed forward. The fighting was brutal, with neither side giving any quarter. Hand-to-hand fighting raged in the gun emplacements and underground passages. However, the battle was soon over, and the Paras took control.

The guns were quickly destroyed and Otway and his men made for their second objective: the high ground close by the village of Le Plein. However, on being informed there were 200 enemy soldiers barring their way, the Paras formed a defensive position. They had nothing to prove, they had fought superbly, and the taking of the Merville Battery was a marvellous feat of arms. But what else would one expect of a para unit?

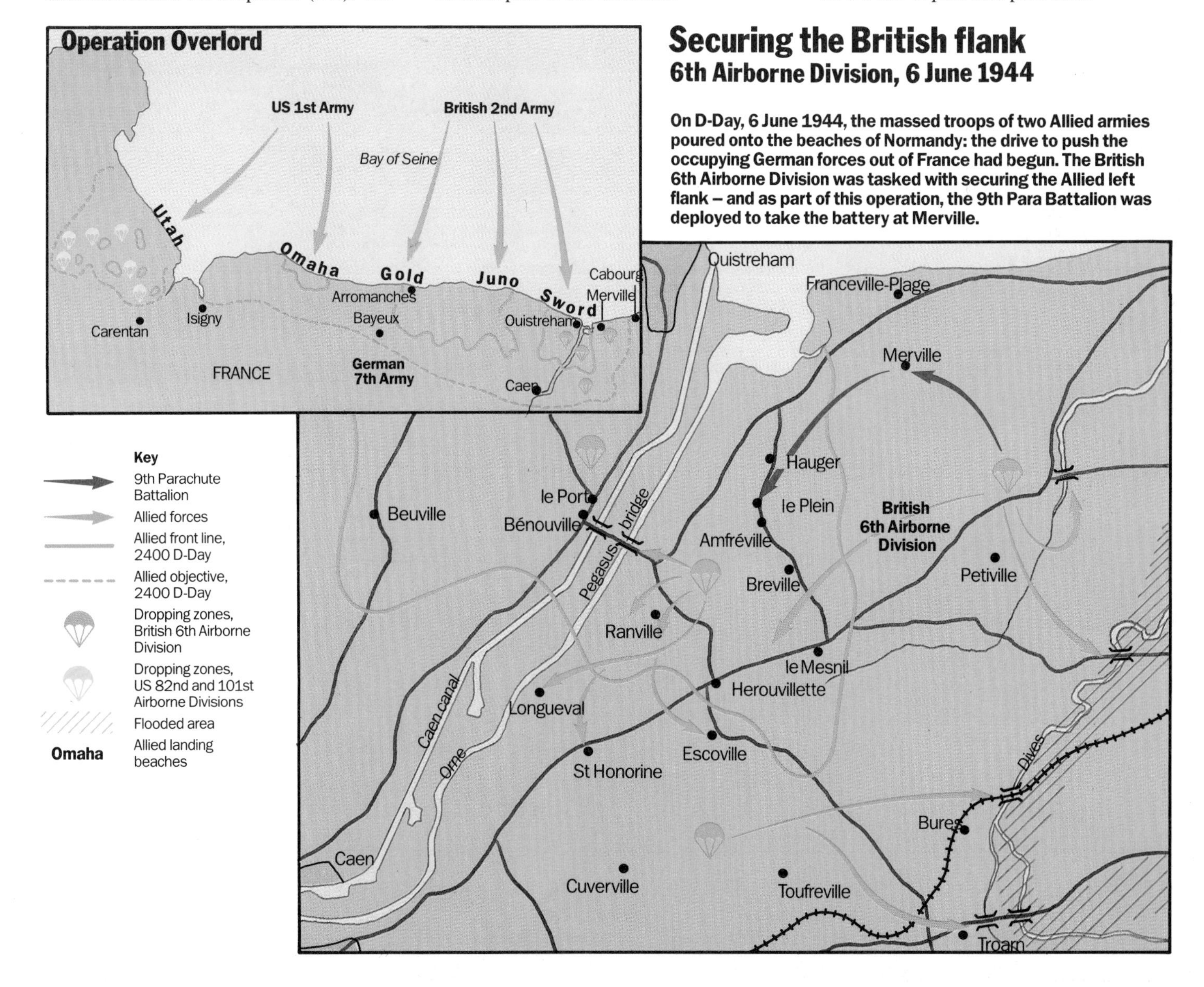

Securing the British flank

6th Airborne Division, 6 June 1944

On D-Day, 6 June 1944, the massed troops of two Allied armies poured onto the beaches of Normandy: the drive to push the occupying German forces out of France had begun. The British 6th Airborne Division was tasked with securing the Allied left flank – and as part of this operation, the 9th Para Battalion was deployed to take the battery at Merville.

16TH INFANTRY REGIMENT, D-DAY, 6 JUNE 1944

On D-Day, the men of the US 16th Infantry Regiment were in the vanguard of the US 1st Infantry Division's assault on Omaha Beach. The regiment was chosen to lead the attack on the beach west of Port-en-Besin-Huppain, near the village of Colleville-sur-Mer. Led by Colonel George Taylor, the 16th was organised into Battalion Landing Teams (BLTs).

The 16th itself formed a Regimental Landing Team (RLT) and landed at 'Easy Red' and 'Fox Green'. Each of the two BLTs of the 16th Infantry RLT comprised a battalion of infantry, a company of Duplex Drive Sherman M4 tanks, two companies of engineers, a beach party, a battalion of field artillery equipped with 105mm howitzers, and a medical detachment.

The plan was for the Shermans to come ashore first, followed by the assault waves of 2 and 3 BLTs. To destroy the beach fortifications, the attack on Omaha would be preceded by a massive aerial and naval bombardment. However, things started to go wrong almost immediately after the preliminary bombardments. First, only two out of the 32 tanks earmarked to support the 16th infantry RLT made it to the beach, and the amphibious trucks carrying the towed artillery met a similar fate. Second, strong offshore currents forced 2 and 3 BLTs to land west of their designated targets on Easy Red and Fox Green. Third, only six of the bulldozers of the Special Engineer Task Force made it to shore, managing to open only a paltry six lanes on Omaha itself.

As the men started to pour ashore, mines, machine-gun and artillery fire exacted a heavy toll. On Easy Red, for example, the Command Group of the 16th Infantry's RCT hit the beach at around 0730 hours, to be met by a hail of fire that killed 35 men out of 103 in one landing craft, including Lieutenant-Colonel Hugh Mathews, the regimental executive officer. The regiment's commander, Colonel George Taylor, seeing his men were simply hugging the embankment, shouted: 'Two kinds of people are staying on this beach, the dead and those who are going to die – now let's get the hell out of here.' Spurred on by this, the men started to push inland. The 16th left behind 27 officers and 935 enlisted men dead or wounded on the beach. It had been a hard fight.

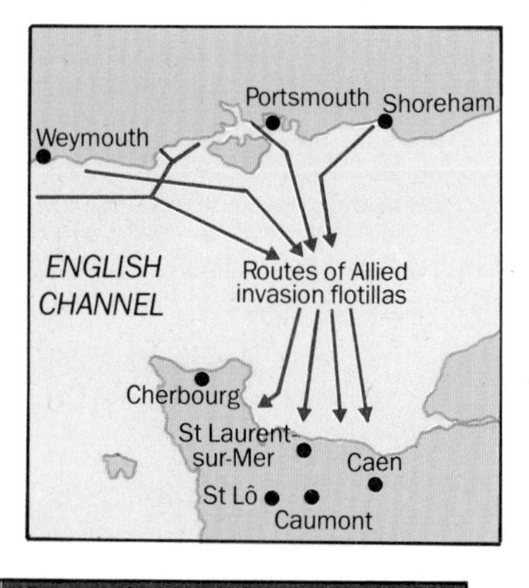

US 16th Infantry Regiment

Omaha Beach, 6-7 June 1944

Allied forces went into action on the beaches of Normandy early on D-Day, 6 June 1944. The US 1st Infantry Division was tasked to land on Omaha beach, and in the forefront of the division were the men of the 16th Infantry Regiment.

At 0700 the leading elements of the regiment's two Battalion Landing Teams neared the beaches. Enemy defences and unpredictable currents combined to make the approach a difficult one and the flat beaches of Omaha became a killing ground. But by the end of the day the regiment was firmly established on French soil.

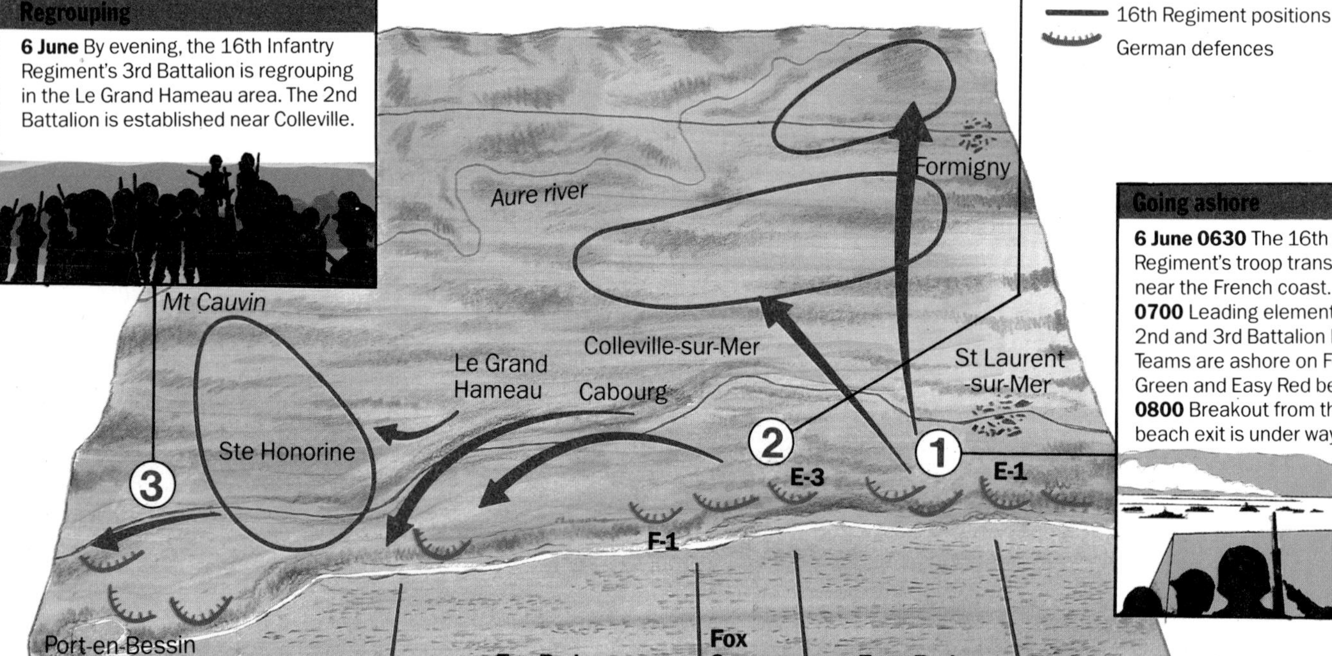

352ND GRENADIER DIVISION, D-DAY, 6 JUNE 1944

The German 352nd Grenadier Division had been formed using remnants of the 389th Grenadier Division that had been virtually wiped out at Stalingrad. In June 1944, the division was stationed on the Normandy coast between Grandcamps and Arromanches. Rested and re-equipped, it was a fine fighting unit that had worked hard on the beach defences.

In the early hours of 6 June, landing craft approached the beach that the Allied planners had codenamed Omaha. The commander of the 916th Grenadier Regiment, Colonel Goth, ordered his men to hold their fire until the enemy was at the water's edge. Then the machine guns opened up, scything through the American troops. Soon the beach was littered with American dead, as well as the burning wrecks of jeeps and tanks, blown up by German artillery.

At 1030 hours, the 1st Battalion, 914th Grenadiers, was having trouble containing troops from the US 116th Regiment and Company B, 5th Rangers, who were fighting their way into Vierville. Despite the slaughter, the Americans were making some headway, forcing the Germans out of the town. Elsewhere, elements of the 916th were engaged in house-to-house fighting in Colleville and St Laurent. The knocking out of the bunkers at Le Ruquet allowed the US 115th Infantry Regiment inland. The 2nd Battalion, 726th Grenadier Regiment, stationed alongside the 352nd Division, started to fall back in disorder.

The 2nd Battalion, 916th Grenadiers, stood firm, repulsing American attacks and mopping up small groups of enemy soldiers. Nevertheless, it was becoming apparent that the 352nd could not hold the ever-increasing numbers of American troops, and so units began to pull back. Some never made it, being caught in the open by US machine guns. By mid-afternoon the fighting had intensified and the 2nd Battalion, 916th Grenadiers, had been almost forced out of St Laurent. The German units in Colleville were cut off by 1800 hours. The end was near.

Though the 352nd Division had not stopped the invaders, it had fought bravely and tenaciously against overwhelming odds, but in the end could not hold back the invasion force.

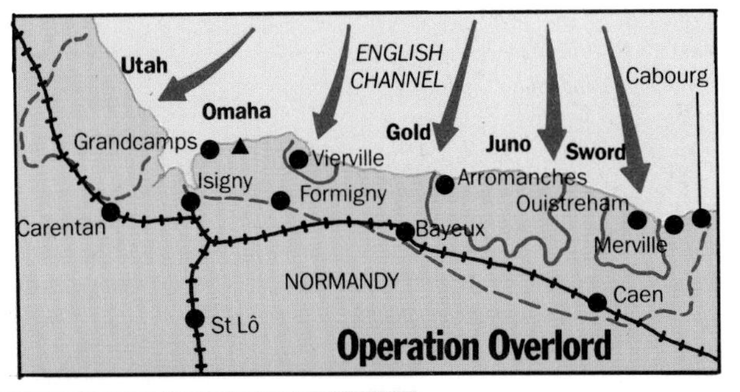

352nd Grenadier Division Omaha Beach, 6-7 June 1944

Early on the morning of 6 June 1944, the US 1st Infantry Division began its attempt to secure a foothold on Omaha Beach, Normandy. Behind a defensive wall consisting of Tellermines, tank-traps, barbed wire and machine-gun positions, the German 352nd Grenadier Division waited for the Allied onslaught.

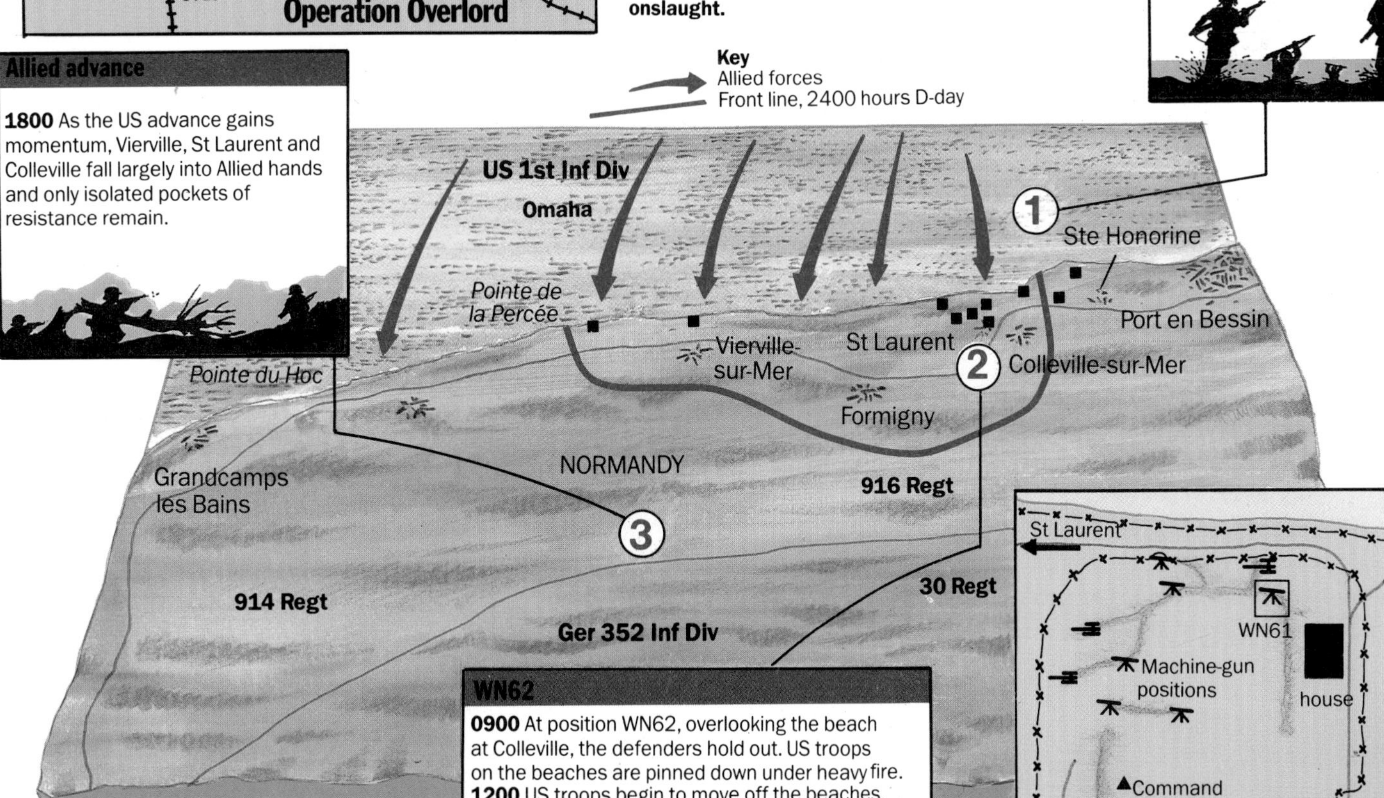

12TH SS PANZER DIVISION HITLERJUGEND, NORMANDY, JUNE -AUGUST 1944

On 6 June 1944, the 20,000-strong 12th SS Panzer Division Hitlerjugend, composed largely of soldiers under the age of 25, was ordered to deploy east of Lisieux, Normandy, where it would be used to halt the Allied invasion forces. The division was grouped west of Caen to participate in a counterattack against the Canadians. However, because of fuel shortages and dispersal, the division could only put together a battle group under the command of Kurt Meyer for the attack.

The orders for the division on the morning of 7 June instructed the Hitlerjugend to throw the enemy into the sea. However, Meyer was more realistic and set a trap around Caen for the advancing Canadians. When the latter were only 80m from the tanks of the Hitlerjugend, the Germans opened up with a devastating barrage. The Panzer Mark IVs and infantry smashed into the flanks of the Canadians as the anti-tank guns fired at point-blank range. The Canadian line buckled, and very soon the villages of Authie and Franqueville were retaken by the young SS soldiers. The Canadians retreated, leaving 30 tanks and 300 dead on the battlefield.

On 8 June Meyer led a night attack along the Caen-Bayeux road. However, in a confused battle at the village of Rots, the Hitlerjugend lost six tanks. Worse was to follow. On 16 June the divisional headquarters 27km southwest of Caen came under heavy naval gunfire, and on 4 July the Canadians took Carpiquet. Between 4 and 9 July, the Hitlerjugend held off a series of attacks by the British I Corps, but the price was high. The division's total infantry strength equalled that of only one battalion, and it had only 65 of its original 150 tanks.

Throughout July and August the Hitlerjugend fought a series of battles with Allied forces, its losses being horrendous: by 22 August the division had been reduced to 300 men, 10 tanks and no artillery. However, its bravery and tenacity on the battlefield were unmatched. The fighting qualities of its soldiers had allowed half the German divisions trapped in the Argentan-Falaise pocket to escape, the SS soldiers holding open the northern side of the pocket.

There was another side to the coin: the atrocities committed by the Hitlerjugend, particularly against the Canadians. In the period between 7 and 16 June, for example, the division murdered 64 British and Canadian prisoners. Nevertheless, in the final analysis it must be considered a unit of exceptional fighting quality.

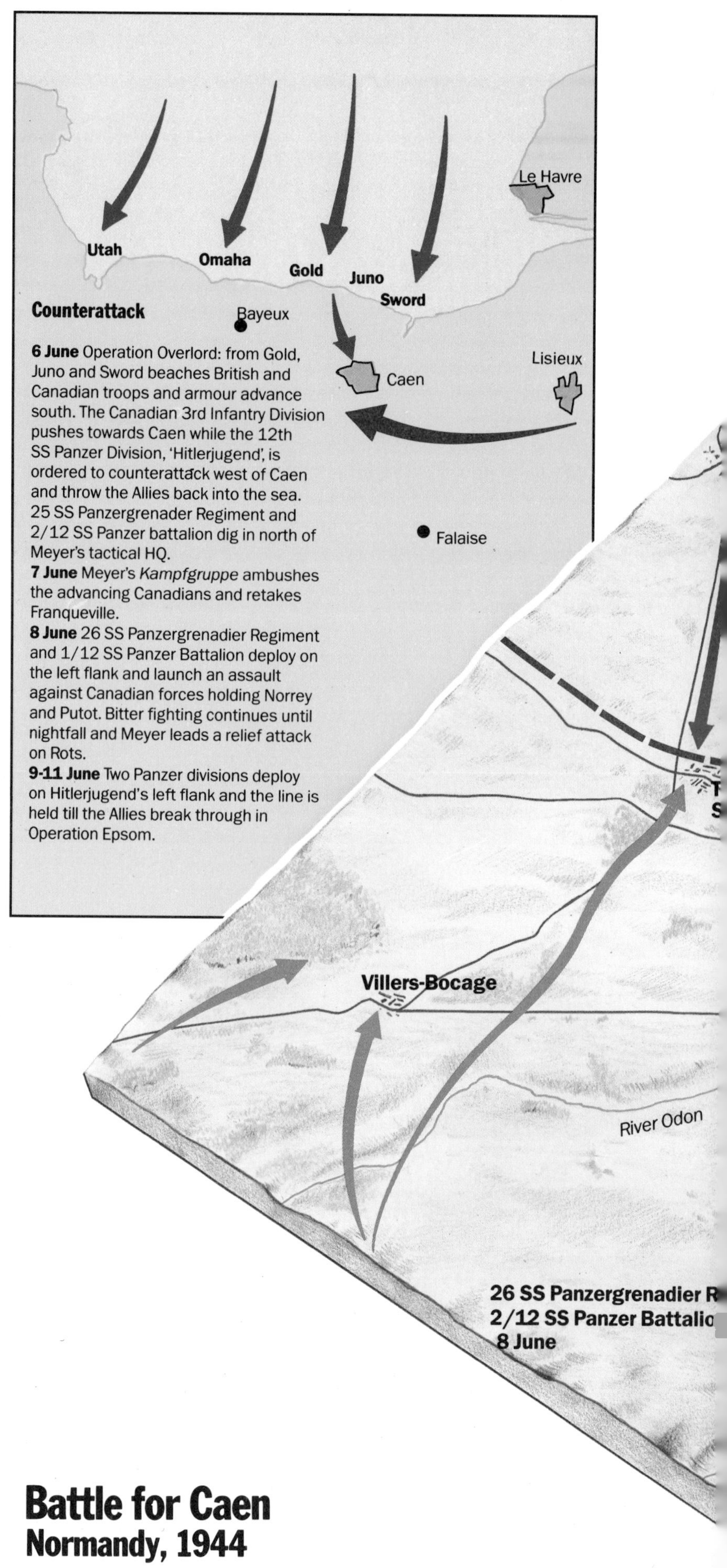

Battle for Caen
Normandy, 1944

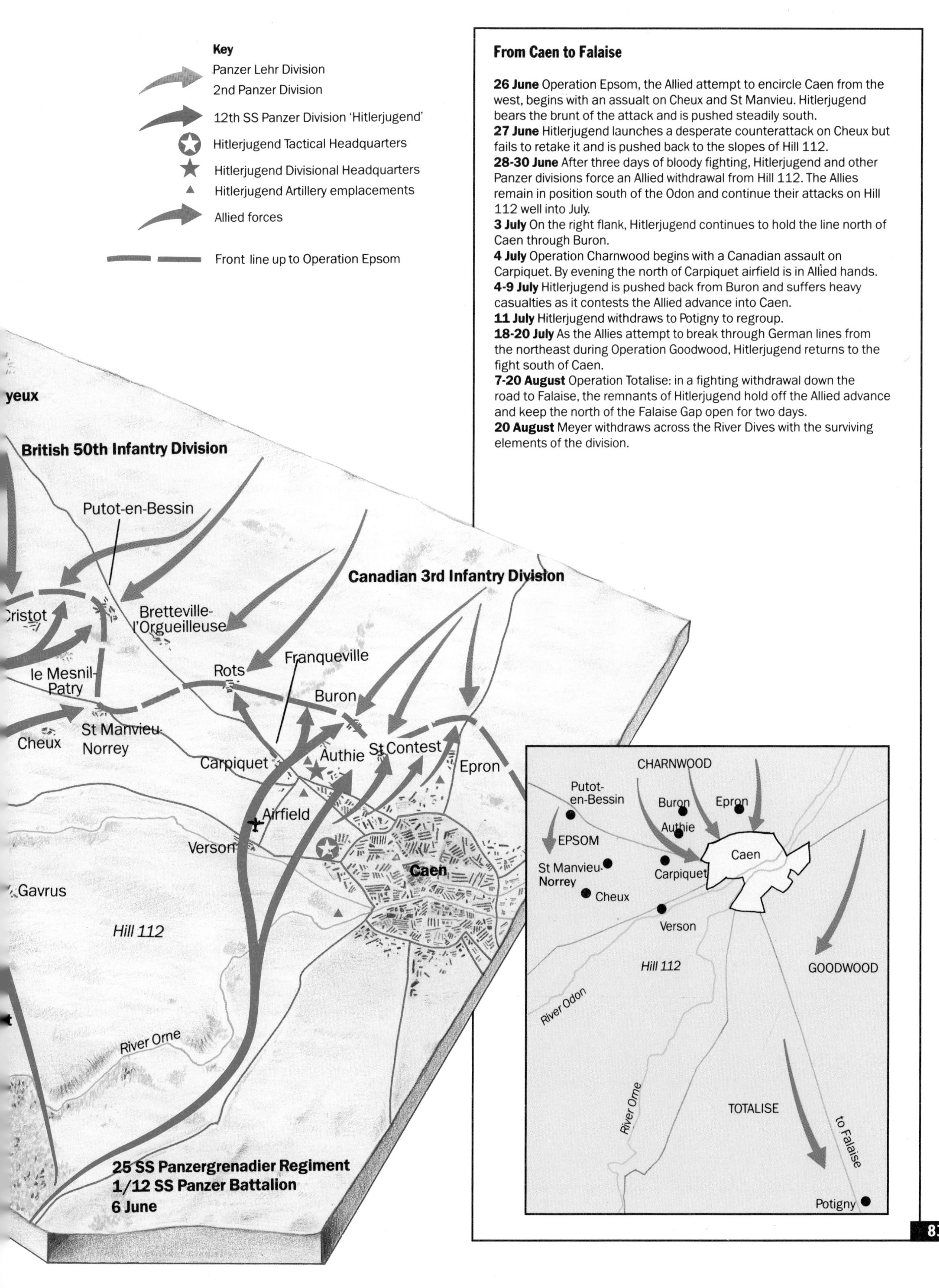

From Caen to Falaise

26 June Operation Epsom, the Allied attempt to encircle Caen from the west, begins with an assualt on Cheux and St Manvieu. Hitlerjugend bears the brunt of the attack and is pushed steadily south.
27 June Hitlerjugend launches a desperate counterattack on Cheux but fails to retake it and is pushed back to the slopes of Hill 112.
28-30 June After three days of bloody fighting, Hitlerjugend and other Panzer divisions force an Allied withdrawal from Hill 112. The Allies remain in position south of the Odon and continue their attacks on Hill 112 well into July.
3 July On the right flank, Hitlerjugend continues to hold the line north of Caen through Buron.
4 July Operation Charnwood begins with a Canadian assault on Carpiquet. By evening the north of Carpiquet airfield is in Allied hands.
4-9 July Hitlerjugend is pushed back from Buron and suffers heavy casualties as it contests the Allied advance into Caen.
11 July Hitlerjugend withdraws to Potigny to regroup.
18-20 July As the Allies attempt to break through German lines from the northeast during Operation Goodwood, Hitlerjugend returns to the fight south of Caen.
7-20 August Operation Totalise: in a fighting withdrawal down the road to Falaise, the remnants of Hitlerjugend hold off the Allied advance and keep the north of the Falaise Gap open for two days.
20 August Meyer withdraws across the River Dives with the surviving elements of the division.

SS Panzer Abteilung 101, Villers-Bocage, 13 June 1944

On 12 June 1944, the British 7th Armoured Division was ordered to head towards Villers-Bocage in an effort to trap the defenders of Tilly, the Panzer Lehr Division, or at least outflank them and force them to withdraw. In addition, once Villers-Bocage had been taken, an advance could be made along the Seulles river valley, to break out from the invasion beaches.

The commander of the 7th, Major-General 'Bobby' Erskine, ordered his assault formation, the 22nd Armoured Brigade under Brigadier Robert Hinde, to spearhead the move. The countryside, known as bocage, was appalling tank country: sunken-track roads, hedgerows, fields and copses. The British Cromwell tanks, Bren gun carriers and trucks moved forward cautiously, and at 0800 hours on 13 June stormed Villers-Bocage. It appeared the outflanking of Tilly was working. However, the situation was about to change.

Heading towards Villers-Bocage was SS Panzer Abteilung 101, sent to plug the gap. Led by SS Obersturmbannführer von Westerhagen, the three companies were immediately deployed to cover the Aure valley. SS Haupsturmführer Michael Wittmann, commander of No 2 Company, decided to conduct a reconnaissance of Villers-Bocage on 13 June. He saw a column of British tanks and Bren gun carriers leaving the village. Then it stopped for a 'brew-up'.

Leaving three Tigers and the single Mk IV to watch the column, Wittmann took his own Tiger, cut behind the British column and entered the village from the northeast. Driving into the village square, he was confronted by four Cromwell tanks. Needing no prompting, his crew began firing, and soon three of the tanks lay burning. The fourth backed through a garden and was missed by the Tiger. The remaining Cromwell then followed the Tiger, the latter unaware of the presence of the British tank. However, as Wittmann approached the western edge of the village, he ran into four British Sherman Fireflies armed with 17-pounder guns. Wittmann ordered a quick about-face which brought him head-to-head with the pursuing Cromwell. The latter was blown out of the way and Wittmann returned to his tanks.

Despite the battle, the column was still in place. Wasting no time, Wittmann's men opened fire. An ammunition truck was hit and exploded, blocking the road, and soon the area was ablaze with knocked-out vehicles. The column had ceased to exist. Wittmann rearmed and refuelled and decided to enter the village with two Tigers and the Mk IV.

Captain Pat Dyas, one of the survivors of Wittmann's original attack, had alerted HQ of the situation, and the latter had despatched three Cromwells and a Firefly. They were joined by a single 6-pounder anti-tank gun and an ambush was set. Wittmann's tank was hit by the 6-pounder as it entered the village. He and his crew baled out as the second Tiger dealt with the anti-tank gun, but both the Tiger and the Mk IV were soon knocked out too. Though the British still held the village, they had lost a total of 20 Cromwells, four Fireflies, three light tanks, three scout cars and a half-track.

The British withdrew, and the next morning (14 June) elements of the 2nd Panzer Division rushed into the area and captured the village. Over the next few days it was hit by 250 Allied bombers and ceased to exist. Wittmann's action on 13 June justifiably earns him the title of tank ace. He had single-handedly torn out the heart of an experienced unit and blunted the Allied drive on Caen.

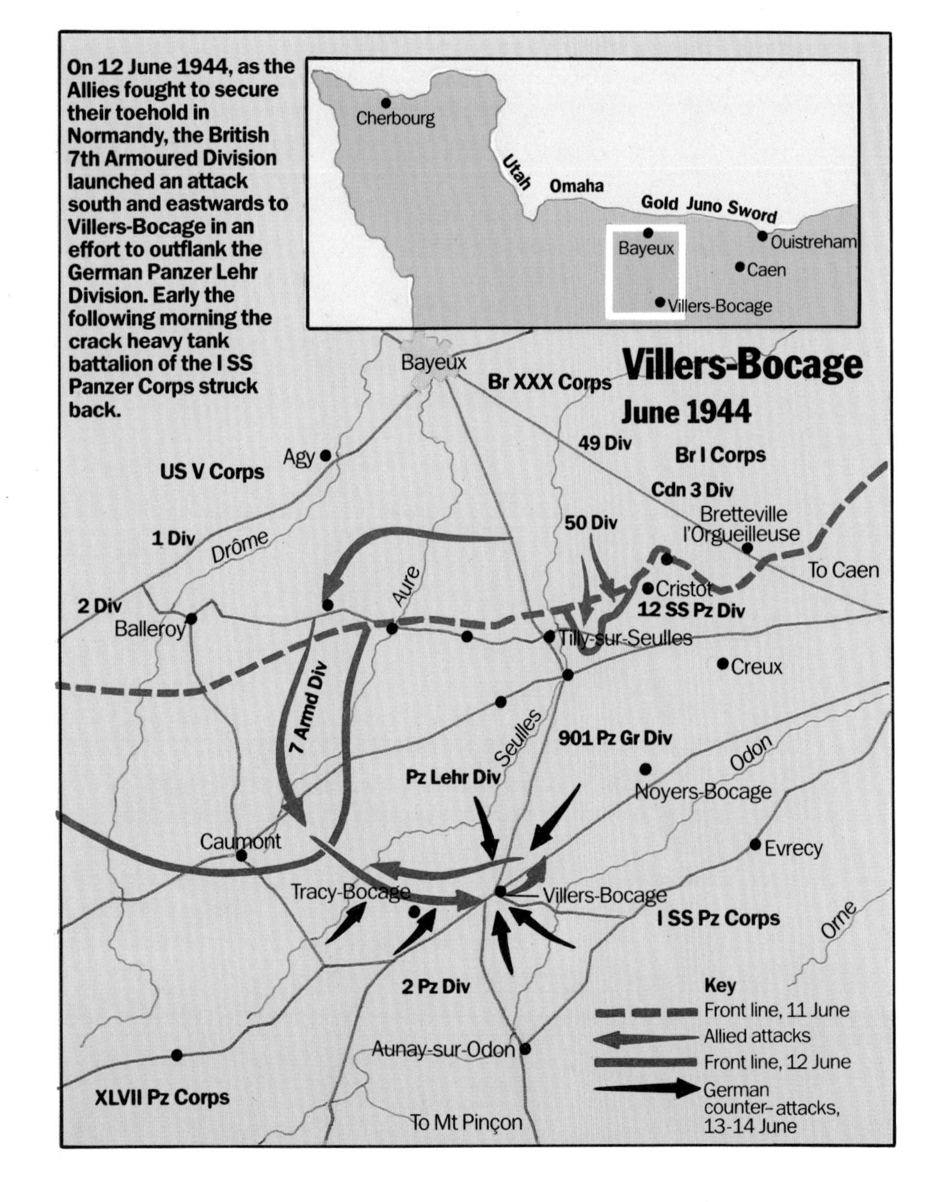

On 12 June 1944, as the Allies fought to secure their toehold in Normandy, the British 7th Armoured Division launched an attack south and eastwards to Villers-Bocage in an effort to outflank the German Panzer Lehr Division. Early the following morning the crack heavy tank battalion of the I SS Panzer Corps struck back.

GUARDS ARMOURED DIVISION, FRANCE AND BELGIUM, JULY-SEPTEMBER 1944

Operation 'Goodwood' was a British attempt to wear down German armoured forces in Normandy and capture Caen in the weeks following the D-Day landings. Scheduled to begin on 18 July 1944, the preliminary bombardment involved 1000 Lancaster bombers, naval gunfire and the artillery of VIII Corps. The latter, led by General Sir Richard O'Connor, comprised the 7th, 11th Armoured and Guards Armoured Divisions.

The 2nd Grenadiers are stopped

At first all went well. When the preliminary bombardment had finished, the armour advanced and started to round up demoralised and shaken German soldiers. However, by mid-morning the leading guards battalion – 2nd (Armoured) Grenadiers – were near Cagny and ran into heavy anti-tank fire. Swinging east towards Emieville with the intention of taking Cagny from the rear, the Sherman tanks were met by panzers of the 503 Heavy Tank Battalion. Very soon, 12 British tanks were ablaze and the rest had beat a hasty retreat. However, one tank commander, Lieutenant J R Gorman of the Irish Guards, discovered a vantage point overlooking the German positions. He fired a shot at the target – four tanks which included two Tigers – only to see the shell bounce off a panzer's hull. Then his own tank's gun jammed and so he ordered a charge.

The Sherman raced forward and smashed into the side of a Tiger, both crews then baling out as the area was hit by an Allied artillery bombardment. Undeterred, Gorman then commandeered a Sherman Firefly which had a powerful 17-pounder gun. Returning to the scene, he destroyed two other enemy tanks, the fourth retiring quickly. Gorman won a Military Cross for his efforts.

'Goodwood', in spite of isolated incidents such as Gorman's, was a disaster, and in its aftermath the Guards Armoured brigades remained in the bocage to clear enemy pockets. By August, however, with Allied armies pushing east, the British guards were around Flers, awaiting the order to cross the Seine. The crossing was carried out on 29 August, the tanks then entering flat, open country serviced by good roads. By 31 August the 5th Guards Armoured Brigade was streaming towards Amiens. Ahead of it, the 2nd Household Cavalry raced forward to seize three bridges over the Somme, codenamed 'Faith', 'Hope' and 'Charity'. The first bridge was reached under the cover of darkness, the Germans unaware of the British approach. The other two were captured shortly after, the demolition charges planted on them being defused by engineers.

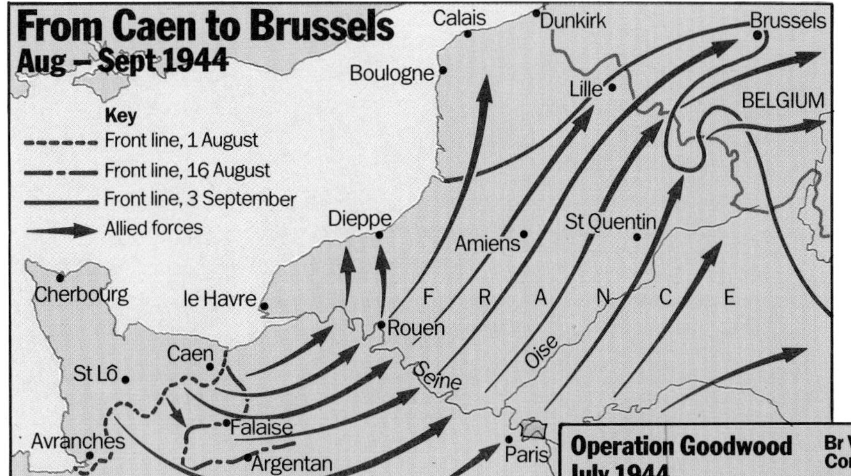

The Germans now launched a number of vigorous counter-attacks. The Cavalry, supported by the French Resistance, beat off the attacks until the guards' Shermans arrived. The tanks began to pour across the river, and, on the left flank, the 11th Armoured Division raced towards Bethune. By early September the decision had been taken for the Guards Armoured Division to strike for Brussels. The advance began at 1700 hours on 3 September, the armoured cars of the Household Cavalry leading the way. By noon, brushing aside light resistance, the guards were over halfway there. During the afternoon the Welsh Guards of the 32nd Brigade became embroiled in a hard-fought action which caused a delay. They then sought permission to race on ahead, their Cromwell tanks being faster than the grenadiers' Shermans. However, the first in the race to liberate Brussels were the armoured cars of the Household Cavalry – the first British unit to reach the city. For the Guards Armoured Division, it had been an excellent end to the campaign which had started poorly in the bocage of Normandy.

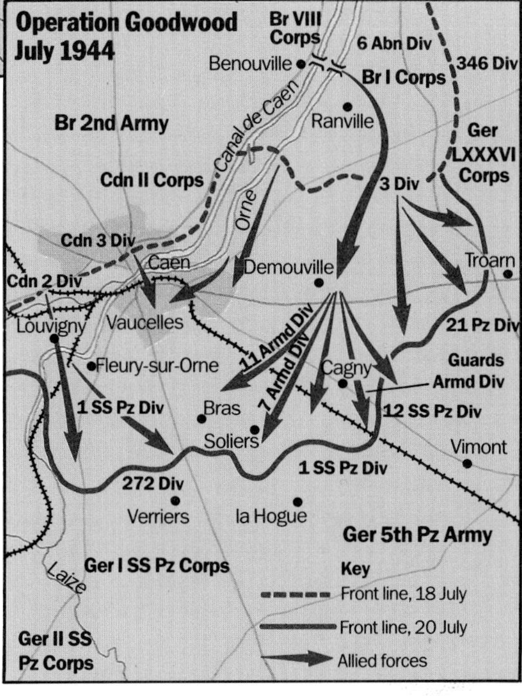

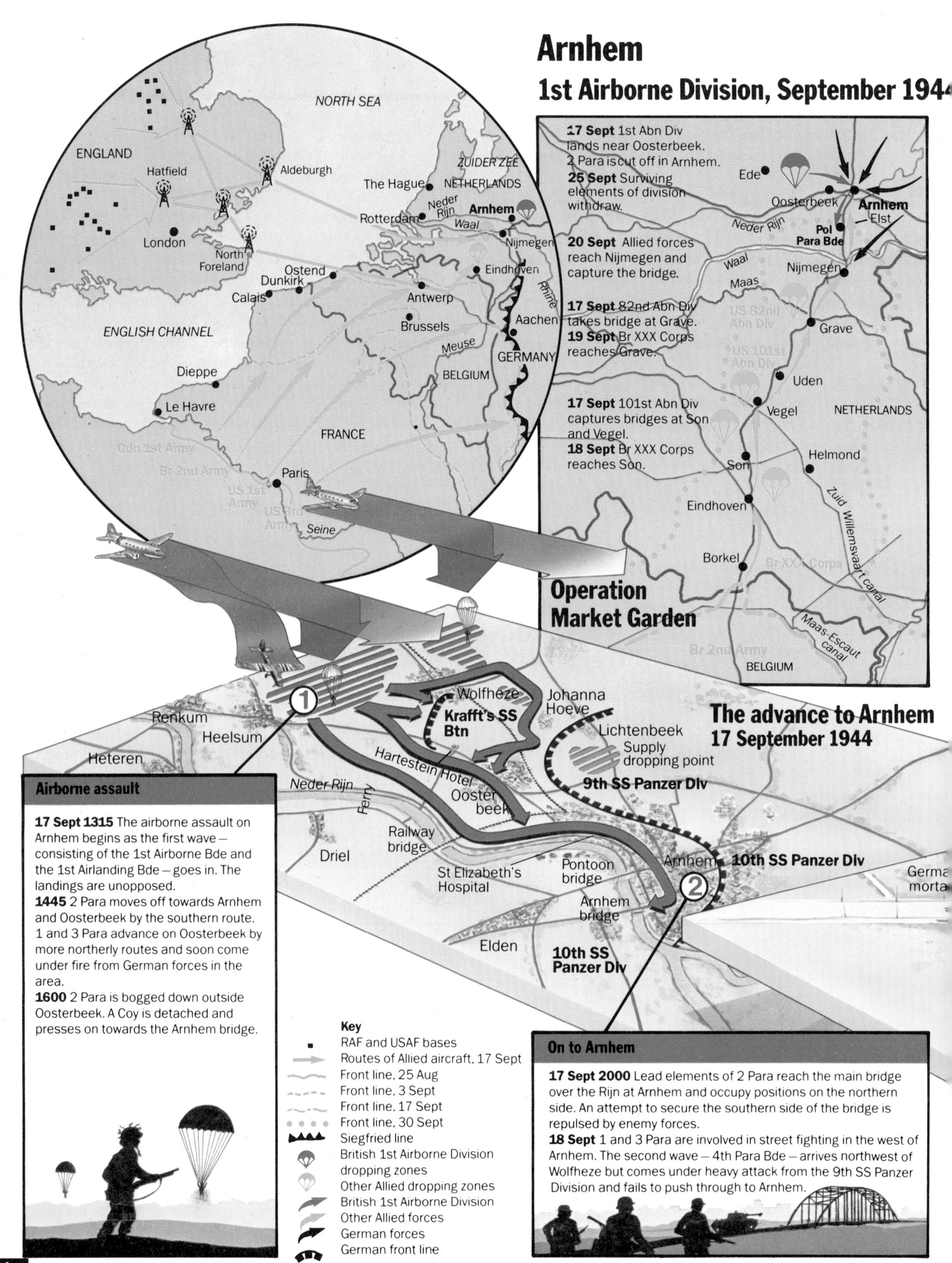
Arnhem
1st Airborne Division, September 1944
NORTH SEA
ENGLAND
Hatfield
Aldeburgh
London
North Foreland
ZUIDER ZEE
The Hague
NETHERLANDS
Neder Rijn
Arnhem
Rotterdam
Waal
Nijmegen
Ostend
Dunkirk
Calais
Eindhoven
Rhine
Antwerp
Brussels
Aachen
ENGLISH CHANNEL
Meuse
GERMANY
BELGIUM
Dieppe
Le Havre
FRANCE
Cdn 1st Army
Br 2nd Army
US 1st Army
US 3rd Army
Paris
Seine
17 Sept 1st Abn Div lands near Oosterbeek. 2 Para is cut off in Arnhem.
25 Sept Surviving elements of division withdraw.
20 Sept Allied forces reach Nijmegen and capture the bridge.
17 Sept 82nd Abn Div takes bridge at Grave.
19 Sept Br XXX Corps reaches Grave.
17 Sept 101st Abn Div captures bridges at Son and Vegel.
18 Sept Br XXX Corps reaches Son.
Ede
Oosterbeek
Arnhem
Elst
Pol Para Bde
Neder Rijn
Waal
Maas
Nijmegen
US 82nd Abn Div
Grave
US 101st Abn Div
Uden
Vegel
NETHERLANDS
Helmond
Son
Eindhoven
Zuid Willemsvaart canal
Borkel
Br XXX Corps
Maas-Escaut canal
Br 2nd Army
BELGIUM
Operation Market Garden
The advance to Arnhem
17 September 1944
Renkum
Heelsum
Heteren
Wolfheze
Krafft's SS Btn
Johanna Hoeve
Lichtenbeek
Supply dropping point
9th SS Panzer Div
Hartestein Hotel
Neder Rijn
Ferry
Oosterbeek
Railway bridge
Driel
St Elizabeth's Hospital
Pontoon bridge
Arnhem
10th SS Panzer Div
German mortars
Arnhem bridge
Elden
10th SS Panzer Div
Airborne assault
17 Sept 1315 The airborne assault on Arnhem begins as the first wave – consisting of the 1st Airborne Bde and the 1st Airlanding Bde – goes in. The landings are unopposed.
1445 2 Para moves off towards Arnhem and Oosterbeek by the southern route. 1 and 3 Para advance on Oosterbeek by more northerly routes and soon come under fire from German forces in the area.
1600 2 Para is bogged down outside Oosterbeek. A Coy is detached and presses on towards the Arnhem bridge.
Key
RAF and USAF bases
Routes of Allied aircraft, 17 Sept
Front line, 25 Aug
Front line, 3 Sept
Front line, 17 Sept
Front line, 30 Sept
Siegfried line
British 1st Airborne Division dropping zones
Other Allied dropping zones
British 1st Airborne Division
Other Allied forces
German forces
German front line
On to Arnhem
17 Sept 2000 Lead elements of 2 Para reach the main bridge over the Rijn at Arnhem and occupy positions on the northern side. An attempt to secure the southern side of the bridge is repulsed by enemy forces.
18 Sept 1 and 3 Para are involved in street fighting in the west of Arnhem. The second wave – 4th Para Bde – arrives northwest of Wolfheze but comes under heavy attack from the 9th SS Panzer Division and fails to push through to Arnhem.

1ST AIRBORNE DIVISION, ARNHEM, SEPTEMBER 1944

The British 1st Airborne Division was dropped into Holland on 17 September 1944 as part of Operation 'Market Garden', General Montgomery's plan to seize bridges at Arnhem, Eindhoven and Nijmegen. Then, the ground forces led by XXX Corps would strike for Arnhem to place the Allies within reach of Germany.

First Airborne was commanded by Major-General Robert 'Roy' Urquhart, and he faced two immediate problems: a lack of transport aircraft and heavy anti-aircraft defences around Arnhem. He decided to commit his division in three separate 'lifts' spread over three days on land to the west of the town. The first lift consisted of the 1st, 2nd and 3rd Parachute Battalions of the 1st Airborne Brigade and three battalions of the 1st Airlanding Brigade. The second lift comprised the rest of 1st Airlanding Brigade and the whole of 4th Airborne Brigade. Finally, the third lift would comprise the 1st Polish Parachute Brigade which would land south of the river to act as a link between the Arnhem defenders and XXX Corps.

Unfortunately, the area was not full of demoralised enemy units, as intelligence had reported. Far from it. Arnhem itself was defended by elements of II SS Panzer Corps. Nevertheless, by 1400 hours on 17 September, all seemed to be going well for the British. 2 Para, under Lieutenant-Colonel John Frost, headed for Arnhem, but was too late to prevent the destruction of the railway bridge. The Paras pushed on, reaching the road bridge at 2000 hours but only managing to secure the northern end.

Frost should have been reinforced by 3 Para, but the battalion never arrived, being pinned down around the Hartenstein Hotel. 1 Para encountered the same fate, being held up by elements of 9th Panzer around Wolfheze. Early on 18 September, 2 Para managed to push into the western suburbs of Arnhem but encountered fierce opposition.

At the road bridge 2 Para had fought off a series of SS attacks, though the continual fighting resulted in the Paras' ammunition running dangerously low. By 19 September the British position was perilous, and so Urquhart ordered 4th Airborne Brigade to disengage and reinforce 2 Para. However, the withdrawal became a rout, with men becoming isolated. Urquhart, on hearing Allied forces were only 16km away, drew his units into a tight defensive ring. However, his men were suffering severely: the 10th Parachute Battalion had ceased to exist, and other units had taken heavy losses.

2 Para at the bridge was in a desperate state. Frost's men had been fighting continuously for over 48 hours and they were short of food and ammunition. It was only a matter of time before the defence crumbled. The tanks of the Guards Armoured Division were halted on 21 September just south of Elst, and at 0900 hours 2 Para surrendered.

At 1715 hours, two battalions of Poles arrived but could not get supplies across the river. On 25 September Montgomery had no alternative but to order a withdrawal. By 27 September, when the operation was finally called off, only 2163 of the original 10,000 soldiers under Urquhart's command had reached the safety of Polish lines.

Holding the bridgehead

18 Sept 2 Para is cut off in Arnhem as the 9th and 10th SS Panzer Divisions launch fierce attacks on the bridgehead, and the expected reinforcements fail to break through.
19 Sept The remainder of the 1st Airborne Division concentrate around Oosterbeek, leaving 2 Para isolated and unable to break out. Enemy forces attack the paras from the north and from across the river.
21 Sept 0900 After holding on without reinforcements or resupply against overwhelming odds, the remnants of 2 Para finally surrender.

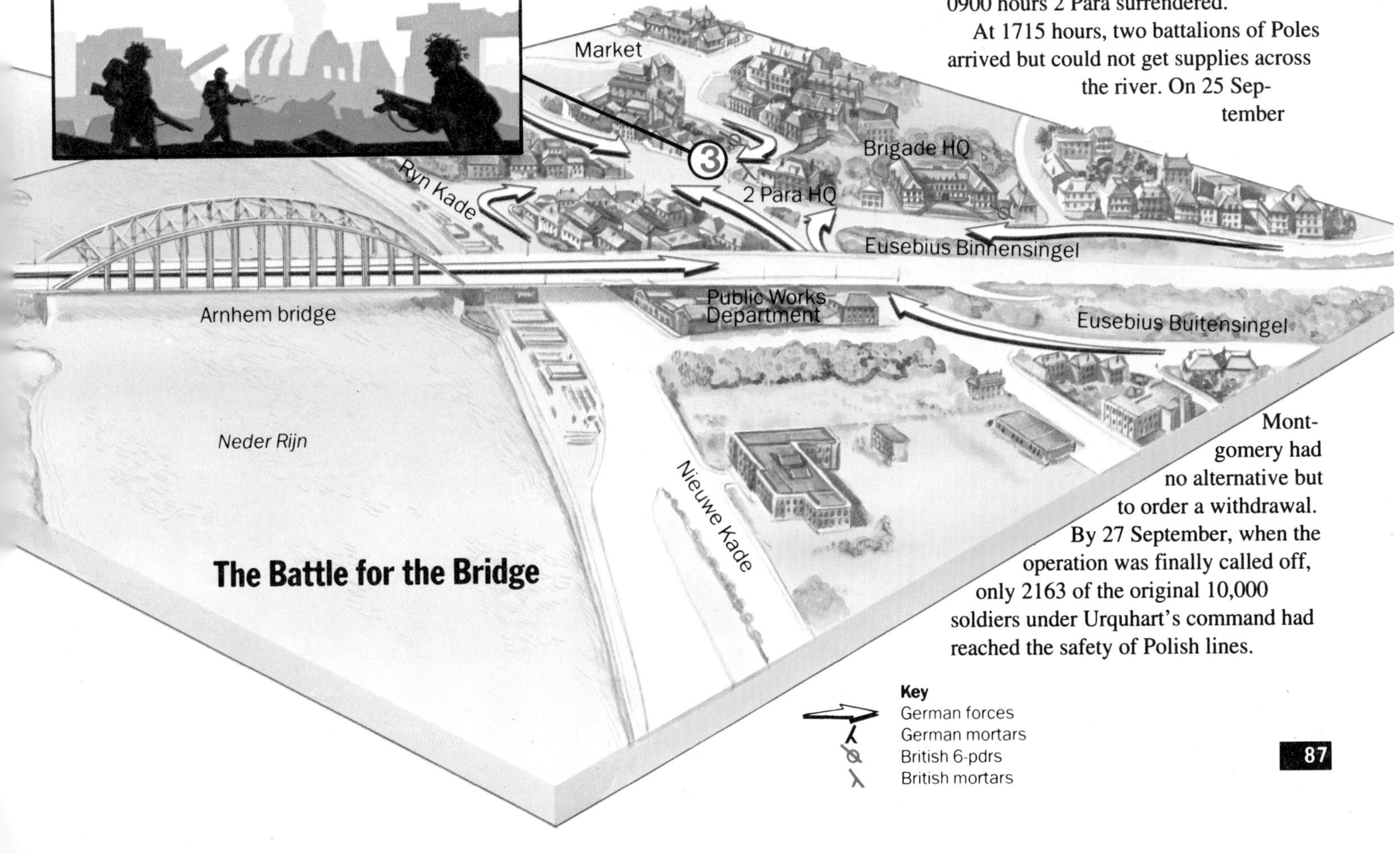

The Battle for the Bridge

2ND ARMOURED DIVISION, ALSACE-LORRAINE, OCTOBER-DECEMBER 1944

In mid-November 1944, the French 2nd Armoured Division was poised to take Strasbourg. The division, led by General Philippe Leclerc, was advancing through the Vosges mountains, seemingly unstoppable. However, the Germans had built a fortified line, the *Vogesenstellung*, to halt its progress. The line consisted of concrete fortifications and concentrations of anti-tank weapons that would make any armoured attack very costly indeed.

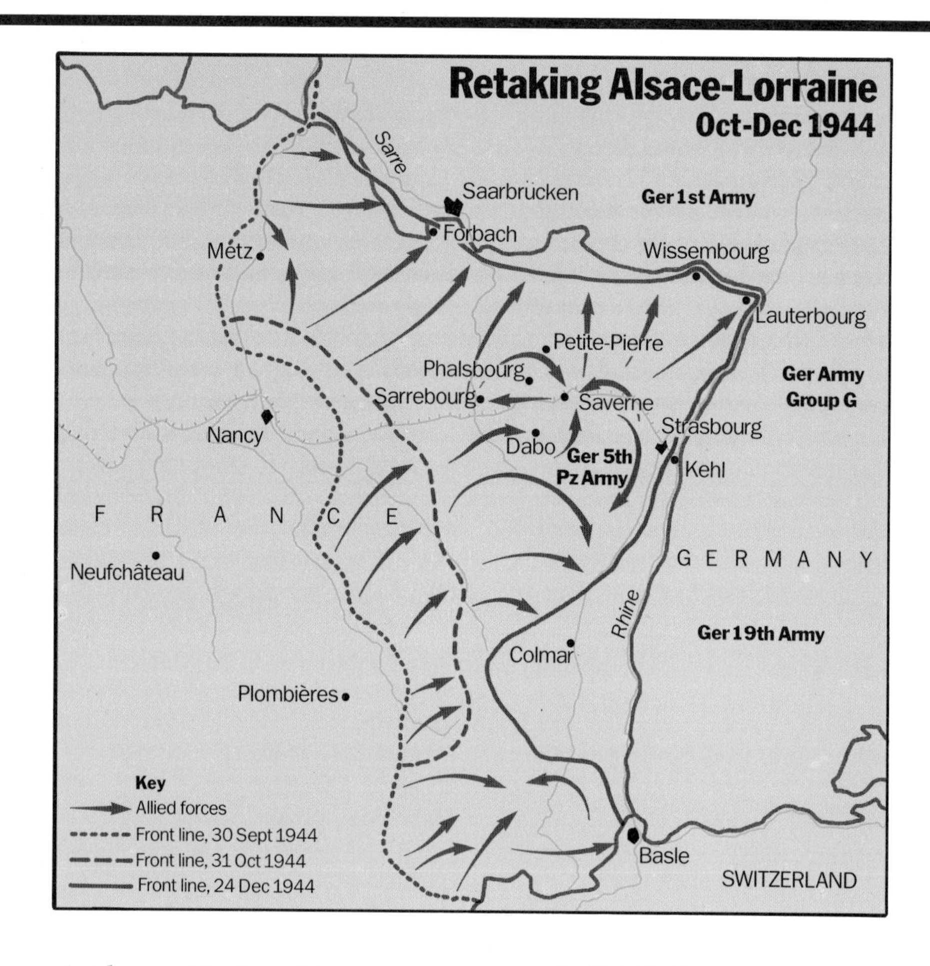

The division is split into units

Leclerc desperately wanted to be in Strasbourg before any other Allied commander. On 13 November, XV Corps began to advance into the Vosges as part of a general Allied push towards the Rhine, and by the 19th Leclerc had advanced far enough forward for him to activate his plan to outflank the Saverne Gap. The plan would rely on the division acting as a number of independent units: four self-sufficient groups named after their commanders – Langdale, Dio, Guillebon and Rémy. Each had its own infantry, tanks, armoured cars and artillery. All commanders had been encouraged to develop initiative and to exploit any opportunities.

The race to Strasbourg

Leclerc's plan was to outflank the German defences at the Saverne Gap in both the north and south. In the north, the Dio group would engage the enemy at Phalsbourg, in the south the Langdale group would take the main mountain route. The Langdale group commenced the attack on 20 November, slipping round the German position at Saint-Michel and then catching up with the retreating German column on a mountain road, the enemy's guns being bulldozed off the road and a host of prisoners being taken. By nightfall, the Shermans had reached Dado, and Leclerc ordered the Guillebon group to move up to the town during the night. Progress was frustratingly slow during the rain-swept night, but by morning the group was ready to support the Langdale group, which was already advancing further forward.

Meanwhile, to the north, the Dio group succeeded in outflanking the German defences at Phalsbourg and by the 22nd both groups were through the mountains and on the broad Alsatian plain. Saverne was taken, along with the German regional commander, General Bruhn. Leclerc moved his HQ to the town to get closer to the frontline and escape from higher command. General Dwight D Eisenhower, the Supreme Commander, had forbidden him to advance any further, fearing an enemy counterattack. Leclerc, however, was determined not to stop.

At 0715 hours on 23 November, the French Shermans started their engines and headed for Strasbourg, 40km away. Leclerc's instructions to his commanders were to avoid any strongpoints and enter the city with all possible speed, pressing on to the Kehl bridge over the Rhine. The armour, acting again in small units, raced ahead and had soon reached the city. The German defenders were taken completely by surprise as the tanks drove down the streets, firing their guns at any targets that presented themselves. However, the German commander in Strasbourg, General von Vaterrodt, managed to escape to Fort Ney and organise a defence, which consisted in the main of a somewhat desultory artillery bombardment. Despite this, by 24 November the French had secured the city and Fort Ney had surrendered.

The men of the 3rd US Infantry Division arrived as reinforcements the next day and the city was secured. For General Leclerc and his 2nd Armoured Division it had been the climax of a magnificent feat of arms. The Free French had taken the city of Strasbourg, the capital of Alsace, which had been seized by the Germans in 1871 and 1940.

KAMPFGRUPPE PEIPER, THE ARDENNES, DECEMBER 1944

The Kampfgruppe (Task Force) Peiper was the spearhead of the 1st SS Panzer Division Leibstandarte Adolf Hitler and was led by Lieutenant-Colonel Joachim Peiper. During the Ardennes offensive of December 1944, its task was to be a spearhead to allow other panzer divisions to break out towards Antwerp.

The Kampfgruppe left its staging area around Blankenheim at 0200 hours on 16 December. At first progress was good, but the force then began to encounter a number of problems. A bridge over the railway line to the east of Losheim was wrecked, and by the time the Kampfgruppe was over it was 10 hours behind schedule. Worse, Peiper was forced to make a fuel-consuming detour to the village of Lanzerath to avoid pockets of American resistance.

The next day saw some progress. The offensive had caused considerable confusion among the Americans, and the Kampfgruppe entered Honsfeld by simply joining a column of retreating US vehicles. Now, however, Peiper was faced with another problem: lack of fuel. Though a petrol supply was secured and the tanks refuelled, it was midday before he could resume the advance. The frustration at not being able to maintain momentum was starting to manifest itself: his men, unknown to him, began to shoot prisoners out of hand.

Peiper led his refuelled tanks towards the town of Ligneuville, encountering and defeating an American column near the town. Some 120 prisoners were taken and then herded into a nearby field and shot. Peiper himself, unaware of what had happened, entered Ligneuville at 1430 hours. Losing no time, he pushed on to Stavelot, which was defended by 13 US servicemen! However, these men halted the German column and allowed the Americans to send forward reinforcements.

Stavelot was taken and Peiper pushed on, but by now the Americans had sent elements of two divisions to surround La Gleize and interdict the supply line at Stavelot. Peiper drew his force – 2000 men and 200 vehicles – into a pocket which included Stavelot. Just as well, because on 19 December the Americans attacked the town. Peiper's panzergrenadiers fought bravely, but by the 24th the Kampfgruppe, given permission to break out, had been largely destroyed.

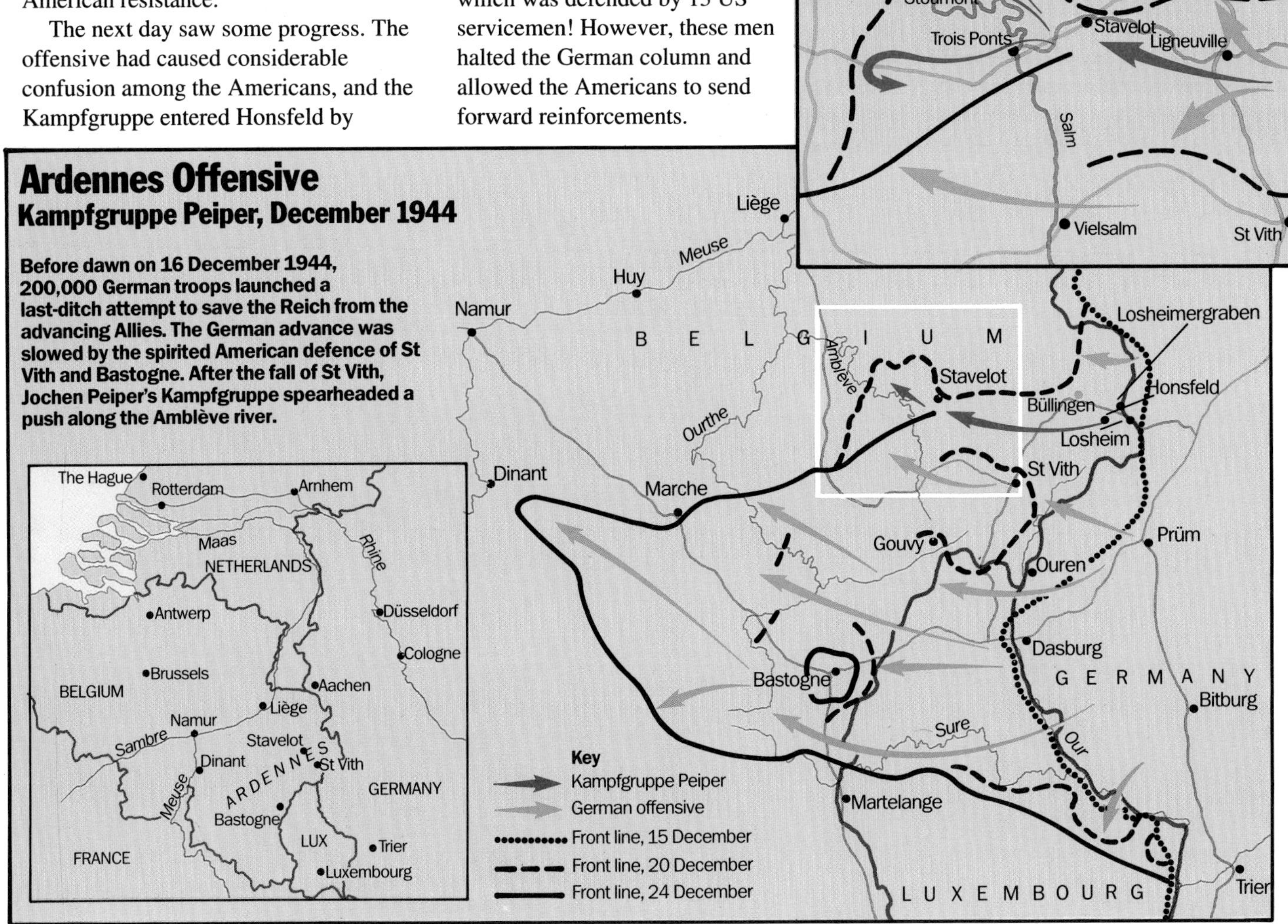

101ST AIRBORNE DIVISION, BASTOGNE, DECEMBER 1944

The Battle of the Bulge
101st Airborne Brigade, Bastogne, December 1944

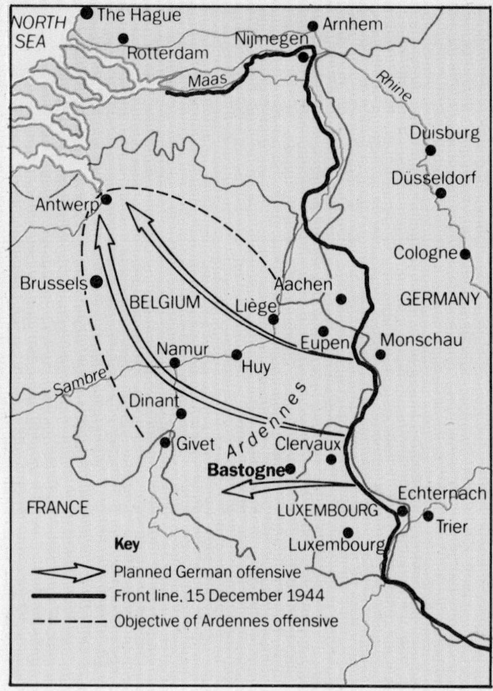

In December 1944, 24 German divisions were thrown into a final offensive against the advancing Allied armies on the Western Front. Hitler's plan called for a breakthrough in the Ardennes, splitting the Allied armies in two, and pushing on to Antwerp. The offensive took the Allies by surprise and from 16 – 20 December the German divisions pushed forward to Stavelot, St Vith, Houffalize and Bastogne. General Eisenhower committed the 101st Airborne Division to the defence of Bastogne, which was situated on a vital crossroads controlling movements north-south and east-west. By 20 December Bastogne was surrounded but the 101st held out, imposing delays on the exploitation of the 'bulge' that were to prove fatal to the German offensive.

By 22 December 1944, the US 101st Airborne Division was under siege in the town of Bastogne, being surrounded by elements of four German divisions: 2nd Panzer, Panzer Lehr, 26th Volksgrenadier and 5th Fallschirmjäger. Hitler's offensive in the Ardennes had taken the Allies by surprise, and had rapidly overrun their thin defensive screen. Bastogne was one of two essential crossroads in the Ardennes, St Vith being the other.

Having surrounded the town, the Germans began to subject it to a heavy artillery bombardment. The Americans hung on, and defeated a number of German assaults, including a major one on Christmas Day. This was the turning point in the battle for the town, as at 1650 hours the leading elements of General Patton's 4th Armored Division crossed the lines of the 101st's defensive perimeter. The garrison, now known as the 'battered bastards of Bastogne bastion', had defended their charge against overwhelming odds.

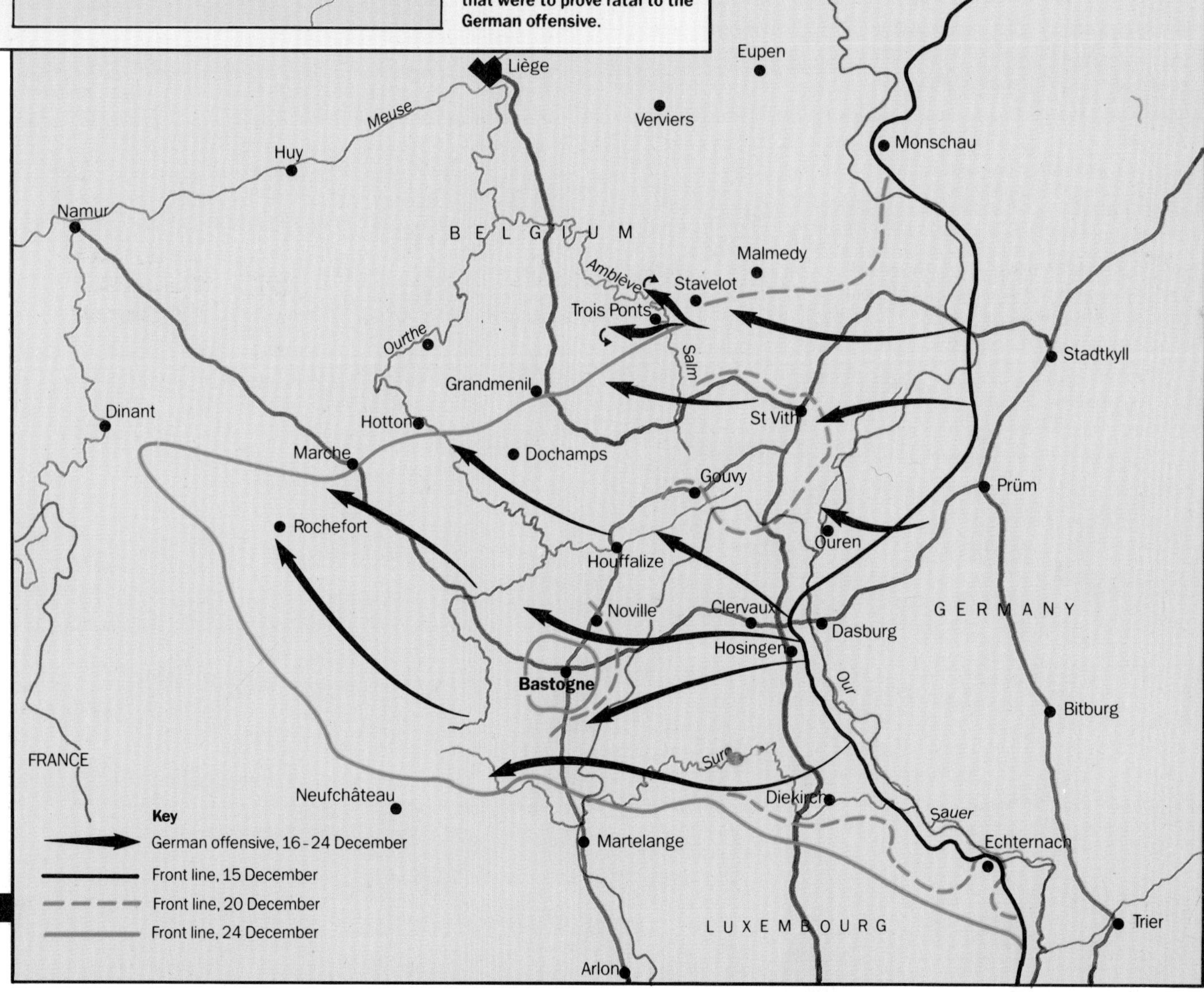

6TH RANGER BATTALION, CABANATUAN, 29-30 JANUARY 1945

When elements of the US Sixth Army landed in the Philippines in January 1945, rumours began to filter through of American prisoners held captive by the Japanese. Fearing the prisoners would be executed by the enemy, it was decided to mount a raid to free them. The men chosen for this mission were the 6th Ranger Battalion and the Alamo Scouts, a specialist long-range reconnaissance unit. Because of the need for secrecy and stealth, only 121 Rangers were selected, plus some Philippine guerrilla units and the Alamo Scouts.

The Rangers left their camp during the afternoon of 27 January and made their way to the guerrilla headquarters of Captain Joson at Lobong. The reinforced company then moved into enemy territory, fording the Talavera river. Travelling throughout the night, by dawn the Rangers had moved to within 8km of the prison camp.

At 0600 hours the Alamo Scouts reported in. Though they had not been able to get near the camp, they had seen many Japanese troops entrenched in positions across the Cabu river and at Cabanatuan City. The Rangers' plan was very simple: hit the camp hard and kill as many Japanese as possible. The Rangers moved towards the camp at 1600 hours on 29 January, but then fell back quickly when the Scouts reported there was a Japanese division moving along the Cabu river. The attack was delayed for 24 hours which gave the Scouts a chance to carry out a recce of the area.

As the Rangers moved out, a six-man bazooka team was tasked with setting up a road block 300m from the camp to stop any enemy tanks that approached once the attack got under way. At 1700 hours on 30 January, the Rangers, Scouts and a party of guerrillas moved into position. Gunfire killed most of the Japanese soldiers guarding the perimeter, and soon the Rangers were pouring into the camp and herding the prisoners out.

They found that many prisoners were so weak that they needed to be carried on carts. By 2046 hours all Rangers and prisoners were across the river and moving towards American lines. The column reached safety a little after 1100 hours on 31 January. For the loss of two Rangers, 516 prisoners had been rescued in a daring raid behind enemy lines.

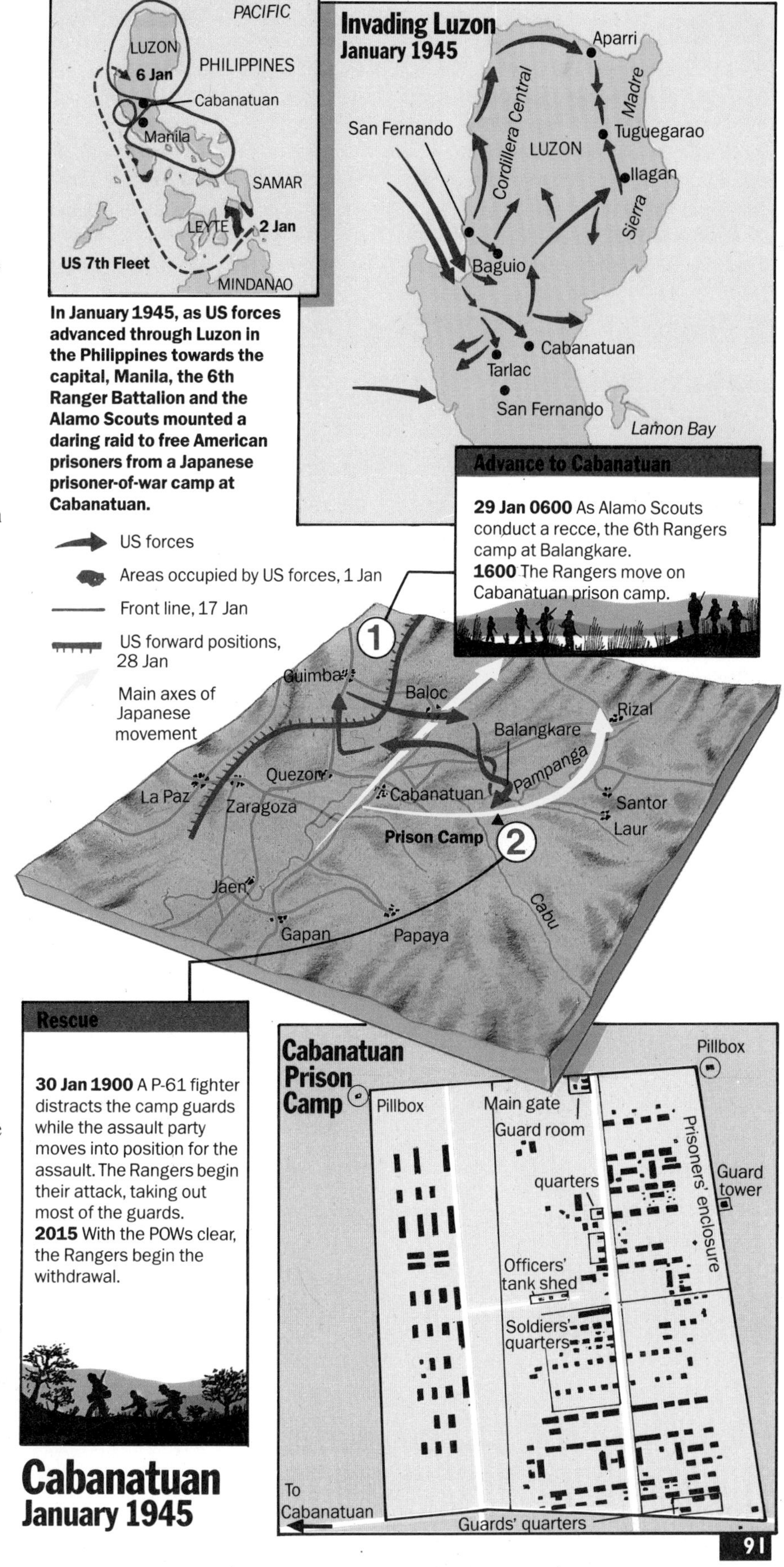

In January 1945, as US forces advanced through Luzon in the Philippines towards the capital, Manila, the 6th Ranger Battalion and the Alamo Scouts mounted a daring raid to free American prisoners from a Japanese prisoner-of-war camp at Cabanatuan.

503RD PARACHUTE INFANTRY REGIMENT, CORREGIDOR, 16-17 FEBRUARY 1945

On 16 February 1945, the 3rd Battalion, 503rd Parachute Infantry Regiment, supported by the men of the 161st Airborne Engineer Battalion and the 462nd Parachute Field Artillery Battalion, landed on the Pacific island fortress of Corregidor, Luzon.

One of the first groups to land did so near the command post of Captain Akira Itagaki, the commander, and killed him with a hand grenade, thus depriving the Japanese of a leader. Around 25 per cent of the paras were killed or injured during the landings and early actions. Despite this, they soon cleared the whole of Topside, and then the amphibious assault began at Black Beach on Bottomside

More paras jumped at 1240 hours, and by the afternoon there were 3000 American paratroopers on the island. The largest enemy attack came at 1600 hours on 18 February, when 600 Japanese attacked Topside. In hand-to-hand fighting, the attack was beaten off, the enemy losing 500 killed. Then the paras began a mopping-up operation, and by 24 February the island was secured. The Americans had lost 225 killed and 645 wounded in this daring operation.

Corregidor

February 1945

By late 1944, the first US foothold in the Philippines – Leyte – was secure except for isolated Japanese forces in the mountains of northwest Leyte. Preparations for the Luzon campaign began with landings on Mindoro in mid-December to secure airbases.

On 9 January 1945, four divisions of the US Sixth Army went ashore at Lingayen Gulf in northwest Luzon. A second landing by the US XI Corps was followed by a drive southwards through the Bataan Peninsula. By 4 February, the Sixth Army had reached Manila.

Guarding the entrance to Manila Bay, Corregidor remained in Japanese hands – and on 16 February a force of US paras made a daring drop on the island.

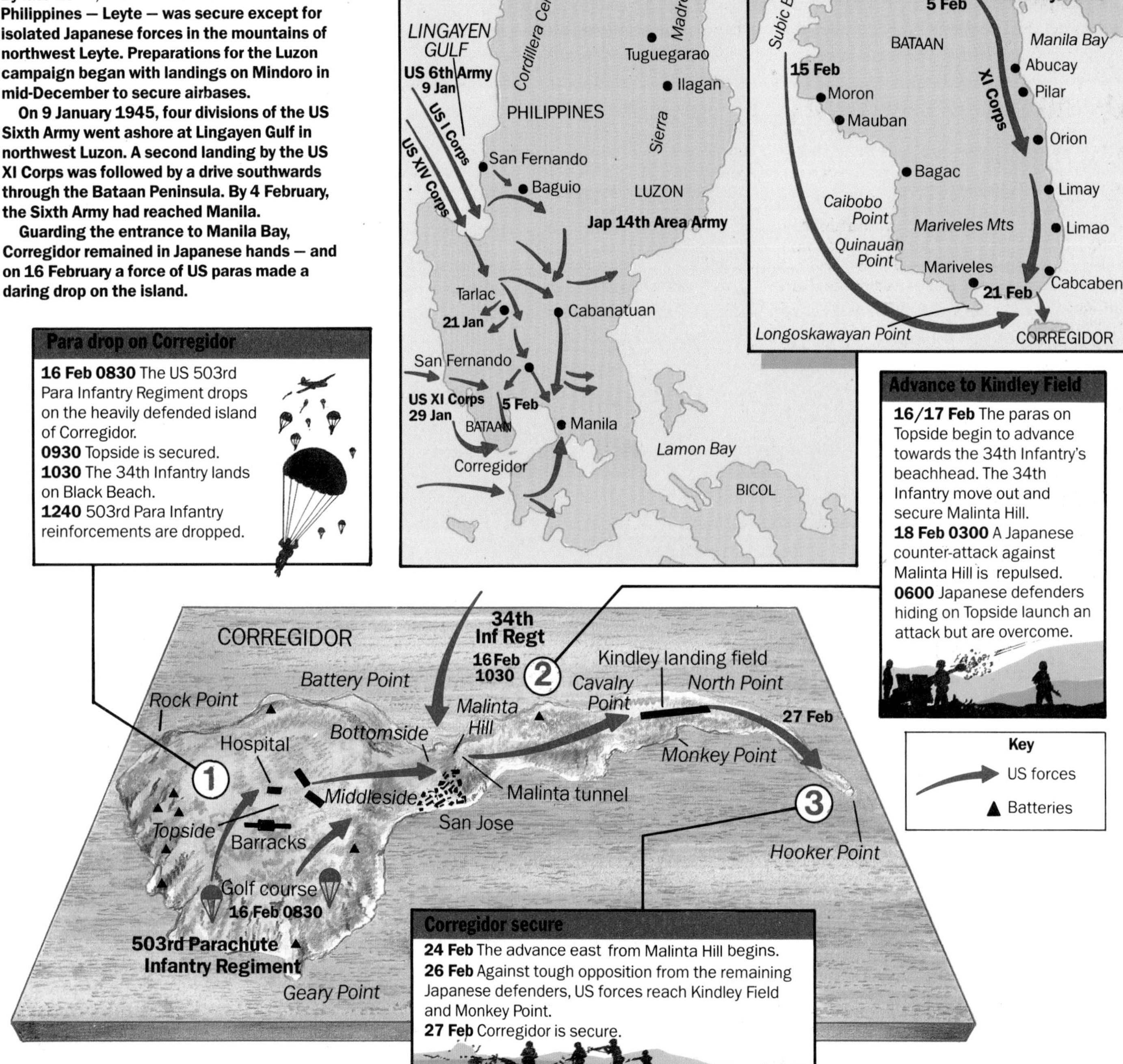

10TH MOUNTAIN DIVISION, NORTH ITALY, 17-23 FEBRUARY 1945

By December 1944, the harsh weather conditions in the Apennine mountains of North Italy had brought a halt to the advance of the Allied Fifth and Eighth Armies. For the coming spring offensive, Major-General Lucien Truscott, commander of the US Fifth Army, chose Highway 64 as his main axis of advance. But he needed to secure the high ground overlooking the highway first. For this operation, code-named 'Encore', he chose the US 10th Mountain Division.

By 28 January the division had been assembled in the Reno Valley, facing the German positions atop the Monte Belvedere-Monte della Torraccia Ridge. The US HQ believed that it was impossible to take the Riva Ridge, which in places rose 400m above the valley. However, the division's commander, Major-General George Hays, reckoned the Germans also thought this and wanted a crack at it. Truscott agreed.

In early February, reconnaissance patrols probed forward to search for routes up the steep face of the Riva Ridge. The 1st Battalion and one company from the 2nd Battalion, 86th Mountain Infantry Regiment, were selected to spearhead the attack on 18 February, and so were given intensive refresher courses in mountaineering. On the night of 17 February, the 1st and 2nd Battalions of the 85th prepared for the assault on the ridge.

The advance began, the men crossing the valley and scaling the rock face. By dawn most of the assault force had reached the summit – then the American troops raced forward and started clearing the bunkers. Soon it was all over. The 86th had secured the Riva Ridge.

With his left flank secure, Hays could now concentrate on the capture of Monte Belvedere. The attack began at 2300 hours on 19 February, and by 0600 hours the 85th Infantry Regiment had taken Monte Belvedere. The 10th Mountain Division had, in the face of a determined enemy, taken the 12km-long Monte Belvedere-Monte della Torraccia Ridge, believed to be impregnable, for the loss of 850 casualties, including 195 dead.

10th Mountain Division

Operation Encore, 17-23 February 1945

By the bitterly cold winter of 1944, the advance of the Allied Fifth and Eighth Armies into northern Italy had bogged down on the slopes of the Apennine mountains. As the troops settled into their billets to sit out the worst of the weather, senior US and British commanders began to plan the next stage of the campaign: the seizure of Bologna and the clearing of the Po valley. Before an all-out offensive could be launched, however, it was decided to unleash the US 10th Mountain Division against a series of heavily defended ridges and mountains that dominated the main road between Rome and Bologna, Highway 64.

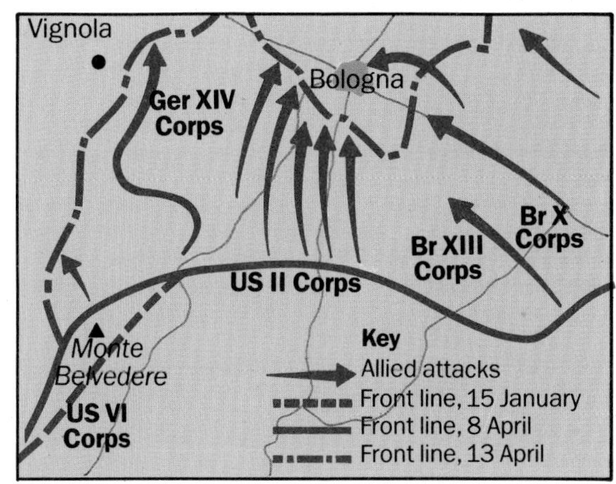

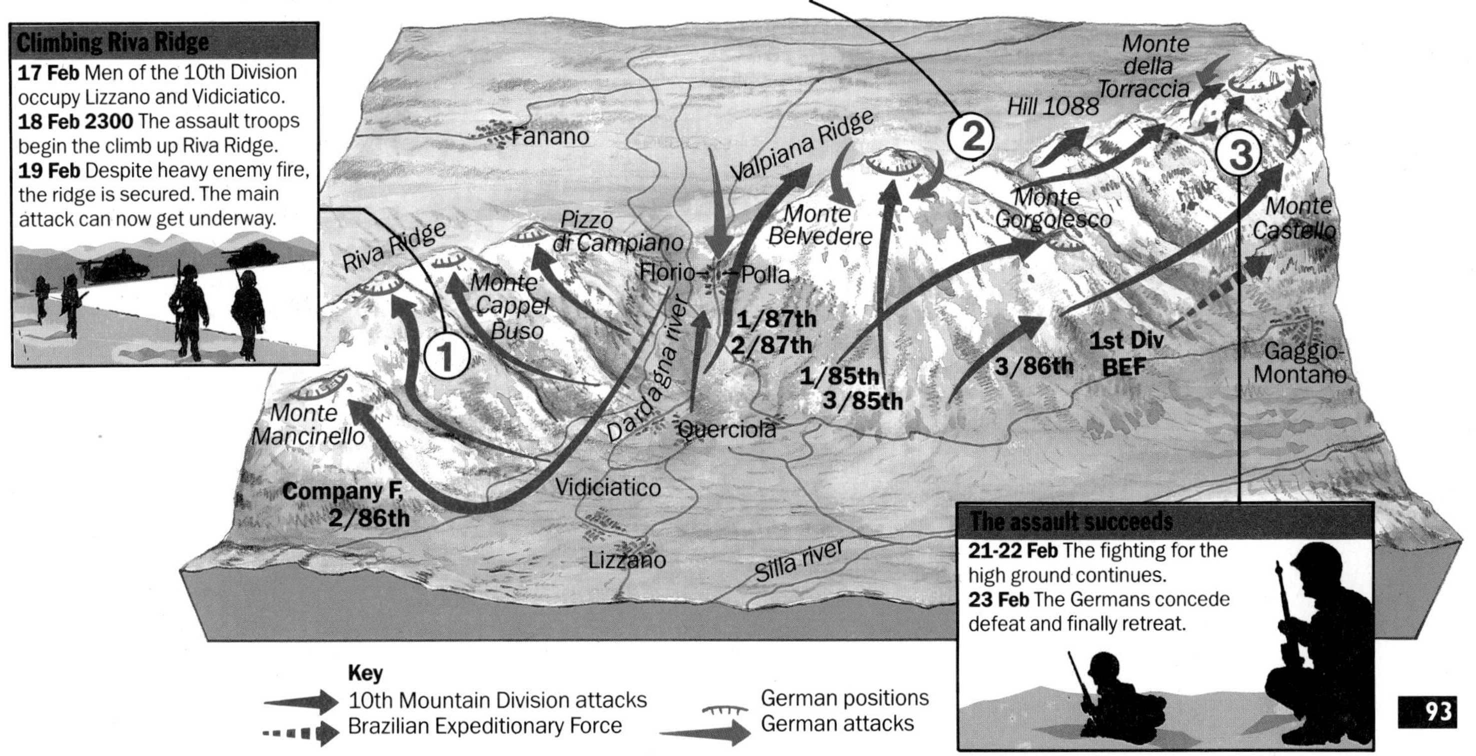

28TH MARINE REGIMENT, IWO JIMA, 19 FEBRUARY-9 MARCH 1945

On 19 February 1945, the US 28th Marine Regiment hit the beaches of the Pacific island of Iwo Jima, its objective being Mount Suribachi. All was initially quiet. Then, the battle erupted as 20,000 Japanese started firing on the Marines as they struggled through the loose black sand, just as the Japanese commander, General Tadamichi Kuribayashi, had planned.

Through a hail of machine-gun, mortar and rifle fire, the 28th advanced, taking fearful casualties. By the end of D-Day there were 30,000 Marines ashore, but Suribachi was still in enemy hands. As long as the Japanese held it, they could observe US forces. Enemy defences were so dense that one company of the 28th inadvertently set up its HQ on a bunker still full of Japanese soldiers!

Though 22 February was a thoroughly miserable day, with little artillery support and no air support, the 28th had managed to surround Suribachi. The mountain was taken the next day, and then the regiment was sent to the north to attack the enemy's main defensive line along the Motoyama Plateau.

Fighting for every metre of ground, the 28th advanced with grim determination. By 9 March, the Marines were in sight of the sea on the northern coast and the remnants of the defenders had been holed up along a ridge overlooking Kitano gorge. Nevertheless, it took a further week of hard fighting to clear this position. Iwo Jima had cost 5931 Marines killed and a further 17,372 wounded. Of the 3900 men of the 28th who had landed on the island, only 600 were fit for duty at the end. Of the garrison, only 250 men were taken alive.

Iwo Jima
3rd, 4th and 5th Marine Divisions, Feb-Mar 1945

As the American central Pacific offensive entered its final phase, three US Marine divisions launched their assault on the island of Iwo Jima. The battle for the island raged for nearly a month before the invading forces could declare it secure – and by then, nearly 6000 marines had lost their lives.

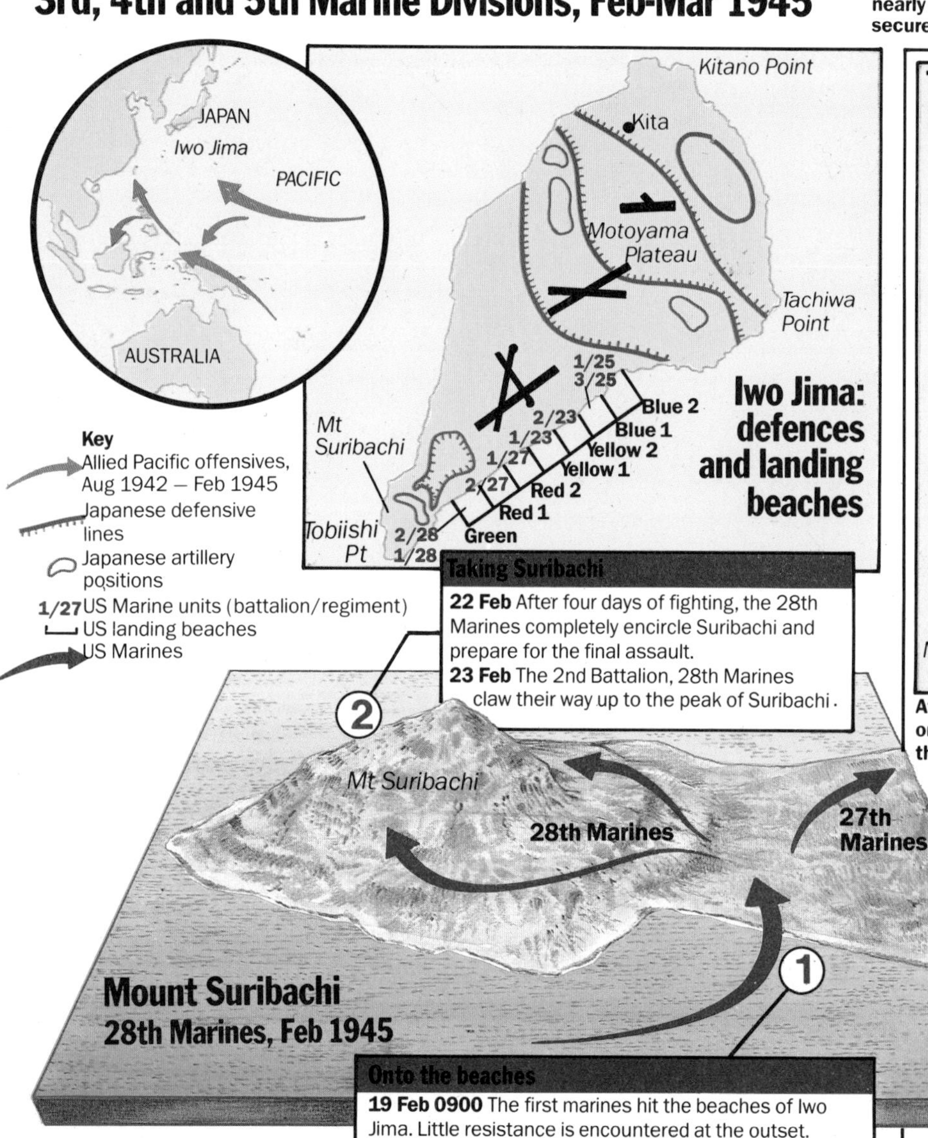

Taking Suribachi

22 Feb After four days of fighting, the 28th Marines completely encircle Suribachi and prepare for the final assault.
23 Feb The 2nd Battalion, 28th Marines claw their way up to the peak of Suribachi.

Onto the beaches

19 Feb 0900 The first marines hit the beaches of Iwo Jima. Little resistance is encountered at the outset. Struggling through the sand, the 28th Marines cross the neck of Iwo Jima and wheel left towards Mount Suribachi.
1030 As the men of the 27th Marines push northwards, and B Coy, 28th Marines, reaches the west shore of Iwo Jima, the bulk of the 28th Marines begins the hard fight for Suribachi. By the end of the day, Japanese resistance has stiffened considerably.

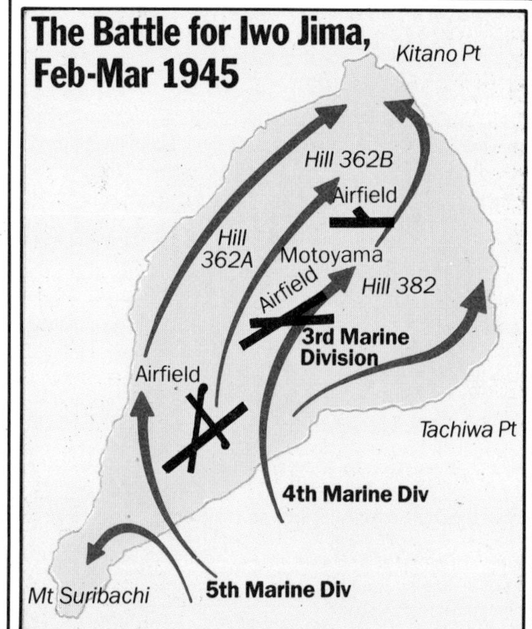

After a massive preliminary bombardment, the assault on Iwo Jima went in at 0900 on 19 February 1945, with the 4th Marine Division on the right flank and the 5th Marine Division on the left. As the leading elements reached positions some 200 yards inland, the marines came under a withering crossfire from the defending Japanese forces – and from that moment onwards the fight for Iwo Jima became a grim and bloody contest.

While the 5th Division struggled to secure the southwest end of the island – with the 28th Marines assaulting Mount Suribachi – the 4th Division pushed north and east. On 24 February, with Suribachi secure, the two divisions, now reinforced in the centre by the reserve 3rd Marine Division, advanced slowly through Iwo Jima's central plateau. After five days of bitter fighting the assault on the complex of tunnels and bunkers on Hills 382 and 362A began. Hill 382 fell on 1 March and Hill 362A was taken the following day after a night attack. The pocket at Kitano Point was cleared by 16 March.

27TH ARMORED INFANTRY BATTALION, REMAGEN, 7 MARCH 1945

Task Force Engeman was part of the US 9th Armored Division and was commanded by Lieutenant-Colonel Leonard Engeman. It consisted of the whole of 27th Armored Infantry Battalion and two companies of 14th Tank Battalion. In March 1945 it was operating west of the Rhine, around Remagen, and on 7 March its lead elements arrived at the still intact bridge.

Reaching the bridge, the Americans saw German troops sheltering in a tunnel on the far bank, where the railway entered a large basalt cliff known as the Erpeler Ley. Brigadier Hoge arrived at Engeman's command post and urged the seizure of the bridge. However, the Germans detonated some charges on the bridge at 1517 hours. When the smoke cleared it was still intact and American infantry raced forward. The Germans then detonated their main charges soon after, but again the bridge remained standing. This was the signal for the Americans to cross the bridge in the face of intensive fire. Moving forward, by 1605 hours there were 75 US troops on the east side of the river. The Germans surrendered at 1630 hours. The bridge had been taken, and the Rhine could be crossed. However, it had been greatly weakened, and it finally collapsed at 1500 hours on 17 March.

Remagen

7 March 1945

During February 1945, as German resistance began to crumble, the Allied armies on the Western Front advanced from the German border to the Third Reich's last line of defence: the River Rhine. By 7 March the 21 Army Group under General Montgomery had established a line along the river from Rheinburg to Düsseldorf, and it was poised to drive into Germany's industrial heartland – the Ruhr. Further south, the US 1st and 3rd Armies under Hodges and Patton advanced on Bonn, Remagen and Koblenz. Soon after midday on 7 March, as lead elements of the US 9th Armoured Division neared Remagen they sighted an intact bridge over the Rhine. Some four hours later the first bridgehead across the Rhine was in Allied hands.

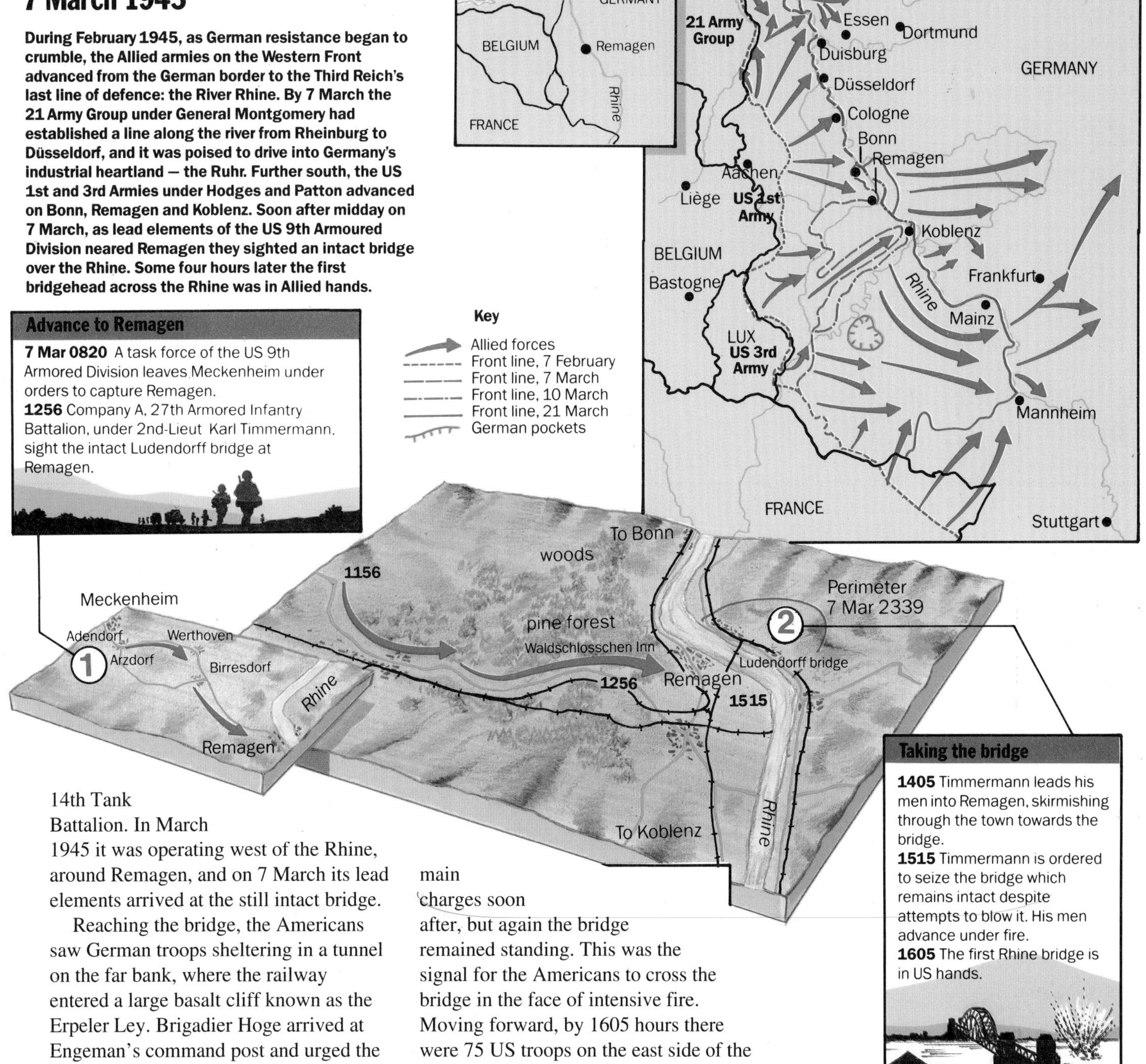

1st Canadian Parachute Battalion, The Rhine, 24 March 1945

Operation 'Varsity' involved 22,000 Allied paratroopers dropping on the east bank of the River Rhine on 24 March 1945, and a component of this formidable force was the 600-strong 1st Canadian Parachute Battalion. Field Marshal Sir Bernard Montgomery planned to use the 6th Airborne Division as part of a two-phase operation to breach the lower Rhine and drive into Germany's industrial heartland. Operation 'Plunder' was the codename for an assault crossing of the Rhine between Rheinberg and Rees, using Lieutenant-General Sir Miles Dempsey's Second Army on the left, and General W H Simpson's Ninth US Army on the right. The defence of this sector of the river was entrusted to the German First Parachute Army. Of concern to Allied planners was the Diersfordter Wald, a thick forest rising 20m above the level of the river. The dense trees afforded the Germans the opportunity of hindering the crossing of the British XII Corps in the Allied centre. Therefore, Major-General Matthew Ridgeway's XVIIIth US Airborne Corps, comprising the veteran British 6th Airborne Division and the inexperienced US 17th Airborne Division, was tasked with seizing the east bank of the Rhine.

The paras land in daylight

The lessons of Arnhem had been learned, and all the Allied commanders were determined that the operation should be well planned and have adequate support. The airborne landing would take place in daylight to allow the paras to concentrate around the landing zones (LZs) quickly. After re-grouping, they would then attack their objectives, which were located well within range of supporting artillery on the west bank of the river. There was to be only one airlift, thus the airborne troops would all be landed within three hours, and the link-up with ground units would take place on the first day of the operation.

The Canadians were tasked with capturing the northwest corner of the woods, believed to be held by the crack troops of the German 7th Parachute Division. The Canadians dropped on the 24th, many of the men being scattered over a wide area (the intensity of the flak had caused the C-47 transports to cross the LZs at speed). Colonel Nicklin, the Canadian commander, was tragically killed by machine-gun fire when he landed, and command of the battalion then passed to Major Fraser Eadie. Advancing aggressively, by mid-afternoon the battalion had taken over 400 prisoners.

The paras then dug in to resist any enemy counterattacks, and throughout the afternoon the battalion was subjected to sporadic shelling from artillery and tanks. A Company repelled two counter-attacks with some ease. Of more concern was a group of German paras in some houses to the north, who raked the western half of the drop zone (DZ) and C Company's positions with mortar and machine-gun fire. But the enemy were incapable of wiping out the Canadians; indeed, it was the latter who were inflicting heavy casualties on the Germans. In one incident, the Machine Gun Platoon wiped out around 40 enemy who were approaching from the Rhine.

The Rhine is secured

Throughout the afternoon the battalion was subjected to minor shelling. Enemy resistance was crumbling, however, and by the early afternoon the 15th Scottish Division had secured its bridgehead on the eastern bank of the Rhine and had linked up with the 6th Airborne Division. The latter had lost 347 men killed in the operation and 731 wounded, while Canadian losses were 24 killed and 32 wounded. The mission had been a complete success: the enemy's artillery and rear defensive positions had been smashed. It was an object lesson in how to conduct an airborne operation.

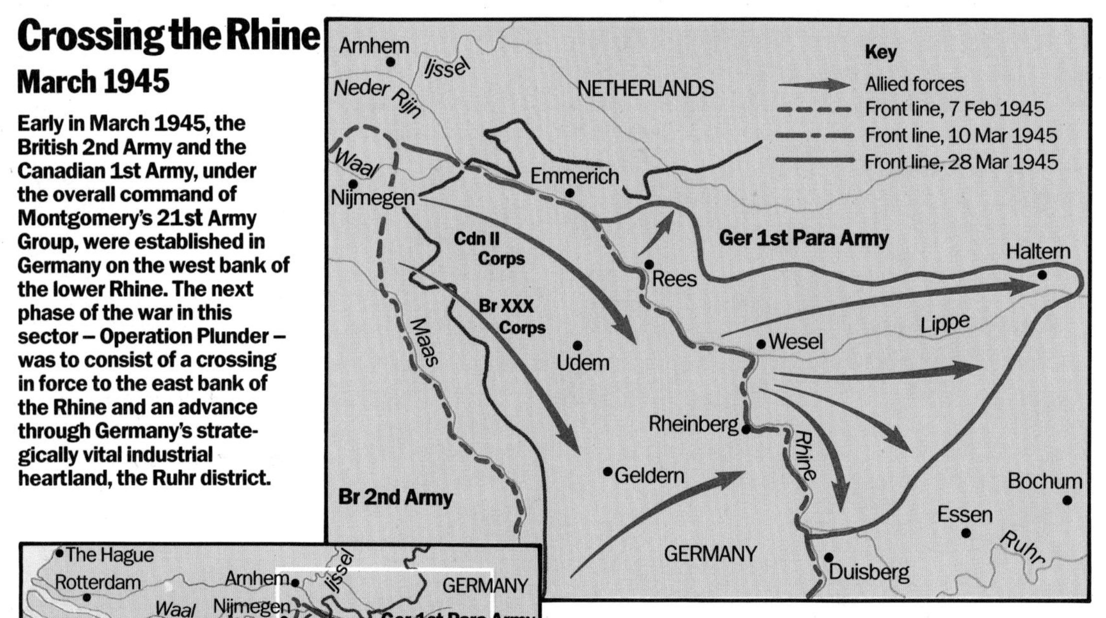

Crossing the Rhine

March 1945

Early in March 1945, the British 2nd Army and the Canadian 1st Army, under the overall command of Montgomery's 21st Army Group, were established in Germany on the west bank of the lower Rhine. The next phase of the war in this sector – Operation Plunder – was to consist of a crossing in force to the east bank of the Rhine and an advance through Germany's strategically vital industrial heartland, the Ruhr district.

ROYAL MARINE COMMANDOS, LAKE COMACCHIO, 2-3 APRIL 1945

On 2 April 1945, four Commandos of 2 Commando Brigade were poised to attack up the length of the spit that divided Lake Comacchio from the Adriatic. The preliminary bombardment began at 0430 hours, and 30 minutes later the first Royal Marines stormed forward. They advanced steadily, and by 0738 hours the enemy had been cleared from the tongue. Under cover of artillery fire, the Commandos then took the 'Acts' position.

Attention now turned to the main enemy positions along the north bank of the river. The Germans had positioned a number of machine-gun nests around Hosea, but PIAT anti-tank guns were deployed against them and they were destroyed. News then arrived that No 9 Commando was having difficulty taking 'Leviticus', so the Royal Marines were then deployed to assist them, and by mid-afternoon of 2 April all the positions on the north bank had been taken.

The next day, the Commandos pushed forward again, coming under machine-gun fire from the barns and cottages of Scaglioca and along the bank of the Valetta canal. Amazingly, Corporal Tom Hunter of 43 Commando raced forward and kicked in the door of one house, wrecked the enemy machine gun and captured its crew, dashed to a second building and repeated the operation, and then cleared a third machine-gun position. As the machine guns along the bank opened up on his comrades, Hunter then turned his Bren gun on them. He disabled two machine guns before being killed. He was awarded a posthumous VC for his actions.

That night the Marines withdrew, and were pulled out of the line the following afternoon. During the Comacchio operation, 2 Commando Brigade had advanced 12km in two days and had taken 450 prisoners for the loss of nine killed and 44 wounded.

Comacchio
April 1945

In August 1944 the British Eighth Army and the US Fifth Army crossed the Gothic Line. The British made good progress initially but German resistance stiffened and it was not until 21 September that Rimini fell. The Eighth Army pushed north along the Adriatic coast and by mid-January Ravenna was in British hands. Further advance was blocked by the marshy expanse of Lake Comacchio.

The western and northern shores of the lake were held by German troops, and the sand spit on the seaward side was manned by a Turkoman division which held a series of strong blockhouses and mined defensive positions. An operation by 2 Commando Brigade was determined upon to seize the far shores of the lake and thus secure the right flank of the planned breakthrough by the Allied armies in the Argenta Gap. On 1 April 1945 the operation was launched: while the army commandos advanced westwards, the Royal Marine Commandos were tasked to fight their way north along the sand spit. The brigade pushed forward some three miles during the next two days, and on 9 April the main offensive was launched.

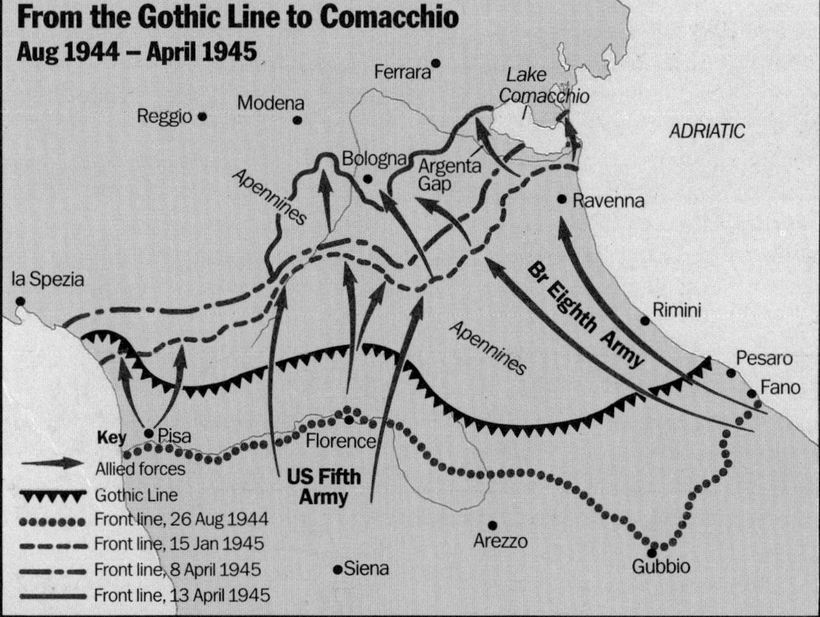

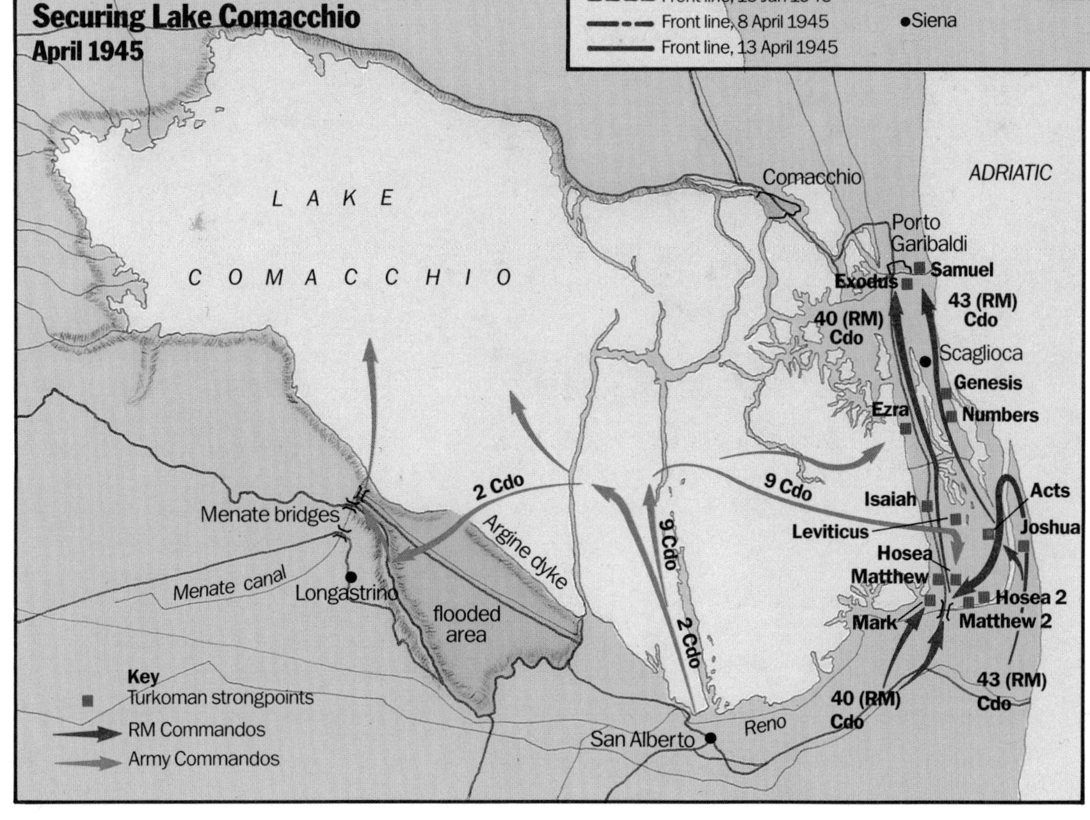

CHAPTER II

KOREA

Perhaps more than any other conflict, the Korean War has been neglected by military historians. Yet in many ways it was one of the most important wars of the twentieth century. To date it is the only battlefield on which China and the United States have met since 1945, and it was the first time an army had conducted a campaign under the banner of the United Nations (UN) to achieve a military objective, the next time being the 1991 Gulf War against Iraq. In terms of casualties the conflict is often seen as being a sideshow, with little happening and losses being relatively small. Nothing could be further from the truth. Though its butcher's bill did not approach that of World War II, casualties were horrendous enough: United Nations losses amounted to 118,515 killed, 264,591 wounded and 92,987 captured (the great majority of whom died of mistreatment or starvation); South Korea lost 70,000 killed, 150,000 wounded and 80,000 captured; and the communists suffered an estimated 1,600,000 battle casualties alone.

Invariably, UN forces were almost always outnumbered in their battles with the communists, especially after the intervention of China in November 1950. This being the case, UN forces were often hard pressed and had to call on all their reserves of fortitude and training. Despite the excellence of UN air and artillery support, communist attacks often broke through Allied lines, resulting in savage close-quarter combat. One of the most memorable examples of this took place at the Imjin river in April 1951, when the 1st Battalion, the Gloucestershire Regiment, blunted the Chinese offensive against Seoul, though at terrible cost. In another incident the same month, the 2nd Battalion, Princess Patricia's Canadian Light Infantry, assaulted by waves of Chinese Infantry, stood its ground and forced the enemy to retreat.

The Korean War was not only about relentless communist drives against outnumbered Allied formations. There were also instances of bold and imaginative use of crack units by UN commanders. The airborne operation involving the US 187th Airborne Regimental Combat Team around Suk'chon and Sun'chon in October 1950, for example, was an example of how paratroopers should be properly employed. But perhaps the boldest, and certainly most famous, operation of the whole war was the US Marine landings at Inchon in September 1950. The brainchild of General Douglas MacArthur, the landings were an unqualified success, being an example of the age-old winning combination of superior generalship and highly trained and motivated troops. The US Marine Corps proved, as it had done during World War II, that it was an elite par excellence, and one that could carry out one of the most difficult of military operations: an amphibious landing in the face of enemy fire.

One reason why UN forces were able to stave off defeat was because of the aerial and artillery support available to them. The Korean War, more so than World War II, emphasized the critical importance of air power. This was especially true during the long retreat from Hagaru made by British and US forces in November and December 1950. Time and time again, the UN troops were saved from annihilation by supporting aircraft and artillery. In the final analysis, however, it was, as always, the quality of the individual men on the ground who decided the outcome. In that, the Korean War was no different from any other conflict.

UN troops manning an anti-aircraft position during the Korean War. North Korean MiG jets were a constant threat to Allied troops.

1ST MARINE DIVISION, INCHON, 15 SEPTEMBER 1950

In early July 1950, the forces of North Korea were driving hard into the southern half of the Korean peninsula. General Douglas MacArthur, displaying inspired generalship, believed that only a daring amphibious assault against the enemy's rear could save the situation.

The Joint Chiefs of Staff agreed to MacArthur's request, and on 7 July the 1st Provisional Marine Brigade was activated. It took most of its assets from the half-strength 1st Marine Division and 1st Marine Aircraft Wing. The core of the ground element was the 5th Marine Regiment, while the air element included three squadrons of F-4U Corsair fighter-bombers. The brigade, 6534 strong, left San Diego on 12 July, but it was not until the 25th that the Joint Chiefs of Staff agreed to MacArthur's request for the complete 1st Marine Division.

By the end of July, the Allied forces in Korea had been pushed back into a defensive position in the southeast corner of the country. Reluctantly, MacArthur agreed to the 1st Provisional Marine Brigade helping the defenders of the so-called Pusan Perimeter. Not until 5 September could the provisional brigade be pulled from the line to prepare for Inchon. As the Marine division began to be pieced together, intelligence reports gave a figure of 21,500 North Korean soldiers in the Inchon area, most of whom were thought to be second-rate.

Ironically, many of the US Navy's amphibious shipping had been given away or allowed to rust after World War II, so for the Inchon landings many landing ships had to be reclaimed from the Japanese, and some came complete with Japanese crews. The plan was to take the island of Wolmi-do on the morning tide, and then land the rest of the division on the evening tide, 12 hours later. The 1st Marine Aircraft Wing would provide air support. After the beachhead was secured, the 7th Infantry Division would land and occupy the area.

The softening up of Wolmi-do began on 10 September with napalm strikes, and then Allied ships pounded the shore. At 0545 hours on 15 September the pre-landing shore bombardment began, and at 0633 hours the first Marines were landed. By noon the fight for Wolmi-do was over, the Marines not having lost one man killed. Throughout the day American naval gunfire and aircraft continued to hit every target available.

At 1645 hours, the second wave steamed towards the shore, with the navy providing covering fire once more. Landing and pushing inland, the Marines captured Cemetery Hill, Observatory Hill, Hill 233 and Hill 94. Before morning the 1st Marine Division had secured all the objectives that had been designated for the first day, losing 22 killed and 174 wounded in the process.

On 17 September MacArthur landed at Inchon, and on the same day the 5th Marines took the vitally important Kimpo airfield. Though there was some heavy fighting in the days ahead, the Marines entered Seoul and had secured it by 27 September. The 1st Marine Division had performed MacArthur's wishes to the letter.

BELOW: *US Marines storm ashore at Inchon. MacArthur's amphibious assault was probably the most daring operation of the Korean War.*

MacArthur's Masterstroke

On 25 June 1950 seven infantry divisions of the North Korean People's Army, backed by a tank brigade, launched an all-out offensive against South Korea. Caught off balance and outnumbered, the South Koreans surrendered their capital Seoul and retreated. Within five days US units were involved in the fighting but were too few to stem the North Korean tide. By the end of July, the South Korean forces and their US allies had been forced back to Pusan in the southeast of the country, where they formed a defensive perimeter. To relieve the pressure on Pusan, General Douglas MacArthur, appointed commander of the UN forces in Korea on 7 July, planned a daring amphibious assault on Inchon, deep behind North Korean lines. With their lines of communication under threat, the North Koreans would have to scale down their attacks on the Pusan perimeter. On 15 September, after weeks of hurried preparation, the first US assault wave hit the Inchon beaches.

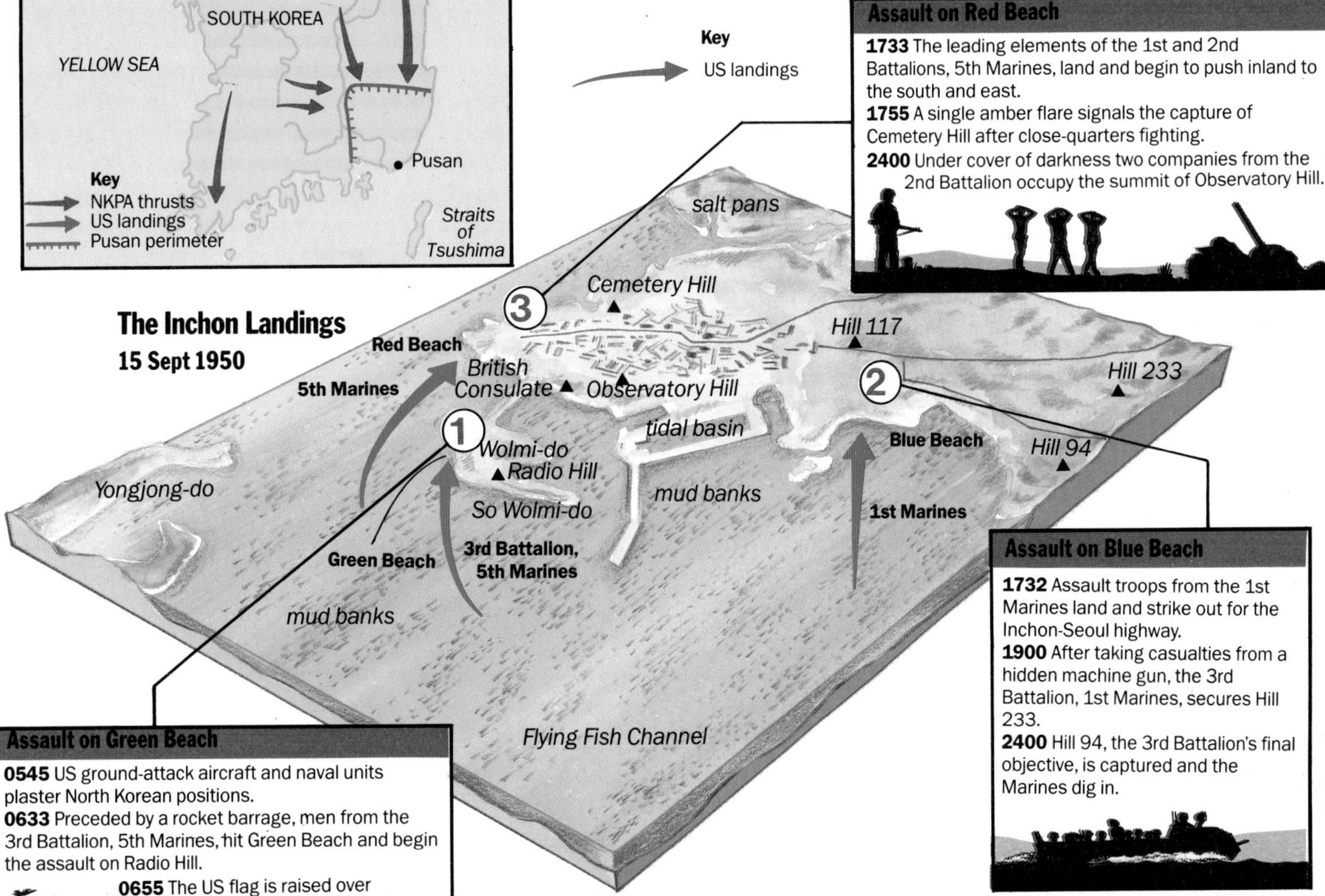

Assault on Red Beach

1733 The leading elements of the 1st and 2nd Battalions, 5th Marines, land and begin to push inland to the south and east.
1755 A single amber flare signals the capture of Cemetery Hill after close-quarters fighting.
2400 Under cover of darkness two companies from the 2nd Battalion occupy the summit of Observatory Hill.

Assault on Blue Beach

1732 Assault troops from the 1st Marines land and strike out for the Inchon-Seoul highway.
1900 After taking casualties from a hidden machine gun, the 3rd Battalion, 1st Marines, secures Hill 233.
2400 Hill 94, the 3rd Battalion's final objective, is captured and the Marines dig in.

Assault on Green Beach

0545 US ground-attack aircraft and naval units plaster North Korean positions.
0633 Preceded by a rocket barrage, men from the 3rd Battalion, 5th Marines, hit Green Beach and begin the assault on Radio Hill.
0655 The US flag is raised over Wolmi-do, but mopping-up operations continue throughout the morning.

By dawn on 16 September, 1st Marine Division had secured Inchon and established a defensive perimeter to the east of the city. To maintain the pressure on the North Koreans, the Marines, backed by regular US and Republic of Korea forces, then struck out for Seoul and Kimpo airfield. Defended by 20,000 North Koreans, the capital proved a tough nut to crack but superior US firepower was used to blast the enemy into submission. By the 20th US troops were on the outskirts of Seoul but it took another seven days of hard fighting before the objective was captured. The North Korean forces were virtually annihilated. MacArthur had won his 'impossible victory'.

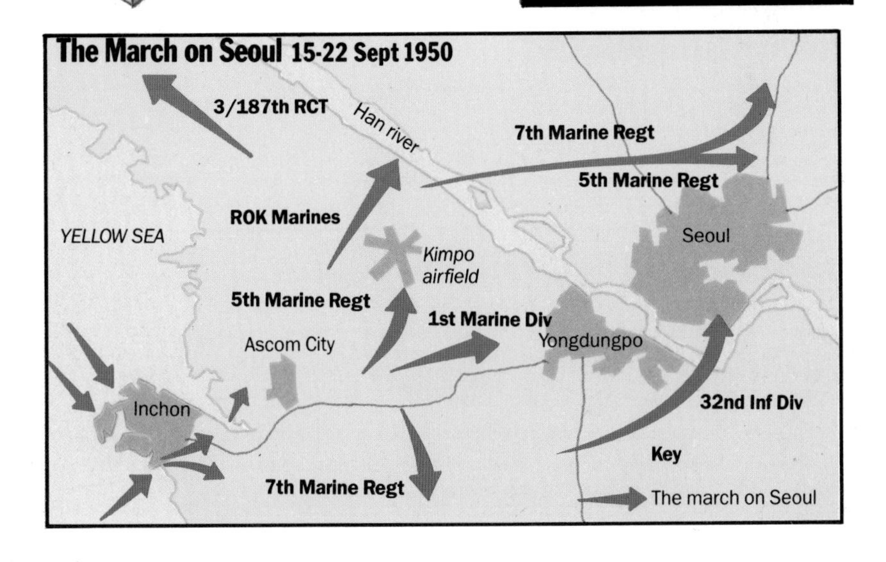

187TH AIRBORNE REGIMENTAL COMBAT TEAM, SUK'CHON, 20-22 NOVEMBER 1950

By October 1950, the North Korean People's Army (NKPA) was in full retreat following the success of the Inchon landings. The commander of the United Nations Command, General Douglas MacArthur, alerted the 187th Airborne Regimental Combat Team to be ready for an air drop north of Pyongyang. He had received intelligence that the North Koreans were moving political officials and American prisoners by rail out of the city and decided to attempt to intercept them.

He ordered the commander of the 187th, Colonel Frank Bowen, to insert his men to block the two railway lines north of the city. Specifically, the men were to be dropped around the towns of Suk'chon and Sun'chon. Bowen's 1000 men were dropped in two lifts on 20 and 21 October. Surprise, essential to all airborne operations, was achieved, the North Koreans putting up little in the way of flak or resistance. Also dropped with the men were trucks, jeeps, 105mm howitzers and pallets loaded with artillery ammunition.

Destruction of the 239th Regiment

Very soon the paras had set up roadblocks around both towns and made contact with a unit of the South Korean 6th Division. However, there were no trains full of officials or prisoners. They had left Pyongyang earlier. The officials had escaped, while the North Koreans had shot the prisoners on the evening of the 20th. The only enemy unit between the 187th and I Corps advancing from the south was the North Korean 239th Regiment, which was deployed between the towns of Yongyu and Opa-ri. The men of the 187th, now reinforced by their comrades of the second drop, advanced and clashed with the 239th just north of Opa-ri. The North Koreans were attacked and thrown back, and they sustained heavy casualties that night when they attempted a break-out.

By dawn on 22 October, the 27th British Commonwealth Brigade was approaching on the main highway to join the airborne troops, reaching the 187th by noon following some fighting north of Yongyu. Caught between the 187th and the Commonwealth Brigade, the North Korean 239th Regiment had been wiped out. The 187th had only suffered 45 jump casualties and 66 battle casualties during the whole operation.

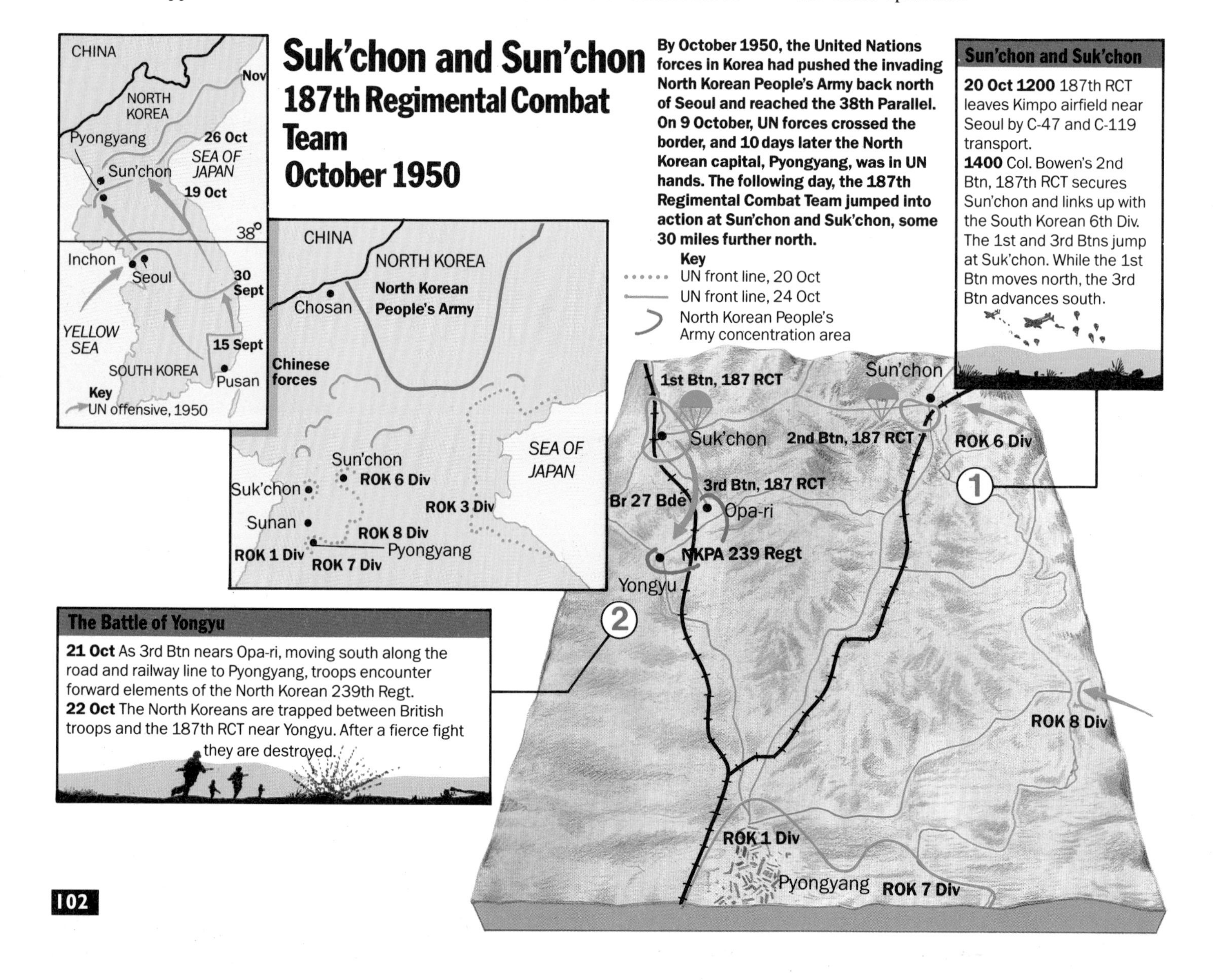

41 (INDEPENDENT) COMMANDO, ROYAL MARINES, HAGARU, NOVEMBER-DECEMBER 1950

On 27 November 1950, the Chinese Communist Forces (CCF) in Korea advanced against the US X Corps in the Chosin area. The 1st Marine Division was in urgent need of reinforcements, and so Lieutenant-Colonel Douglas Drysdale was ordered to take a relieving force from Koto-ri to Hagaru. The column, which included the British 41 (Independent) Commando, set off at 0700 hours on 29 November.

Soon the column came under withering fire, and 41 Commando was tasked with destroying an enemy stronghold that was blocking the way. The Royal Marines advanced and cleared the Chinese from their foxholes. Pushing on into the night, the column was constantly subjected to enemy mortar, sniper and artillery fire. The Chinese let the vanguard of the column through a defile and then blocked the way for the rest – Drysdale's command was now split.

Some Marines were in the vanguard, but the bulk remained with the main column under the command of Major Dennis Aldridge. They were soon attacked by Chinese infantry, though US fighter-bombers staved them off. Reaching Hagaru at last, 41 Commando had lost 65 men killed, missing or wounded.

41 Commando was given the task of securing the perimeter. On 6 December, orders arrived for the withdrawal to Koto-ri, and 41 Commando, along with the 5th US Marines, formed the rearguard. The column comprised 10,000 men and 1000 vehicles, and as it made its way south the US and British Marines at Hagaru were subjected to ferocious Chinese attacks.

There were now seven Chinese divisions concentrated against the column. However, the morale and fighting spirit of the British Commandos was superb, and held up during the exhausting march from Koto-ri to the Hungnam bridgehead.

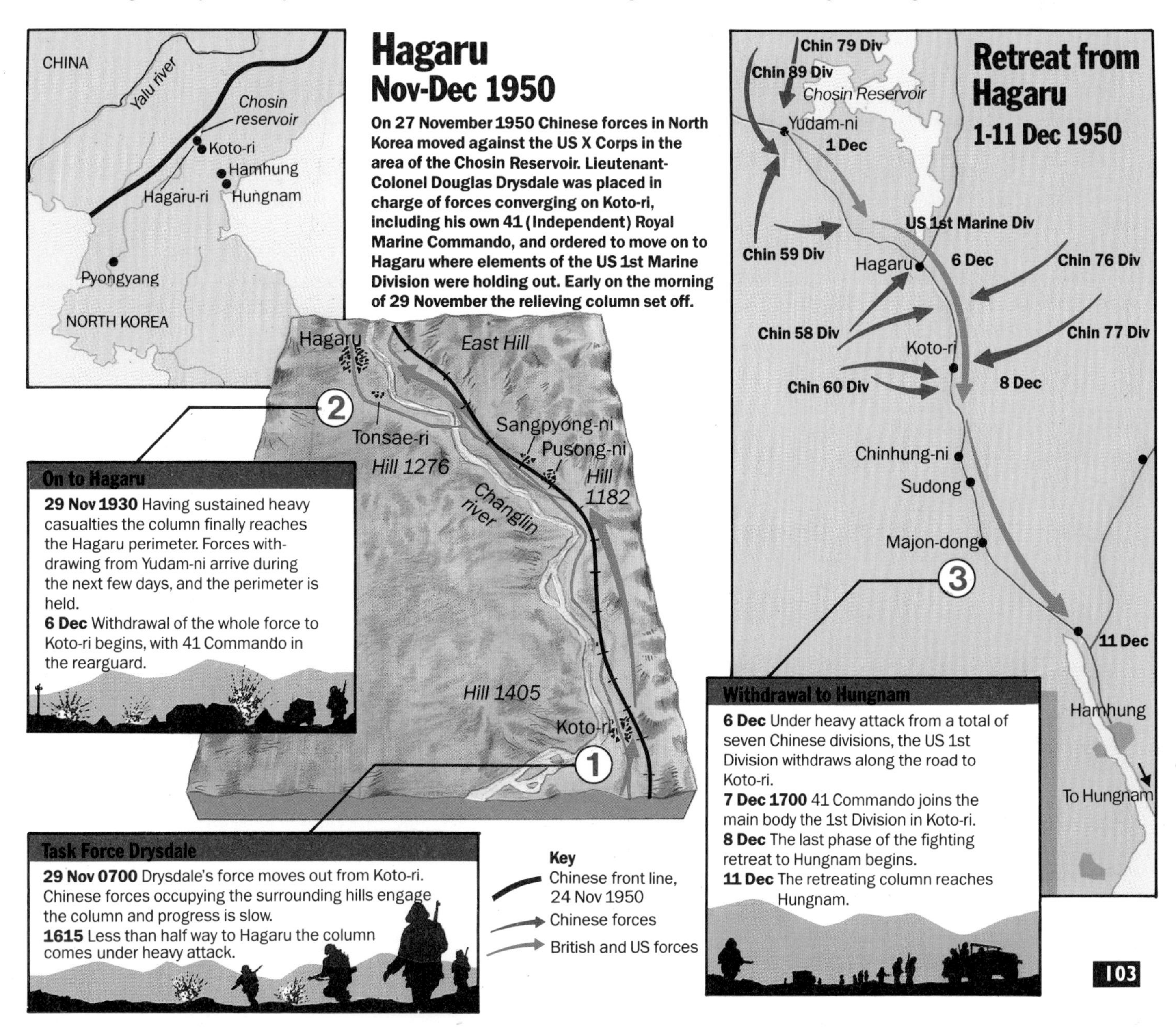

PRINCESS PATRICIA'S CANADIAN LIGHT INFANTRY, KAPYONG VALLEY, 24-26 APRIL 1951

In April 1951, the 2nd Battalion, Princess Patricia's Canadian Light Infantry (2 PPCLI), under the command of Lieutenant-Colonel J R Stone, was tasked with holding Hill 677 on the western side of the Kapyong valley. It was the second year of the Korean War and the Chinese were hitting the United Nations (UN) forces hard. Supporting the Canadians were a battalion of Australians and an American heavy tank battalion. The Australians were attacked by wave after wave of Chinese on the morning of 24 April, and by the evening it had become obvious that they would not be able to hold their position the next day. Therefore, they were withdrawn in the evening, leaving 2 PPCLI in the frontline.

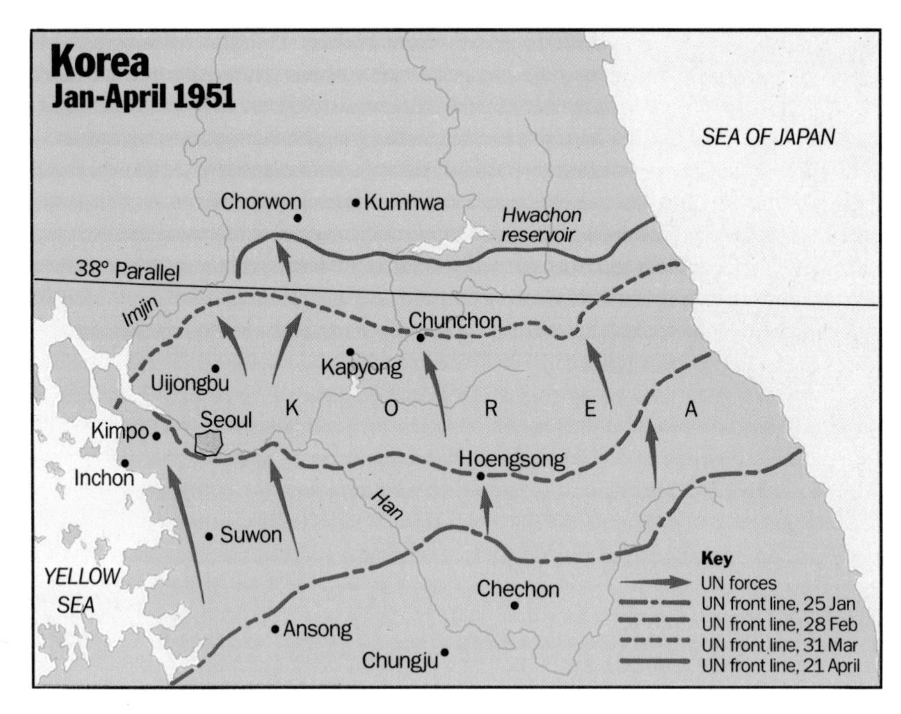

Blunting the Chinese attacks

At 2200 hours Chinese mortar shells began falling on the Canadians' trenches, to be followed by 200 infantry scrambling up the hill towards them. The attack was stopped by a combination of UN mortar fire and by rolling hand grenades down the hill. Another Chinese attack, on the battalion's headquarters and mortar platoon, was defeated when the Canadian mortars blew the enemy infantry to pieces at a range of 200m and machine guns killed the rest. There was fighting during the rest of the night, with a particularly large attack being launched against the northwest corner of the Canadian position.

Hordes of Chinese soldiers charged forward, to be met by a hail of rifle and machine-gun fire. However, the enemy kept coming, and before long were engaged in savage hand-to-hand fighting with D Company, 2 PPCLI, under the command of Captain Mills. In the fighting, Lieutenant Mike Levy's 10 Platoon was virtually wiped out, but not before it had killed 30 enemy soldiers. The machine gunners performed particularly well, as Mills later stated: 'The machine-gunners immediately fired on the enemy with such deadly accuracy that the enemy stopped his main attack on 10 Platoon. The enemy then directed his main assault against the MMG [medium machine gun] position, thus relieving the pressure on 10 Platoon.'

The battalion is surrounded

Captain Mills, fearing his position would fall, asked for artillery fire to be directed onto his position in a desperate attempt to stop the Chinese. As the Canadians sheltered in their trenches, 25-pounder shells rained down on them. Miraculously, not one of them was hurt, and by dawn they were able to reclaim their forward trenches. However, the battalion as a whole was by this time surrounded. Lieutenant-Colonel Stone stated: 'Our supply route had been cut and I had no way of knowing how long we might have to hold our position and how aggressive the enemy might become. We were pretty well out of food, water and ammunition.'

Stone requested an air drop, and six hours later several American aircraft arrived during the afternoon and delivered food, water and ammunition, with only four parachutes falling outside the battalion's area.

The daylight hours of the 25th were fairly quiet, the Canadians being subjected to some desultory shelling. By 1400 hours, patrols from B Company reported that the road back to brigade headquarters was clear of the enemy, and Stone requested that additional supplies be brought forward as soon as possible. However, the enemy did not renew the attack, and after an uneventful night an exhausted but jubilant 2 PPCLI was pulled out of the line.

Light Canadian casualties

Despite the ferocity of the Chinese attack, the Canadians had lost only 10 dead and 23 wounded. The enemy had used 6000 men to try to punch a hole through the Allied line. However, the Canadians had stopped it dead. Their reward was to be awarded the Presidential Unit Citation, along with the Australians and the US tank battalion.

1ST BATTALION, THE GLOUCESTERSHIRE REGIMENT, IMJIN RIVER, 22-25 APRIL 1951

In April 1951, the Gloucestershire Regiment was one of the three battalions that made up the 29th Brigade that was tasked with stopping the Chinese and North Korean assault on Seoul. The 657 men of the Glosters were placed across the Imjin river, and there awaited the Chinese attack.

The Chinese attack started during the evening of 22 April, and by 24 April the battalion was completely surrounded. The Glosters threw back the enemy time and time again; the Chinese were subjected to artillery and napalm strikes. However, with no hope of relief, the order was given to abandon the position.

Only 63 reached safety, the rest being captured by the Chinese or killed in the battle. The Chinese 63rd Army had sustained 11,000 casualties in its attempt to reach Seoul, its hopes crushed by the Glosters. In recognition of this, the 1st Battalion, the Gloucestershire Regiment, was awarded a US Presidential Citation.

Imjin river

The 1st Battalion the Gloucestershire Regiment, 22-25 April 1951

As the UN forces in Korea under General Douglas MacArthur pushed north towards the 38th parallel the Chinese prepared their counter-offensive. The UN established a front along the Imjin river guarding the route to the South Korean capital, Seoul. On 22 April Chinese forces crossed the river in stength. The Glosters held positions south of the crossing near Choksong against massed Chinese attacks for three successive nights, breaking the momentum of the enemy advance and gaining sufficient time for a new front to be established.

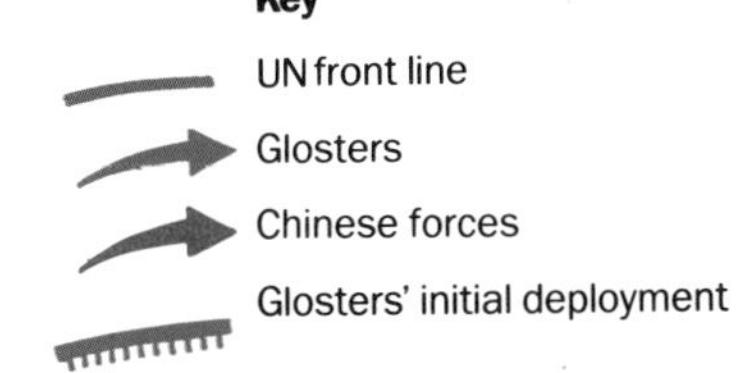

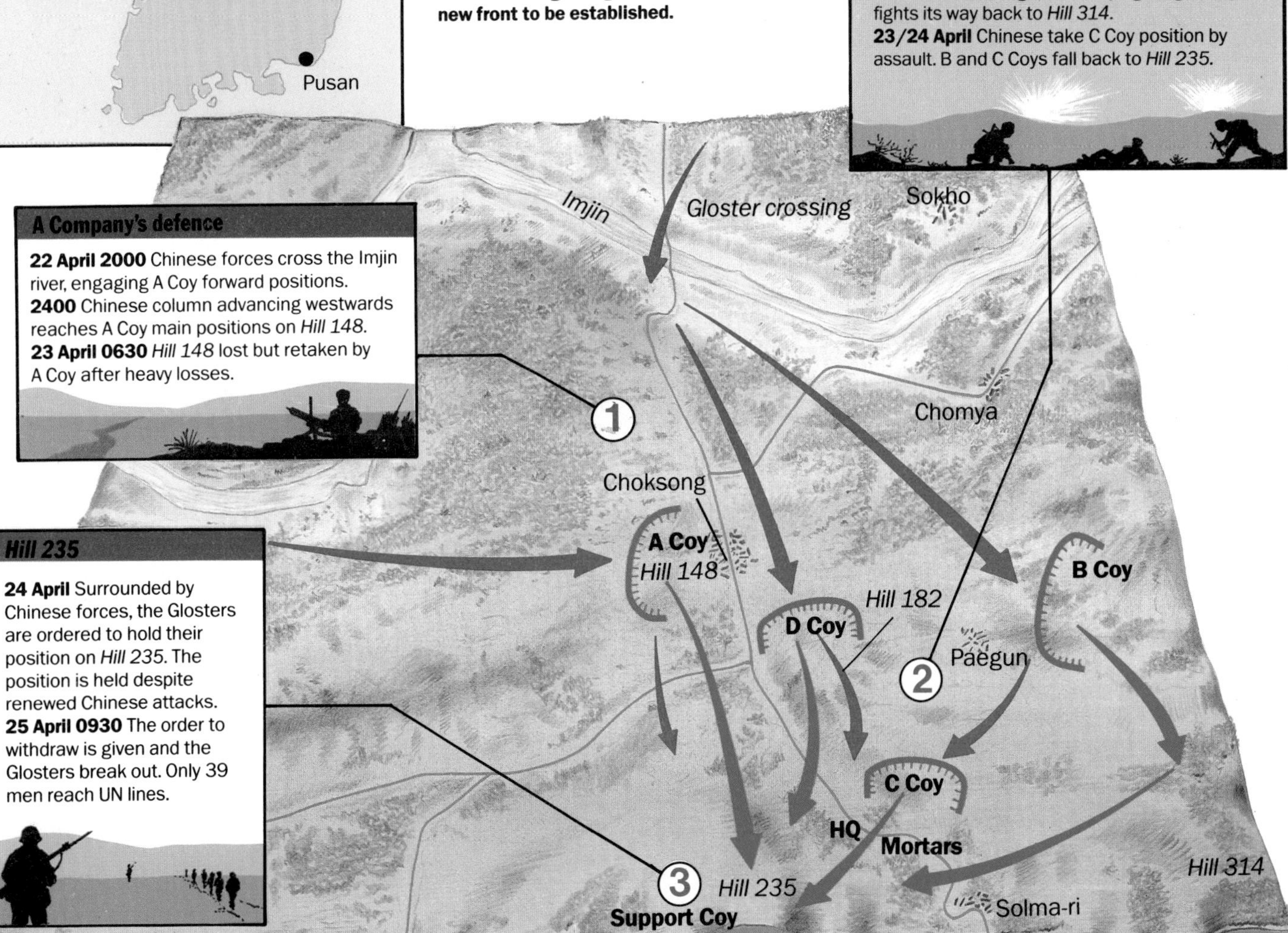

1ST MARINE DIVISION, BUNKER HILL, 11-17 AUGUST 1952

In the summer of 1952, the US 1st Marine Division was on the left flank of the US Eighth Army's Jamestown Line in Korea. Across No-Man's Land lay the Chinese 194th and 119th Divisions. The Korean War was starting to resemble World War I, with no movement, massive trench systems and huge underground complexes. In July 1952, the 1st Marine Regiment moved up to the centre of the division's sector. On its right were the 5th Marines, on its left the 1st Korean Marine Corps Regiment. The 1st's 3rd battalion had in its sector Hill 201, Hill 58A and also Paekhak Hill (Hill 229). The Chinese forces opposite held Hill 122, soon to be more commonly known as Bunker Hill, and behind that a mountain called Taedok-san.

American aircraft pound the hill

Shortly after midnight on 9 August, the Chinese pushed the Marines off Hill 58A. When daylight came American aircraft pounded the hill as a preliminary to an attack mounted by a company of the 1st Battalion, 1st Marine Regiment, which was successful. However, they were themselves pushed off the hill by the enemy, and the Marines also abandoned Hill 56A (Samoa).

Undeterred, the Marines made another assault during the night of 9/10 August. For four long hours the battle raged, until at daybreak the Marines were forced to retreat again, losing the hill for a third time along with 17 dead and 243 wounded. As intensive artillery fire from Hill 122 had been responsible for the Marines losing 58A, it was decided to mount an attack on this position. Planned for the night of 11 August, a diversionary attack was to be made against 58A by tanks and artillery. To gain surprise, it was decided that there would be no softening up barrage against Hill 122, but the 5th Marines (on the right) would fire a false barrage to mislead the enemy.

The attack against Hill 58A – Siberia – began at 2110 hours, and by midnight the hill was taken without much

difficulty. The Marines tasked with taking Bunker Hill also met with success, taking it just before dawn on the 12th, the Chinese putting up a spirited fight before they withdrew. However, by mid-afternoon heavy Chinese artillery and mortar fire was falling on Bunker Hill and the Marines were forced back to a reverse slope position. Just as victory seemed within their grasp, it appeared certain that the Marines would have to fall back yet again.

Then the Americans were hit by a force of around 350 Chinese infantry, the enemy managing to take the hill's north slope while the Marines held the south slope. There then followed two Chinese attacks: one against Hill 48A which was a diversion, and another against Bunker Hill. The two US companies on Bunker Hill were severely tested, but were saved by a heavy artillery barrage launched by the 11th Marines. The night's action on Bunker Hill had cost the Marines 24 dead and 214 wounded, the enemy's losses being estimated at 700 dead. Most importantly, however, was that the Marines were still on Bunker Hill.

The enemy is thrown back

Throughout 13 August the Chinese shelled Bunker Hill and then launched an attack in the evening. They were repulsed with heavy loss, a pattern that would be repeated on the 14th, 15th and 16th. The attacks were intensive and the Marines were hard pressed. As often happens in war, just as it seemed the Chinese would overwhelm the US soldiers the assaults lessened. Even though there were seven more Chinese attacks before the end of the month, those mounted after the 17th were not of the same intensity and the crisis had passed. The Battle of Bunker Hill was over. The Marines continued to hold on to the hard-won Hill 122. Total Chinese losses were estimated at 3200, the Marines losing 48 killed and 313 seriously wounded in the eight-day battle. It had been a hard-fought action for the possession of a few square kilometres of seemingly unimportant earth.

ABOVE: *A Marine 75mm howitzer prepares to shell enemy positions near the North Korean border. Artillery and air support were to prove invaluable to UN operations in the Korean War, often defeating enemy human-wave attacks.*

K-1496

CHAPTER III

VIETNAM

The US armed forces lost no battles during the Vietnam War – a fact often forgotten in the political controversy surrounding the conflict. And although the military machine faced enormous problems, the war also afforded the military the opportunity to experiment with a number of new tactical and strategic doctrines, which bore fruit in later conflicts, notably the Gulf War of 1991 against Iraq. For example, the Americans pioneered the mass use of helicopters on the battlefield. As early as 1965, for instance, the heliborne operations of the US 1st Cavalry Division in the la Drang Valley proved the worth of the airmobility concept. In addition, the war also led to the creation of a new special forces unit: the SEALs (Sea, Air and Land teams). The SEALs' operations in the Mekong Delta between 1966 and 1972 were highly successful, proving the point that the US could raise, train and equip an elite force in a short space of time. Similarly, the Civilian Irregular Defense Group (CIDG) Program was a notable success for the US Special Forces, but one that was subsequently wasted by the government of South Vietnam.

The communist Tet Offensive of January 1968 was a major surprise to both the Americans and the South Vietnamese, and hastened US withdrawal from the conflict. However, paradoxically, on the battlefield Tet was a disaster for the communists. Their losses amounted to 46,000 dead and 9000 wounded. American and South Vietnamese forces acquited themselves well, especially the US Marines, who retook the city of Hue after desperate fighting, and prevented the base of Khe Sanh being overrun.

Though the war was largely conducted by the forces of the United States and the government of South Vietnam, there was also Australian involvement in the conflict. There are two separate Australian actions listed in this chapter, both of which illustrate the fine fighting qualities of the individual Australian soldier. The first concerns the actions of two companies of the 6th Battalion, The Royal Australian Regiment, in Phuoc Tuy province in August 1966. Its subsequent engagement with the Viet Cong was to win the Diggers a US Presidential Citation. The second was to win one of the Australians involved a Victoria Cross, one of the highest awards for valour in the world. In May 1969, members of the Australian Army Training Team were operating with Montagnard and South Vietnamese units around Ben Het, in the highlands of South Vietnam. The subsequent rescue of wounded personnel by Keith Payne was a display of courage and perseverance of the highest kind, and rightly won him a VC. But all the Australians in the battle performed admirably, and prevented the retreat becoming a rout.

Finally, there is one action included that precedes American involvement in Vietnam, a battle of an earlier, though just as painful, war: the French defeat at Dien Bien Phu. It is included not because it was a great military triumph – it was not. Rather, it is one more example of the fighting qualities of France's Foreign Legion. Dien Bien Phu was a tragedy, one made inevitable by the gross underestimation by the French of the capabilities of the Viet Minh, especially their commander, General Giap. Indeed, the actions of the French High Command in Indochina comes close to gross incompetence. Fortunately for France, her honour was saved by the heroism of the Foreign Legion. As ever, the Legionnaires paid the price for their masters' mistakes.

A US Marine opens up with an M60 machine gun against Viet Cong snipers south of Da Nang during the Vietnam War.

FRENCH FOREIGN LEGION, DIEN BIEN PHU, NOVEMBER 1953-MAY 1954

In 1953, the French High Command in Indochina, fighting a losing war against the Viet Minh guerrillas, decided to force a battle: the plain of Dien Bien Phu, a remote village on the border of Laos and northern Vietnam. The intention was to supply the base of Dien Bien Phu from the air, and use its artillery to defeat anything the Viet Minh could throw at it.

ABOVE: *Battered and bloodied but unbowed. A wounded Legionnaire mans the defences at Dien Bien Phu.*

Viet Minh strength

By March 1954 the garrison of Dien Bien Phu numbered 10,814 men, including colonial troops and French Foreign Legionnaires. Artillery support was provided by 24 105mm and four 155mm howitzers, three 120mm mortar companies and a squadron of 10 M-24 Chaffee light tanks. Where the French calculations had gone wrong, however, was in the assessment of Viet Minh strength. They did not believe General Vo Nguyen Giap, the Viet Minh field commander, could deploy more than a few troops against the base. In fact, he concentrated 37,500 men around Dien Bien Phu, as well as heavy artillery. At 1700 hours on 13 March, his guns commenced firing. The initial artillery bombardment was extremely effective. It reduced many of *Béatrice*'s defences to rubble and inflicted many casualties among the Legionnaires. For over eight hours the defenders of *Béatrice* held on in the face of heavy pressure. By 0300 hours on 14 March, it was obvious that the Legionnaires in *Béatrice* could only be saved by retreating. Therefore, Colonel Christian de Castries, the base commander, ordered what was left of them to abandon their position.

It was *Gabrielle*'s turn next. Held by Algerians and a Legion mortar unit, the stronghold was attacked by the Viet Minh during the evening of 15 March, only one sector of the bastion remaining in French hands by dawn. The fate of *Gabrielle* was in the balance, therefore de Castries launched a counterattack. However, he only sent in two companies of Legion paras, a battalion of Indochinese and a troop of Chaffee tanks. When this composite force reached the ford of the Nam Yum, it came under heavy fire. The Indochinese broke and scattered, one of the tanks was hit and the rest turned back, only the Legionnaires pressed forward to help the defenders of *Gabrielle*. However, they were too few to make a difference, and that afternoon the stronghold was abandoned. Giap had won the strategic ridges to the north and northeast of Dien Bien Phu. He could now pound the French at will, the agony of Dien Bien Phu had begun.

On 17 March the T'ai battalion holding *Anne-Marie* deserted en masse, and the bastion fell. Giap's force had now swelled to over 40,000 men, and his units began to pound the airstrip ceaselessly and cut trenches to within rifle shot of *Huguette*, *Claudine*, *Dominique*, *Eliane* and *Isabelle*. By 23 March, all flights in and out of the base had been halted by Viet Minh artillery. For the rest of the siege, the French were supplied by parachute, though the aircraft could only pass over at night because of the heavy flak during the day.

The beginning of April saw the Viet Minh try to take *Isabelle*. However, the position was strong and the many assaults were beaten off. Reinforcements arrived by air during the night of 11/12 April in the shape of a battalion of Foreign Legion paras, though many were killed in the air or when they landed in the midst of the action.

The fighting raged on, the burden of the defence falling on the Legionnaires and the Colonial paras, many of the North Africans deserting their posts. In early May the Viet Minh redoubled their attacks on *Claudine* and *Huguette*. The end was near now as the French fought desperately to prevent the inevitable. *Eliane* fell and the enemy were closing in on Castries's command post. By the afternoon of 7 May it was all over. The garrison had suffered 4000 dead, with the rest being led into captivity, few ever to return. Giap had not won a light victory, though: his losses amounted to at least 8000 dead and 15,000 wounded.

Dien Bien Phu

French Foreign Legion, November 1953 – May 1954

At 1035 hours on 20 November 1953 French forces carried out Operation Castor, parachuting into dropping zones Natasha and Simone and establishing a base from which they could patrol Viet Minh invasion routes into Laos. By late February the Legionnaires were under sporadic artillery fire, and they awaited the inevitable Viet Minh offensive.

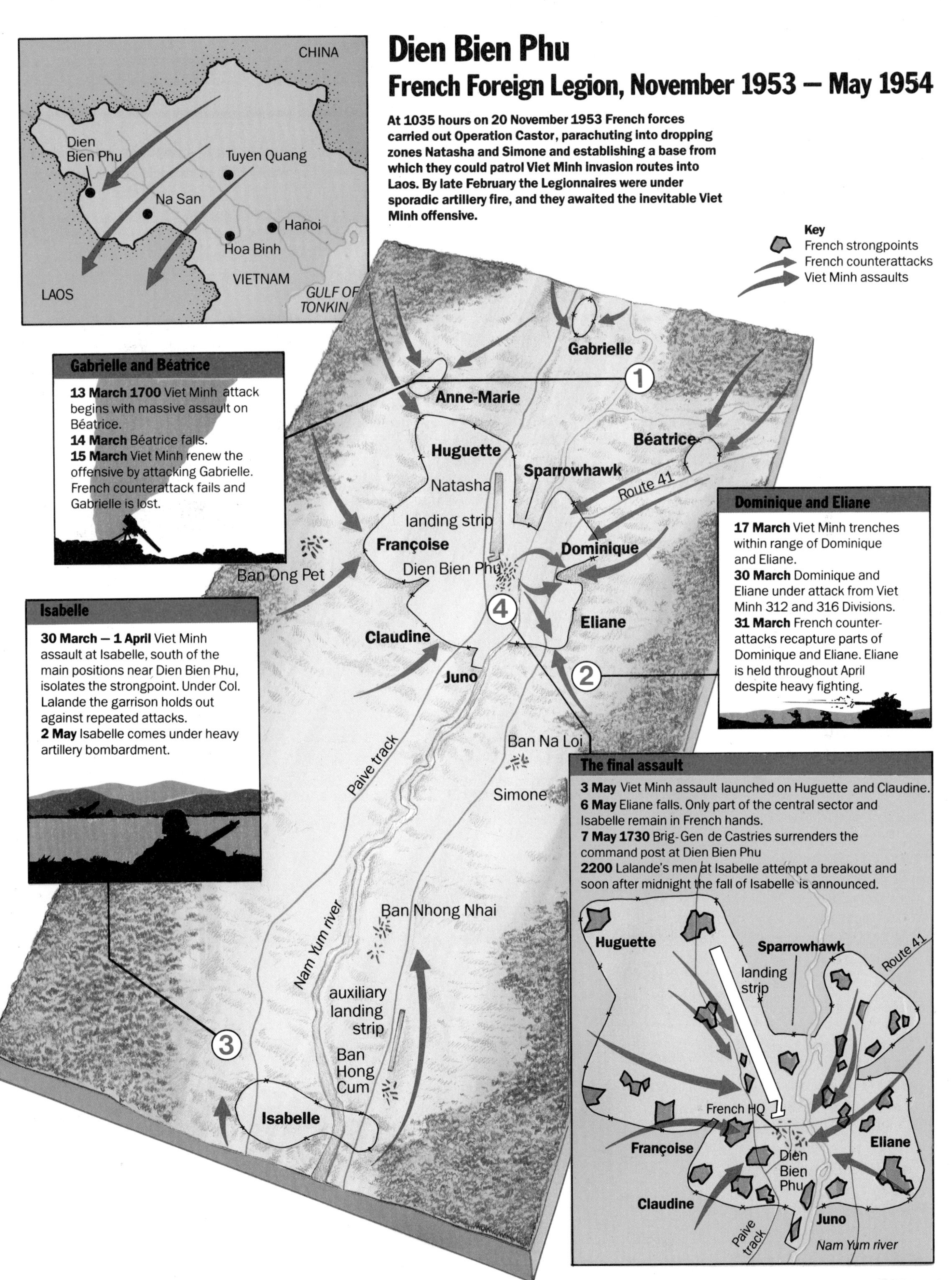

1ST CAVALRY DIVISION (AIRMOBILE), IA DRANG VALLEY, OCTOBER-NOVEMBER 1965

In October 1965, the US 1st Cavalry Division (Airmobile) was about to go into action against the North Vietnamese Army (NVA) in the Central Highlands of Vietnam. Led by Major-General Harry Kinard, the division specialised in the helicopter insertion of its men onto the battlefield. Its strengths were speed and firepower, with the basic tactical unit being the Eagle Flight: six UH-1Cs armed with rockets and mini-guns, and seven troop-carrying UH-1Ds.

The division was about to take part in what would become known as the Battle of the Ia Drang Valley: the attempt by the NVA to cut South Vietnam in two. Initially, the division was used to support the South Vietnamese Army around Pleiku. At 1730 hours on 23 October, the NVA hit a relief column and the Air Cav was called up. Reacting with speed, the helicopters headed into battle and shot up the NVA forces, the latter withdrawing quickly. General William C Westmoreland, Commander of the US Military Assistance Command, Vietnam (MACV), then ordered the division into the pursuit.

For the next 12 days much of the division's 1st Brigade was deployed to the west of Pleiku to engage the enemy. The airmobility concept was proving its worth: the location of the enemy was fixed by flying patrols and then massive air and ground firepower was brought down. Several actions involved the deployment of airborne units at night – on 3 November troops were flown into a defensive perimeter under heavy fire during the hours of darkness.

The 1st Brigade was withdrawn from the Ia Drang battles on 9 November, after killing some 200 NVA soldiers, wounding another 180, and capturing large quantities of weapons and ammunition. It was replaced by the 3rd, consisting of the 1st and 2nd Battalions, 7th Cavalry, and was supported by the 2nd Battalion, 5th Cavalry. By this time the division was operating southeast of Plei Me, and on 14 November the 1st Battalion, 7th Cavalry, began a sweep along the base of the Chu Pong range. At 1017 hours, a preliminary bombardment began and was quickly followed by an aerial attack. The choppers came into Landing Zone (LZ) X-Ray and soon the troops were fanning out to secure a perimeter. However, they came under NVA fire, and several Hueys that came in to deliver more men were hit.

By mid-afternoon it was obvious that the cavalrymen were fighting for their lives against determined opposition. Fighting continued throughout the night, but by 1000 hours on 15 November air strikes and aerial rocket artillery had blasted the NVA soldiers out of their positions. By 0930 hours on 16 November, the Americans had been withdrawn. They had suffered 200 casualties, but had inflicted over three times that number on the NVA. The importance of the Ia Drang battles was that they had illustrated air cavalry units could respond to any situation quickly and maintain contact with the enemy for longer than was previously thought possible.

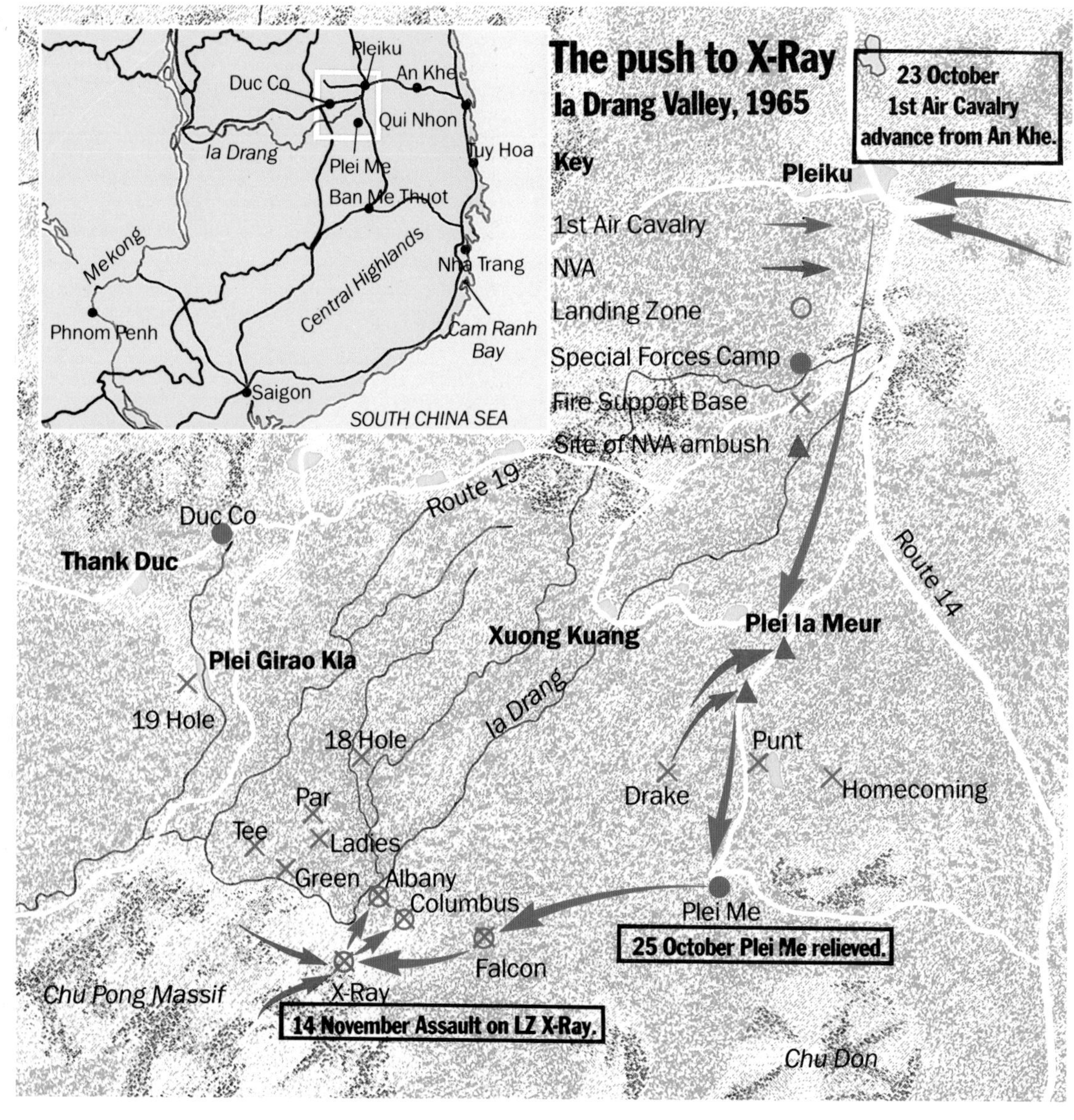

CIDG PROGRAM, VIETNAM, 1961-1971

In the Vietnam War, the Central Highlands were strategically vital, and so the allegiance of the inhabitants – the so-called 'Montagnards' – was also critical. Since the Montagnards had little reason to trust the South Vietnamese government – they had been discriminated against for years – they were ripe for communist infiltration. The US Special Forces had other ideas, however, and poured considerable military and financial resources into winning them over.

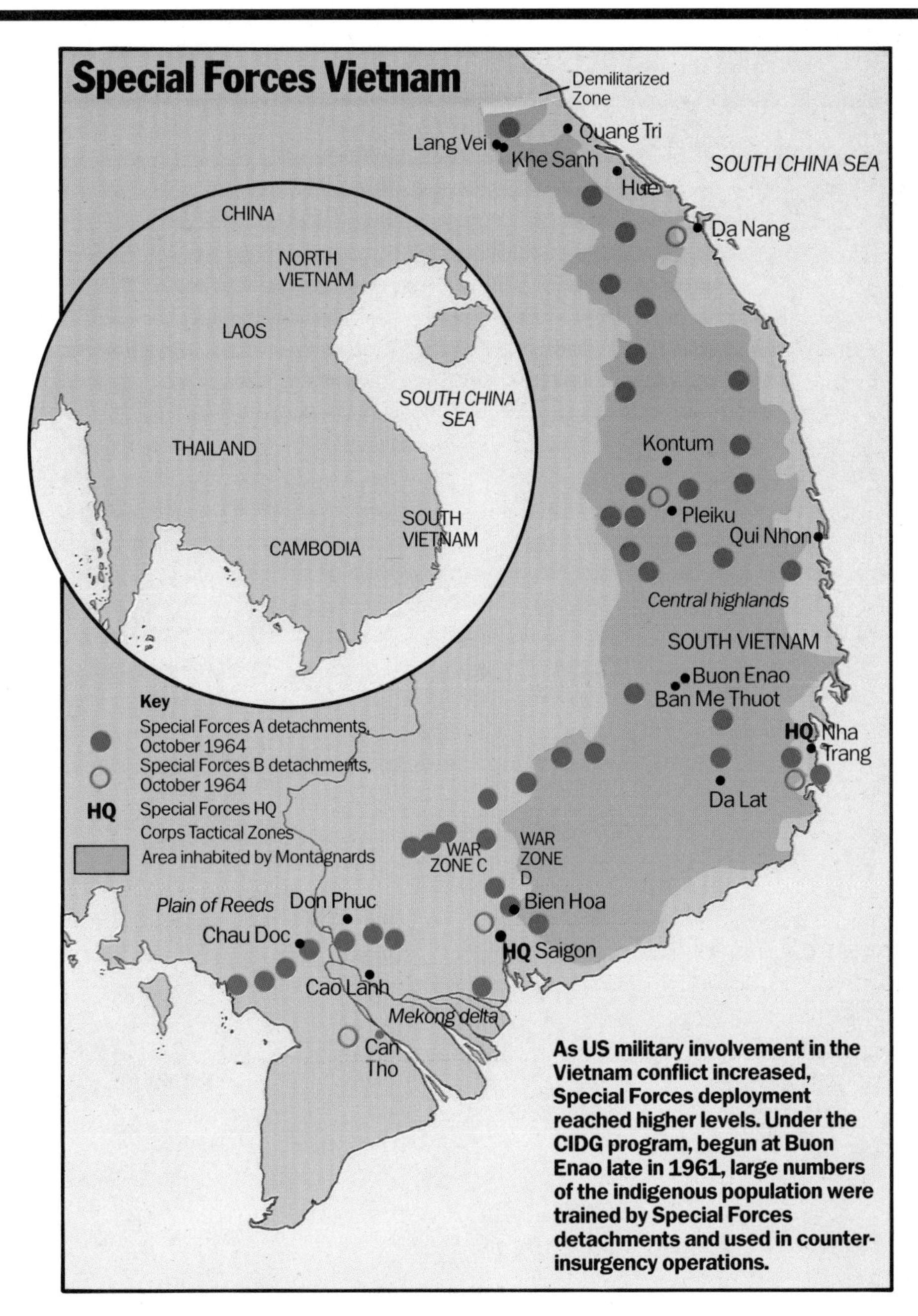

As US military involvement in the Vietnam conflict increased, Special Forces deployment reached higher levels. Under the CIDG program, begun at Buon Enao late in 1961, large numbers of the indigenous population were trained by Special Forces detachments and used in counter-insurgency operations.

The 'cidgees' against the VC

The tactic was to set in motion a civic action programme which included arms, money, medical aid and other benefits. A detachment of Green Berets and the Vietnamese Special Forces (LLDB) would move into a village and begin military training. By the end of 1963, the US Special Forces, with the aid of the LLDB, had trained 18,000 strike force troops and more than 43,000 hamlet militiamen. The campaign became known as the Civilian Irregular Defense Group (CIDG) Program, and by early 1963 the 'cidgees', as they were known, had begun aggressively patrolling against the Viet Cong (VC), with some success. The Montagnards thus quickly expanded their role to become effective military operatives against the enemy.

The CIDG Program assessed

The majority of the indigenous CIDG personnel came from the Rhada tribe of Montagnards, but other recruits included ethnic Cambodians, ethnic Chinese, Nungs and even religious sects. Enlisting these groups created its own problems, because animosities often existed between them. In addition, there was often friction between the mountain people and the South Vietnamese, as well as between the Green Berets and the LLDB. Naturally, there were failures. However, despite all the difficulties, the US Special Forces managed to create an effective contribution to the war effort out of the CIDG Program.

With the build-up of American forces in Vietnam between 1965 and 1966, CIDG units took part in a number of operations, for example the 'Greek-Letter' Projects: Delta, Omega, Sigma and Gamma. The Mobile Strike (Mike) Forces that evolved out of the CIDG Program were widely used in both the Greek-letter projects and a number of other military operations. For example, in the so-called 'Blackjack' operations, mobile guerrilla forces would be inserted into enemy territory, where they would be reinforced by Mike Force battalions. The reconnaissance platoons used in these operations constituted the elite of the Mike Forces.

The CIDG forces inflicted numerous defeats on the VC during the so-called Tet Offensive of January 1968, when enemy units were repulsed from cities garrisoned by Mike Forces, such as Ban Me Thuot and Nha Trang.

By early 1970 it was decided to end the Program and absorb the CIDG units into the South Vietnamese Army, and the cidgees' effectiveness declined sharply. Overall, the CIDG Program made a very real contribution against the VC. For the US Special Forces, it was a 'hearts and minds' triumph, but not one shared by the government of South Vietnam.

6TH BATTALION, ROYAL AUSTRALIAN REGIMENT, LONG TAN, 17-18 AUGUST 1966

The province of Phuoc Tuy was an important area of South Vietnam: a rich rice-producing area that was also the back door of Saigon. The North Vietnamese-backed Viet Cong (VC) were active in the province, and they carried out a number of attacks in and around the provincial capital of Bia Ria and the coastal town of Vung Tau.

Two units stationed in Phuoc Tuy were two companies of the 6th Battalion, Royal Australian Regiment. On 18 August 1966, having endured a VC shelling of their camp at Nui Dat the previous day, the Australians deployed to go and find 'Charlie'. It was an operation that would win the Diggers a US Presidential Citation.

The Diggers run into the VC

D Company, commanded by Major Harry Smith, moved out and entered the rubber plantation near Long Tan. As the afternoon wore on, the sweat-soaked Australian soldiers encountered a group of VC and quickly engaged them, killing them all. The company pushed on, and ran straight into an ambush in a small clearing halfway through the plantation. However, the officers and men of the 6th Battalion were made of stern stuff, and Smith quickly deployed his unit: 11 Platoon at the front, 10 Platoon on the left and 12 Platoon and the HQ group in the rear. However, 11 Platoon was soon in trouble, a heavily armed ambush party had been placed across the Australians' line of advance and was now being rapidly reinforced. 11 Platoon's commander was then killed, leaving Sergeant Bob Buick in charge.

Lieutenant Graham Kendall led his 10 Platoon forward to 11's relief. Coming across a VC force about to charge 11 Platoon's flank, Kendall's men

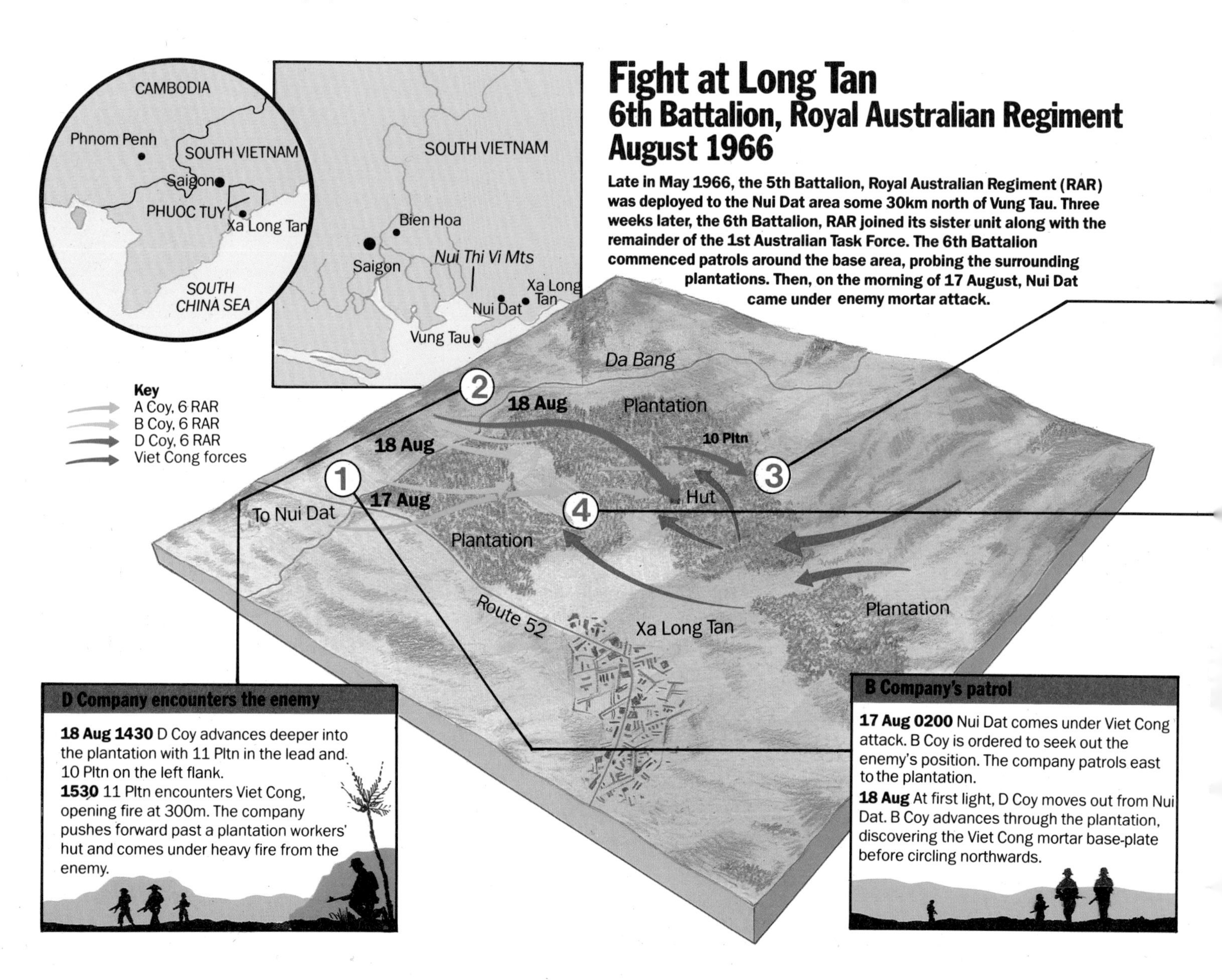

instinctively dropped to their knees and began firing at the enemy, who were decimated by the accurate barrage and quickly fell back. A second wave came at Kendall's men, only to be stopped again. 11 Platoon was still isolated, although not yet in a critical position. The Diggers had recovered from their initial shock and were calmly trading fire with the enemy, the latter having the worse of it. The Australians were tough soldiers and easily beat off each attack, but the two platoons were facing three enemy regiments: D445, the 27th and the 45th, consisting of almost 3000 North Vietnamese Army (NVA) regulars and VC. Eventually numbers would tell.

The fighting was furious but sporadic, as each side sought to test the other. Smith decided to send forward 12 Platoon, and at the same time requested an artillery strike on the enemy position. Within minutes, 105mm shells from the Royal Australian Artillery were crashing into the VC ranks. With the enemy now preoccupied, Smith gave the order to withdraw. 12 Platoon linked up with 10 and covered the latter's retreat, but 11 Platoon still had to be reached. Skirting to the south, 12 Platoon charged forward and reached their beleaguered mates. The two units then fell back, maintaining a steady fire at the enemy all the time.

Back at base, B and A Companies moved out to back up their comrades. The VC, thinking the Australian retreat was a rout, charged forward, only to be met by disciplined fire that scattered them. The resolution and professionalism of the Australians was frustrating the enemy – the fact that the Aussies were a tiny force was also very galling – while the artillery fire from Nui Dat was very effective, blowing many VC and NVA soldiers to pieces. When B and A Companies entered the fight, crashing into the enemy and forcing them back as night came, the VC and NVA had to pull back, and the battle was over.

ABOVE: *Searching for 'Charlie', a photograph that amply conveys the type of terrain encountered by the Australians at Lon Tan.*

D Company's fight

Under attack from a large force of enemy troops, D Coy adopts defensive positions and holds the Viet Cong at bay. 10 Pltn, still on the left flank, circles in and opens fire on the enemy, taking them by surprise and driving them back. Under cover of friendly artillery, 10 and 11 Pltn push the enemy further before withdrawing with 12 Pltn to the main D Coy position.

Rescue

1830 As the Viet Cong renew their attacks on the Australians' position, reinforcements advance through the plantation. B Coy pushes forward,south of D Coy's perimeter, while A Coy moves up to the north and south. Hard pressed, the Viet Cong pull back.

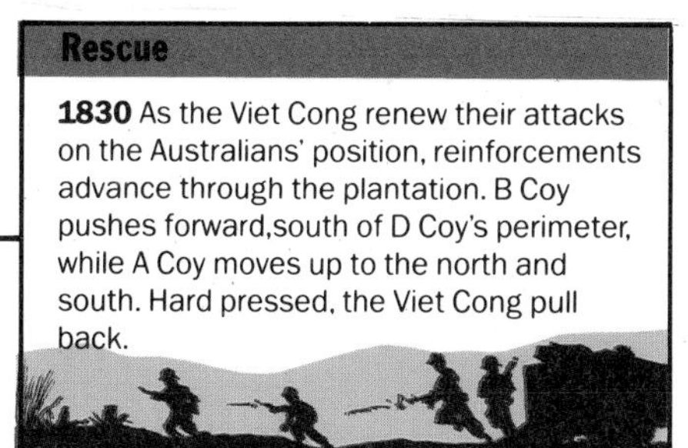

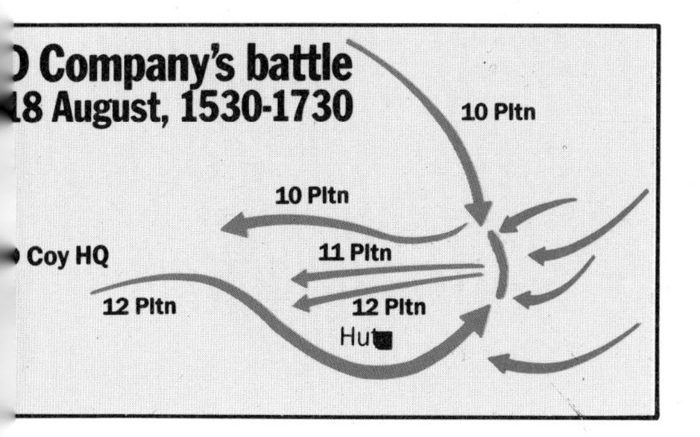

US NAVY SEALS, THE MEKONG DELTA, 1966-1972

By 1966, there were some 80,000 Viet Cong (VC) members operating in the Mekong Delta, the area of open water, swamp and rich paddies in the corner of South Vietnam. However, a new American unit, the US Navy SEALs, was sent to the area to combat the enemy. The men of the SEALs were tough, dedicated and highly trained. On arrival in Vietnam, the SEAL teams operated by setting up observation and listening posts along the waterways and trails used by the VC. They would then mount raids or ambushes to cut enemy supply lines.

The SEALs were also used in the Sung Sat Special Zone south of Saigon, where three-man detachments would be inserted into enemy territory using 'Mike' boats: heavily armed riverine patrol craft. The SEALs often laid booby traps. For example, at ambush sites they would lay demolition cord along the ditches on either side of the trail to catch any VC diving for cover when the SEALs opened up.

The SEALs were essentially a highly mobile force, trained to operate anywhere from the Arctic wastes to the jungle. In the Delta they were often transported in 'Boston Whalers', 3m-long fibreglass craft with a very shallow draft and high-power outboard engines. For operations in swampland, choppers from the Naval Light Helicopter Attack Squadrons were available.

In 1966 the SEALs, along with the US Army Special Forces, became involved in the Intelligence and Exploitation Program which was aimed at destroying the VC infrastructure within South Vietnam. The SEALs' performance was impressive: they killed and captured many VC, spearheaded search and destroy missions, as well as infiltrating North Vietnam for intelligence purposes. In Operation 'Crimson Tide' in September 1967 and Operation 'Bold Dragon III' in March 1968, they scouted and blew up a number of enemy installations. The Phoenix Program, a combination of intelligence gathering and counter-terrorism, involved the SEALs working closely with the Provincial Reconnaissance Units – very effective indigenous troops – and the results were extremely impressive: between 1967 and 1971, it is estimated that VC numbers within Vietnam were cut from 100,000 to less than 2000.

The SEALs also trained their Vietnamese counterparts, the Lin Dei Nugel Nghai (LDNN), and conducted many joint operations, most of which were successful. The last SEALs were officially out of Vietnam by 1971 or 1972, though there is reason to believe that a number were operating in the country right up to the fall of Saigon in April 1975.

The Mekong Delta

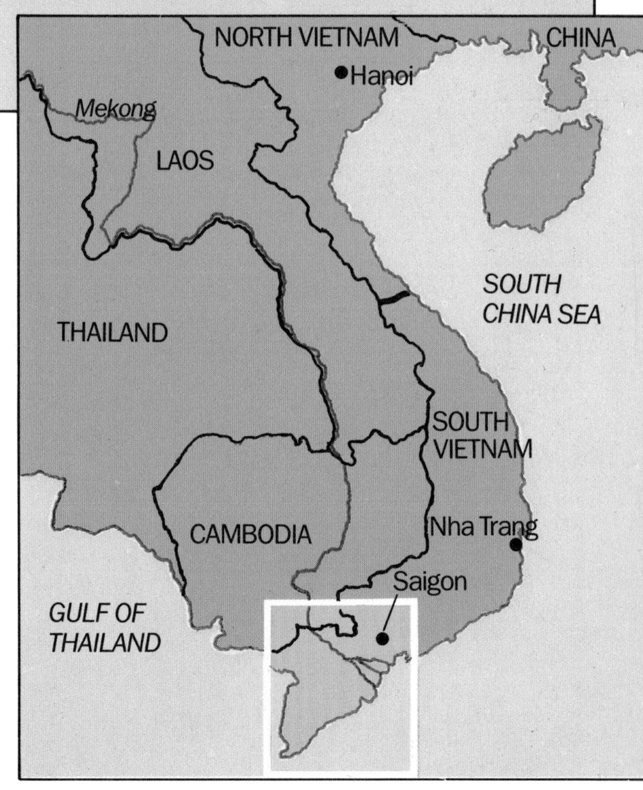

25TH INFANTRY DIVISION, THE BATTLE FOR SUOI TRE, 19-21 MARCH 1967

In March 1967, Colonel Marshall Garth, commander of the 3rd Brigade of the 25th 'Tropic Lightning' Infantry Division, ordered his 3rd Battalion, 22nd Infantry Regiment, to establish a fire base near the hamlet of Suoi Tre, War Zone C, Vietnam. This was part of Operation 'Junction City' which took place between February and May 1967. It was designed to convince Hanoi that War Zone C was no longer safe for the Viet Cong (VC). The tactic was to establish fire support bases by making airmobile assaults, with helicopters carrying infantry battalions and 105mm artillery to selected spots to establish the base. The infantry would then sweep the surrounding areas on foot, the artillery providing support in the event of a contact.

Fire Support Base Gold, the base set up by Garth, was to prove 'hot' from the beginning. The night of 19/20 March was quiet. There was no enemy activity throughout the 20th and into the early hours of the 21st. At 0630 hours on 21 March, however, the VC attacked.

Supporting fire was called from 105mm artillery units at a nearby fire support base. However, the VC attack was relentless – the base was in great danger of falling.

Though air strikes had been called up and reinforcements were on the way in the shape of the infantry and armoured battalions, the VC attack continued unabated. By 0840 hours, the perimeter had shrunk and the enemy were within hand grenade range of the the command post. The base looked set to fall. However, at 0900 hours the relief force arrived and the VC were driven off. The men of the 3/22 and 2/77 had won because they had done everything correctly: they had dug in deep, prepared secondary and primary perimeters, and had set up the base within the range of the artillery of other bases.

The Battle for Suoi Tre

25th Infantry Division, 19-21 March 1967

On 22 February 1967 South Vietnamese and US forces launched the first phase of Junction City, a major sweep against Viet Cong units in War Zone C to the west of Saigon. The second phase of the offensive began on 18 March. A day later troops from the US 25th Infantry Division were ordered to establish Fire Support Base Gold. During the early morning of the 21st, they faced a mass frontal assault.

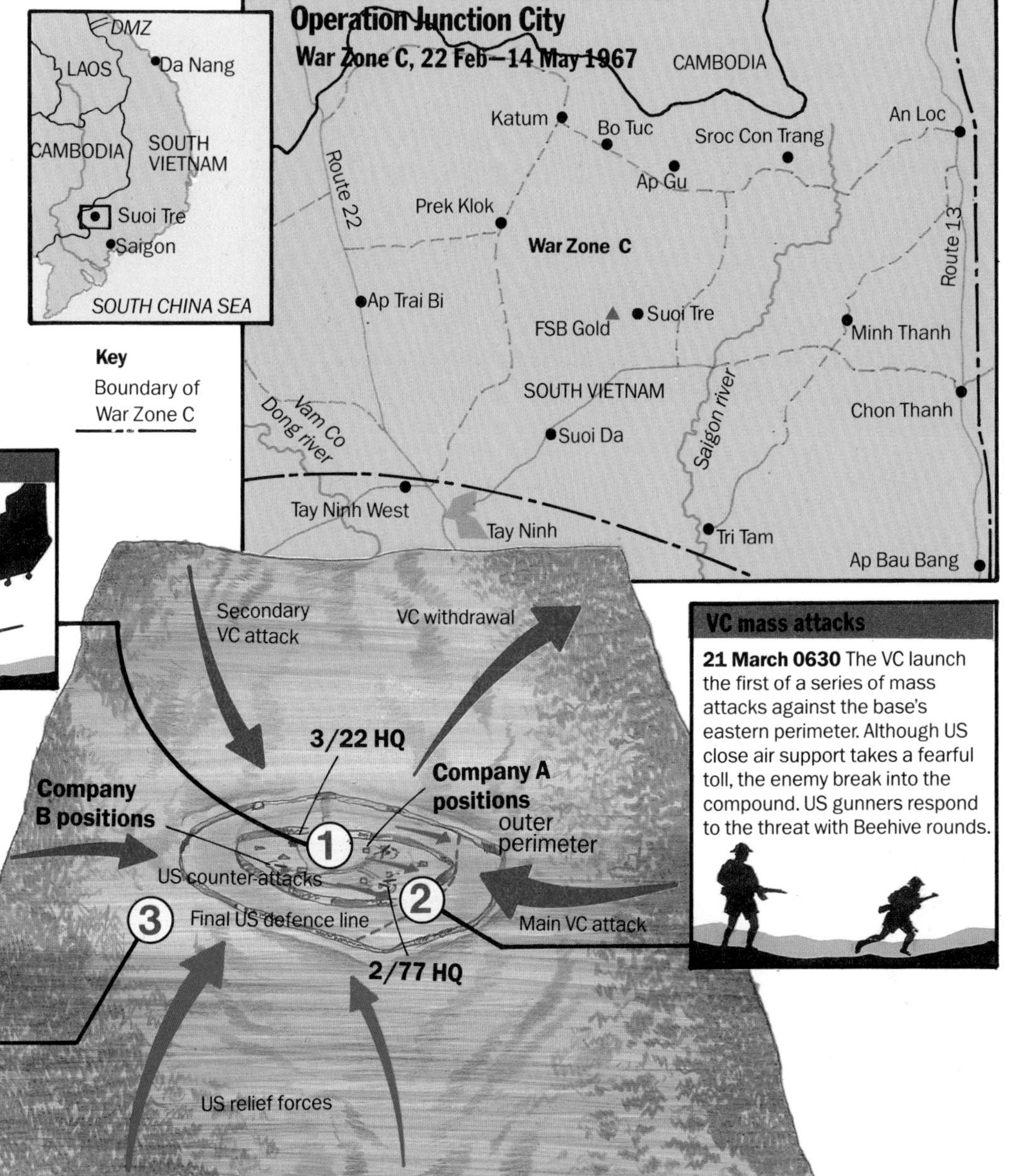

Tropic Lightning flies in

19-20 March Elements of the US 25th Tropic Lightning Division are flown into a clearing near the village of Suoi Tre. Despite taking casualties, the assault troops build a fire base.

The relief force arrives

0840 The base's eastern sector falls.
0845 The gunners run out of Beehive rounds and resort to high explosive to keep the VC at bay.
0900 The first units of the US relief force reach the battlefield.
0930 Caught between two forces, the VC are thrown out of the base and retreat to the northeast.

MOBILE RIVERINE FORCE, CAN GIOUC, 19 JUNE 1967

Beginning in June 1967, the newly formed US Mobile Riverine Force (MRF) conducted intensive operations in the Mekong Delta against the Viet Cong (VC). One of these missions was a strike against the VC in the Can Giouc District. On 18 June, the Mobile Riverine Force Base (MRB) was moved to an anchorage at the junction of the Soi Rap and Van Co rivers, and a battery of 155mm self-propelled guns was positioned in an old fort just opposite the junction.

The terrain afforded little cover, and therefore the US soldiers were instructed to use dispersed formations and to move by bounds from covered position to covered position. The plan was for an attack from north to south, with the boats entering the waterways as the tide was rising, permitting greater speed and a longer period at high-tide level immediately following entry. The method of operation was to split the combat area into a large number of intermediate objectives, phase lines and zones. Thus, the MRF had the capacity to change the direction of the attack – tactical flexibility that was to have many benefits.

On 19 June the infantry companies of the 2nd Brigade's 3rd and 4th Battalions of the 47th Infantry Regiment fought a series of engagements in Can Giouc, the most bloody of which was that fought by A Company, 4th Battalion, which engaged a VC force near a spot called Objective 18. The company ran straight into an entrenched VC position and suffered accordingly; it lost all its officer platoon leaders at the onset of being fired upon and 40 men were killed in total. However, by 2000 hours the infantry had done considerable damage to the VC with the twin assaults of the rifle companies of both the 3rd and 4th Battalions of the 47th, and with the combined firepower of artillery, naval gunfire, helicopter gunships and an unending series of air strikes, all of which continued into the night.

The next day the infantry were back on the line, engaging withdrawing VC units and inflicting casualties on the enemy. B and C Companies, 3/47th, made contact with the VC in the Rach Giong Ong. However, despite artillery and air strikes, the enemy proved difficult to destroy and the Americans were forced to sit tight throughout the night. In the morning the VC were gone, the survivors having floated or swum down river to the southeast. The MRF continued to sweep the area, engaging small groups of the enemy, but in reality the battle was over. The VC had lost an estimated 250 dead, but more importantly the MRF had helped drive the enemy from the area, and was free to drive deeper into the Delta.

BELOW: *Vessels of the Mobile Riverine Force on duty in the Mekong Delta.*

Can Giouc
19 June 1967

In June 1967 the newly-formed joint US Navy-US Army Mobile Riverine Force (MRF) began a series of operations in the Viet Cong-dominated areas of the Mekong Delta and the Rung Sat Special Zone to the south of the South Vietnamese capital, Saigon. On 18 June the MRF moved to a new anchorage on the Soi Rap river ready to go into action against Viet Cong forces in the Can Giouc district.

Mobile Riverine Force

19 June 1000 A battalion-size Viet Cong force is sighted near Objective 20. MRF forces move in by assault boat and helicopter and converge on the VC positions.
1150 As company-size units of the US 47th Infantry Regiment converge on them, the Viet Cong open fire.

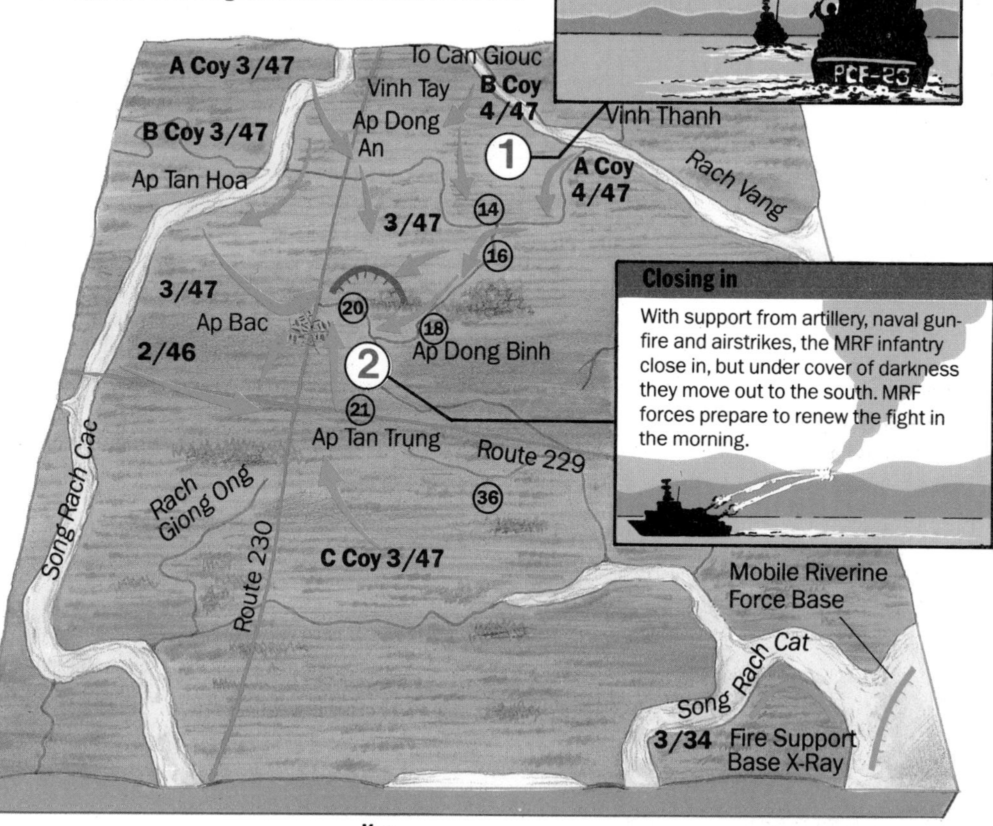

Closing in

With support from artillery, naval gunfire and airstrikes, the MRF infantry close in, but under cover of darkness they move out to the south. MRF forces prepare to renew the fight in the morning.

Can Giouc
20-21 June 1967

On 20 June 1967, the MRF troops of the 47th Infantry Regiment swept forward in pursuit of a large Viet Cong force encountered on the previous day. By the following morning, a Viet Cong headquarters had been taken, and the 5th Nha Be Battalion had been effectively eliminated.

Key
- Viet Cong positions
- US forces
- 3/47 US battalions
- (20) US objectives

Renewing the fight

20 June At first light, the MRF infantry move off in pursuit of the enemy, engaging isolated groups as the day progressed.
1700 All MRF companies are in position around the main body of Viet Cong.

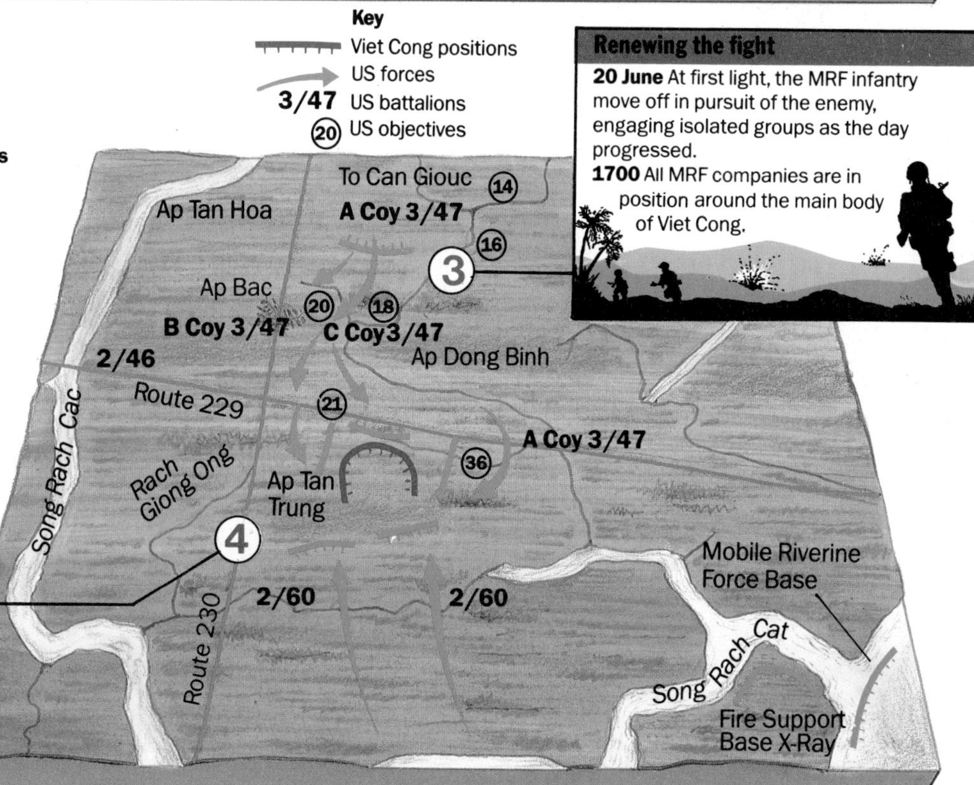

The enemy surrounded

20/21 June Resupply and casualty evacuation is carried out during the night. At first light, B Company, 3/47, sweeps through the enemy position encountering no resistance. MRF forces continue operations against isolated groups of Viet Cong.

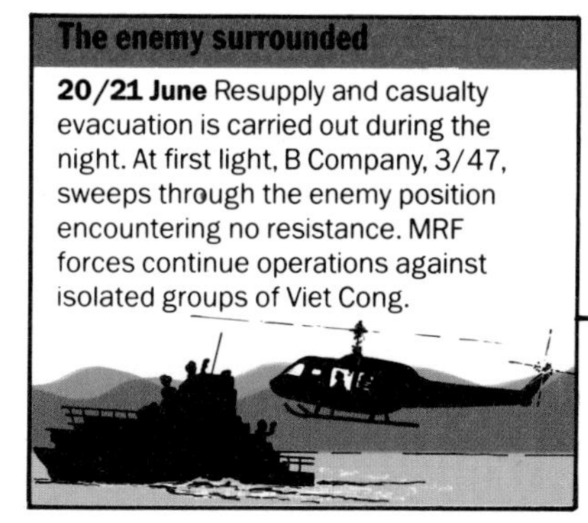

196TH LIGHT INFANTRY BRIGADE, HILL 63, 22-25 NOVEMBER 1967

In late November 1967, the men of the US 196th Light Infantry Brigade prepared to engage the North Vietnamese Army (NVA) in the Que Son Valley. They were after the NVA's 2nd Division. In addition, there were also Viet Cong (VC) units in the area.

Closest to the enemy was Task Force Dorland under the command of Major Gilbert N Dorland. Composed of two 100-man rifle companies and two armoured units, plus four M48 tanks, it contacted the enemy on Hill 63 at 0710 hours on 23 November. Soon a furious firefight developed, and Dorland called up the tanks. To prevent the enemy escaping, Dorland called in artillery strikes from a fire base 7km to the south.

Dorland was fighting as he should, placing as much firepower as possible on the enemy positions to fix and eliminate them. Reinforcements were airlifted forward by helicopter: Company B of the 3rd Battalion, 21st Infantry. The tanks were locating and destroying bunkers with high-explosive rounds, the shells slamming into the structures and then ripping them apart.

As the battle raged, at brigade level the immediate task was to seal off the area to prevent the enemy from escaping. By nightfall 60 enemy dead had been found by the Americans, while the latter had lost seven killed and 50 wounded. The fighting continued until the 25th. When the battle was over, the bodies of some 151 enemy soldiers were found, together with their equipment. The 196th had fought a professional battle.

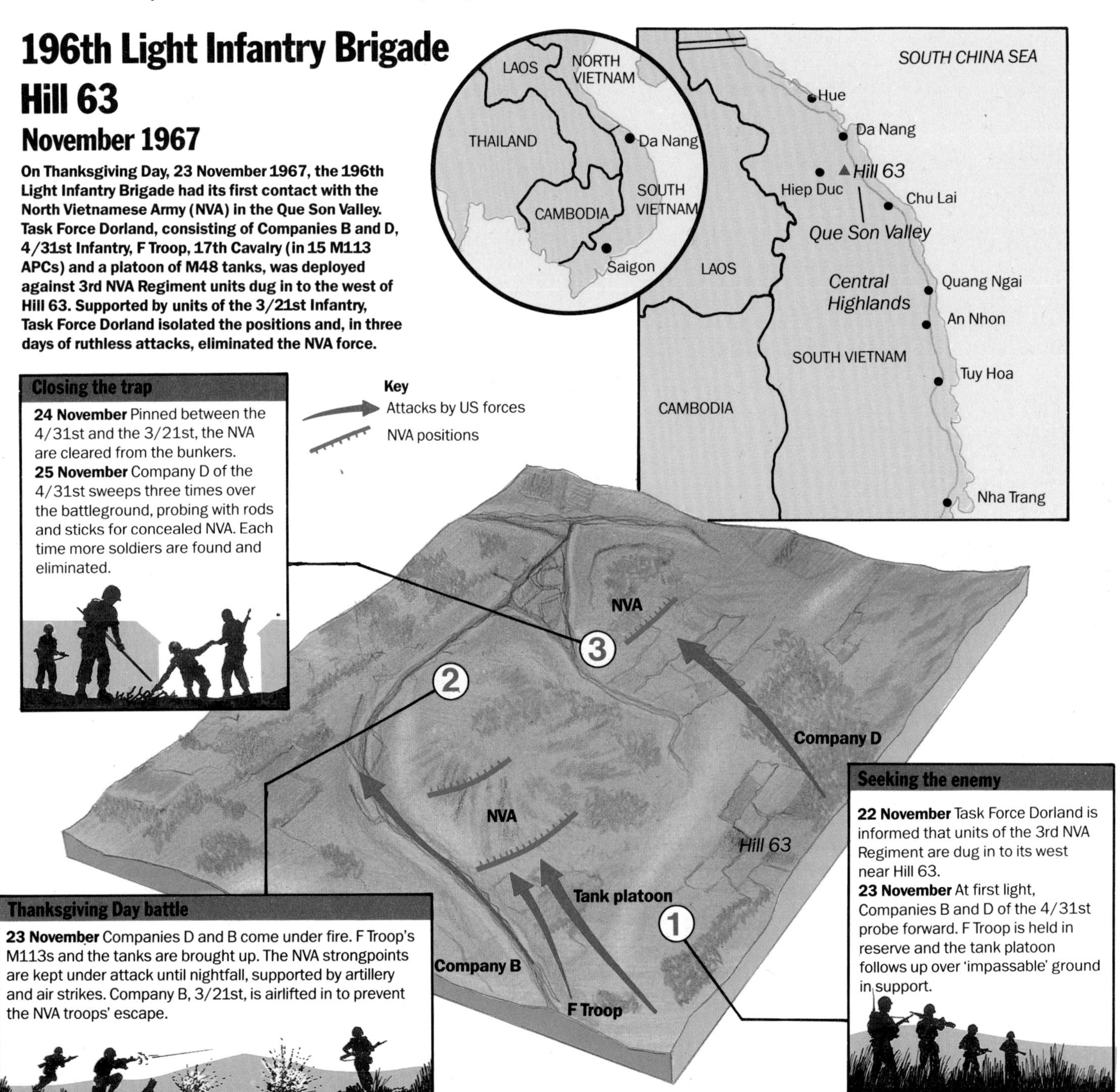

173RD AIRBORNE BRIGADE, THE BATTLE OF DAK TO, 1-7 NOVEMBER 1967

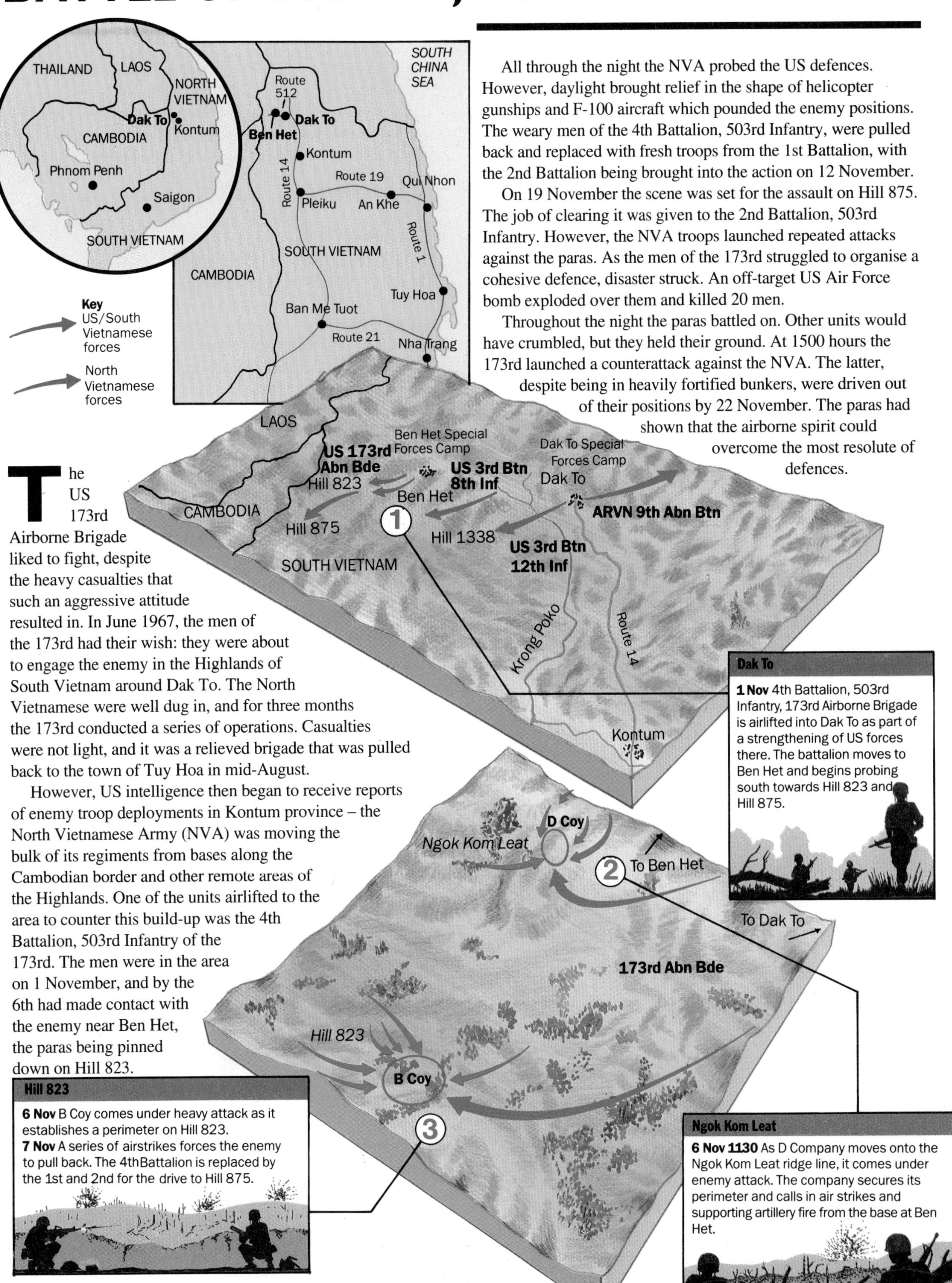

The US 173rd Airborne Brigade liked to fight, despite the heavy casualties that such an aggressive attitude resulted in. In June 1967, the men of the 173rd had their wish: they were about to engage the enemy in the Highlands of South Vietnam around Dak To. The North Vietnamese were well dug in, and for three months the 173rd conducted a series of operations. Casualties were not light, and it was a relieved brigade that was pulled back to the town of Tuy Hoa in mid-August.

However, US intelligence then began to receive reports of enemy troop deployments in Kontum province – the North Vietnamese Army (NVA) was moving the bulk of its regiments from bases along the Cambodian border and other remote areas of the Highlands. One of the units airlifted to the area to counter this build-up was the 4th Battalion, 503rd Infantry of the 173rd. The men were in the area on 1 November, and by the 6th had made contact with the enemy near Ben Het, the paras being pinned down on Hill 823.

All through the night the NVA probed the US defences. However, daylight brought relief in the shape of helicopter gunships and F-100 aircraft which pounded the enemy positions. The weary men of the 4th Battalion, 503rd Infantry, were pulled back and replaced with fresh troops from the 1st Battalion, with the 2nd Battalion being brought into the action on 12 November.

On 19 November the scene was set for the assault on Hill 875. The job of clearing it was given to the 2nd Battalion, 503rd Infantry. However, the NVA troops launched repeated attacks against the paras. As the men of the 173rd struggled to organise a cohesive defence, disaster struck. An off-target US Air Force bomb exploded over them and killed 20 men.

Throughout the night the paras battled on. Other units would have crumbled, but they held their ground. At 1500 hours the 173rd launched a counterattack against the NVA. The latter, despite being in heavily fortified bunkers, were driven out of their positions by 22 November. The paras had shown that the airborne spirit could overcome the most resolute of defences.

1ST AND 5TH MARINE REGIMENTS, HUE, JANUARY-FEBRUARY 1968

During the Vietnam War, Hue was the most important city in the northern provinces of South Vietnam. During the Tet Offensive of January 1968, it was attacked by North Vietnamese Army (NVA) units. Backed up by local Viet Cong units, the NVA soon controlled most of the Old City.

The nearest US Marine units were at the Phu Bai combat base under Brigadier-General Lahue (elements of the 1st and 5th Marine Regiments). He despatched A Company, 1st Battalion, 1st Marines, to investigate Hue, but the unit was quickly pinned down by NVA forces. Another force of Marines under Lieutenant-Colonel Marcus Gravel was sent to help A Company. Gravel pushed his small force through to the Phu Cam canal and entered the city. He was then ordered to make contact with South Vietnamese forces in the northern corner of the Old City, but he could not get beyond the Nguyen Hoang bridge.

By 4 February more Marines had arrived, including Colonel Stanley Hughes of the 1st Marines. His men faced a different type of warfare from the one they usually fought in Vietnam: there was no mobility, the fighting was at close quarters and often hand-to-hand. The attackers had to fight their way in and pull out the defenders one by one. The communists had turned every bit of cover and every building into a strongpoint. The Marines had a few M48 tanks and some 'Ontos', tracked vehicles mounting six recoilless rifles.

The worst fighting occurred in the Old City, where the buildings were tightly packed together. Crouching behind walls, setting up as much covering fire as they could, the Marines inched forward. By the end of February it was all over – the qualities of the Corps had won through.

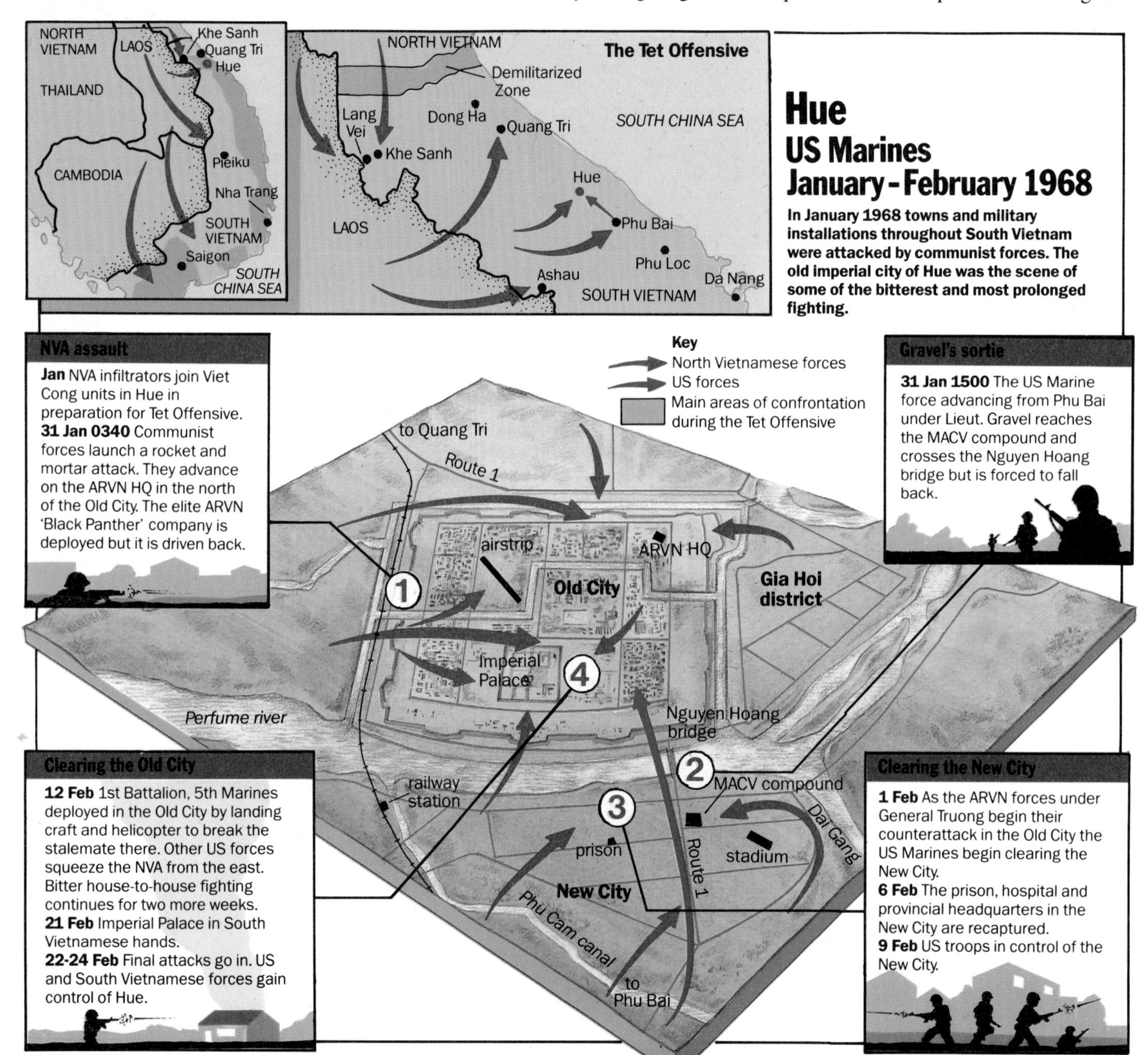

Hue
US Marines January-February 1968

In January 1968 towns and military installations throughout South Vietnam were attacked by communist forces. The old imperial city of Hue was the scene of some of the bitterest and most prolonged fighting.

NVA assault

Jan NVA infiltrators join Viet Cong units in Hue in preparation for Tet Offensive.
31 Jan 0340 Communist forces launch a rocket and mortar attack. They advance on the ARVN HQ in the north of the Old City. The elite ARVN 'Black Panther' company is deployed but it is driven back.

Gravel's sortie

31 Jan 1500 The US Marine force advancing from Phu Bai under Lieut. Gravel reaches the MACV compound and crosses the Nguyen Hoang bridge but is forced to fall back.

Clearing the Old City

12 Feb 1st Battalion, 5th Marines deployed in the Old City by landing craft and helicopter to break the stalemate there. Other US forces squeeze the NVA from the east. Bitter house-to-house fighting continues for two more weeks.
21 Feb Imperial Palace in South Vietnamese hands.
22-24 Feb Final attacks go in. US and South Vietnamese forces gain control of Hue.

Clearing the New City

1 Feb As the ARVN forces under General Truong begin their counterattack in the Old City the US Marines begin clearing the New City.
6 Feb The prison, hospital and provincial headquarters in the New City are recaptured.
9 Feb US troops in control of the New City.

26TH MARINE REGIMENT, KHE SANH, JANUARY-MARCH 1968

Beginning in January 1968, the US Marine Corps' 26th Regiment was besieged in Khe Sanh Combat Base by two North Vietnamese divisions. The Marines had studied the battle for Dien Bien Phu in an earlier Vietnamese war, when French forces had been defeated at the hands of the Viet Minh because they had allowed the latter to deploy large quantities of artillery in the hills surrounding their position. The Marines at Khe Sanh were determined not to repeat this mistake, and therefore occupied some of the high ground around their position. This allowed the Americans to engage the enemy and observe likely North Vietnamese routes of advance on the base.

One of the most important hills was 881S which overlooked Route 9 and was quickly occupied by the Marines. No supplies reached the base by road: everything had to be flown in. At first the aircraft were able to land, but when the flak became too intense only parachute drops were feasible. The Marines on the surrounding hills could only be reached by helicopter. Each hill was held by a company-sized unit, all part of or attached to the 26th Marines. Hill 881S was held by Company 1 ('India') and two platoons and the headquarters of Company M ('Mike'), 3rd Battalion, 26th Marines. With a section of 81mm mortars, 106mm recoilless rifles and a detachment of 105mm howitzers, the party totalled some 400 men.

There was heavy skirmishing around the hill on 18-20 January, with the enemy having the worst of it. Khe Sanh was attacked on the 21st, but Hill 881S was left alone. However, the mortars on the hill gave support fire all through the day, the tubes becoming so hot that a 'daisy chain' of Marines had to form to urinate on them to keep them cool!

On the 22nd the base was hit again. Fire came in from two sources: 152mm and 130mm guns situated in Laos, and 122mm Russian-made rockets fired in salvoes of 30 to 50 at a time. The North Vietnamese also turned their attention to Hill 881S, pounding it with well-dug-in 120mm mortars. By early February, the combined effects of the mortars and flak had cost Companies India and Mike 150 casualties and six helicopters. Such losses would normally have resulted in the position falling very quickly – but the Marines found a solution to the problem.

Operation 'Super Gaggle' was mounted in mid-February. On a pre-arranged signal, the mortars fired white phosphorus against all known anti-aircraft positions, and then a flight of four Marine A-4 Skyhawks attacked the positions marked by the mortars, closely followed by a second flight dropping napalm. Then two more A-4s dropped delayed-fuse bomblets. The mortars fired more white phosphorus and then 10 Marine CH-46 helicopters came in carrying externally slung supplies. A-4s laid thick smoke to hide their approach, and the choppers swooped in. Other lifts brought in men and more supplies, and although there was still enemy mortar and flak, it was largely ineffective.

The Marines constantly observed enemy positions, bringing heavy amounts of fire onto the North Vietnamese. The siege of the base wound down in March, with India Company having only 19 of the original 200 Marines who had taken up the defence of Hill 881S. Mike had fared little better. It was a heavy price to pay – but it led to success.

ABOVE: *This Marine at Khe Sanh has no doubts about his perilous position.*

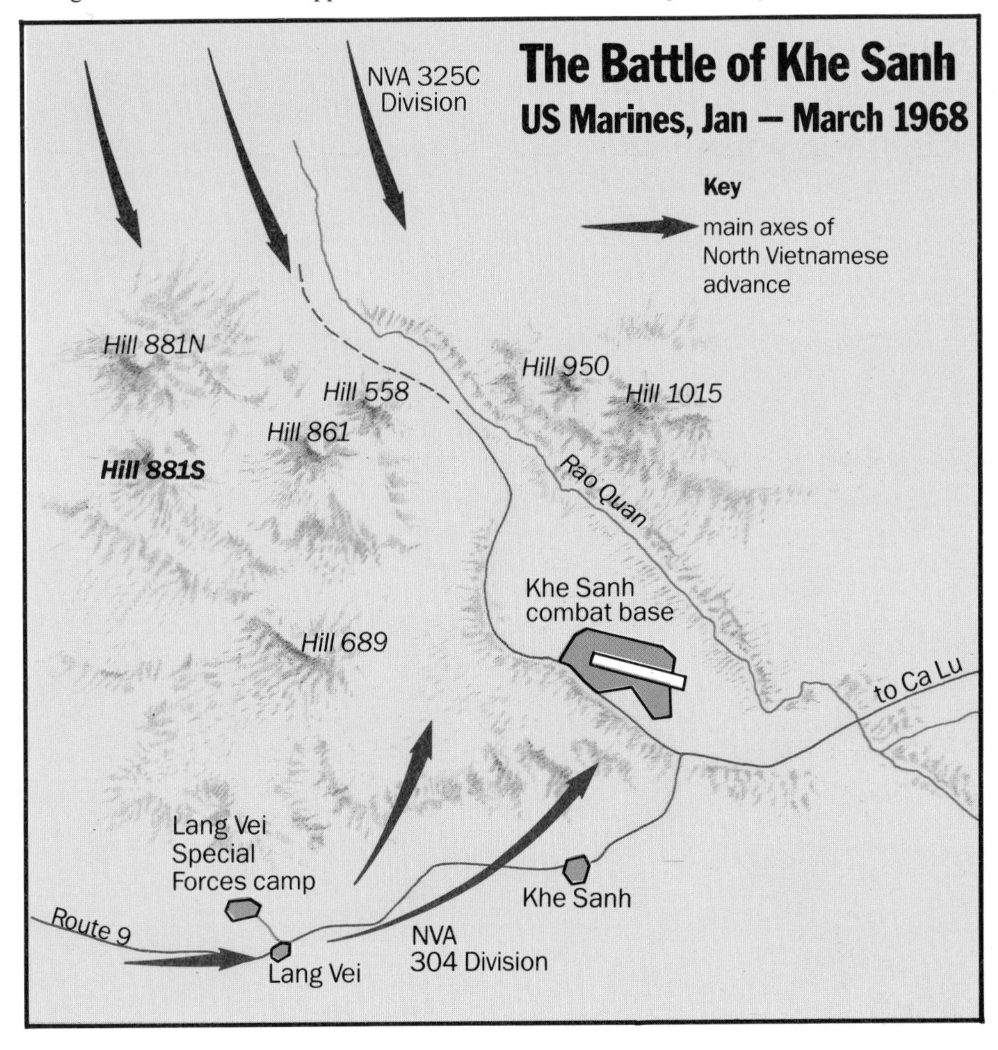

AUSTRALIAN ARMY TRAINING TEAM, BEN HET, 18-24 MAY 1969

In May 1969, a Mike (mobile strike) Force battalion of Montagnards was attacked and badly mauled by a regiment of the North Vietnamese Army (NVA) deep in the jungle highlands of South Vietnam. The battalion withdrew in disarray, leaving the wounded to their fate in enemy territory. Their subsequent rescue is an extraordinary tale of the heroism of one man.

The enemy hits Ben Het

Keith Payne was a member of the Australian Army Training Team, Vietnam (AATTV), which was tasked with advising field units of both the Army of the Republic of South Vietnam (ARVN) and paramilitary forces. Payne was based in Pleiku Province and commanded the 212th Company in the 1st Mike Force Battalion of recruited Montagnards. His unit was deployed in the tri-border area of Laos, Cambodia and Vietnam. There was increased NVA activity in the area in April and May 1969, and in late May the enemy laid siege to the village of Ben Het, which lay astride Route 512 and would provide the NVA with an important infiltration line into South Vietnam if it fell. The NVA's 24th Regiment was besieging the village, but it was believed that the 66th Regiment was also approaching from Laos. Payne's battalion was tasked with finding and engaging the 66th Regiment.

The NVA holds the ridge

The three companies of the battalion – the 211th, 212th and 213th – were commanded by Warrant Officer Tolley, Payne and Sergeant Montez respectively. Payne had 89 men in his company, but many of them were ill-trained Montagnards. On 18 May, the battalion was lifted to a ridge line 9km southwest of Ben Het. Four days later, the 5th Mike Force was landed by helicopter on a ridge 4km to the south and Payne's battalion joined it the same afternoon. The next morning the unit was ordered to move out and locate the 66th Regiment. Tolley's company was the first to move, running straight into the enemy and being forced to withdraw. Montez's company tried next, but it too was forced to withdraw.

That night orders came through for the 1st Battalion, with the 5th in support, to clear the enemy from the ridge. An air strike preceded the ground troops, but when the latter advanced they soon ran into heavy, concentrated small-arms fire which caused many Montagnard casualties. In fact, the enemy had pulled back to escape the air strikes and were now moving forward to trap the battalion. Withering fire from four machine guns, rockets and highly accurate mortars tore into the position. An NVA company then wedged itself between the two forward companies and Tolley's and began firing on Tolley. Things were starting to go badly wrong.

The Montagnards crack

Tolley's company became isolated from the rest of the battalion, and efforts by the other two to relieve him came to nothing. Payne ran from position to position, encouraging his men and firing at the enemy with everything he could lay his hands on. His leadership was superb: in one incident, for example, a rocket-propelled grenade exploded near him, decapitating his radio operator and whipping Payne's Armalite out of his hands. He grabbed an M60 machine gun and continued to fire at the enemy, now bleeding heavily from a head wound. Faced by his determined action the enemy faltered, then pressed forward once more. The half-trained Montagnard tribesmen began to run in panic, though Payne, cutting across the exposed ground, managed to stem the disordered retreat. He was now seriously wounded, having been wounded a second time by mortar and rocket splinters in his hands and arms, but he reorganised the companies into a temporary defensive line in the valley, approximately 350m from the ridge. All the time North Vietnamese fire continued to pour down onto them.

The action had resulted in very heavy casualties: Payne, Montez, Latham, Lieutenant Forbes (the US artillery coordinator), and Lieutenant James (the acting battalion commander) had all been wounded. In addition, several Montagnard soldiers had been killed and many more wounded.

Payne goes behind enemy lines

However, many men were left wounded in enemy territory, with others being unaccounted for. Payne requested, and received, permission to go and collect as many men as he could. He set off alone at dusk. He knew that he would have the best chance alone: there were no other advisors available and it was no use taking any Montagnards, as he did not speak their language and they would only make a noise and increase his chance of being detected. Therefore, Payne set off armed with only an Armalite and carrying a radio. Few thought they would ever see him again.

Payne is awarded the VC

In fact, he made four separate trips, each time collecting more stragglers and wounded, though he himself came close to physical and mental exhaustion. When he returned with the last band he found the battalion had gone (it had left to establish contact with the 5th). Payne decided to follow it, and so the party slipped and staggered through 1000m of jungle at night, until it reached safety at 0310 hours on 25 May. After the mauling it had received, the 1st Mike Force was withdrawn for a rest, re-equipping and re-training. It returned to Ben Het some time later, though by then the NVA, severely battered and somewhat demoralised, had withdrawn. For his actions Payne was awarded the Victoria Cross. Indeed, such was the quality of the AATTV that it finished the war in Vietnam with a staggering four Victoria Crosses and numerous other Imperial, American and Vietnamese awards, a fine testament to a unit that numbered on average only 100 soldiers.

Ben Het

1st Mike Force Battalion, May 1969

During April and May 1969 the North Vietnamese Army built up its forces in the South Vietnamese province of Kontum close to the Laotian and Cambodian borders. The 24th and 27th NVA Regiments laid siege to the village of Ben Het, guarding what was potentially a major infiltration route into the Vietnamese central highlands. With the suspected arrival of the 66th NVA Regiment in the area, the 1st Mike Force Battalion (MFB) was deployed with orders to find and engage the enemy.

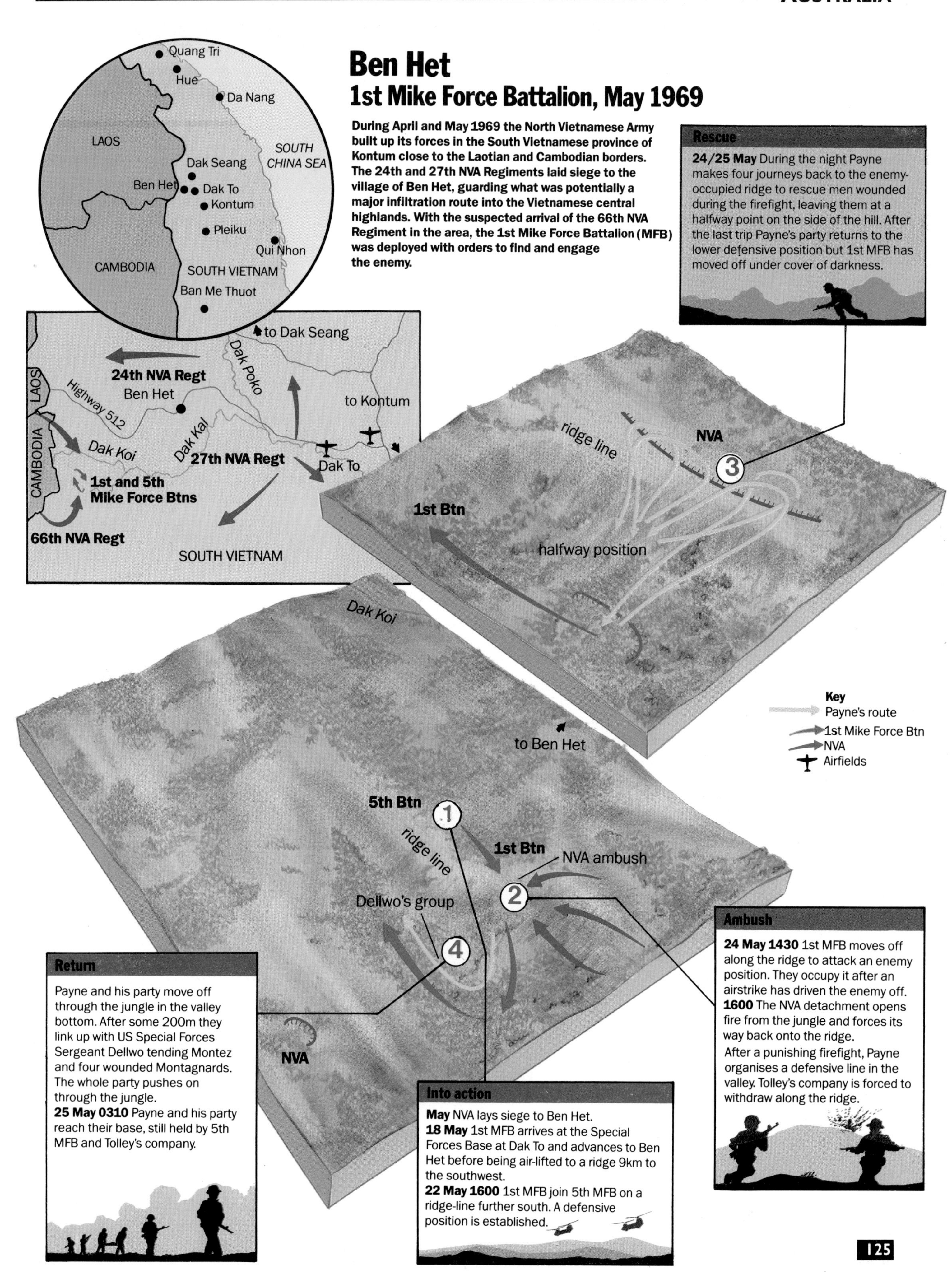

101ST AIRBORNE DIVISION (AIRMOBILE), HAMBURGER HILL, 10-20 MAY 1969

The taking of Hamburger Hill – or Hill 937 – was one of the most famous incidents of the Vietnam War, and one that illustrates the fighting spirit of the American airborne soldier. The US 101st Airborne Division's 3rd Brigade had been lifted into the area on 10 May, and the next day began to comb for enemy troop concentrations and supply dumps (the area was a prime infiltration route for North Vietnamese heading across the Ho Chi Minh Trail).

The first contact was made with the enemy on 11 May, machine-gun fire halting the advance of Company B of the 3rd Battalion, 187th Infantry. Calling in artillery and air strikes, the company waited until the area in front of it had been pulverised with napalm and shells before advancing. However, the US troops again ran into small-arms fire. The enemy had not budged. By the following day, 12 May, Lieutenant-Colonel Honeycutt, the battalion commander, had committed all four of his companies to the struggle for Hill 937. The enemy had stayed put, and the Americans were intent on destroying him.

Throughout the day the enemy were subjected to artillery and air strikes, while Companies C and D worked their way up the forward slopes of the hill. However, they ran into intense fire – the North Vietnamese were dug in to incredibly strong emplacements which offered interlocking fields of fire. Very soon the two companies had suffered four dead and 33 wounded and were forced to retire.

The next day Companies B, C and D went up, only to be sent packing again. Undeterred, Colonel Joseph Conmy, 3 Brigade's commander, and Honeycutt prepared for another assault on the 15th. Throughout the night AC-47 gunships poured fire into the enemy positions with their 7.62mm miniguns. However, the next day witnessed another grim battle. Companies A and B moved forward, accompanied by helicopters which blasted the enemy bunkers with rockets.

BELOW: *US airborne troops engage North Vietnamese forces in May 1969.*

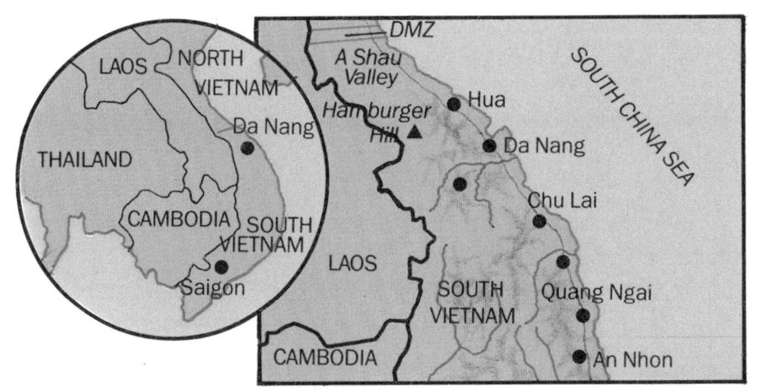

101st Airborne Division (Airmobile)

Hamburger Hill, 10-20 May 1969

Early in May 1969, the US 101st Airborne Division was tasked with blocking the movement of NVA forces from Laos along the A Shau Valley into South Vietnam. The operation, codenamed Apache Snow, began on 10 May. The division's 3rd Brigade deployed by helicopter near Hill 937, known as Hamburger Hill, and began a series of assaults on NVA defensive positions in the area.

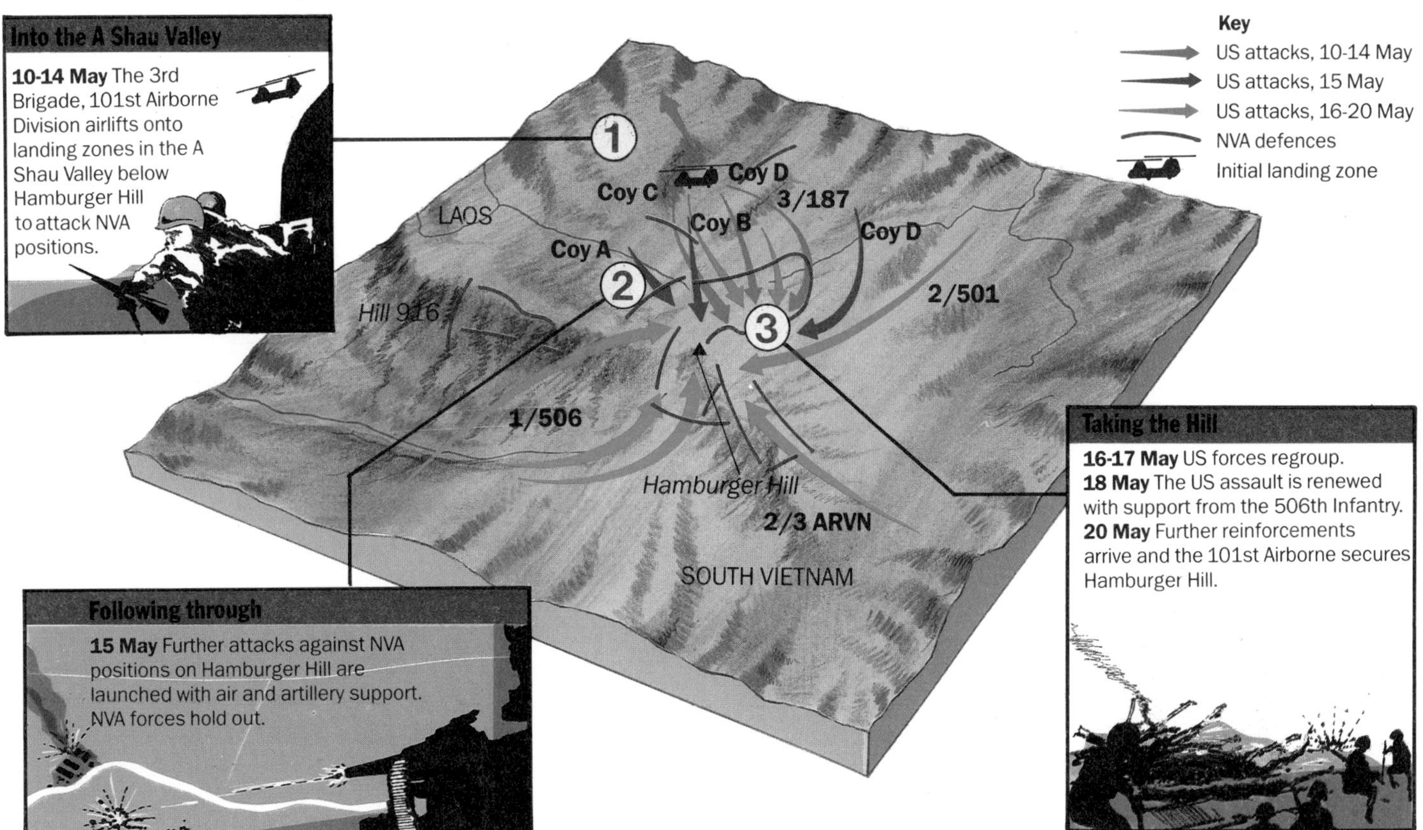

Bunker after bunker fell, the enemy had been overrun and the US soldiers could see the crest of the hill. Then, disaster struck. The coordination between air and ground units went desperately wrong, and a gunship swooped down, pouring fire into the flanks of Company B. As men started to fall the attack fell apart.

Nevertheless, both Conmy and Honeycutt believed the hill had to be taken, regardless of cost. Honeycutt was wounded three times but refused to be evacuated. Another attack went, this time involving the 1st Battalion, 506th Infantry as well the 187th. The fresh attack began on the 18th, the 3rd Battalion going in again where so many of its men had fallen, chewed to mincemeat, hence the name – Hamburger Hill. The terrain was a moonscape: shell-blasted trees and churned up earth. Despite enemy fire and booby traps the airborne soldiers again had victory within their grasp. Then, in the early afternoon, it began to rain heavily, turning the slopes into a quagmire. Men became stuck in the mud, and soon, demoralised, they had fallen back under the constant enemy fire. The battalion had lost 14 killed and 64 wounded in the day-long battle. Morale nose-dived.

Another unit, the 2nd Battalion, 501st Infantry, was air-lifted in, together with a battalion of the South Vietnamese Army. On the ground there was much hostility towards Honeycutt, with the men believing he wouldn't be satisfied until he had got them all killed. Despite all the complaining, the men of the 101st went up the hill again on the 20th. At last the enemy had been worn down, and the men went up almost unmolested. By noon the 3rd of the 187th had reached the crest of the hill and began clearing the enemy positions bunker by bunker. The men were soon joined by the 1st of the 506th, which had broken through from the west. By nightfall Hamburger Hill had been taken, but at what cost? The Americans had lost 60 dead and 300 wounded, and the position was abandoned one week after it had been taken. Nevertheless, it was a superb example of the sheer guts of the American airborne soldier.

US SPECIAL FORCES, SON TAY, 21 NOVEMBER 1970

The 1970 Son Tay raid was an ambitious, though ultimately unsuccessful, operation mounted by the US Special Forces. It proved that the North Vietnamese were vulnerable to attacks within their territory, and also illustrated the flexibility and expertise of America's Green Berets. Its origin was the discovery of American POWs at a prison 37km west of Hanoi, at Son Tay. Brigadier-General Donald Blackburn, the Special Assistant for Counter-insurgency and Special Activities, was tasked with preparing the mission. The raid was led by Colonel 'Bull' Simons, the party being called the Joint Contingency Task Group (JCTG) and the mission codenamed 'Ivory Coast'.

The optimum time for the raid appeared to be between 20/25 October, when the weather and moon would be most favourable. Some 85 men, mostly from the 6th and 7th Special Forces Groups, were chosen for the raid. A mock-up of the prison compound was built at Eglin Air Force Base in Florida (it was designed to be dismantled during the day and set up at night to deceive Soviet spy satellites). Detailed planning of the raid began on 9 September.

Planning for perfection

The assault force comprised three assault groups: the compound assault force of 14 men; the command and security group of 20 men; and the support group of 22 men led by Simons himself. Five HH-53 and one HH-3 helicopter would carry the assault troops, all being refuelled in mid-air during the flight. Other aircraft that would be involved included three C-130s and A-1 strike aircraft.

The actual assault was practised many times, with alternative plans being formulated in case one of the three teams failed to make it to the target. In addition, Simons had his force equipped with special hardware for the operation: 12-gauge shotguns, 30-round M16 magazines, CAR-15s for the compound assault force, M-79 grenade launchers, LAWs, bolt cutters, cutting torches, chainsaws and special goggles.

Simons and his men then moved to Southeast Asia, and President Nixon

Assault on the compound

21 Nov 0218 Son Tay camp is illuminated by a C-130 flare-ship and strafed. Meadows' assault force lands inside the compound and goes into action, firing and rushing forward to cell blocks 'Opium Den,' 'Cat House' and 'Beer House'. The command group under Sydnor lands outside and blasts its way through the compound's south wall.
0226 Having cleared the enemy at the 'secondary school' site, Simons' group is heli-lifted to the Son Tay compound to assist with mopping up enemy forces.
0236 The first helicopter returns from the holding area and withdrawal of the raiding force begins.

LEFT: *An HH-53 helicopter, similar to those employed in the Son Tay raid, undergoes aerial refuelling over South Vietnam. These aircraft are ideal for operations behind enemy lines, being rugged, having a comprehensive avionics suite and a large fuselage that can contain up to 37 fully equipped troops.*

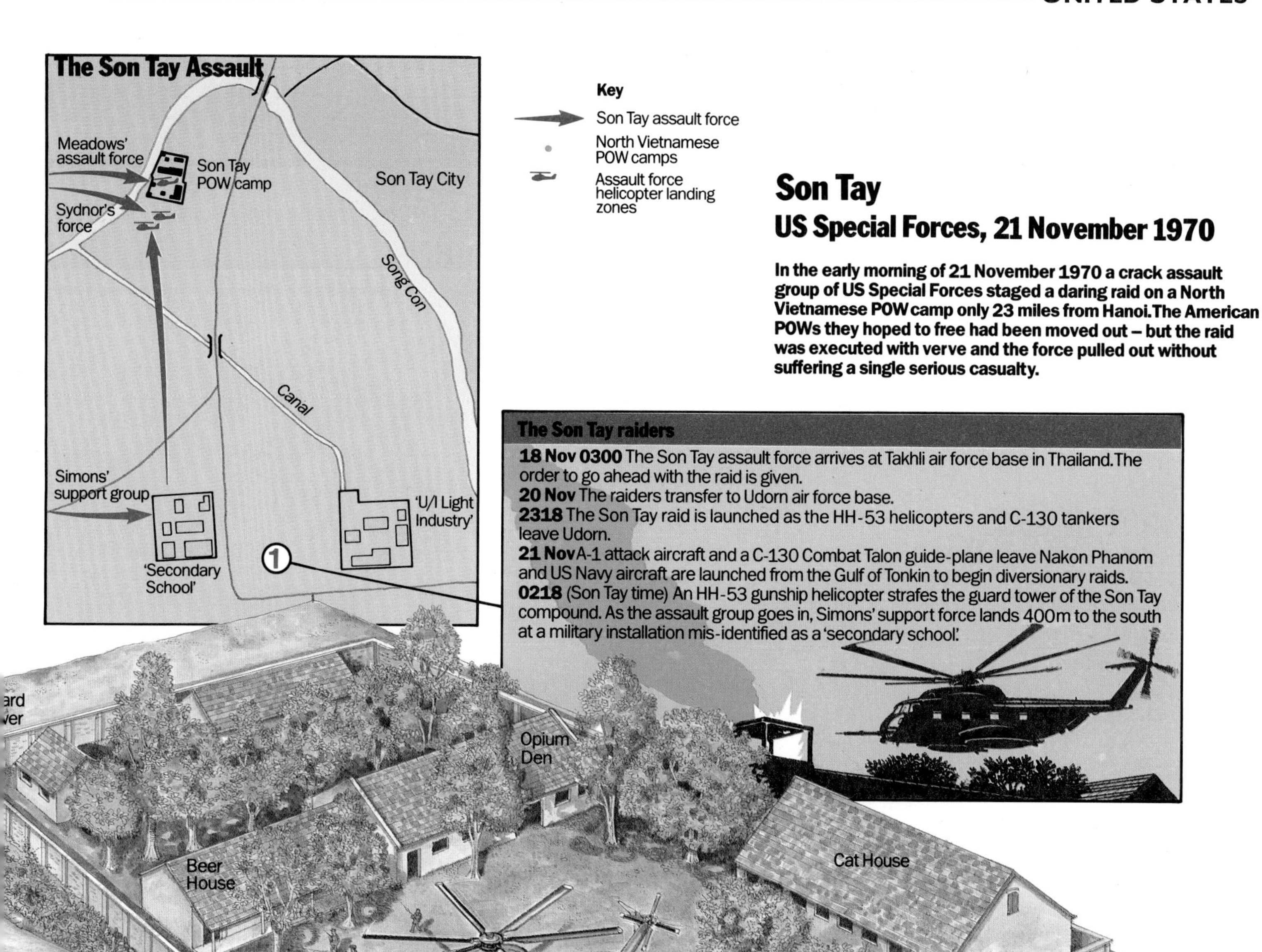

Son Tay

US Special Forces, 21 November 1970

In the early morning of 21 November 1970 a crack assault group of US Special Forces staged a daring raid on a North Vietnamese POW camp only 23 miles from Hanoi. The American POWs they hoped to free had been moved out – but the raid was executed with verve and the force pulled out without suffering a single serious casualty.

The Son Tay raiders

18 Nov 0300 The Son Tay assault force arrives at Takhli air force base in Thailand. The order to go ahead with the raid is given.
20 Nov The raiders transfer to Udorn air force base.
2318 The Son Tay raid is launched as the HH-53 helicopters and C-130 tankers leave Udorn.
21 Nov A-1 attack aircraft and a C-130 Combat Talon guide-plane leave Nakon Phanom and US Navy aircraft are launched from the Gulf of Tonkin to begin diversionary raids.
0218 (Son Tay time) An HH-53 gunship helicopter strafes the guard tower of the Son Tay compound. As the assault group goes in, Simons' support force lands 400m to the south at a military installation mis-identified as a 'secondary school.'

gave the go-ahead. The raid began at 2318 hours on the evening of 20 November, with carrier aircraft being launched to create a diversion by staging a fake raid over Hanoi. At the compound all went well, except that there were no prisoners – they had been moved elsewhere some weeks before the raid. This had not been picked up by US intelligence because no one had wanted to risk putting in any agents on the ground, and far too much reliance had been placed on photographic intelligence.

Within 30 minutes the helicopters were off the ground and heading for Thailand. Casualties were light: only one man was wounded. In addition, the support group, though landed 400m off course, had destroyed a building containing Soviet or Chinese advisors, preventing the latter from reinforcing the prison guards.

The Son Tay raid was not a complete failure; it did result in the North Vietnamese tying down additional troops to guard sensitive areas, and it had also resulted in the deaths of dozens of foreign advisors without a single US casualty. In addition, the North Vietnamese lost some credibility with the Chinese and Russians, who feared that the US would continue to mount raids into North Vietnam. Finally, it led to some improvement in the treatment of POWs. It also demonstrated that the US Special Forces had the flair and imagination to plan, mount and successfully execute what was an extremely ambitious project.

CHAPTER IV

ARAB-ISRAELI WARS

The state of Israel has some of the finest soldiers in the world. In every war the Jewish state has fought since its creation in 1948, her armies have been victorious (albeit in 1956 aided by France and Britain). Israeli troops have always been highly motivated, well trained and, perhaps most importantly, aggressively yet intelligently led. The latter point cannot be over-stressed. Men such as Ariel 'Arik' Sharon, Rafael Eitan, Israel Tal, Mordecai Gur and Moshe Dayan led their men with imagination and flair. Often they got themselves into tricky situations, an example being Ariel Sharon's 202nd Parachute Brigade at the Mitla Pass in October 1956. However, the daring and elan of the Israelis usually won through.

It is no coincidence that many of the actions featured in this chapter concern Israeli paratroopers. The paras are an elite within what is an elite army, and it is no surprise that they have won some of the most famous victories in Israel's history: the capture of the Old City of Jerusalem in 1967, the bloody engagement at 'Chinese Farm' in 1973, and the clearing of Sidon of Palestine Liberation Organisation (PLO) guerrillas during the invasion of Lebanon in 1982. Other Israeli units featured in this chapter include the Golani Brigade, whose capture of Beaufort Castle in 1982 is an object lesson in how to attack supposedly impregnable positions; the 7th Armoured Brigade's epic defence of the Golan Heights against overwhelming numbers of Syrian tanks in the Yom Kippur War; and the daring assault made by Israeli commandos on the Egyptian radar station on Green Island in 1969.

It is unfortunate for the Arab nations that they have such a capable adversary. This has resulted in their suffering a number of defeats. In the 1967 Six-Day War, for example, the Israelis lost nearly 700 killed, but the Arabs lost 3000 killed, 6000 wounded and 12,000 prisoners, as well as large amounts of military equipment destroyed. There have, nevertheless, been some Arab successes, most notably during the initial stages of the 1973 Yom Kippur War, when Egyptian Commandos captured the east bank of the Suez Canal. The Egyptians then spilled into the Sinai and destroyed large numbers of Israeli aircraft and tanks with their dense anti-aircraft defences and anti-tank weapons. Despite this, Israel managed to gain the upper hand and eventually won the war, giving the Syrians a particularly bloody nose on the Golan Front. The 1982 Israeli invasion of Lebanon again demonstrated the superior fighting skills of Israel's soldiers, particularly in Beirut and Sidon, where PLO guerrillas and Syrian troops had to be dislodged from entrenched positions.

A battle-scarred Israeli Centurion tank near the Jordanian border. Israeli tank crews have traditionally been well trained and highly motivated.

JORDANIAN ARAB LEGION, JERUSALEM, MAY 1948

At 1800 hours on 18 May 1948, Lieutenant-General John Glubb, commander of the Jordanian Arab Legion, sent 1 Garrison Company into the Old City of Jerusalem during the first Arab-Israeli War. The Legion succeeded in driving back the surprised Israelis, but Glubb realised that he quickly needed reinforcements if he was to hold back the enemy, who had superior numbers and armaments. Therefore, he signalled his field commander, Brigadier Norman Nash, for help. The latter despatched Major Bob Slade, Suffolk Regiment, who was commander of the Legion's 2nd Regiment. Slade's column consisted of an armoured car squadron and the 6-pounder and 3in mortar platoons from his own regiment, plus two companies of the 5th Regiment and 8 Company of the 6th Regiment, altogether 500 men.

Slade had to fight his way through the suburb of Sheikh Jarrah, which took time and cost casualties, and he himself was wounded. Nevertheless, by 1400 hours the armoured cars arrived at the Damascus Gate. Though the Legion had control of the Old City, platoons and sections were spread dangerously thin, and it was clear more troops were needed.

The battle for the Old City

As a consequence, the 3rd Regiment under Lieutenant-Colonel Gordon Newman was ordered to Jerusalem. It set off on the evening of 20 May and fought its way to the Notre Dame de France monastery, where its leading companies were then pinned down by Israeli fire. The battle raged for the next three days. Inside the Old City, meanwhile, the Legion fought desperately for possession of the old streets. This was a soldiers' battle, the senior commanders being able to do little to influence the fighting.

By 25 May it was clear to Glubb that his men could not continue to take such crippling casualties; they were being bled to death (in fact, the Israelis were in an equally desperate state). Newman was told to cease attacks on the Notre Dame de France, and both sides halted to lick their wounds. The Old City had been taken, but only just. The battle for Jerusalem had been a keenly fought contest, but the Arab Legion had prevailed in the face of overwhelming odds by the professionalism of its mainly British officers and the elan, training and dedication of its men. In particular, the despatch of an armoured column into an enemy-held urban area without aircraft or artillery support was totally against the rules of war, but it had worked.

The Legion's Offensive
May 1948

On 14 May 1948, following the United Nations' decision to partition Palestine, Britain withdrew her forces and open confronation broke out between Arab and Jew. The fledgling state of Israel struggled to survive as the combined armies of her Arab neighbours invaded. The Israelis' most formidable opponents were the British-trained and officered men of the Jordanian Arab Legion.

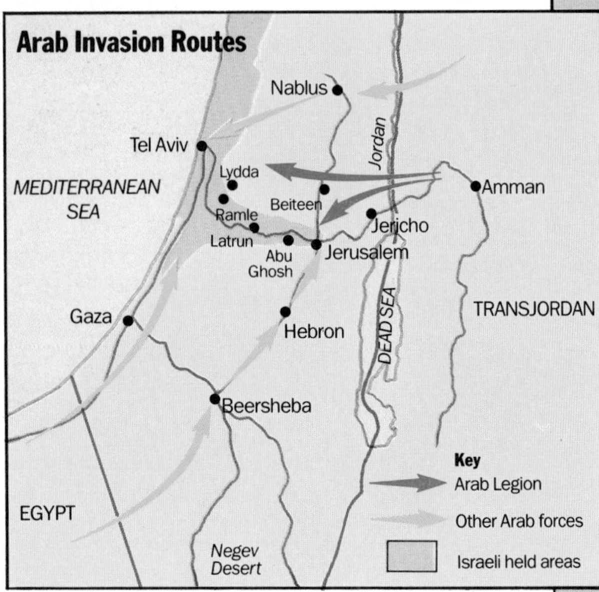

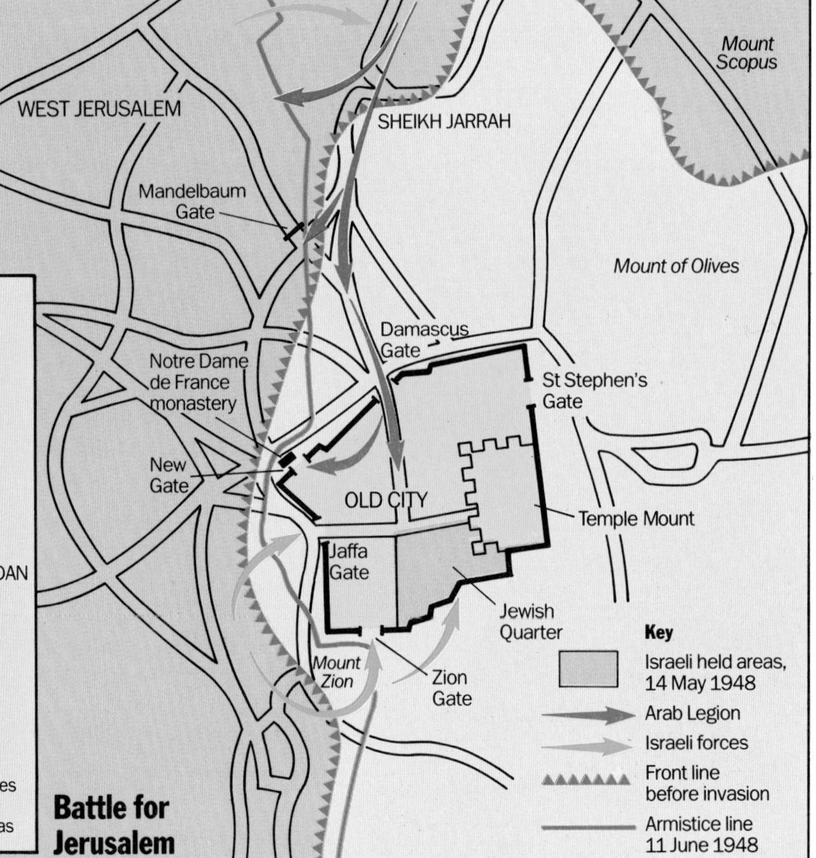

202ND PARACHUTE BRIGADE, THE MITLA PASS, 29-31 OCTOBER 1956

When the 395 men of the 1st Battalion of the newly formed Israeli 202nd Parachute Brigade jumped into the Mitla Pass on 29 October 1956, it was a gamble. The lightly equipped men were to seize the strategically vital Pass and hold it until they linked up with the rest of the brigade under Colonel Ariel 'Arik' Sharon, as part of the surprise Israeli attack on Egypt. The paras, led by Lieutenant-Colonel Rafael 'Raful' Eitan, made a good landing and, after clearing the Pass of some Egyptian guards, dug in and awaited their comrades who were driving west into the Sinai to link up with them. Sharon's force, consisting of the other two battalions of the 202nd, two battalions of half-tracks, 13 AMX-13 tanks, a battery of 25-pounders and a heavy mortar company, smashed through the Egyptian defences at El Kuntilla and headed for El Thamad, 60km to the west.

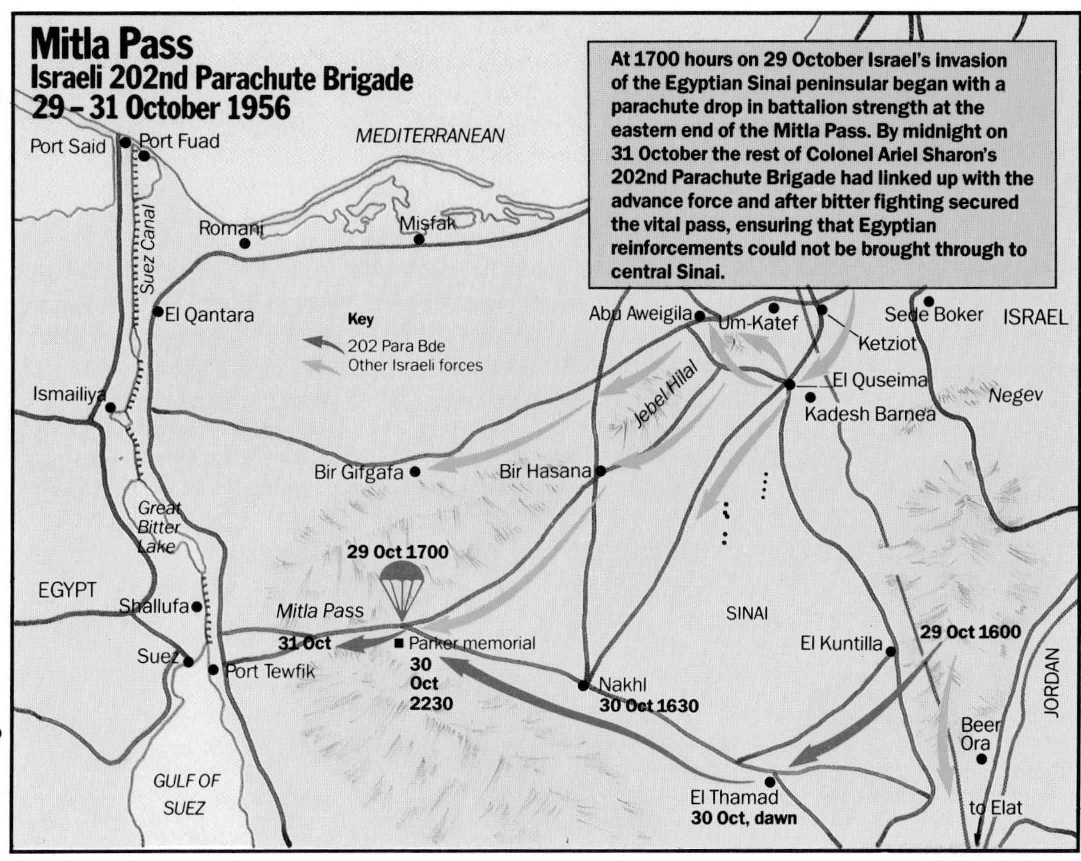

This was a tough nut to crack, being defended by two Sudanese companies ensconced behind barbed wire and a minefield. Nevertheless, Sharon's men, the sun at their backs, attacked vigorously at dawn on the 30th, the paras driving their half-tracks into the heart of the Sudanese defences. They took the position, scattering the enemy for the loss of only four killed and six wounded. Then Sharon had to call a halt: his men were exhausted after the two actions.

Pushing on, the column reached Nakhl and drove off the garrison. Mitla was only 65km away. Driving hard, Sharon linked up with Eitan at 2230 hours. However, the Israelis' problems weren't over. Elements of the Egyptian 2nd Brigade had reached the area by the 30th, and had taken up position around and in some caves on the Jebel Heitan that lay along the southern edge of the road from Suez, and in dug-outs along a ridge to the north. Every section of the Pass had been turned into a killing ground.

Sharon was unaware of this, but he realised that his paras were exposed to air attack and so sought to move deeper into the Pass. He despatched two reinforced companies under 'Motta' Gur into the defile to reconnoitre the area. Gur's force entered the Pass and was ambushed. However, despite taking heavy losses the vehicles pressed on until they reached the middle of the Pass, where they were forced to halt.

Sharon was forced to send another column, under Aharon Davidi, to rescue Gur. The Egyptian positions were located using a sacrificial jeep, driven by a volunteer, which drew the enemy's fire. Having pinpointed their enemies, the paras waited until dark and then crawled beneath the caves. Armed with Uzis and hand grenades, the paras then began clearing the caves: lobbing in grenades and then firing their sub-machine guns. The battle raged for two and a half hours, the paras eventually holding the Pass by midnight. The cost, however, had been high: 38 dead and 120 wounded. The paras' fighting spirit had overcome an ambush that would have defeated lesser units, but it was a timely reminder of the cost of engaging units that were in well-defended positions.

ABOVE: *Lietenant-Colonel Eitan (right), who fought at the Mitla Pass.*

3RD BATTALION, THE PARACHUTE REGIMENT, SUEZ, 5-6 NOVEMBER 1956

All airborne operations are risky, but what makes the difference is good planning, timely support for the men when they hit the ground, and a degree of luck. Operation 'Musketeer', the Anglo-French attempt to regain control of the Suez Canal after it had been seized by Egypt's President Nasser, was certainly well planned. It involved 80,000 men who were spearheaded by the British 16th Independent Parachute Brigade and 3 Commando Brigade, Royal Marines. Leading the French forces were their 10th Parachute Division and the 7th Mechanised Division.

The Paras landed during the morning of 5 November 1956. The machine-gun fire was intense as the men drifted down from their Valetta transports. When they hit the ground they quickly located their equipment canisters and began engaging the enemy. Individual Egyptians fought bravely, and engaged in savage battles with the British soldiers. After a series of vicious close-quarter encounters, the enemy fled towards Port Said.

It had been a good day, and an excellent example of how a parachute drop should be conducted. All of 3rd Battalion's objectives had been secured. The unit had done well in the face of an enemy with strong numbers and armour.

Suez
3rd Battalion, The Parachute Regiment 5-6 Nov 1956

Spearheading the Anglo-French effort to reopen the Suez Canal after its closure by President Nasser of Egypt, 3 Para carried out a successful assault on Gamil airfield, to the west of Port Said, early on 5 November 1956. As the amphibious assault on Port Said was launched the following day, 3 Para provided vital covering fire from its positions to the west and was heavily engaged throughout the day's fighting.

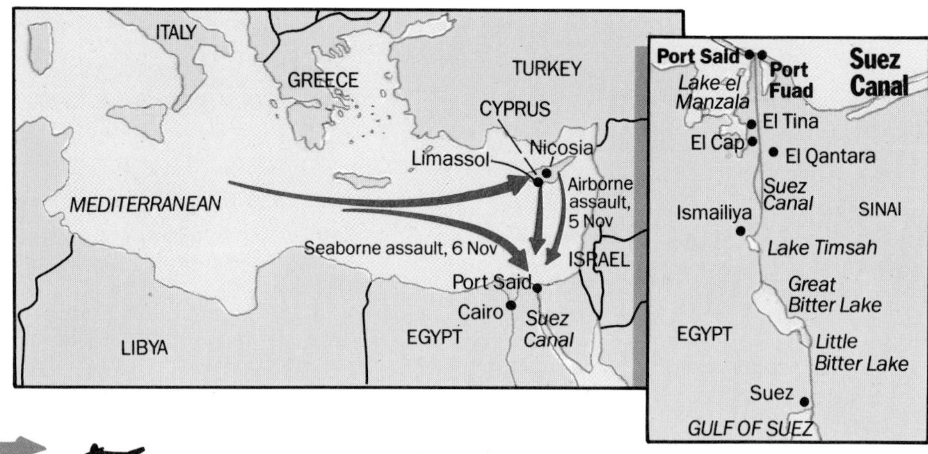

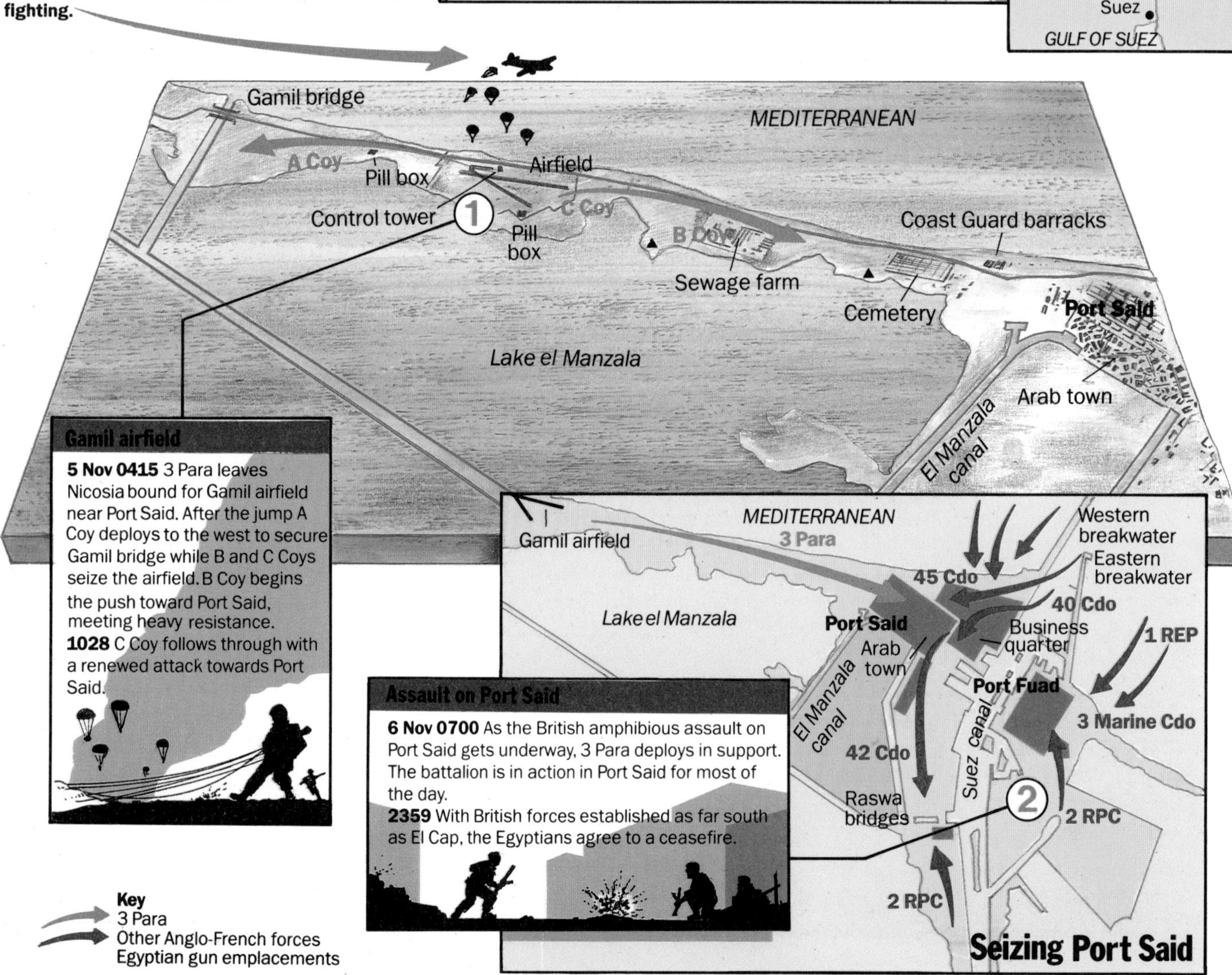

ROYAL MARINE COMMANDOS, SUEZ, 5-6 NOVEMBER 1956

The men of 40 and 42 Commandos, Royal Marines, were to be the first Allied troops into Port Said as part of Operation 'Musketeer', the Anglo-French seizure of the Suez Canal in November 1956. The Marines were landed in tracked amphibious vehicles (LVTs), each one capable of carrying 30 men, while Royal Navy ships pounded the shoreline during the run-in. Overhead, Fleet Air Arm aircraft strafed the beach. The naval bombardment was forbidden to go farther than the second row of buildings on the beach; after that the Marines were on their own.

Hitting the beach, the Marines were pleasantly surprised to discover that the Royal Navy had done its stuff: there was no enemy fusillade. In fact, the Egyptian Army had withdrawn to the hinterland, many men having thrown away their weapons. The next stage of the operation could now be mounted: a dash through the town in amphibious vehicles, supported by the Centurion tanks of C Squadron, 6th Royal Tank Regiment, to secure the Nile Cold Storage Depot and the Port Said power station.

Driving through an enemy town, where every building and roof-top could contain a sniper or anti-tank team, and where every road can be mined, is not easy. Fortunately, there was little resistance that day. Had there been, the fact that, because of an oversight, the sides of the amphibious vehicles had not been fitted with armoured plate, could have turned the drive into a bloody shambles.

In fact, the column actually pressed too far forward, ran into an Egyptian Army camp, and so withdrew to the Cold Storage Depot. While waiting for further orders, they heard that a temporary cease-fire had been called: there would be no more fighting. What the Marines had done that day was to conduct an almost perfect amphibious landing and had then gone on to clear a large part of Port Said at little cost. They had won the battle for the town with classic military efficiency.

Suez: assault on Port Said
5-6 Nov 1956

On 26 July 1956, President Nasser of Egypt nationalised the Anglo-French Suez Canal Company, provoking an international crisis that resulted in a joint British and French assault on Port Said. As Britain and France prepared for war, gathering an expeditionary force in the Mediterranean, secret meetings were held with the representatives of the Israeli government. On 29 October, Israel invaded Sinai. An Anglo-French ultimatum to withdraw from the canal zone was rejected by Egypt and the way was open for the RAF to neutralise Egyptian air force bases in the area.

Early on 5 November, 3 Para and 2 RPC made advance airborne landings, and the following morning the main assault went in.

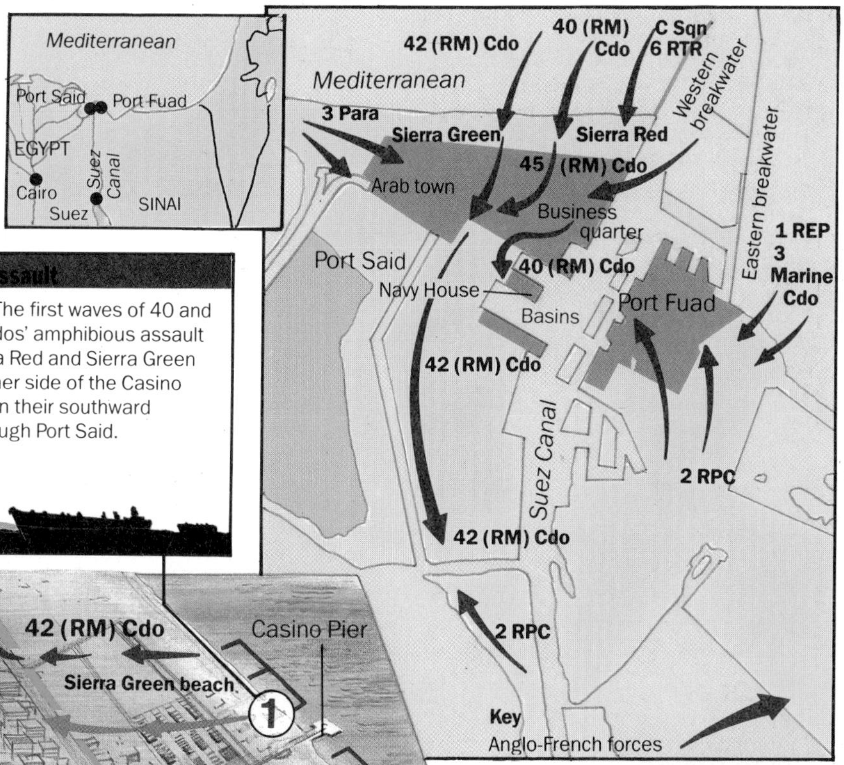

Seaborne assault

6 Nov 0430 The first waves of 40 and 42 Commandos' amphibious assault land on Sierra Red and Sierra Green Beaches, either side of the Casino Pier, and begin their southward advance through Port Said.

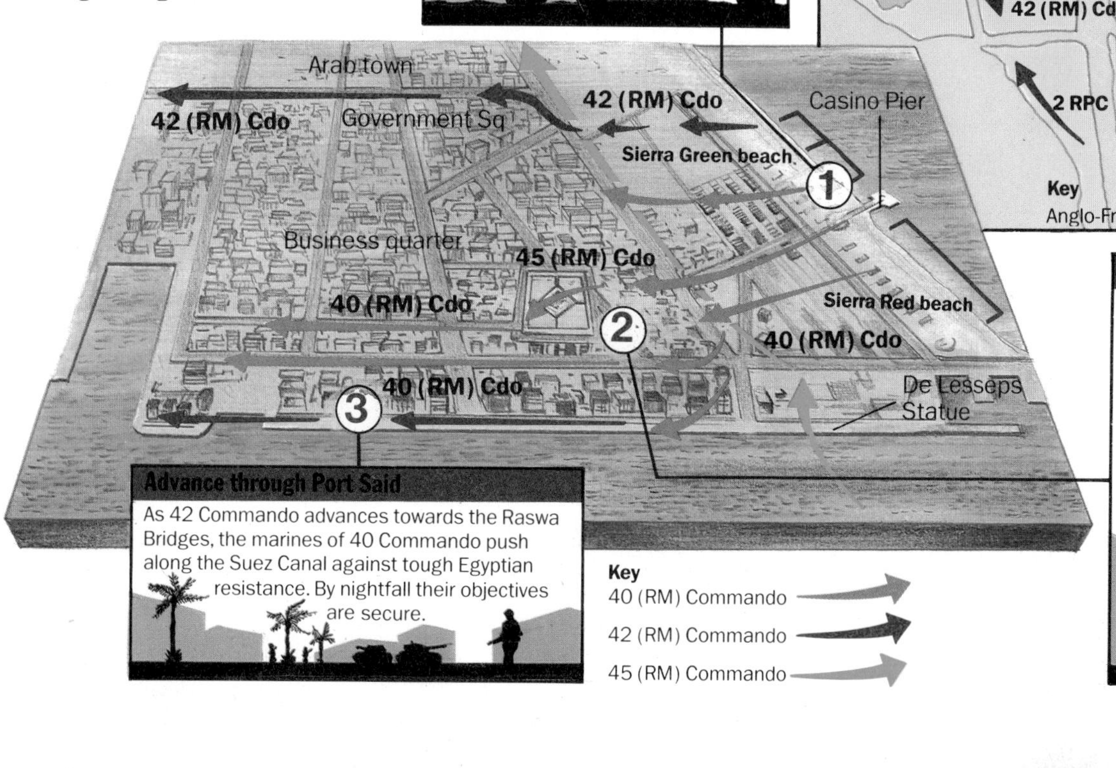

Airborne assault

0530 As 40 and 42 Commandos advance through Port Said, 45 Commando's heliborne assault begins. The marines land by helicopter near the statue of de Lesseps and begin a westward drive, linking up with 3 Para before nightfall.

Advance through Port Said

As 42 Commando advances towards the Raswa Bridges, the marines of 40 Commando push along the Suez Canal against tough Egyptian resistance. By nightfall their objectives are secure.

Key
40 (RM) Commando
42 (RM) Commando
45 (RM) Commando

Key
Anglo-French forces

202ND PARACHUTE BRIGADE, THE GAZA STRIP, 5-6 JUNE 1967

During the Six-Day War of 1967, the Israeli 202nd Parachute Brigade, led by Rafael Eitan, was tasked with clearing Egyptian forces from the Gaza Strip and Sinai. The war began in the early hours of 5 June, with Israeli aircraft conducting bombing and strafing runs. Eitan's main problem was keeping his formations in order. One of the Israeli tanks was knocked out, but the main force managed to get behind the Egyptian lines and immediately destroyed a company of enemy tanks. Scything through the flanks of the Egyptians, the Israelis quickly reached the road between Rafah and El Arish.

Eitan then gave the order to advance to Rafah junction. However, his tanks were in trouble. Some had only an hour's worth of fuel left in their tanks, others had no ammunition left. Undeterred, he ordered the tanks with low fuel to advance as far as they could, while the ones with no ammunition were not to shoot! The force, which had no more than five tanks, charged forward. The result was amazing: hundreds of Egyptian soldiers fled to the west.

The next day the 202nd was detailed to help clear the enemy from Gaza. Though lacking clear instructions, Eitan decided to head for Khan Yunis, which was stormed by the paras. The excellent training and the superb leadership qualities of their officers, especially Eitan himself, was beginning to pay off.

Later that day he was ordered to head south to the Suez Canal. The first enemy encountered were Egyptian tanks, but these were soon knocked out. Pressing on, and despite losing Eitan wounded, the 202nd reached the Suez Canal on 8 June.

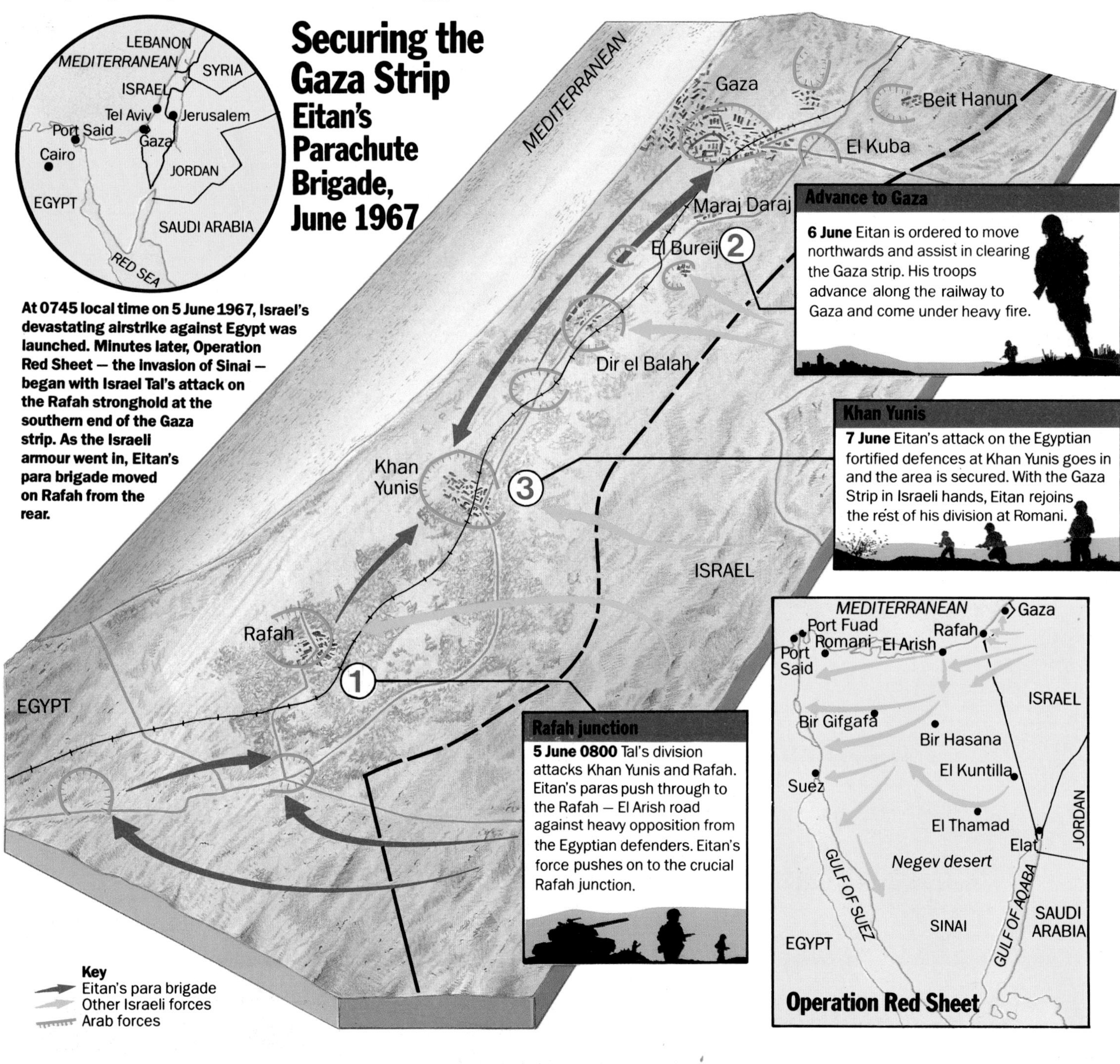

55TH PARACHUTE BRIGADE, JERUSALEM, 6-7 JUNE 1967

The capture of Jerusalem by the Israeli 55th Parachute Brigade during the 1967 Six-Day War is a testament to the fighting qualities of the Israeli airborne soldier. The unit was trained to expect shock action and to be in the forefront of any Israeli offensive. Under its commander, Colonel Mordechai Gur, it had been turned into a seasoned, aggressive force which was itching to get to grips with the enemy.

The paras needed all their aggressive fighting qualities. During the assault on Jerusalem they fought through a daunting set of obstacles: barbed wire, concrete pillboxes and a maze of narrow streets and buildings that had been fortified by the Jordanians. The paras were heavily laden with extra magazines for their Uzis, while bergens filled with grenades interfered with mobility. They had to blast a way in using Bangalore torpedoes – many of which failed to work properly and merely revealed the attacker's position. Even when they reached the streets, the Israelis found it very hard to clear areas completely of the enemy. Snipers and lone Jordanian positions were an irritant throughout the whole of the fighting, and inflicted many casualties.

It was, therefore, a considerable achievement that by 0800 hours on 6 June the 55th Brigade had secured all its objectives. Twenty-four hours later, Gur was ordered to take the Old City via the Lion's Gate. He met little resistance: the Jordanian leader, Brigadier Ata Ali, had been forced to withdraw, having been cut off by Israeli forces in the north and south. At 1000 hours the paras reached the Wailing Wall; the heavy casualties had been worth it.

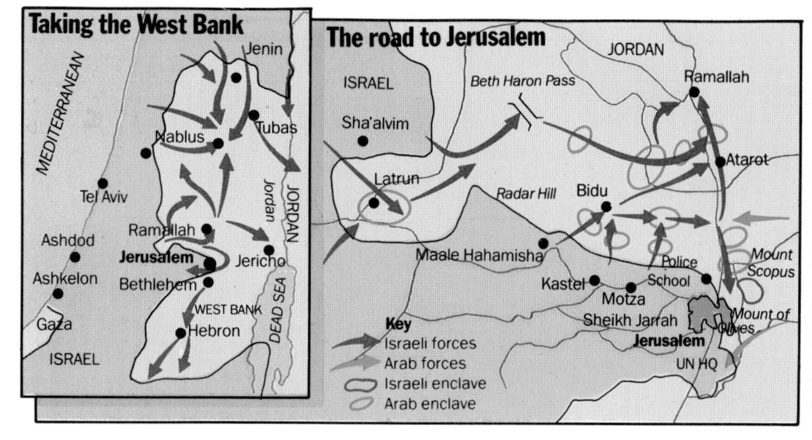

Battle for Jerusalem

Israeli 55th Parachute Brigade, June 1967

At 1100 hours on 5 June 1967 Jordanian artillery and aircraft began attacking targets in Israel. Faced with the problem of defending the corridor to Jerusalem against a Jordanian advance, the Israelis deployed an armoured brigade to secure the high ground north of the corridor. With the northern flank secure the 55th Parachute Brigade began its attack on Jerusalem, entering the Old City early on 7 June. Meanwhile, Israeli forces were clearing the rest of the West Bank, and that evening hostilities between Israel and Jordan ended.

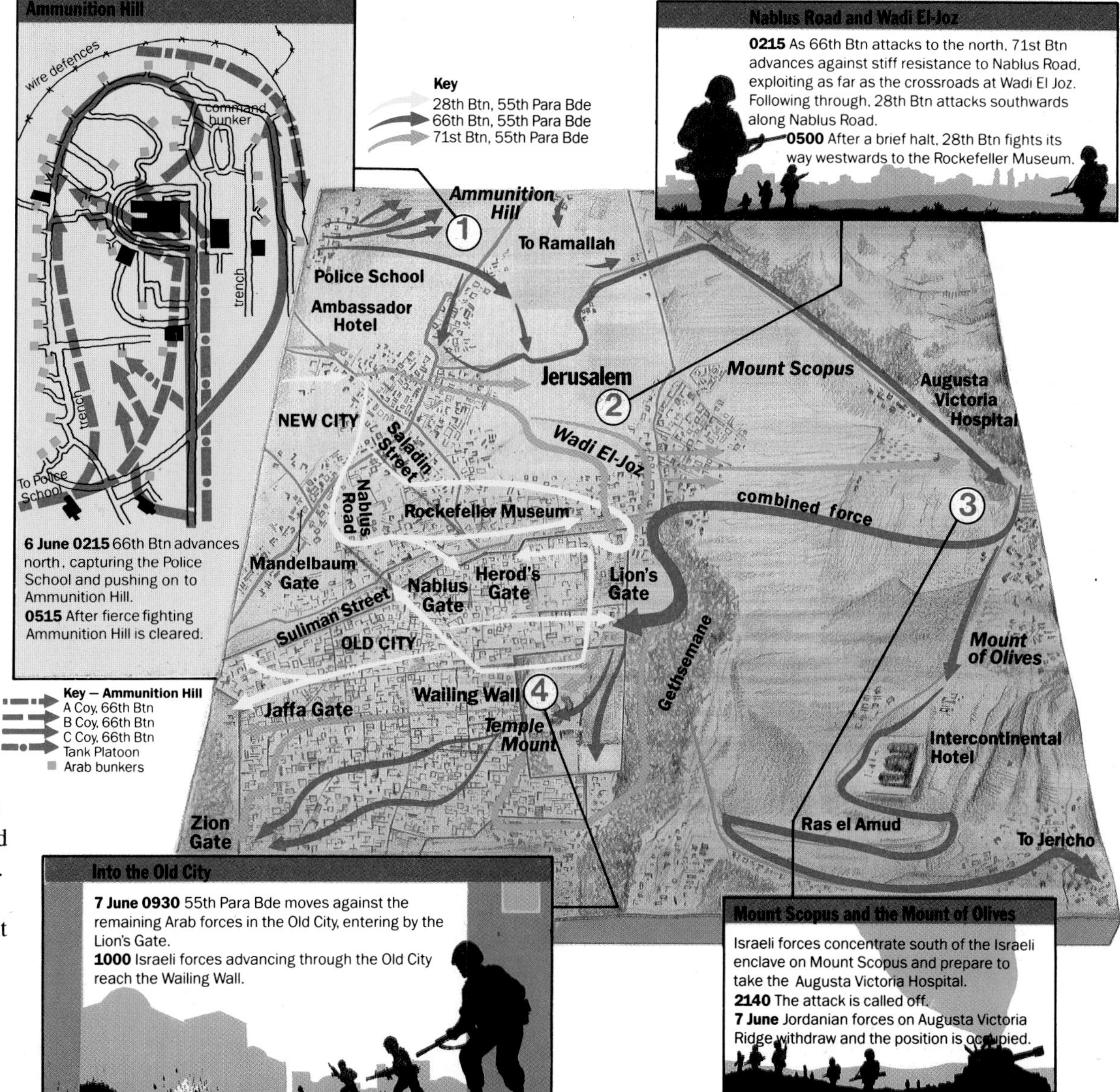

ISRAELI COMMANDOS, GREEN ISLAND, 19-20 JULY 1969

Daring has always been a vital part of special forces operations. The Israeli attack on the Egyptian radar station on Green Island in July 1969, during the so-called War of Attrition, displayed this quality in abundance. One of a series of Israeli reprisals mounted in response to air, artillery and commando attacks undertaken by Egypt after the Six-Day War of 1967, the destruction of the radar station on the island was crucial to the planned series of air assaults against Egypt.

If the radar was destroyed, IDF jets could hit the Egyptian naval base at Ras Adabia and deal with a number of artillery batteries that were shelling Israeli positions along the Suez Canal and in Sinai. The raid was given to Lieutenant-Colonel Zeev Almog of the elite naval commandos. They would need all their skills for the Green Island raid. The island fort was formidable to say the least: reinforced concrete fortifications housed 100 Egyptian soldiers; there were six emplacements mounting 37mm and 85mm anti-aircraft guns; and 14 well-sited heavy machine guns. In addition, there were a number of 20mm cannon.

The plan was for Almog's men to split into three assault teams before they reached the island; two would attack the fort and radar station, with the third providing covering fire. The raid was launched on the night of 19/20 July. Surprise was total as the Israelis breached the perimeter and dealt with the garrison with grenades and small arms. Almog's team was soon in possession of the radar emplacement, allowing the demolition squad to come forward to do its work. While the men laid their charges, other commandos headed for their secondary objectives. Speed was now vital as the Egyptians had recovered from their initial shock and were organising a counterattack.

The Israelis began to take casualties: one officer shot through the neck and killed, another riddled by tracer fire from hidden machine-gun pits. Nevertheless, they forged on, clearing the perimeter and then descending into the courtyard and clearing it of Egyptian positions. Almog realised it was time to go. Very soon the Egyptians on the western shore of the gulf would respond to the raid. Shouting above the noise of the remaining small-arms fire, he ordered his men to the rendezvous point, where they would be picked up by inflatable dinghies.

When they were in the waters of the gulf the commandos glanced back to see the charges they had laid detonate, wrecking the fort and radar station. For the loss of six men killed and 10 wounded, they had dealt a severe blow to the Egyptian early warning system along the Suez Canal.

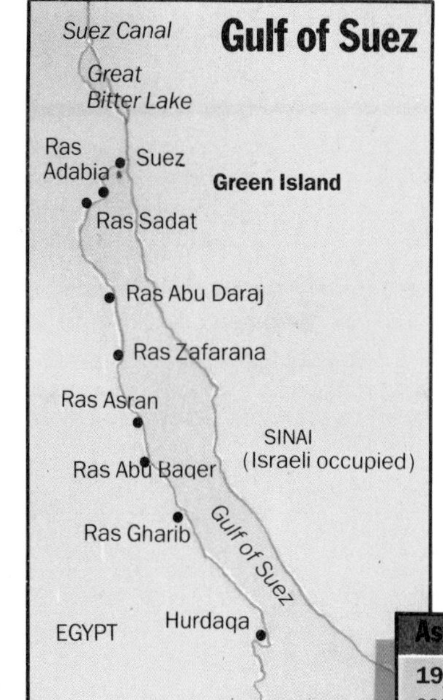

Green Island
19/20 July 1969

In July 1969, at the height of the War of Attrition between Israel and her Arab neighbours, a small team of Israeli naval commandos was sent in to blow up the Egyptian radar installations and defences on Green Island in the Gulf of Suez. The heavily defended island, a tiny fortress some three miles from the Israeli held east shore, was a vital keystone in the Egyptian radar network defending Egyptian bases such as the naval base at Ras Adabia. The commandos landed unobserved, overcame the garrison in a fierce firefight, and blew up the installation before withdrawing.

Assault on Green Island

19/20 July Under cover of darkness, Israeli naval commandos move out in inflatable assault boats from the Israeli-held eastern shore of the Gulf of Suez and set course for Green Island, some three miles away. Covering the last part of the journey underwater, two assault teams silently land on the island while a covering force establishes itself further south.

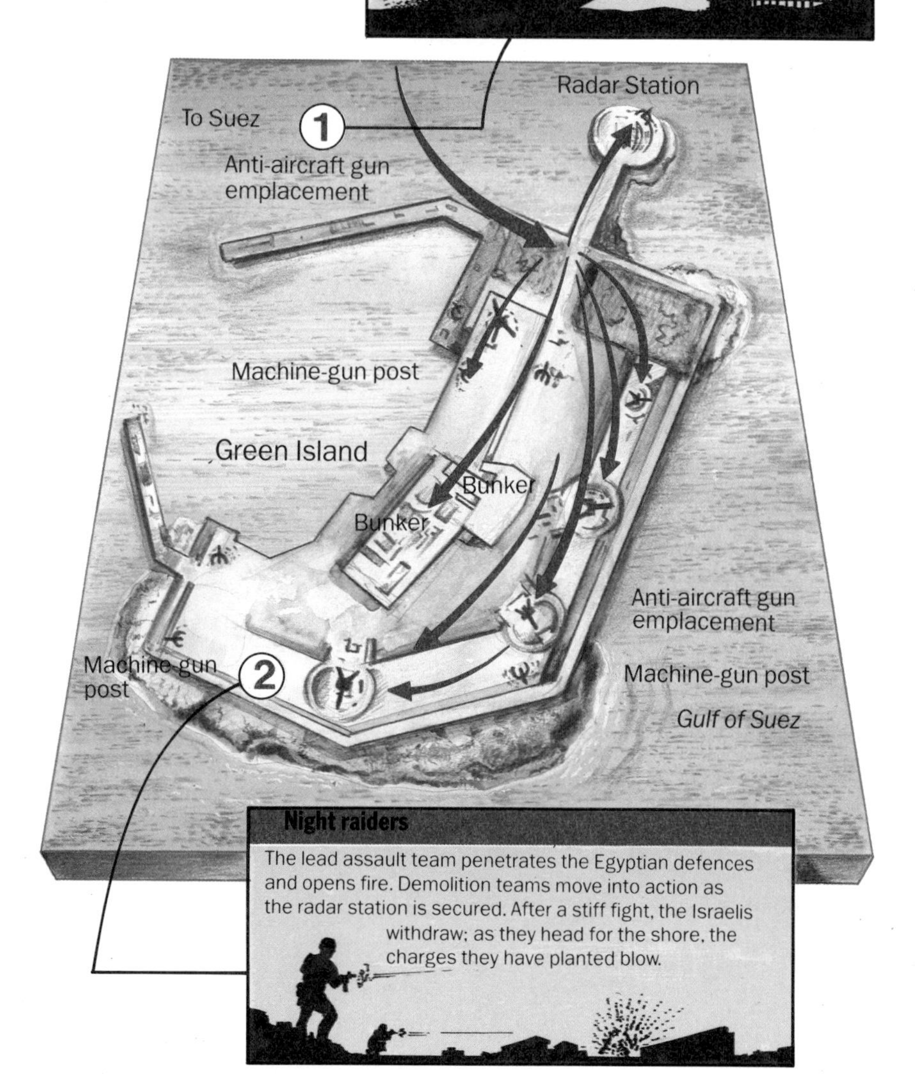

Night raiders

The lead assault team penetrates the Egyptian defences and opens fire. Demolition teams move into action as the radar station is secured. After a stiff fight, the Israelis withdraw; as they head for the shore, the charges they have planted blow.

EGYPTIAN COMMANDOS, CROSSING THE SUEZ CANAL, 6-7 OCTOBER 1973

Following their humiliating defeat in the 1967 Six-Day War, the Arab nations, particularly Egypt, were desperate to regain some of their lost prestige. Therefore, the Egyptian commandos who attacked the Israeli Bar-Lev Line in the early hours of 6 October 1973 were highly motivated, as well as being well trained. They were prepared to take high losses, and had trained for months to deal with the Israelis on the right bank. The Egyptians faced two main problems: how to breach the Line, and how to deal with the Israeli armour that would rush towards the Suez Canal to aid the Bar-Lev garrisons.

Under the cover of air strikes, the commandos crossed the Canal in rubber dinghies and then stormed up the sand ramparts. To their surprise, they found only 16 of the Bar-Lev positions were manned and resistance was variable. In the south, at the Quay, the Israelis held out for a week until its commander was authorised to negotiate surrender through the Red Cross. Others were taken relatively easily, while the defenders of some posts managed to beak out and flee east.

As Israeli tanks sped west in response to the attack, many were ambushed by the commandos with Sagger AT-3 Anti-Tank Guided Weapons (ATGWs) and RPG-7 rocket launchers. In the marshy northern sector, Israeli tanks had to operate with restricted visibility because enemy small-arms fire forced them to close all their hatches. Within 24 hours, Major-General Mandler's armoured division had lost 170 tanks.

Shazli's helicopter insertion operations went less well. In one incident Israeli jets attacked a group of helicopters flying over Ras Suda, shooting down 14 and killing most of the 250 commandos being transported. Though the garrison beat off an armoured attack, a unit of commandos managed to cut it off during the night of 6 October. When the Israelis tried to send tanks to its relief, they were ambushed. Three were disabled before the force retired. The Israelis tried twice more in the morning, being repulsed each time.

The commandos had contributed significantly to the success of the Egyptian operation, spearheading the crossing and inhibiting Israeli attempts to make an armoured counterattack.

Crossing the Bar-Lev Line

Egyptian commandos, October 1973

On the afternoon of Yom Kippur, 6 October 1973, the troops manning the Bar-Lev defensive line along the Suez Canal in Israeli-occupied Sinai were the victims of a surprise assault spearheaded by crack squads of Egyptian commandos. By the following day most of the Bar-Lev Line was in Egyptian hands.

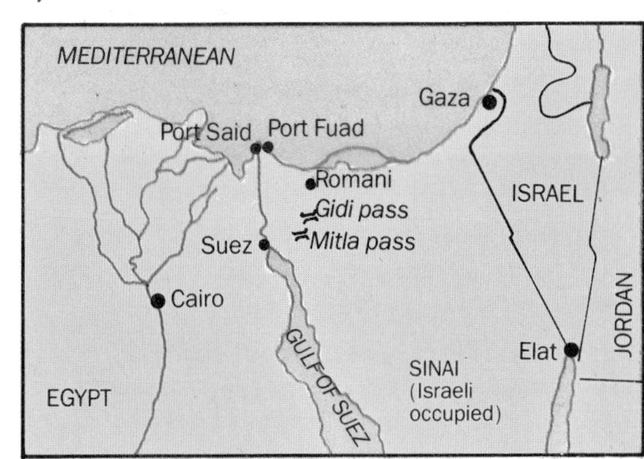

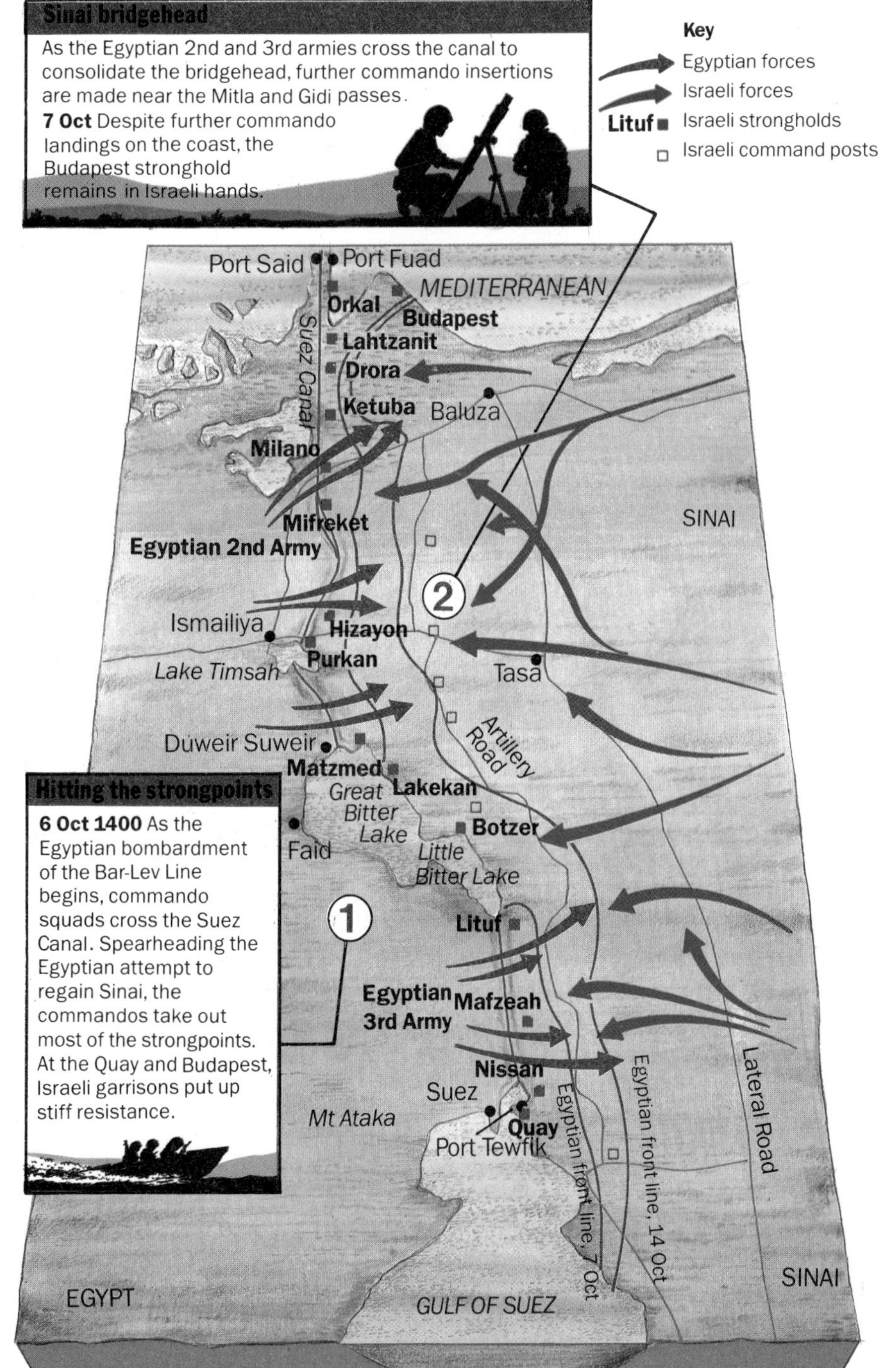

7TH ARMOURED BRIGADE, THE GOLAN HEIGHTS, 6-7 OCTOBER 1973

On 5 October 1971, on the eve of the Jewish festival of Yom Kippur, the Israeli 7th Armoured Brigade was emplaced on the Golan Heights, facing the Syrians. The Yom Kippur War was about to break out. The 7th had 17 strongpoints, each holding 20 men and three Centurion tanks. In addition, there were minefields and a deep, four-metre wide anti-tank ditch which ran from the lower slopes of Mount Hermon to Rafid. Any Syrian advance would encounter few natural obstacles, but the Israelis hoped they could slow any attack long enough for reserves to be brought up to plug the gap.

The Syrian attack

For their part, the Syrians were equipped with Soviet T-62 tanks armed with 115mm guns backed by large amounts of artillery and anti-aircraft batteries. They began their assault at 1400 hours on 6 October. The Israelis were heavily outnumbered. Could they hold on until reinforced?

The 7th's first action consisted of a company under the command of Captain Meir Zamir halting and then throwing back the Syrian 43rd Armoured Brigade in a night battle around the town of Kuneitra, an action that prevented the collapse of the central sector of the Golan Heights. But this was just a taster. The 7th's main action was fought in the north.

The 7th is cut off

The Syrians attacked in the north with 500 tanks and 700 armoured personnel carriers, and the battle between Mount Hermon and 'Booster' Hill took place in an area that was later called the 'Valley of Tears'. The Israelis could call upon no reserves – the 7th was on its own. Though the Syrians knew that the Israelis had turned every crossing point over the anti-tank ditch into a killing ground, they were highly motivated and prepared to take heavy casualties. Although their bridgelayers were knocked out one by one, and then dozens of tanks were stopped, still the Syrians came on, their infantrymen filling in parts of the ditch with their entrenching tools. The Syrians drove on, only to be cut down by artillery, tank and machine-gun fire. Overhead Israeli aircraft strafed the enemy lines. More tanks and men filled the places of the burning hulks and falling bodies, until the Syrians were only a few metres from the defences. Some broke through, only to be destroyed by Centurion tanks in adjacent bunkers, their 105mm guns punching holes through the Soviet tanks' thin rear armour. Then the guns were swung around the face the front again, just in time to deal with the next Syrian line.

Night came but the battle still raged. The Syrian tanks were equipped with night-sights, unlike the 7th's, and so the Syrians were able to press their attacks at close range. The Syrians sensed victory, for if they broke through the 7th there was nothing to bar their way to the Jordan river.

The Israelis organised a scratch force of 20 battle-damaged tanks crewed by wounded men and threw them into the action in the early hours of the 9th. They arrived at the front at a critical time: some of the Centurions were down to only three or four shells. They crashed into the Syrian flank and began to destroy the enemy's armour. The Syrians, after fearsome losses which included 500 tanks and armoured personnel carriers, began to withdraw. The battle had lasted for 30 hours, but the 7th, against the odds, had held.

Two days later the 7th counterattacked, capturing the Syrian part of the Golan heights. But it was the battle in the 'Valley of Tears' which marked out the 7th as a crack armoured unit, filled with highly trained and motivated tank crews who drew a line in the sand and refused to budge, despite overwhelming odds.

ABOVE: *A row of Israeli Centurion tanks. Centurions in Israeli service during the Six-Day War had up-rated engines, an improved cooling system, and were armed with the formidable British L7 105mm gun.*

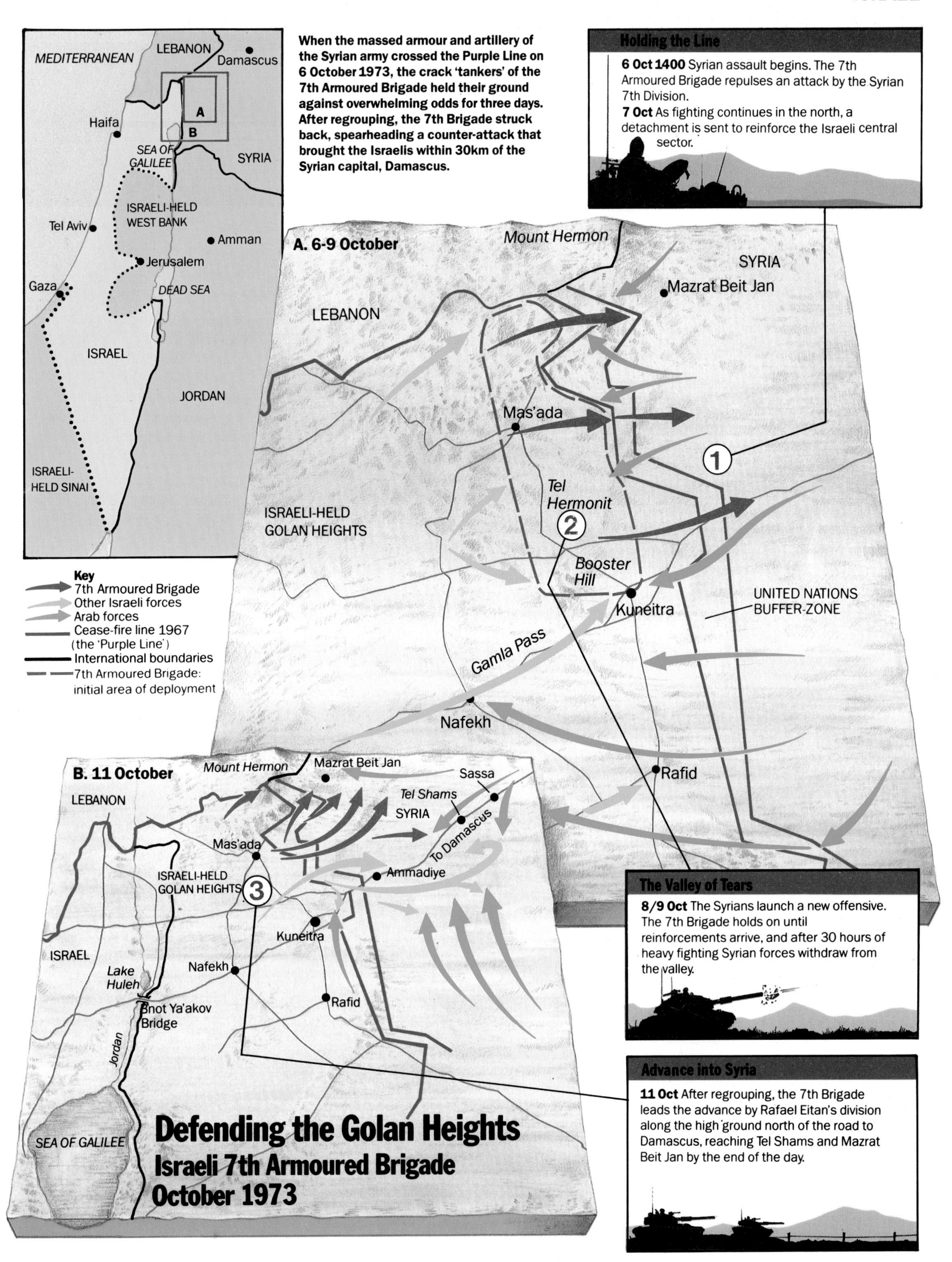

When the massed armour and artillery of the Syrian army crossed the Purple Line on 6 October 1973, the crack 'tankers' of the 7th Armoured Brigade held their ground against overwhelming odds for three days. After regrouping, the 7th Brigade struck back, spearheading a counter-attack that brought the Israelis within 30km of the Syrian capital, Damascus.
Holding the Line
6 Oct 1400 Syrian assault begins. The 7th Armoured Brigade repulses an attack by the Syrian 7th Division.
7 Oct As fighting continues in the north, a detachment is sent to reinforce the Israeli central sector.
The Valley of Tears
8/9 Oct The Syrians launch a new offensive. The 7th Brigade holds on until reinforcements arrive, and after 30 hours of heavy fighting Syrian forces withdraw from the valley.
Advance into Syria
11 Oct After regrouping, the 7th Brigade leads the advance by Rafael Eitan's division along the high ground north of the road to Damascus, reaching Tel Shams and Mazrat Beit Jan by the end of the day.
MEDITERRANEAN
LEBANON
Damascus
A
B
Haifa
SEA OF GALILEE
SYRIA
ISRAELI-HELD WEST BANK
Tel Aviv
Amman
Jerusalem
Gaza
DEAD SEA
ISRAEL
JORDAN
ISRAELI-HELD SINAI
Key
7th Armoured Brigade
Other Israeli forces
Arab forces
Cease-fire line 1967 (the 'Purple Line')
International boundaries
7th Armoured Brigade: initial area of deployment
A. 6-9 October
Mount Hermon
SYRIA
Mazrat Beit Jan
LEBANON
Mas'ada
1
Tel Hermonit
2
ISRAELI-HELD GOLAN HEIGHTS
Booster Hill
Kuneitra
UNITED NATIONS BUFFER-ZONE
Gamla Pass
Nafekh
Rafid
B. 11 October
Mount Hermon
Mazrat Beit Jan
Sassa
Tel Shams
SYRIA
LEBANON
To Damascus
Mas'ada
Ammadiye
ISRAELI-HELD GOLAN HEIGHTS
3
Kuneitra
ISRAEL
Nafekh
Lake Huleh
Bnot Ya'akov Bridge
Rafid
Jordan
SEA OF GALILEE
Defending the Golan Heights
Israeli 7th Armoured Brigade
October 1973

35TH PARATROOP BRIGADE, CHINESE FARM, 15-18 OCTOBER 1973

The Israeli capture of the Chinese Farm, a former agricultural settlement in the Sinai Desert, during the 1973 Yom Kippur War, was originally given to the 14th Armoured Brigade under the command of Colonel Ammon Reshef. The Farm lay across the main axes of advance and would provide Israeli forces with a safe corridor to the Suez Canal. The attack began in the early evening of 15 October. It began well, but then got bogged down, and by the next day Reshef had lost 60 per cent of his tanks. Knowing the importance of the Chinese Farm, the high command despatched the 35th Paratroop Brigade to clear it.

Lieutenant-Colonel Mordecai arrived with his parachute battalion and prepared to clear what they thought was a small garrison. They were thus only lightly armed with small arms and light anti-tank weapons. The battalion arrived on the 16th, the paras moving slowly forward as they probed the Egyptian positions. Colonel Uzi Ya'ri, the brigade commander, ordered the pace to be quickened. The paras did so, only to be stopped by Egyptian fire. The commander of B Company was killed, and Mordecai was forced to send in reinforcements to rescue it. Then C Company also became pinned down by fire, and both units began to take heavy casualties. Mordecai ordered E Company, his reserve, forward to see if it was possible to launch a further assault. However, it, too, came under heavy fire.

The Israelis are pinned down

During the night, under heavy fire, the Israelis managed to extricate 60 wounded, placing them behind a hill which became known as 'Wounded Hill'. Mordecai ordered his men to hold on, but it was obvious that the paras were up against a much larger force than expected and were being decimated. General Adan, realising how important it was to get a bridge across the Suez, ordered his armour to head towards the crossing point. Meanwhile, Mordecai urgently requested aid. Attempts to evacuate the wounded resulted in a hail of Egyptian fire which often cut down the stretcher bearers.

Egyptian artillery and anti-tank rockets pounded the paras' positions. A tank battalion of the Israeli 460th Armoured Brigade under Lieutenant-Colonel Ehud managed to reach the paras, but they came under heavy fire and within half an hour all of them were on fire: the rescuers had to be rescued.

The paras hold on

The paras now showed why the Israeli airborne forces are among the best troops in the world. Going forward in the face of murderous fire, they managed to pull many men from the burning tanks before they exploded. Though the Egyptians threw everything they had at the paras, for the next 14 hours Mordecai's men, against incredible odds, held, pulling back only when receiving orders to do so. Away from the carnage, the paras took stock of their situation. The cost had been high. The battalion had lost 40 killed and 100 wounded.

Though they did not take the Farm, the paras had held the Egyptians long enough to allow other forces to bypass it and head for the Canal.

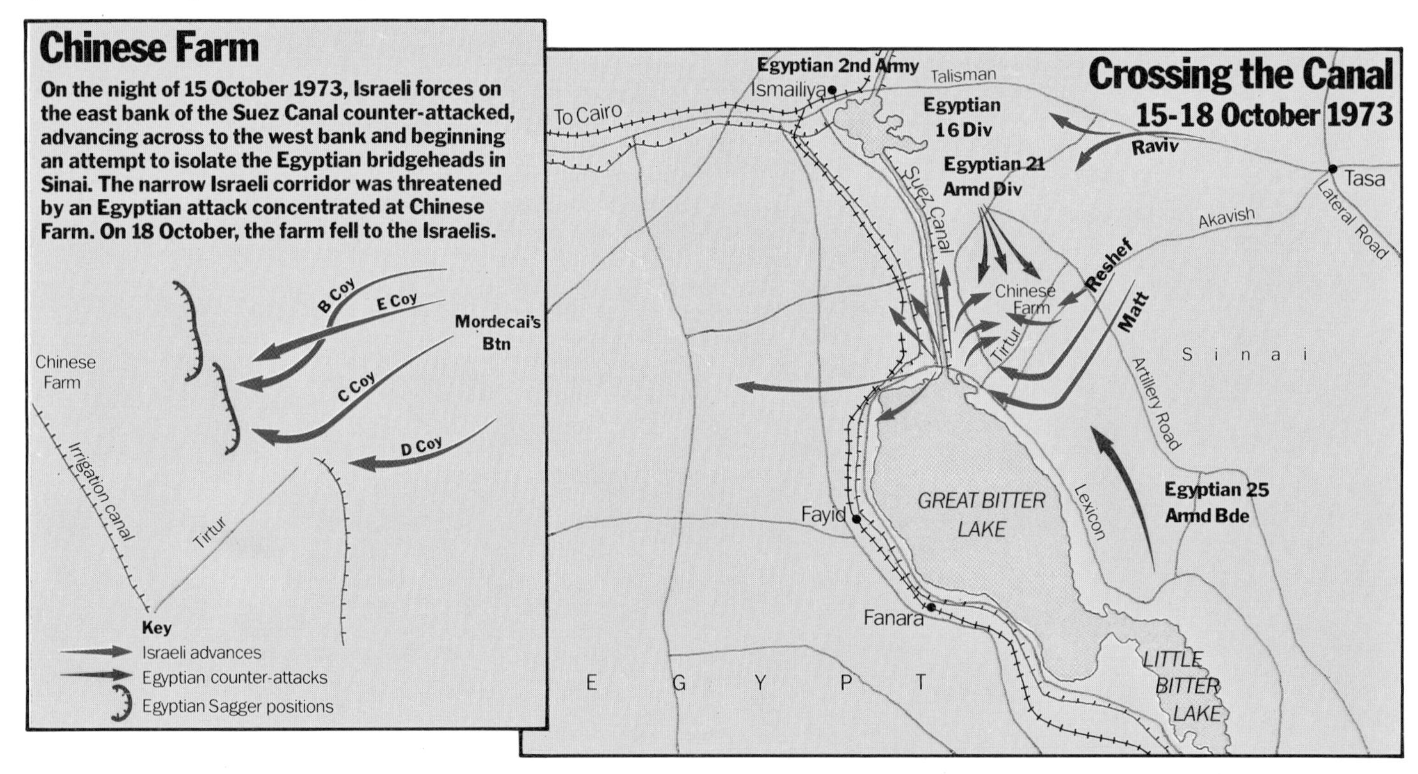

ISRAEL PARAS, SIDON, JUNE 1982

It is often the case that paratroopers are called upon to fulfil military roles they are not really trained for. Fighting in built-up areas is a case in point. However, paras in general have certain qualities that are useful for the bloody, frustrating work of clearing urban areas: determination, abundant amounts of raw courage, and the drive to get the job done no matter what the cost. In addition, when it comes to man against man, and that is what street fighting often comes down to, there is a better than average chance that the determined para will come out on top, irrespective of who the opposition is.

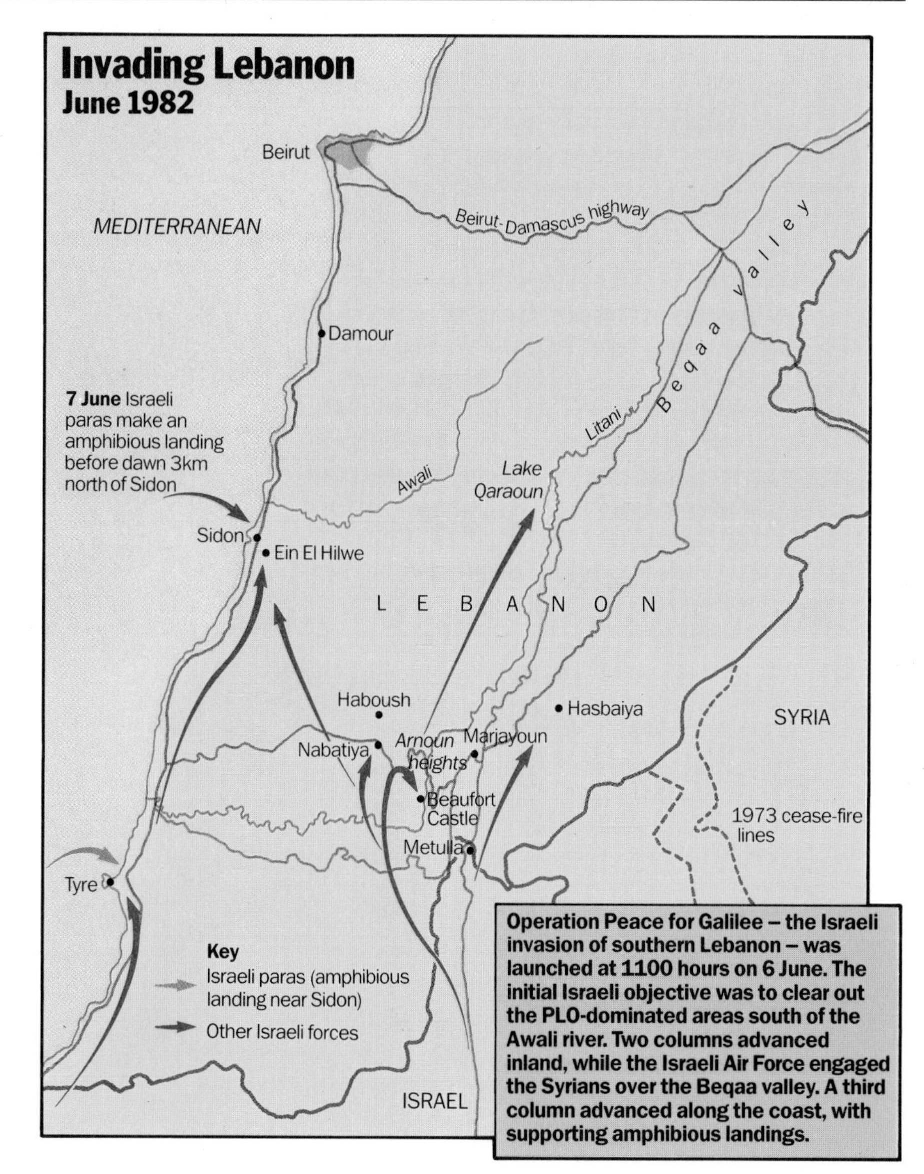

Operation Peace for Galilee – the Israeli invasion of southern Lebanon – was launched at 1100 hours on 6 June. The initial Israeli objective was to clear out the PLO-dominated areas south of the Awali river. Two columns advanced inland, while the Israeli Air Force engaged the Syrians over the Beqaa valley. A third column advanced along the coast, with supporting amphibious landings.

Tactics for clearing built-up areas

So it was in June 1982, when Israeli paras were tasked with clearing the Lebanese port of Sidon of Palestine Liberation Organisation (PLO) guerrillas entrenched there during Operation 'Peace for Galilee' (which began on 6 June). The tactics were simple: suppress sniper fire with tank and artillery shells and air strikes, enter the building, mop up, exit, rest and regroup – then do it all again.

The main PLO concentrations were in the ancient Casbah area of the town and in the Ein El Hilwe refugee camp; Sidon also served as an Al Fatah naval base (Fatah was the most important group within the PLO). The PLO defences were based on a closely built network of high-rise buildings and concealed bunkers.

General Israeli tactics in Lebanon were to outflank and completely encircle enemy towns. This, it was hoped, would have a strong psychological effect on the foe and soften resistance. Pressure would then be exerted from the fringes, and increased as the troops came nearer to the main areas of resistance. The defenders comprised some 1500 guerrillas from the El Kastel Brigade, reinforced by units retreating from the Israeli invasion of the south. The El Kastel Brigade had also built fortifications in the mountains overlooking the coastal strip and was supported by the Palestinians in the Ein El Hilwe camp.

At first the job of clearing a path through Sidon was allocated to one of the forces moving north, but because of the fierce resistance it was decided to send in the paras. The assault began at noon on 8 June, the paras advancing down the main street in two lines, keeping close to the buildings on both sides. Closely following them were tanks and 155mm self-propelled artillery (their guns could elevate to hit the top floors of apartment blocks, unlike tank guns).

Resistance was slight at first – sporadic bursts of sniper fire – and was silenced by point-blank artillery fire. However, the deeper the paras advanced into the port the heavier the fighting became, and the para commanders realised they could not clear the town in one day. The next day the assault was resumed, more urgent now in order to clear the main road so supplies could be got to the armoured columns advancing on the Lebanese capital, Beirut. Under intense artillery, tank and aircraft fire, the paras cleared the main street, but the Casbah remained a problem. Rather than fight in the narrow, twisting alleyways of the old market, Israeli artillery reduced parts of it to rubble, forcing the remaining PLO guerrillas to surrender. The paras, thankful for not having to fight in the ancient Casbah, headed off to join up with Golani units for the attack on Ein El Hilwe

The Israeli paras at Sidon had been at the centre of an inter-arm coordinated exercise involving armour, artillery and aircraft, but ultimately it was their raw courage and tenacity that had been the deciding factor.

GOLANI BRIGADE, BEAUFORT CASTLE, JUNE 1982

In June 1982, when Israeli forces invaded Lebanon, Beaufort Castle overlooking the Litani river in southern Lebanon was a Palestine Liberation Organisation (PLO) stronghold. Parts of the ancient castle had been rebuilt and had been further fortified with gun positions, sandbag defences and trench systems. The PLO used the castle as a forward observation post and artillery base, from which the Israeli settlements in the Galilee panhandle and the Lebanese Christian enclave in southern Lebanon were constantly shelled. The capture of the castle was essential if the Israelis were to control the mountain passes of the south, and so the Golani Brigade was given the job. This was no easy task, for by all accounts Beaufort was impregnable; indeed, repeated bombings by the Israeli Air Force had done little to dislodge the PLO guerrillas stationed there.

The first assault

The Bokim HaRishonim battalion of the brigade reached the castle during the evening of 6 June, the tanks and the forward patrol unit then advancing in the face of intense PLO fire. However, the Israelis suffered a number of casualties and the forward patrol unit's armoured personnel carrier (APC) was hit; the assault stalled and then fell apart. As the Golanis attempted to reorganise themselves, Major Giora 'Gonni' Hernik came up and took over command. His presence was very important, his men respected his leadership and, because of

BELOW: *Golani infantry, mounted on M113 armoured personnel carriers, advance into Lebanon during the Israeli invasion of June 1982. The brigade saw some vicious fighting in the war.*

Beaufort Castle
Golani Brigade, June 1982

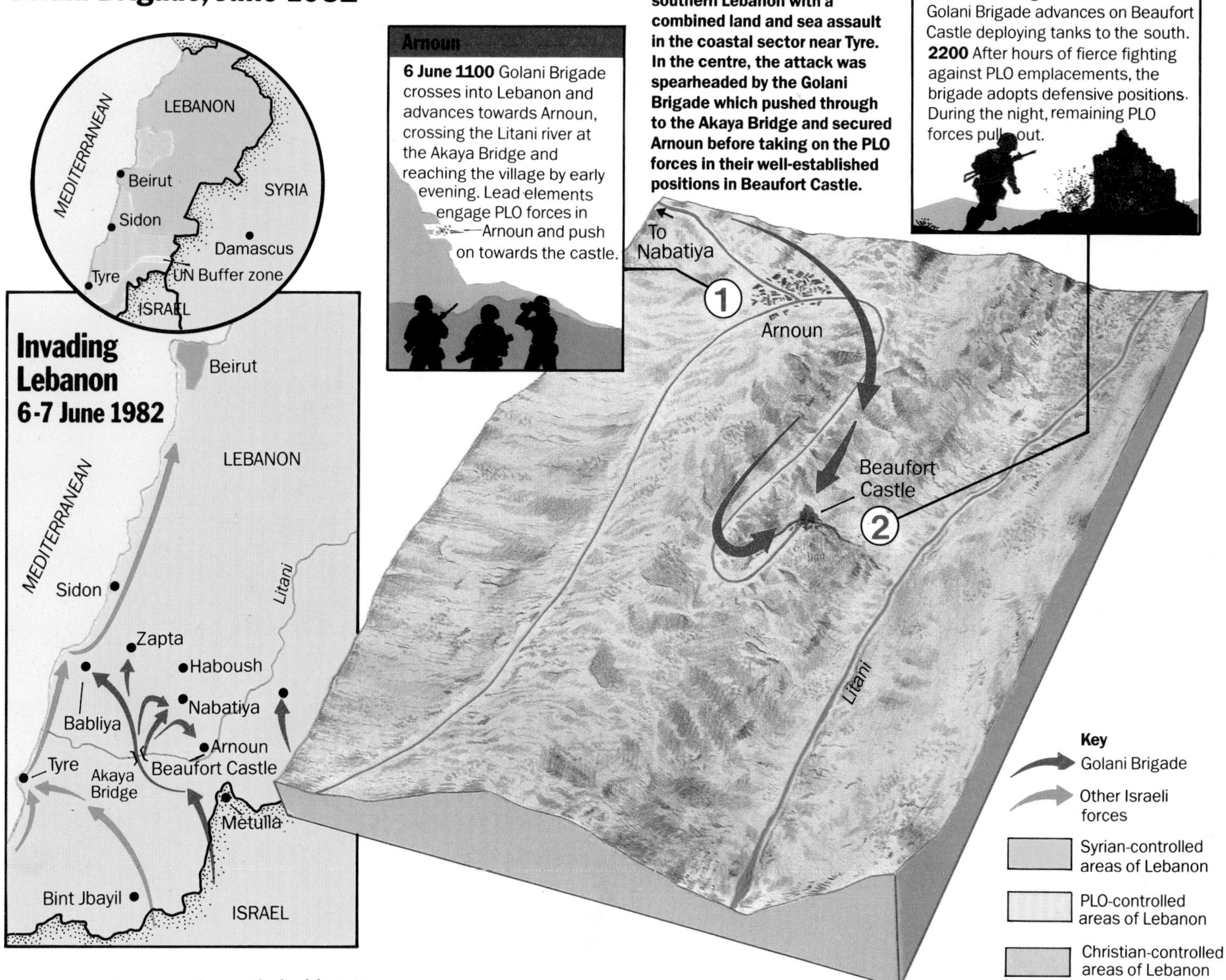

exercises, he knew the castle inside out. He nearly died early on in the battle, when the driver of his APC lost control of the vehicle and turned it over. Remarkably, the crew sustained only minor injuries and Gonni, despite a very painful blow to the back, grabbed his assault rifle and ran 700m forward to catch up with the leading elements of the attack force.

He quickly reorganised his men and re-assessed the situation. The original plan had been for an APC-mounted assault on the fortress, supported by tanks, but now it was dark and he decided to launch an attack on foot. PLO fire still poured from the castle and the village of Arnoun.

As the Israelis advanced, groups of Golani soldiers and PLO fighters came face to face with each other in the rabbit warren of the fortress. Fighting was especially bitter on the northern side, with the Israelis breaking through but taking heavy casualties. An Israeli officer who took part in the battle describes the scene: 'We put down a barrage of cannon and anti-tank fire, then attacked with our improvised force again...We were then able to turn our attention back to the central bunker from where small-arms fire was coming all the time. We fired anti-tank shells and threw explosives and grenades into the bunker until the enemy fire was silenced.'

From 2200 hours until first light, the battle for Beaufort continued as a static action. In one incident Gonni was hit by a bullet and killed instantly. It was a sad loss, but the attack continued. The Israelis reorganised themselves: the wounded were taken to a central point. Then a Golani unit was detailed to secure the roof of the fortress and provide covering fire for the others. A single tank was placed to cover the assault, and very soon the roof was taken. Finally, the trenches were cleared of PLO fighters. Some Palestinians escaped from the castle, but many were killed in the fighting. By first light the Israelis were in control of Beaufort after a fierce fight.

CARTRIDGES 40MM
LINKED
LINKS

CHAPTER V

HOSTAGE RESCUE

In the 1960s and 1970s, there was an explosion in international terrorism. It was largely waged by two distinct groups. On the one hand, extremist political groups, mostly left-wing but also including a smattering from the right, fought a war of liberation against their 'imperialist oppressors' or class enemies. Thus, in Italy the Red Brigade began a campaign of assassination and bombing – a line also taken in France by Direct Action – as part of the drive to establish a communist society.

Other groups used terrorism to try to win self-determination for their homelands, with varying degrees of support from the people they were supposed to be liberating. These formed the second group of terrorist organisation: the liberation groups. In Northern Ireland, the Irish Republican Army and the Irish National Liberation Army began a reign of terror in Ulster and elsewhere in Europe against the British government and its armed forces, a campaign that still continues. Similarly, in Spain the Basque separatist group ETA wages a war for the 'liberation' of its people. Perhaps the most 'famous' liberation group is the Palestine Liberation Organisation (PLO). Set up to free Palestine from Israeli control, its operatives have committed terrorist acts throughout the Middle East and Europe.

To combat these groups, Israel and the West were forced to establish dedicated anti-terrorist and hostage-rescue groups. Trained to storm buildings, railway carriages, aircraft and ships, these units were armed with state-of-the-art weaponry and were issued with other sophisticated equipment. However, the real key to their winning edge was the endless hours of training these units undertook. The British SAS, for example, has a building called the 'Killing House', in which its men practise hostage-rescue drills until they are second nature. The American counter-terrorist unit Delta Force has a similar building entitled the 'House of Horrors'. Very soon every Western nation, as well as Israel, had its own dedicated anti-terrorist unit, and these formations quickly began to achieve successes. The spectacular rescue of hostages at Entebbe by Israeli commandos in 1976 was quickly followed by GSG 9's success at Mogadishu in 1977, and that of the British SAS at the Iranian Embassy in London three years later. These units are elite in every way, containing as they do some of the finest soldiers in the world. Their sharpness and skills are constantly being refined by endless exercises and cross-training with other hostage-rescue formations, both civil and military.

Hostage-rescue units are by their nature small and highly trained. However, there have been occasions when conventional forces have been used on a large scale both to secure military objectives and to free potential hostages. The intervention by US forces in Grenada and Panama concerned issues such as regional power politics and the crushing of extremist regimes and dictators, but they were also about the rescue of large numbers of American citizens who were living in those countries at the time. For this reason, these two operations are included in this chapter.

An American soldier keeps watch for enemy personnel during Operation 'Just Cause', the US intervention in Panama in December 1989.

GIGN, DJIBOUTI, 4 FEBRUARY 1976

Shortly before 0800 hours on 3 February 1976, four members of the Somali Coast Liberation Front (FLCS) hijacked a school bus containing 30 children as it made its way from the airbase in Djibouti to the school in the town's port area. The driver was forced to drive to within 180m of the Somali border, where a fifth hijacker boarded the bus. They issued their demands: the immediate independence of the French territory of Afars and Issas, or they would start to cut the children's throats.

Negotiations between the local French commander and the terrorists began immediately, but there was concern for the children, who were on the bus in the blistering desert heat. As the talks dragged on, the government in Paris decided to despatch the crack counter-terrorist unit *Groupement d'Intervention de la Gendarmerie Nationale* (GIGN), under the command of Lieutenant Prouteau. This unit, though untried, was highly trained and expert in a wide range of police and military skills, including scuba diving, parachuting, weapons training and hand-to-hand combat. Each member was superbly fit and an expert shot, and had his own FR-F1 sniper rifle and Manurhin 73 revolver.

The unit as a whole is equipped with a host of surveillance and detection hardware, as well as specialised pyrotechnical devices and weaponry. However, all this equipment merely enables the GIGN soldier to get into a position whereby he can do his main job: neutralise his target. In 1976 the unit was untried, but Prouteau had unshakable confidence in his men.

When they arrived in Djibouti, the GIGN men were deployed around the bus, each man in contact with Prouteau by means of a throat microphone. Each marksman had been assigned to watch over a particular section of the bus; it was essential that the terrorists were eliminated at the same time to avoid a general massacre of the children. To get the children out of the line of sight, a meal containing tranquillisers was sent to the bus at 1400 hours. At 1547 hours only the terrorists were visible in the snipers' sights, the children were asleep.

This was the moment Prouteau was waiting for: he gave the order to fire and all four terrorists were killed. Somali border guards opened up on the GIGN men, but were fired upon themselves by French Foreign Legionnaires. GIGN members rushed forward and quickly began to evacuate the children. Sadly, another terrorist had got onto the bus from the Somali side and, though he was shot dead, he managed to kill a schoolgirl. Nevertheless, 29 other children had been rescued by France's crack hostage-rescue unit.

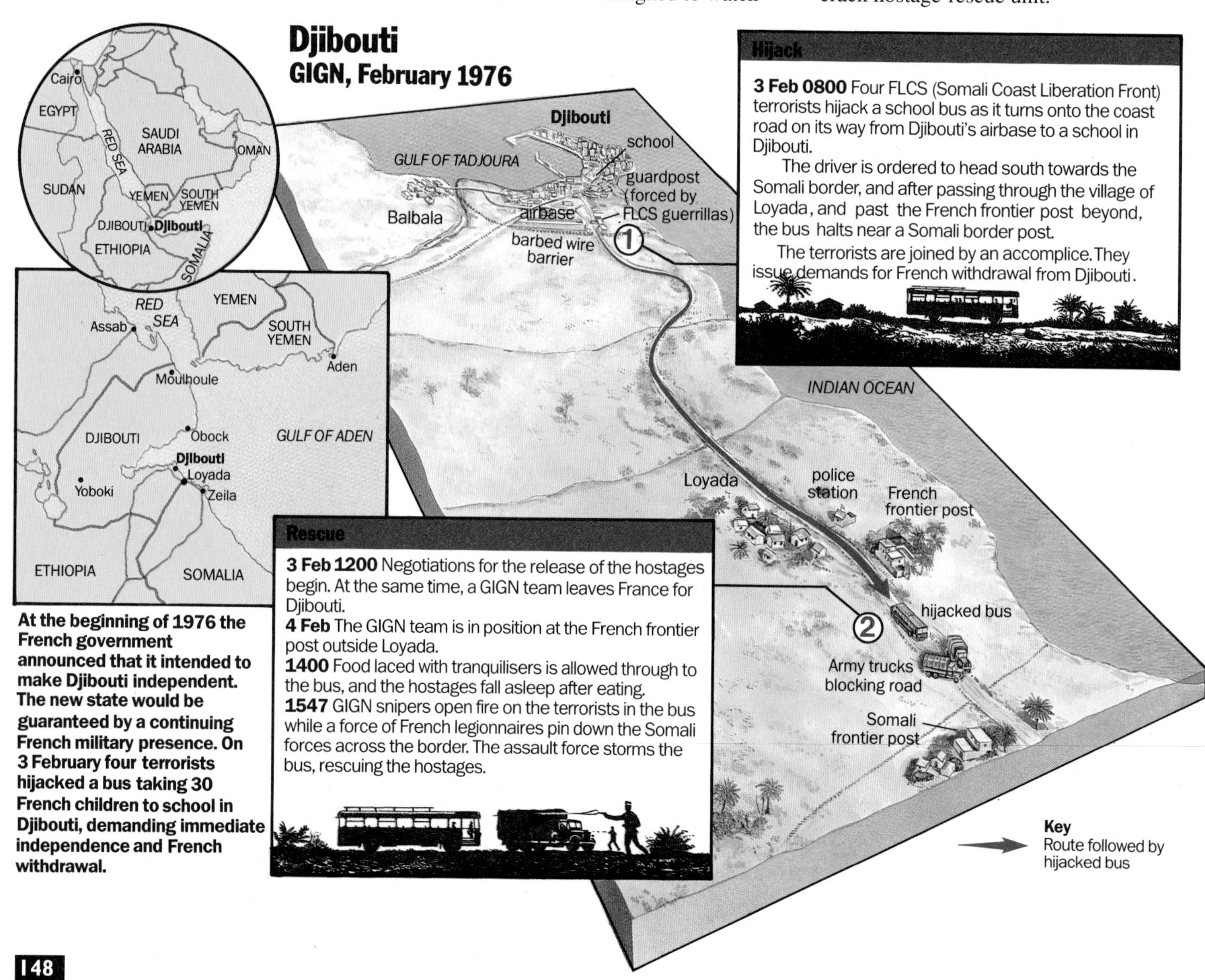

At the beginning of 1976 the French government announced that it intended to make Djibouti independent. The new state would be guaranteed by a continuing French military presence. On 3 February four terrorists hijacked a bus taking 30 French children to school in Djibouti, demanding immediate independence and French withdrawal.

ISRAELI PARAS, ENTEBBE, 3-4 JULY 1976

The rescue by Israeli paras of civilians being held hostage by German and Palestinian terrorists at Entebbe airport in July 1976 remains a classic example of a hostage-rescue operation carried out with split timing and ruthless professionalism, all the more remarkable because it was conducted at a distance of nearly 5000km from Israel.

Initially, the Israeli government had been unwilling to risk the lives of non-Jewish passengers in a rescue attempt. However, when the terrorists released the non-Jewish passengers from the Boeing 707 they had hijacked, the administration accepted a daring plan drawn up by Major-General Dan Shomron, the director of infantry and paratroopers, to free the remaining 105 Jewish hostages.

First of all, however, it was necessary for the Israelis to build up a detailed picture of the situation at Entebbe. This was achieved when some non-Jewish passengers, who had just been released, were interviewed by Israeli undercover agents at Orly airport near Paris. Details were quickly assembled concerning the number of terrorists, their weapons, routine and clothing.

Intelligence was also collected from Israelis who had worked in Uganda and from Israeli Air Force officers who had trained Ugandan pilots. After all the intelligence had been assessed, it was decided to conduct an airborne landing at Entebbe using a force of crack paras.

Israeli paras, who formed the assault teams, were loaded onto four C-130

BELOW: *Jubilant freed hostages arrive in Israel following their daring rescue by Israeli paras. The operation sent a message to terrorists all over the world: Israel would always strike back.*

Entebbe

Israeli paras, July 1976

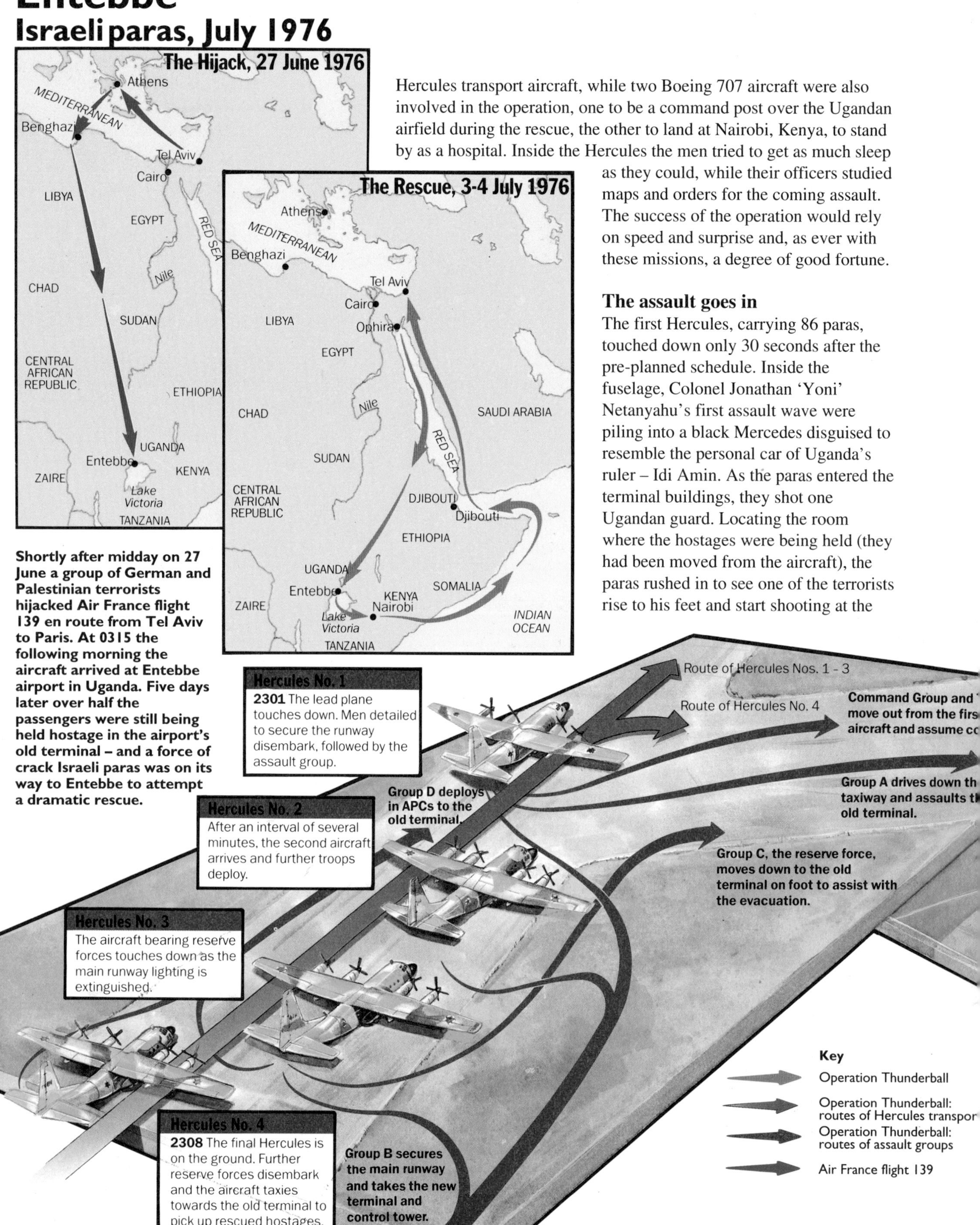

Shortly after midday on 27 June a group of German and Palestinian terrorists hijacked Air France flight 139 en route from Tel Aviv to Paris. At 0315 the following morning the aircraft arrived at Entebbe airport in Uganda. Five days later over half the passengers were still being held hostage in the airport's old terminal – and a force of crack Israeli paras was on its way to Entebbe to attempt a dramatic rescue.

Hercules transport aircraft, while two Boeing 707 aircraft were also involved in the operation, one to be a command post over the Ugandan airfield during the rescue, the other to land at Nairobi, Kenya, to stand by as a hospital. Inside the Hercules the men tried to get as much sleep as they could, while their officers studied maps and orders for the coming assault. The success of the operation would rely on speed and surprise and, as ever with these missions, a degree of good fortune.

The assault goes in

The first Hercules, carrying 86 paras, touched down only 30 seconds after the pre-planned schedule. Inside the fuselage, Colonel Jonathan 'Yoni' Netanyahu's first assault wave were piling into a black Mercedes disguised to resemble the personal car of Uganda's ruler – Idi Amin. As the paras entered the terminal buildings, they shot one Ugandan guard. Locating the room where the hostages were being held (they had been moved from the aircraft), the paras rushed in to see one of the terrorists rise to his feet and start shooting at the

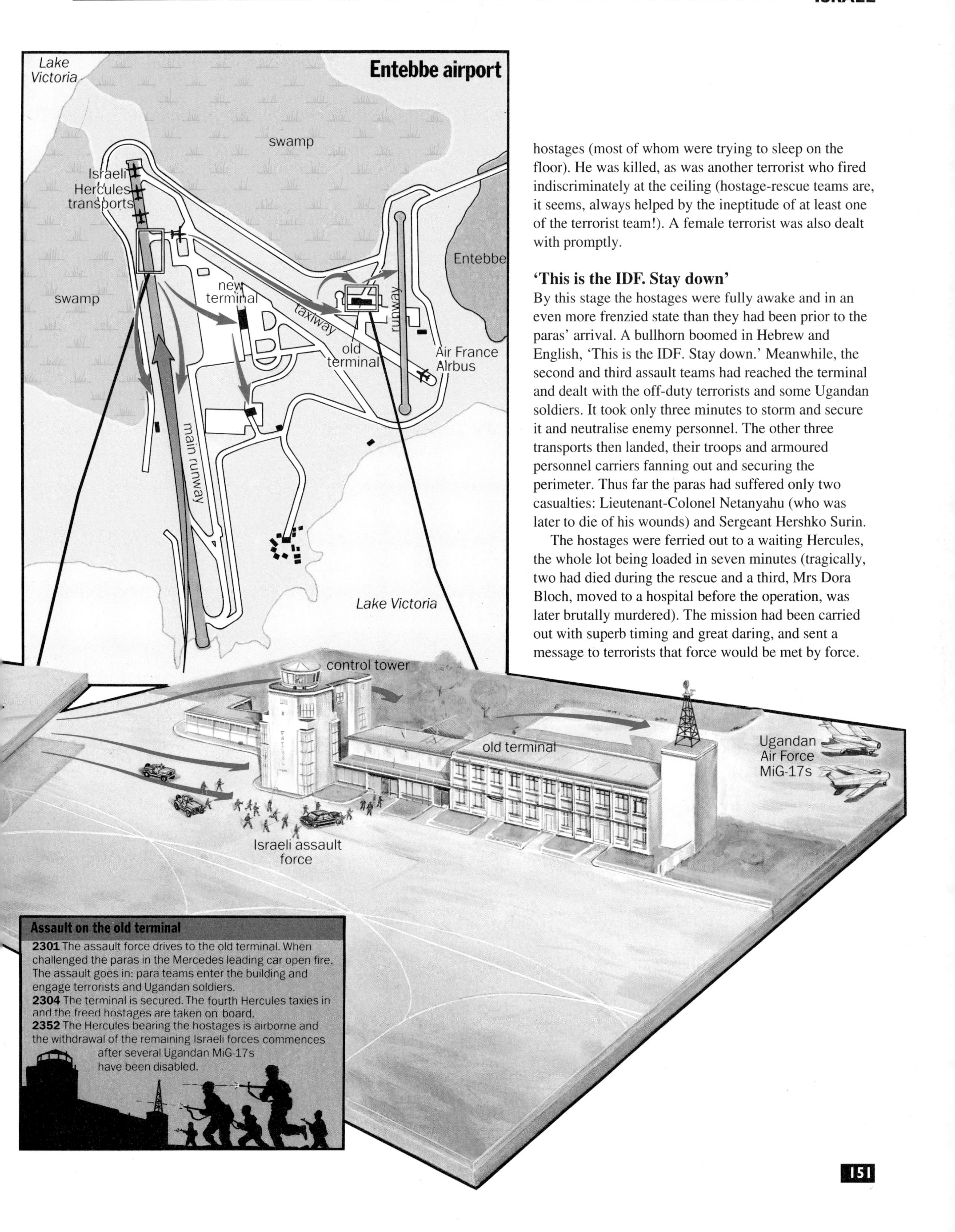

hostages (most of whom were trying to sleep on the floor). He was killed, as was another terrorist who fired indiscriminately at the ceiling (hostage-rescue teams are, it seems, always helped by the ineptitude of at least one of the terrorist team!). A female terrorist was also dealt with promptly.

'This is the IDF. Stay down'

By this stage the hostages were fully awake and in an even more frenzied state than they had been prior to the paras' arrival. A bullhorn boomed in Hebrew and English, 'This is the IDF. Stay down.' Meanwhile, the second and third assault teams had reached the terminal and dealt with the off-duty terrorists and some Ugandan soldiers. It took only three minutes to storm and secure it and neutralise enemy personnel. The other three transports then landed, their troops and armoured personnel carriers fanning out and securing the perimeter. Thus far the paras had suffered only two casualties: Lieutenant-Colonel Netanyahu (who was later to die of his wounds) and Sergeant Hershko Surin.

The hostages were ferried out to a waiting Hercules, the whole lot being loaded in seven minutes (tragically, two had died during the rescue and a third, Mrs Dora Bloch, moved to a hospital before the operation, was later brutally murdered). The mission had been carried out with superb timing and great daring, and sent a message to terrorists that force would be met by force.

ROYAL NETHERLANDS MARINE CORPS, DE PUNT TRAIN HIJACK, MAY-JUNE 1977

In May 1977, 13 South Moluccan terrorists seized 80 hostages on board a train travelling between Rotterdam and Groningen, Holland. Stopping at De Punt, the terrorists issued their demands: the Dutch government was to exert pressure on the Indonesians to grant independence to their homeland of South Molucca. In addition, several of their compatriots were to be released from Dutch jails, and a Boeing 747 jet was to be made ready at Schipol airport for their departure. To reinforce their demands, they murdered the train driver and dumped his body on the tracks.

A pregnant woman is released

Though negotiations were to drag on for over two weeks, the Dutch government considered a military option from the start. Dutch Marines of the BBE (literally 'Different Circumstances Unit', perhaps better translated as 'Special Operations Unit') were on the scene from the beginning. Food trolleys were allowed to go the train, but the terrorists insisted the porters – supposed to be Red Cross personnel – had to be naked to prove they were unarmed. In fact, the porters were policemen gathering intelligence (in any hostage-rescue operation the gathering of intelligence is vital). Intelligence can also come from released hostages, and a pregnant woman who was released was thoroughly debriefed by the authorities. Thus the Marines built up a detailed picture concerning how many terrorists there were, what weapons they carried, how many were on guard at a given time, and so on.

The Marines go in

By 10 June the negotiations had stalled and the Dutch decided to send in the Marines. Explosives had been planted in front of the train, to be used as a noisy diversion when the attack went in. At first light on 11 June, the BBE Marines prepared for action. They were formed into two bodies – one to storm the train, the other to provide covering fire. The attack platoon was equipped with highly accurate Heckler & Koch MP5 submachine guns and Smith and Wesson handguns. Three members of the assault party placed explosive charges on the train doors, while others placed small scaling ladders against the carriages. At zero hour, Dutch Starfighter aircraft flew over the train and kicked in their afterburners. The whole train shuddered with the vibration caused by the jets and the hostages threw themselves on the floor. The charges in front of the train were detonated, and the covering group opened fire with a blistering fusillade of fire (interestingly, the British Special Air Service had offered the Dutch Marines a number of stun grenades to disorientate the terrorists just prior to the assault, but the offer was turned down).

The two-minute firefight

The terrorists had no time to recover before the doors were blown in and the Marines stormed inside. Ordering the hostages to get down, the terrorists were engaged with accurate small-arms fire. Seven were shot and six were captured; only two hostages were killed in the firefight, which lasted only minutes (the skill of the Marines is reflected in the low casualties among the hostages: it could have been a blood bath). At zero hour plus two minutes the train was secure and all the hostages freed. Despite the fact that the Dutch government considered the operation only a qualified success (because of the two hostages who died), the Marines had proved that they were a highly trained anti-terrorist unit, and had proved that the Dutch were no soft touch when it came to taking on terrorists.

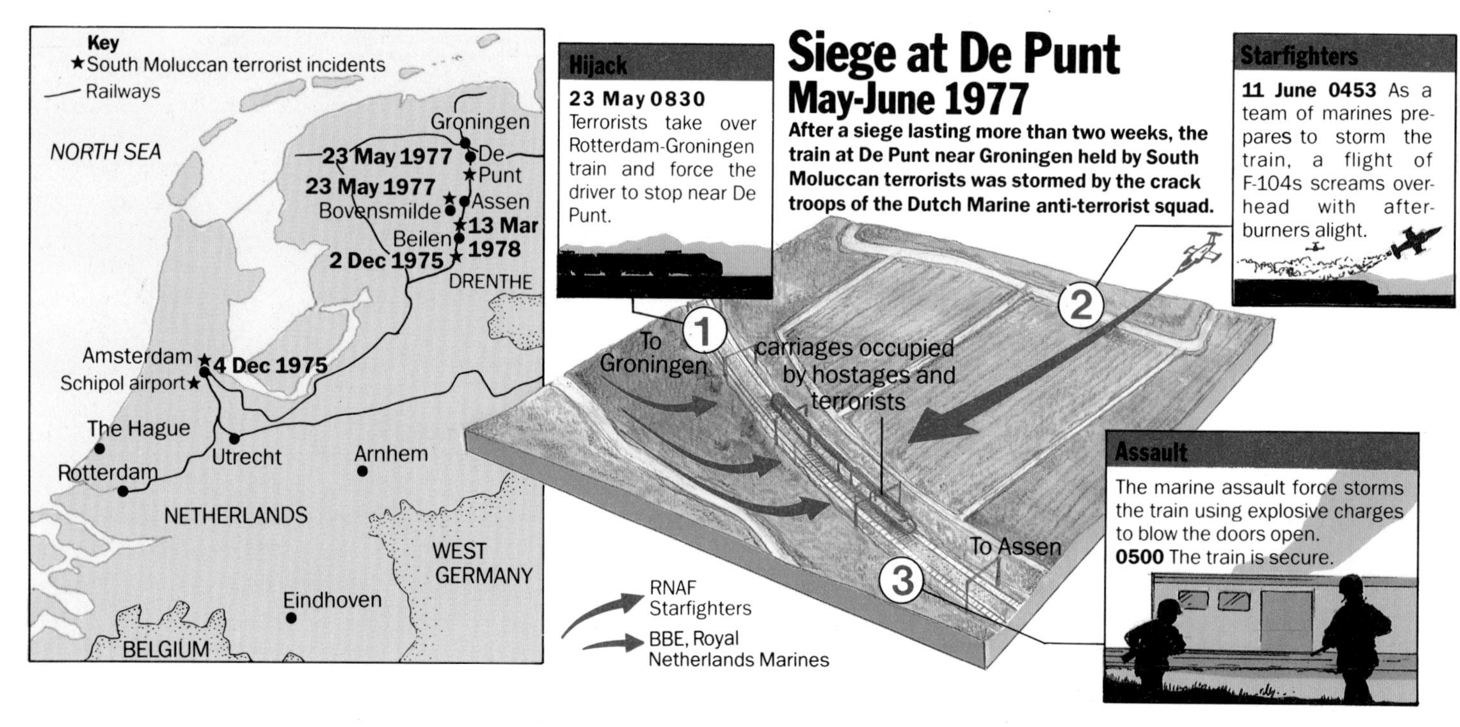

FRENCH FOREIGN LEGION, KOLWEZI, 19-20 MAY 1978

The 2nd Foreign Legion Parachute Regiment (2 REP) is an elite unit par excellence, combining as it does the qualities of two elite corps: Foreign Legionnaires and paratroopers. As such, it was well equipped to deal with the crisis that occurred in Shaba Province in south Zaire in May 1978.

Shaba, under the name of Katanga, had attempted to break away from the newly independent Congo in 1960. Though the breakaway movement had been defeated, relations between the province and the central government remained poor, and sporadic fighting continued. In 1978 the province was invaded by separatist rebels who took over the town of Kolwezi. Kolwezi was inhabited by over 3000 Europeans, mainly mining experts and their families, who were regarded as potential hostages by Major Mufu and his 4000 separatist Katangan 'Tigers'.

A drop of Zairean paratroopers into the town on 16 May was a fiasco. The Zairean leader, President Mobutu, had discussed the affair with his French counterpart to arrange foreign intervention if necessary; it was now very necessary.

Colonel Philippe Erulin's 2 REP was put on standby. The first elements to leave were 1, 2 and 3 Companies, and part of the HQ Company, in five DC8 aircraft on the night of 17/18 May. The Support and 4 Company would follow later. Flying to Kinshasha, the Legionnaires were packed into four C-130s and one Transall aircraft for the drop: 500 paras in very cramped conditions.

It was broad daylight when the paras landed near Kolwezi, but fortunately the Tigers were caught off guard. A command post was quickly established and the men began to regroup. Even before all the paras had landed, the first groups fanned out and advanced to their objectives. Although the Tigers outnumbered the paras, their discipline and morale had crumbled. Resistance did stiffen, but nothing could halt the ruthless momentum of the attack. As the Legionnaires cleared parts of the town, white settlers began to emerge from cover, most of them hungry, thirsty and suffering from shock. Tragically, those held in the Impala Hotel were killed before the Legionnaires reached them.

Within two hours of the initial jump, the Legionnaires were in almost complete control of the town. A second wave of aircraft carrying 4 Company, Support Company and the rest of HQ Company was ordered by Erulin to fly on to Lubumbashi to avoid a night drop. Meanwhile, on the ground the Legionnaires continued to patrol and engage the enemy, killing many Tigers and suffering only six casualties.

Assault on Kolwezi
2 REP, 19-20 May 1978

To Luilu
Metal Shaba
4 Coy
Reconnaissance and mortar sections
Camp Forrest
Gendarmerie
Reconnaissance and mortar sections
BRAVO
ALPHA
Gecamines
Impala Hotel
2 Coy
1 Coy
3 Coy
Hospital
Hippodrome
OLD TOWN
Post Office
NEW TOWN
2 Coy
To Kapata
Manika Hotel
Lycée Jean XXIII
MANIKA
To Lubumbashi
Key
2 REP
Dropping zone

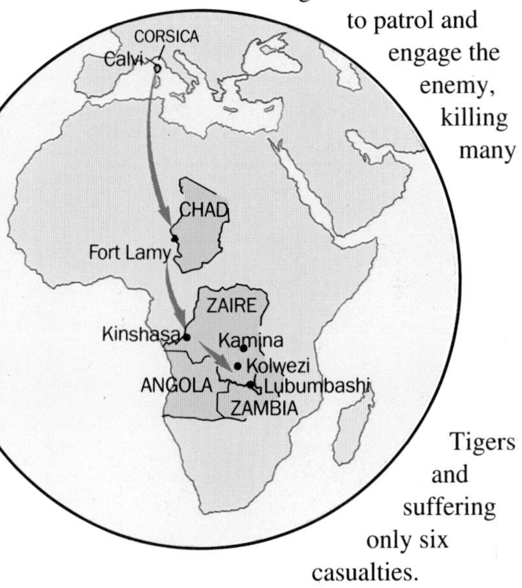

The second wave dropped in during the early hours of 20 May, but there was little overall fighting until the afternoon, when 4 Company ran into heavy resistance near Metal Shaba. The Tigers mounted an attack, but were stopped by Support Company's 81mm mortars and 89mm anti-tank rockets. The Tigers fled, leaving 80 dead. This was the last major action at Kolwezi, the paras then conducting mopping-up operations. For the men of 2 REP, the operation confirmed their status as elite soldiers.

22 SAS, IRANIAN EMBASSY, 5 MAY 1980

At 1132 hours on 30 April 1980, six armed terrorists of the Democratic Revolutionary Front for the Liberation of Arabistan (Arabistan was their description of a predominantly Arab province of Iran) burst into the Iranian Embassy in Princes Gate, London, and seized 26 hostages. Within minutes the building was surrounded by the police, including 'Blue Beret' D11 marksmen and C7, Scotland Yard's Technical Support Branch.

Storming a building full of armed terrorists and terrified hostages is never easy, but in the SAS the British government has a first-rate counter-terrorist unit. Its members, as well as being excellent soldiers, are rotated through anti-terrorist training at the Regiment's barracks at Hereford. In particular, recruits spend hours perfecting their close-quarter hostage-rescue skills in the 'Killing House', a building specially designed to simulate hostage-rescue scenarios. The SAS also has the right equipment for the job: Heckler & Koch submachine guns, reliable and accurate; Browning High Power handguns, carried by all assault team members as a back-up; stun grenades, designed to disorientate the terrorists long enough for them to be neutralised; and the black assault suits and face masks that would become so famous at Princes Gate.

The government, having such a splendid unit, were confident it could bring the siege to a successful conclusion. Obviously it tried to bring a peaceful end to the whole affair, but this became impossible when the terrorists shot an embassy press officer and dumped his body on the pavement. The SAS went in.

Storming the building front and rear, the SAS soldiers lobbed in stun and CS gas grenades and then swept through the building (see map, No 2). Firing their submachine guns from the hip, the black-clad men located the hostages in the embassy's telex room (see map, No 3).

ABOVE: *An SAS trooper storms the Iranian Embassy. His black assault suit is fire-resistant – just as well!*

The terrorists demanded the release of 91 Arabs being held in Iranian jails, and for Arab ambassadors to mediate on their behalf with the British government. The usual threats were issued. If their demands were not met the death of the hostages and the destruction of the building would be the consequences. Negotiations started, allowing the security forces to build up an intelligence picture of the terrorists (see map, No 1): where they were located in the building, their number, and so on. An SAS Special Projects Team had also been deployed to the area, and it began its own preparations.

Five of the six terrorists were gunned down and killed in the building, the other was captured. Only one hostage was killed during the operation, shot by a terrorist before the SAS reached the scene. The operation was over in 17 minutes, the SAS having suffered no casualties. Princes Gate remains a classic example of how to conduct a hostage-rescue operation, and created a legend about the SAS which endures still.

1
2
3

US RANGERS, GRENADA, 25 OCTOBER 1983

Operation 'Urgent Fury', the US invasion of Grenada in October 1983, involved a number of American special forces units, including the SEALs, Rangers and the 82nd Airborne Division. The last two conducted low-level parachute drops onto the island during the operation, and conducted a very speedy conquest of enemy forces once they had landed.

A coup in 1979 had brought Maurice Bishop, a popular radical nationalist, to power on Grenada. However, he was deposed in October 1983 by his former deputy, the Marxist Bernard Coard. This was extremely unpopular throughout the island and public order soon deteriorated, especially when the army shot Bishop. The Organisation of Eastern Caribbean States called on President Reagan to provide military intervention and the US President eagerly agreed. The operation would involve a combined force of elite strike units, whose job was also to rescue US students on the island.

The invasion began in the early hours of 25 October, when SEALs and Marines landed by sea and air. Meanwhile, 550 Rangers of the 1st and 2nd Battalions, 75th Infantry (Ranger) Regiment were approaching Point Salines in the west in C-130 transport aircraft. They were dropped from a low level to minimise the threat to the aircraft posed by the anti-aircraft batteries around the airport, and to minimise the time the men were in the air, thus cutting down the chances of their being hit by small-arms fire. A few members of the 82nd Airborne also jumped over Point Salines.

Once on the ground, the Rangers secured the airstrip and cleared the oil drums on the runway to allow aircraft to land. They then set up their mortars and began to shell enemy positions on the bluff overlooking the airstrip. Supported by A-7 Corsair and A-6 Intruders and Spectre gunships, the Rangers surged forward and knocked out the enemy mortar and machine-gun positions. By 0715 hours the heights were secure and

BELOW: *American M102 105mm artillery in action during Operation 'Urgent Fury'. The M102 was the standard divisional direct support piece throughout the Vietnam War.*

Grenada
US Airborne Forces, October 1983

On the morning of 25 October 1983 the United States launched Operation Urgent Fury with an airborne assault on the airstrip at Point Salines and a heliborne landing near Pearls airport. As a second Marine task force worked its way down from Grand Mal Bay, the airborne forces at Point Salines overcame Cuban and Grenadan resistance and pushed northwards. St George's fell late on 26 October and mopping up operations began.

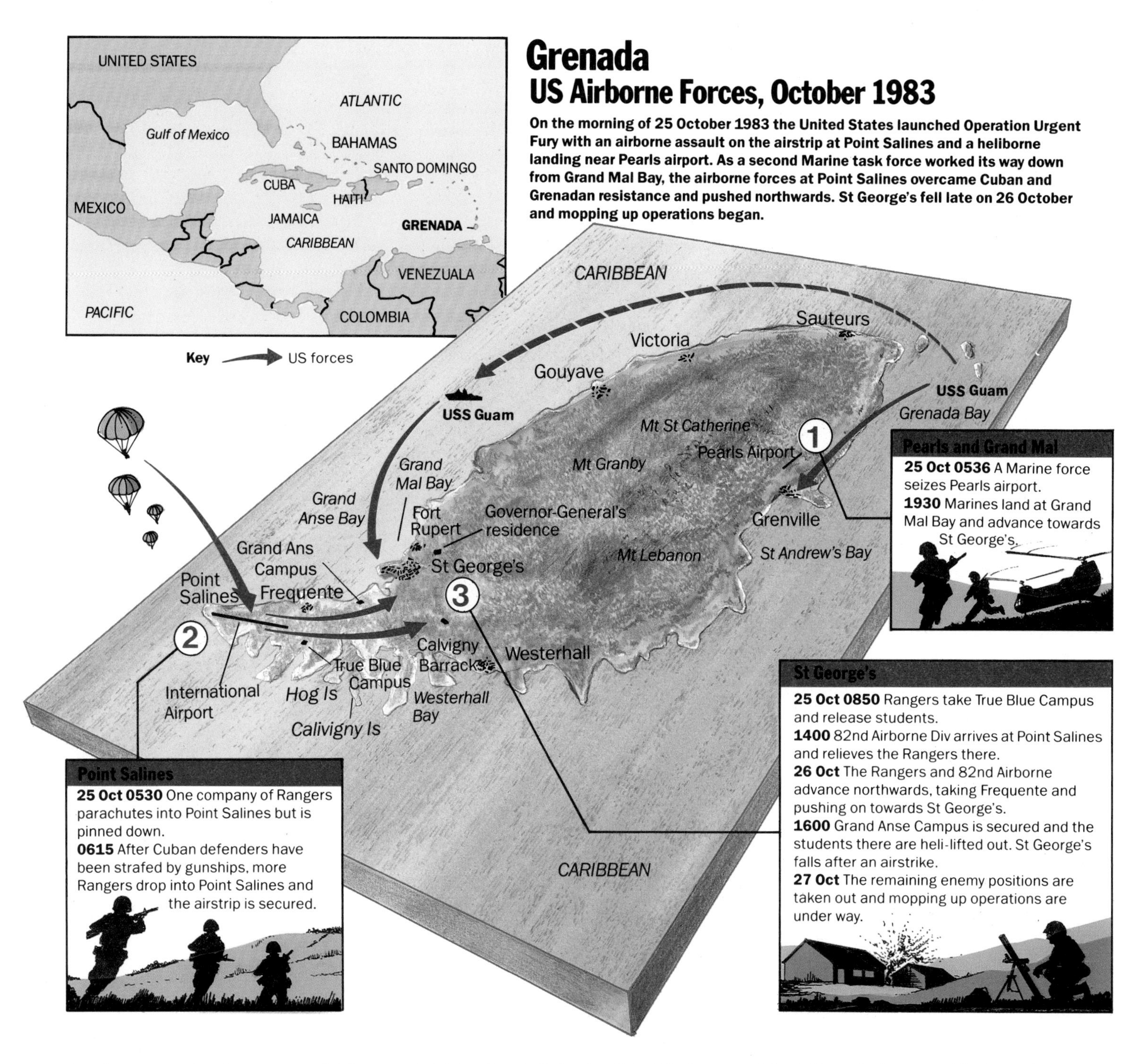

they began clearing the runway of debris to allow aircraft to land. The Cuban soldiers in the area attempted to make two counterattacks, but their armoured personnel carriers were blown apart each time by recoilless rifles and light anti-tank weapons.

The Rangers then moved out to rescue the 130 American students at the St George's Medical College. By 0850 hours it was secure, though the Rangers were then informed that more students were at the Grand Anse campus. At Point Salines the cleared runway meant the Division Ready Brigade of the 82nd Airborne could be flown in (eventually over 5000 men of the division would be landed on Grenada). The rescue of the students at Grand Anse now became a priority, and so the 2nd Battalion, 75th Rangers, carried in Marine helicopters, landed on the site during the afternoon of 26 October and escorted them to safety.

The only major point of resistance left by the 27th was the Cuban barracks at Edgmont, which was taken in spectacular fashion by men of the 82nd Airborne and spearheaded by Rangers in Black Hawk helicopters. The latter lost three killed and 15 wounded, but the barracks was taken. Despite some minor hitches, Operation 'Urgent Fury' demonstrated the ability of US forces in general to deploy rapidly, and it also proved that the Rangers could fulfil their traditional role as spearhead troops, living up to their motto of 'Rangers lead the way'. In addition, it also demonstrated the 82nd Airborne's ability to deploy rapidly: the first paras had arrived over Point Salines within 17 hours of being alerted.

US AIRBORNE FORCES, PANAMA, 20 DECEMBER 1989

The December 1989 invasion of Panama by American forces, codenamed 'Just Cause', might seem a case of overkill: there were 26,000 US personnel committed, including 1700 Rangers and 3300 paras who parachuted in. However, there were a number of problems for the Americans, not least of which was the fact that the Panamanian forces wore the same uniforms and carried much the same equipment as their adversaries!

The main American tactical formations employed in 'Just Cause' were multi-battalion task forces: Atlantic, Bayonet, Pacific and Red. Apart from armoured personnel carriers (APCs), the Army's only other armoured vehicles used in Panama were the 82nd Airborne Division's M551A1 Sheridan light airborne assault vehicles of the 3rd Battalion, 73rd Armor Regiment.

'Just Cause' was the culmination of the deterioration in relations between Panama, specifically its dictator, General Noriega, and the United States. In October 1989 there was an abortive coup against Noriega which had been encouraged by the USA. In mid-December Noriega had himself appointed 'Maximum Leader' and persuaded the Panamanian legislature to declare that a state of war existed with the US. The Panamanian Defence Forces (PDF) and US forces in-country began to watch each other closely. On 16 December four US Marine officers travelling in Panama were fired on when they refused to stop at a roadblock: a

BELOW: *Noriega's world crumbles as US forces launch Operation 'Just Cause'. The invasion went smoothly, and the Panamanians were able to mount only sporadic attacks on the Americans.*

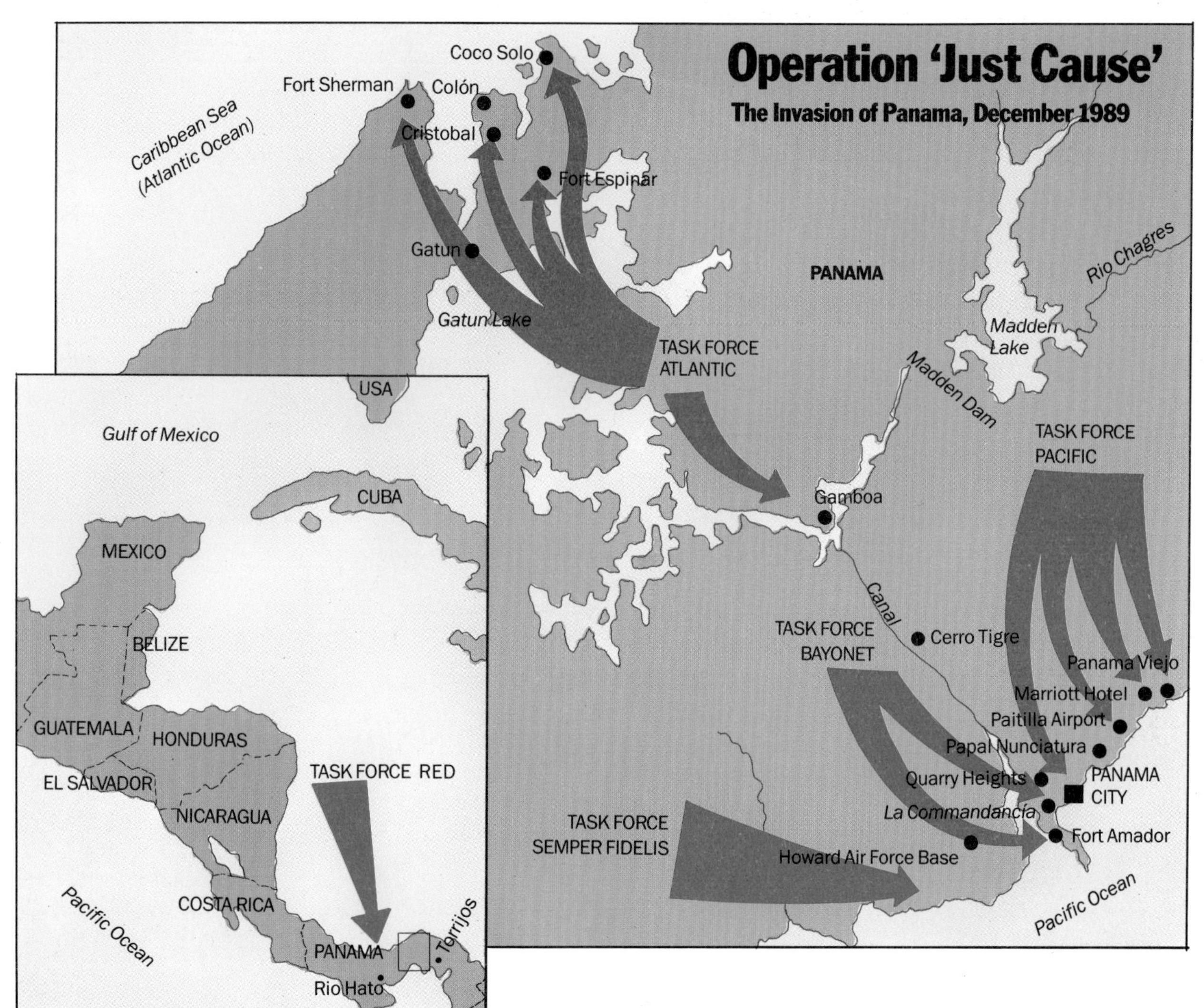

young lieutenant was killed. A US Navy officer and his wife who witnessed the shooting were detained – he was beaten and his wife threatened with rape. The next day President Bush ordered the implementation of 'Just Cause'.

US units already in Panama (in the Canal Zone) included elements of the 82nd Airborne, two infantry brigades and Marines, but the main force would come from the United States: 1st Brigade, 82nd Airborne; 3rd Brigade; 7th Infantry Division; 193rd Infantry Brigade; and the 75th Ranger Regiment. The PDF, for its part, was, thanks to Noriega, a largely corrupt military machine which numbered some 15,000 personnel, including the brutal Dignity Battalions which were often filled with criminals and thugs.

The first men to drop into Panama were paras of the 82nd Airborne forming part of Task Force Pacific, who parachuted onto Torrijos airport at 0210 hours on 20 December. After securing the airport, the paras were then air-assaulted in Black Hawk helicopters into Panama La Viejo on the Pacific coast. Another company drove from the airport to link up with the heliborne troops, the paras taking two Sheridans. However, they came under enemy fire and had to bring up two more Sheridans before breaking through. In the afternoon the paras secured the Marriott Hotel and other locations along the coast, blowing up four PDF V-300 armoured cars in the process. The fight for Paitilla airport was short but intense, the enemy losing 13 dead and 10 destroyed armoured cars before melting away.

Units of the 82nd were also a part of Task Force Atlantic which captured the Madden Dam, Gamboa and the northern areas of the country. In one incident, UH-1H, AH-1S and OH-58 helicopters landed in a prison compound, shot up the guards barracks and freed all the prisoners.

Task Force Bayonet, involving the 82nd's Armor Regiment, seized the well-defended La Commandancia. Throughout the day on the 20th, it was pounded with mortars, anti-tank rounds and the Sheridans' 152mm guns. However, it held out, until the defences were breached in the early evening, the PDF suffering heavy casualties. From 22 December the paras and other units conducted stability operations (security and civil tasks throughout Panama City) until relieved by units of the 7th Infantry Division on 10 January.

Though the US had used overwhelming force in 'Just Cause', the units had interacted superbly and had quashed resistance very quickly. The 82nd Airborne Division in particular had once again proved its rapid response capability, and its men fought bravely and professionally when on the ground – no mean achievement when one considers that they dropped into 'hot' landing zones at night.

CHAPTER VI

BRUSHFIRE WARS

Brushfire wars usually erupt with little warning, and if not contained can spread very quickly. Therefore, to suppress them often requires a sort of military fire brigade: a force that can deploy rapidly to destroy the enemy before he has time to act, or to stabilise a difficult situation. This type of warfare requires soldiers who are adaptable, quick-thinking and can operate in small groups deep inside enemy territory if required. The men of Britain's Special Air Service are one such group. It is, therefore, hardly surprising that they were sent to Oman in the 1950s and 1970s when that country was beset by internal rebellion and dissent, first in the north of the country, and then in the south. The two campaigns the SAS conducted in Oman remain a superb example of how a small force, if containing the right kind of soldiers and used correctly, can achieve remarkable results. Two actions from those campaigns are included in this chapter. One is the Battle of Mirbat in 1972, when a nine-man SAS team, aided by a handful of local tribesmen and armed policemen, defeated an enemy force of 250 heavily armed communist fighters.

Africa provides many of the actions for this chapter, specifically the operations of South African and Rhodesian forces. Surrounded as they were, and in the case of South Africa still is, by the black 'frontline states', both countries were forced to establish rapid reaction/counter-insurgency units. The Rhodesian Light Infantry was one such force, and its highly successful series of operations into Mozambique is included below.

The South African Defence Force (SADF) has probably the best troops in Africa. Its reconnaissance commandos, for example, are trained to operate deep inside enemy territory, a task similar to the one performed by the now disbanded Rhodesian Selous Scouts. Indeed, many former members of the Scouts joined South Africa's reconnaissance specialists. The commandos are elite troops in every sense of the word, being trained in parachuting, tracking and survival techniques.

Finally, the 1991 Gulf War between Iraq and the forces of the United Nations is examined. Though this conflict was a large-scale affair, it bore all the hallmarks of a brushfire war: the sudden invasion of Kuwait by Saddam Hussein in August 1990, the rapid build-up of United Nations troops in Saudi Arabia, and the short but violent campaign to eject Iraqi troops from Kuwait. There is no doubt that Saddam Hussein would have invaded Saudi Arabia if allowed to do so, and that the rapid deployment of American units to the country in August 1990, codenamed Operation 'Desert Shield', stopped this (though the Iraqis did have an opportunity to occupy northern Saudi Arabia at least in the days following their conquest of Kuwait). The rapid and efficient deployment of mostly US troops and equipment to the region made any further Iraqi aggression impossible, and laid the foundations for the speedy liberation of Kuwait – Operation 'Desert Storm' – during which the Iraqi armed forces were systematically destroyed in a land war that lasted only 100 hours.

South African deep-penetration forces search for enemy guerrillas on the veldt.

GREAT BRITAIN

22 SAS, THE JEBEL AKHDAR, 26-27 JANUARY 1959

Taking fortified enemy positions is never easy. A commander can attempt it in a number of ways: starve the garrison into surrender, storm the defences, or try to entice the besieged into capitulation. However, if the stronghold consists of an almost inaccessible mountain plateau containing well-armed rebels who know the terrain, then the commander has problems.

Such was the task facing Lieutenant-Colonel Tony Deane-Drummond, commander of 22 SAS, in late 1958 when D Squadron of the elite British regiment was flown to Oman in the Middle East. The Jebel Akhdar (which means Green Mountain) range rises from the Omani desert to form a massive and formidable massif, topped by a plateau and surrounded by jagged peaks. For over two years it had been the stronghold of rebel forces opposing the regime of the repressive Sultan Said bin Taimur, and had successfully resisted all attacks by the British-trained Sultan's Armed Forces (SAF).

Establishing positions on the Jebel

The task required specialist soldiers, hence the SAS. The men of the Special Air Service get results largely by stealth and guile, allied to superb combat skills and the daring to try almost anything. Arriving at the Jebel in November 1958, the SAS were assisted by RAF Venoms which blasted the rebel positions with rockets. However, the rebels were good shots and cover was sparse: the SAS men quickly developed a healthy respect for their foes.

The SAS were deployed to the north and south of the Jebel, the northern force under Captain Rory Walker establishing a number of sangers on the heights of Aquabat al Dhafar. The SAS men began acclimatising themselves to the conditions and had a number of brushes with the enemy. By Christmas, though, the rebels were still firmly entrenched on the Jebel, and it was clear that the SAS would have to storm it by force. Needing reinforcements for the task, A Squadron arrived in Oman and was shipped north. In mid-January 1959, several attacks were launched in the north and the south, but these were only part of a ruse. The SAS soldiers were heavily outnumbered; if the assault was to succeed, the element of surprise had to be exploited to the full.

Word was spread among the Arab donkey handlers that the attack would take place from Tanuf. They were told that this information was confidential, on pain of death; needless to say, the rebels had this news within a few hours. The

BELOW: *British aircraft drop supplies to waiting SAS trucks in northern Oman, early 1959. The assault on the Jebel Akhdar was a classic operation.*

Jebel Akhdar
22 SAS, January 1959

When D Squadron, 22 SAS, was first deployed in Oman in November 1958, the mountain stronghold of the Jebel Akhdar was held by well-armed and entrenched rebel forces. Early in January A Squadron arrived, and 22 SAS started preparations for a decisive assault on the Jebel. At 0300 on 26 January the first phase of the operation began with A Squadron's attack on the Aquabat al Dhafar.

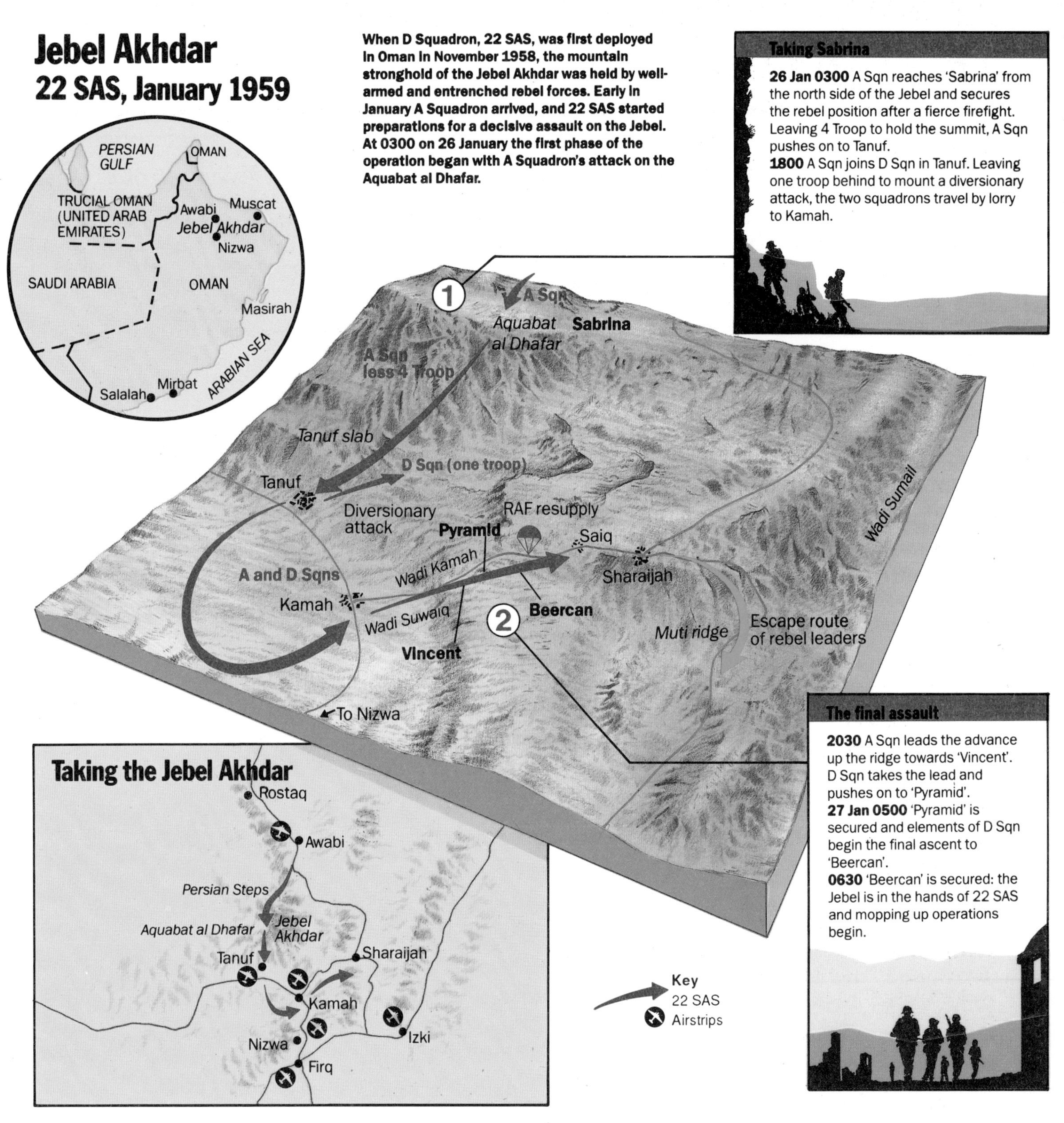

attack, of course, was from a totally different direction. The SAS soldiers were superbly fit – they had to be. Scaling up a precipitous mountain track at night heavily loaded with weapons and ammunition takes a special kind of soldier. Major Johnny Cooper, A Squadron, describes it thus: 'It was bloody difficult and we were carrying a hell of a lot of weight.'

In fact, so successful was the ruse that the SAS encountered little opposition when they made it onto the plateau, suffering only two dead and two wounded. The rebels were dumbfounded. The SAS quickly mopped up the pockets of resistance and by 5 February had control of the whole Jebel. It had been a classic example of how a small body of highly trained men, coupled with imaginative planning, can achieve results out of all proportion to their size. But that is what Britain's Special Air Service is all about.

22 SAS, THE BATTLE OF MIRBAT, 19 JULY 1972

The defence of the Omani town of Mirbat by a nine-man SAS team and a few local soldiers and policemen against 250 communist insurgents is one of the more remarkable feats in the history of an elite regiment. The British SAS specialises in fighting in small units – usually four-man teams – its soldiers all highly trained in all aspects of special forces work: demolitions, languages, first aid, parachuting, combat diving, as well as elite weapons skills. The latter came into play at Mirbat, when the SAS team gave the enemy a lesson in accurate firepower.

The SAS was in Oman assisting the Sultan, Qaboos, against the forces of the communist People's Front for the Liberation of the Occupied Arabian Gulf (PFLOAG) in Dhofar Province in the south. The insurgents received aid from neighbouring South Yemen, and so they were a force to be reckoned with. The SAS had done well, recruiting ex-communist fighters, called *firqat*, and assisting the local population. The people of Dhofar were starting to turn against the *adoo*, as the communists were known. Thus the communists needed a victory to convince the waverers that their cause was the one that would prevail. The town of Mirbat was chosen.

ABOVE: *An SAS mortar pounds* Adoo *positions in Dhofar, southern Oman, in the mid-1970s. The weapons skills of individual SAS soldiers are legendary.*

The *adoo* attack begins

The attack was well planned. It took place, for example, in the monsoon season, which made air support for the defenders difficult. In addition, the 250 assailants were armed with heavy machine guns, mortars, rocket launchers and recoilless rifles. They also hoped that they would achieve total surprise when they attacked. In this they were wrong. The *adoo* were spotted by a patrol of the Dhofar Gendarmerie as they crept forward and were fired upon. The SAS commander, Captain Mike Kealy, rushed to his HQ – the 'Batthouse' – and assessed the situation. The *adoo* were pressing their attack against a fort held by around 25 Gendarmes, beside which was a gun-pit holding a 25-pounder field gun. There was also the Wali's Fort held by 30 *askars* (armed tribesmen).

The *adoo*, sensing victory, pressed the attack hard. However, the SAS soldiers were returning accurate, deadly fire: Lance-Corporal Pete Wignall and Corporal Roger Chapman with machine guns, Lance-Corporal Harris with a mortar in a pit beside the Batthouse, as well as Corporal Labalaba furiously firing the 25-pounder with the assistance of an Omani gunner. The Gendarmerie Fort looked set to fall, but the *adoo* were held off by the machine guns of Wignall and Chapman.

By 0700 hours the first *adoo* attack had been stopped, but Mirbat was still in danger. Labalaba had been wounded and his place taken by Trooper Savesaki. Kealy took Trooper Tobin and made a mad dash to the Gendarmerie Fort, just as another *adoo* attack erupted. Labalaba was killed, then Tobin. Kealy radioed the Batthouse for fire to be brought down on the gun-pit, and this was carried out. Then, during a break in the clouds, Omani Strikemaster jets raced down and poured cannon fire into the enemy.

Reinforcements arrived in the shape of 23 members of G Squadron from Salalah. G Squadron mounted a ferocious counterattack which drove off the startled *adoo*. The Battle of Mirbat was over. The ground was littered with enemy dead, the SAS for its part losing only two men killed. It had been a salutary lesson in weapons skills and tactical awareness.

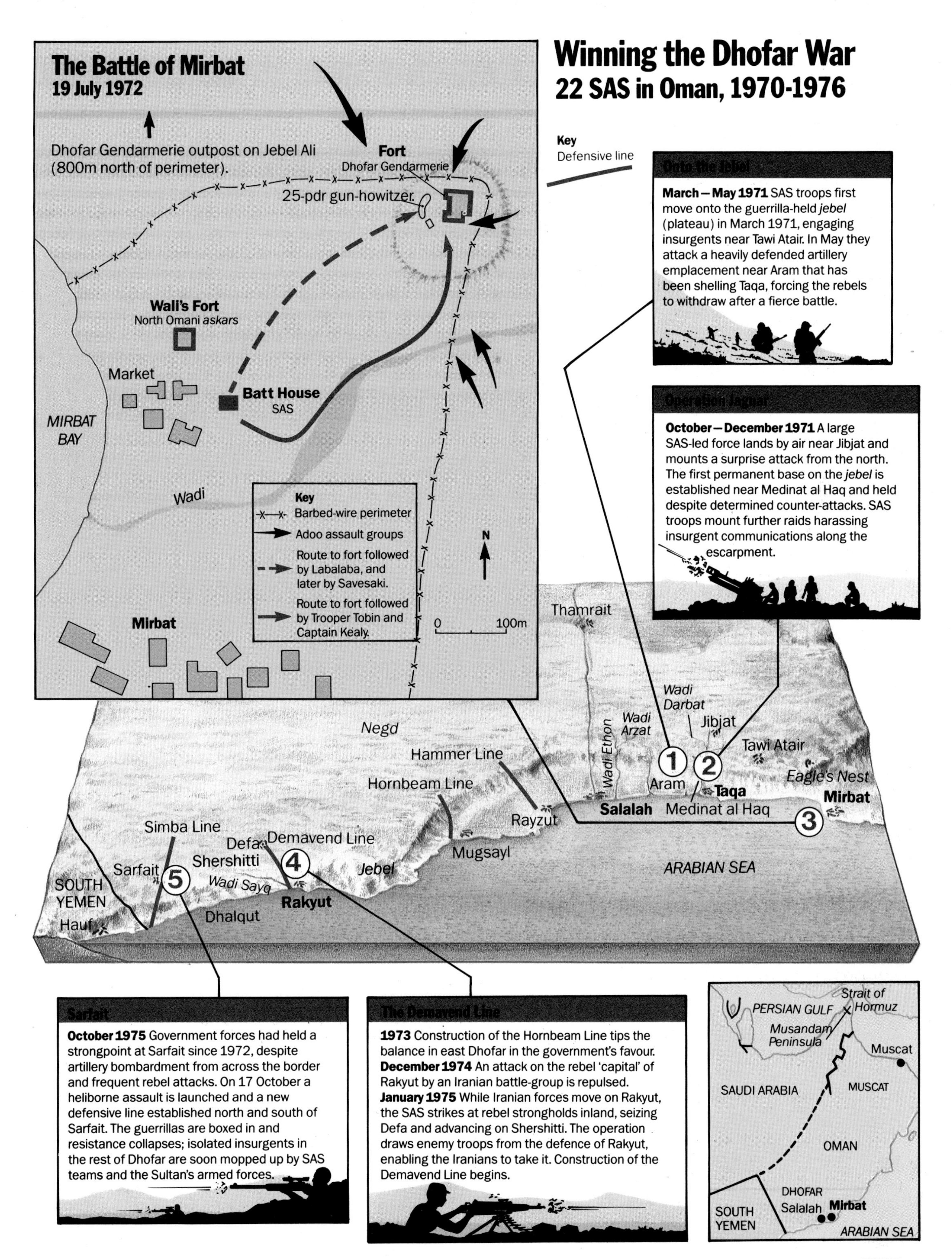

Winning the Dhofar War
22 SAS in Oman, 1970-1976
Key
Defensive line
The Battle of Mirbat
19 July 1972
Dhofar Gendarmerie outpost on Jebel Ali (800m north of perimeter).
Fort
Dhofar Gendarmerie
25-pdr gun-howitzer
Wali's Fort
North Omani askars
Market
Batt House
SAS
MIRBAT BAY
Wadi
Key
Barbed-wire perimeter
Adoo assault groups
Route to fort followed by Labalaba, and later by Savesaki.
Route to fort followed by Trooper Tobin and Captain Kealy.
N
0 100m
Mirbat
Onto the Jebel
March – May 1971 SAS troops first move onto the guerrilla-held jebel (plateau) in March 1971, engaging insurgents near Tawi Atair. In May they attack a heavily defended artillery emplacement near Aram that has been shelling Taqa, forcing the rebels to withdraw after a fierce battle.
Operation Jaguar
October – December 1971 A large SAS-led force lands by air near Jibjat and mounts a surprise attack from the north. The first permanent base on the jebel is established near Medinat al Haq and held despite determined counter-attacks. SAS troops mount further raids harassing insurgent communications along the escarpment.
Thamrait
Wadi Darbat
Wadi Arzat
Jibjat
Tawi Atair
Wadi Ethon
Eagle's Nest
Aram
Taqa
Mirbat
Salalah
Medinat al Haq
Negd
Hammer Line
Hornbeam Line
Rayzut
Simba Line
Defa
Demavend Line
Shershitti
Mugsayl
Jebel
ARABIAN SEA
Sarfait
Wadi Sayq
SOUTH YEMEN
Rakyut
Hauf
Dhalqut
1
2
3
4
5
Sarfait
October 1975 Government forces had held a strongpoint at Sarfait since 1972, despite artillery bombardment from across the border and frequent rebel attacks. On 17 October a heliborne assault is launched and a new defensive line established north and south of Sarfait. The guerrillas are boxed in and resistance collapses; isolated insurgents in the rest of Dhofar are soon mopped up by SAS teams and the Sultan's armed forces.
The Demavend Line
1973 Construction of the Hornbeam Line tips the balance in east Dhofar in the government's favour.
December 1974 An attack on the rebel 'capital' of Rakyut by an Iranian battle-group is repulsed.
January 1975 While Iranian forces move on Rakyut, the SAS strikes at rebel strongholds inland, seizing Defa and advancing on Shershitti. The operation draws enemy troops from the defence of Rakyut, enabling the Iranians to take it. Construction of the Demavend Line begins.
PERSIAN GULF
Strait of Hormuz
Musandam Peninsula
Muscat
SAUDI ARABIA
MUSCAT
OMAN
DHOFAR
Salalah
Mirbat
SOUTH YEMEN
ARABIAN SEA

RHODESIAN LIGHT INFANTRY, COUNTER-INSURGENCY OPERATIONS, 1979

By the mid-1970s, the black nationalist guerrillas of Robert Mugabe's ZANU organisation were operating in eastern Rhodesia from bases inside Mozambique. Rhodesian forces needed to launch pre-emptive raids against the insurgents; and to this end, the Rhodesian Light Infantry (RLI) airborne Fire Forces were created, to seek and destroy terrorist units in the bush. High mobility and operational flexibility, combined with heavy firepower, were the keys to success.

Operating from Grand Reef airfield, the tactics were to fly in four-man 'stop groups' by helicopter. If they could deal with the terrorists, all well and good. If not, then RLI paras would be dropped to act as 'beaters' to drive the enemy towards the stop groups.

Contacts were invariably short but violent, with confused individual firefights breaking out in the bush once the men were on the ground. The Rhodesians were armed with FN rifles and FN MAG machine guns, while their adversaries, the guerrillas of the Zimbabwe African National Liberation Army (ZANLA) were invariably armed with Russian or Chinese AK series assault rifles.

Each Fire Force usually consisted of three four-man sticks transported in 'G-Cars' (Alouette helicopters) and another four four-man sticks available to parachute in from a 'Para-Dak' (DC-3 Dakota). During an operation, there was always an Alouette 'K-Car' (command helicopter) that circled the area. If extra fire support was needed, then the men could call in Lynx aircraft armed with rockets and napalm, or even Venom and Canberra jets of the Rhodesian Air Force.

Though the RLI contained foreign nationals who had fought with many elite units – the SAS, US Special Forces, and French Foreign Legion, for example – and although its record was extremely good against the guerrillas, minority rule could not be maintained and so, in 1980, shortly after the end of hostilities, the RLI was officially disbanded.

ABOVE: *Rhodesian troops hunt for black nationalist guerrillas of Robert Mugabe's ZANU movement.*

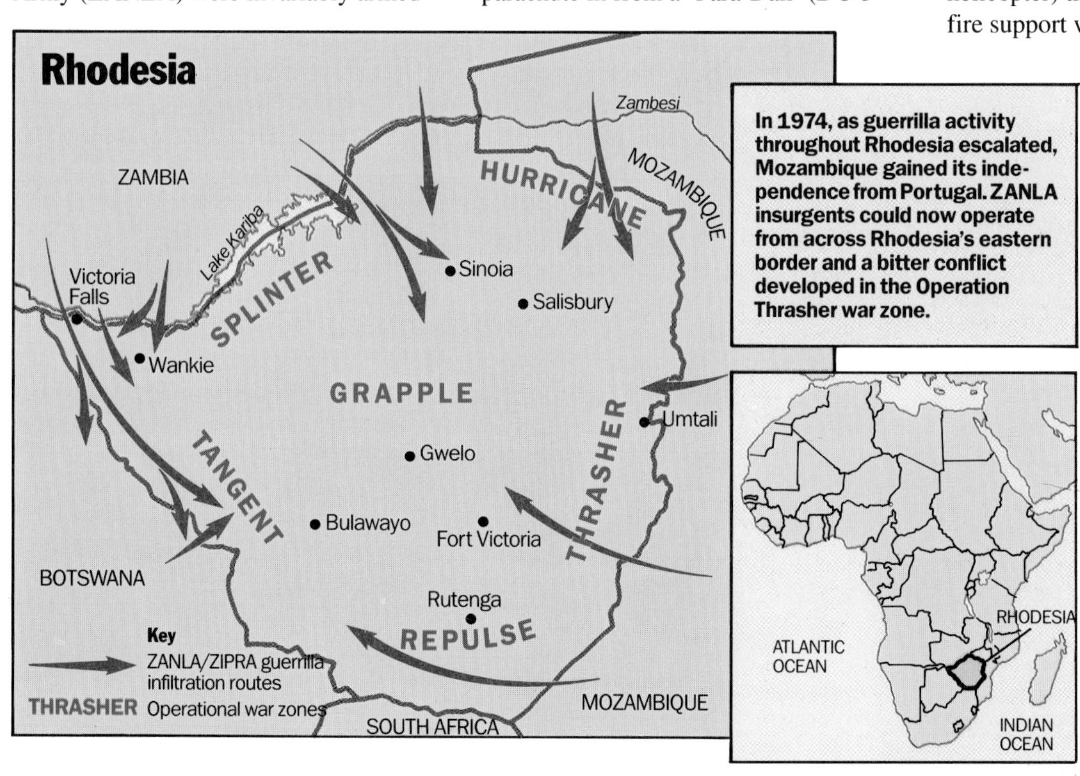

In 1974, as guerrilla activity throughout Rhodesia escalated, Mozambique gained its independence from Portugal. ZANLA insurgents could now operate from across Rhodesia's eastern border and a bitter conflict developed in the Operation Thrasher war zone.

32 BATTALION, SOUTH AFRICAN DEFENCE FORCE, NAMIBIA, 1980S

The South African Defence Force's (SADF's) 32 Battalion was composed of white ex-Rhodesian military personnel and black troops from the National Liberation Front of Angola (FNLA), as well as white mercenaries. The men and their families were housed in a secret camp near Rundu. It was created in 1975-76 and was distinct from other SADF units; indeed, contact between it and other troops was positively discouraged.

The battalion operated against the Popular Armed Forces for the Liberation of Angola (FAPLA), the troops usually carrying Soviet-made AK-47 assault rifles and machine guns. In fact, in their appearance the men of 32 Battalion differed little from Angolan units. This was deliberate: should any casualties be left behind, there would be no evidence that the SADF was engaging in clandestine operations beyond the borders of South Africa.

32 Battalion was organised into seven companies, each containing three or four platoons. In addition, there was a separate 81mm mortar company and a reconnaissance element. Unlike other SADF units, it was deployed solely on counter-insurgency operations. Its specific missions were not known at the time, although it is known that it carried out a number of very successful strikes against both the People's Liberation Army of Namibia (PLAN) – the military wing of the South West African People's Organisation – and the Popular Armed Forces for the Liberation of Angola (FAPLA).

Discipline within the unit was strict: serious misdeeds could result in a trooper being flogged, and in some cases death was meted out to maintain the respect of the men. It seemed to work. In one particular incident, a 32 Battalion patrol was ambushed while operating in Angola. The enemy fire was intense and cut down 23 men – though, amazingly, only one was killed. Rather than try to run, those who had survived the initial contact stood and charged headlong at the enemy. They killed six of them and drove the rest off, retrieving a seemingly lost situation.

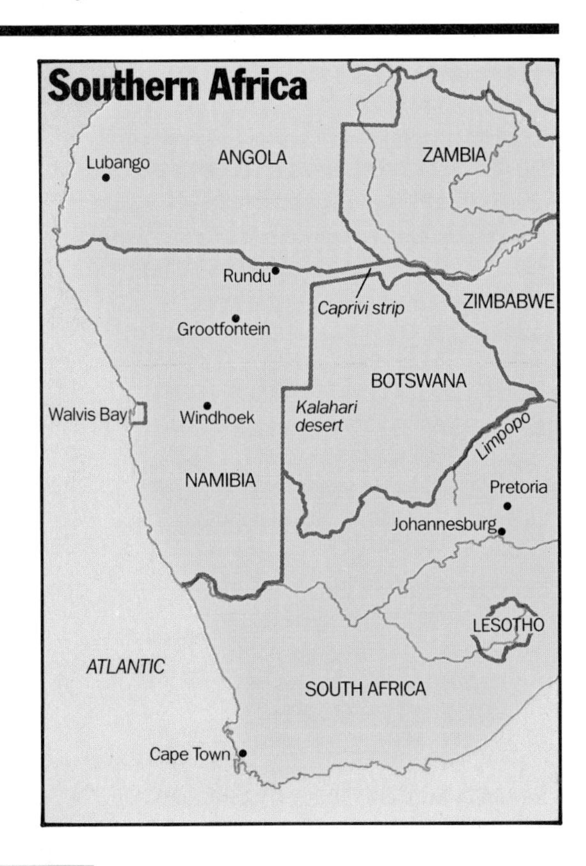

Soon 32 Battalion became known as the 'Terrible Ones' to its enemies. The South African government drew a veil of secrecy over the activities of 32 Battalion, but there is no doubt that when it was in existence it carried out its masters' bidding without question. In the shady world of covert counter-insurgency operations, the battalion proved itself to be an expert.

LEFT: *White special forces soldiers on a mission deep inside Namibia during the early 1980s hunt for guerrillas as part of South Africa's secret war.*

SOUTH AFRICAN RECCE COMMANDOS, NAMIBIA, 1978-84

The Reconnaissance Commandos are the elite of the South African Defence Force (SADF). They were formed to deal with military threats at sea and on land that cannot be countered by conventional methods. Their training is therefore orientated towards the development of techniques of infiltration, reconnaissance and counter-insurgency. Composed mainly of white officers and men, there is also a contingent of black ex-SWAPO (South West African People's Organisation) guerrillas who became disillusioned with the cause of African nationalism.

All white Recce Commandos undergo an intensive training schedule that includes tough tests: a 5km cross-country run in 20 minutes, a 200m dash carrying a man in a fireman's lift in one minute, and a 15km route-march carrying a 30kg load in two hours. Psychological tests determine whether they will be able to stand the strain of operating behind enemy lines for long periods. The basic training lasts for three months and includes parachuting and realistic battle simulations. Then there are eight months of special orientation for their future role. Those who fail at any stage – and quite a few do – are returned to their original unit. Once trained, the new recruit joins an operational unit. Recce Commandos receive additional allowances and extra pay during operations.

The Commandos were employed by the SADF throughout the 1970s and 1980s, examples being the 1975-76 'Angola March' and in 1980 during the anti-terrorist operations 'Sceptic' and 'Smokeshellbasis'. They have been used in many short-duration, hit-and-destroy attacks, their targets being reached by parachute, on foot, in vehicles, by helicopter or across water.

When operating in areas that are entirely populated by blacks, the white Recce Commandos tend to black-up all exposed flesh, even carrying enemy weapons to add to the ruse. Though South African forces have now withdrawn from Namibia, there is no doubt that the Recce Commandos stand ready to go back in should the South African government feel threatened by events north of their border. Whatever happens, the elite Recce Commandos are prepared.

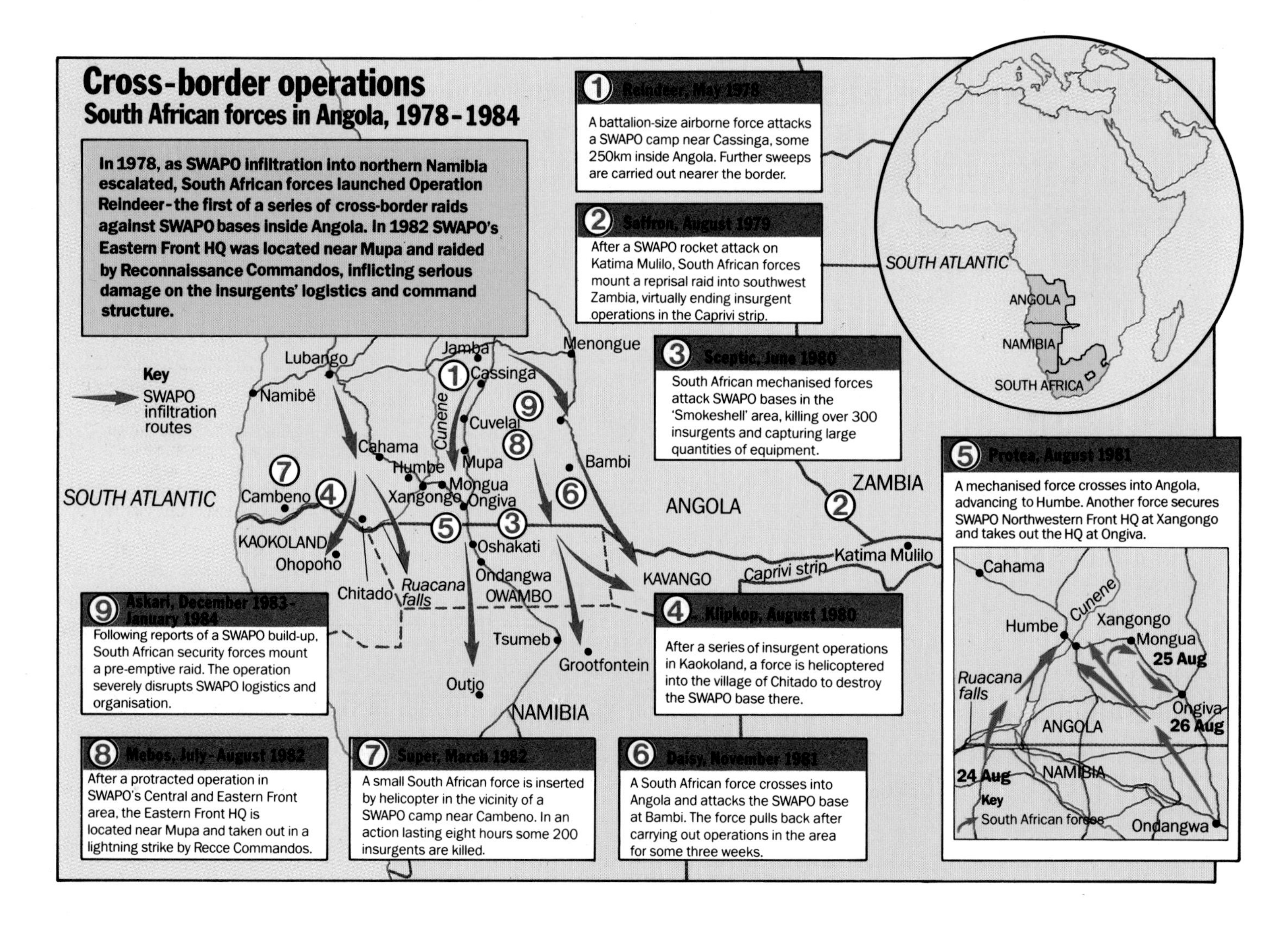

PATHFINDER COMPANY, 44 PARACHUTE BRIGADE, ANGOLA, 1981

The Pathfinder Company of 44 Parachute Brigade, South African Defence Force (SADF) was activated in 1980 and contained many foreign nationals. By early 1981 there were enough personnel to be deployed on active service in Angola. The men were mounted on a number of vehicles: three Toyota Landcruisers mounting machine guns and cannon, three Land Rovers also equipped with machine guns, and three Unimog trucks carrying extra fuel, ammunition and supplies.

The vehicles arrived at Murrayhill, the Pathfinders' base, and then the whole convoy moved to the operational area: Sector 10, the region of Namibia that borders Angola. The first operation was a dawn attack on a SWAPO (South West Africa Peoples' Organisation) base. Following air strikes, the base was to be assaulted by 32 Battalion, with the Pathfinders providing close support. The company struck north, crossing the Angolan border and linking up with 32 Battalion.

The air strike went in at dawn the next day. Though the enemy did put up some ineffective flak and fired rockets on likely ground approach routes, as the ground forces advanced it became clear that the terrorists had fled. Though the camp was destroyed, the element of surprise had been lost and so the operation was only a partial success.

During the summer of 1981 the Pathfinders mounted ceaseless combat patrols into Angola. However, the major action of that year was a large-scale invasion of Angola to deliver a crushing blow to SWAPO's ability to mount raids into Namibia, as well as force FAPLA (Popular Armed Forces for the Liberation of Angola) to reconsider its support for SWAPO. Operation 'Protea' was about to commence.

Tank hunters

The Pathfinders were given the role of tank hunters, ready to deploy as required. On 25 August the company was attached to Battle Group 30, and made ready to stop any FAPLA vehicles coming down from Cahama. A column of vehicles was ambushed that night. By morning the Pathfinders were on the move again, checking all known enemy camps around Chibemba. They were all deserted. The rest of the operation was largely uneventful for the unit, the company continuing its sweeps but finding only sporadic enemy resistance.

The Pathfinders were undoubtedly tough troops and, because many were Rhodesians with long service records, were always eager to get to grips with the enemy. The training process was amazingly tough. For example, a full ammunition box was always carried by each man on every run, and a 5-10km run rounded off every day's training. The result was the finest strike troops on the African continent.

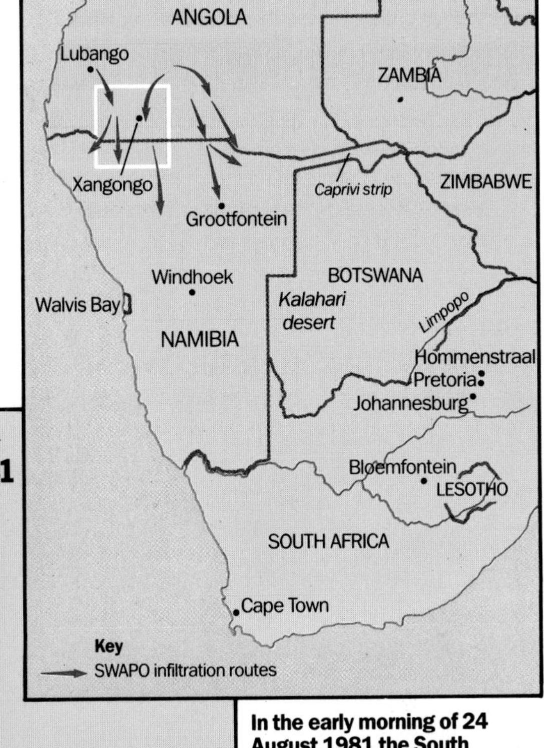

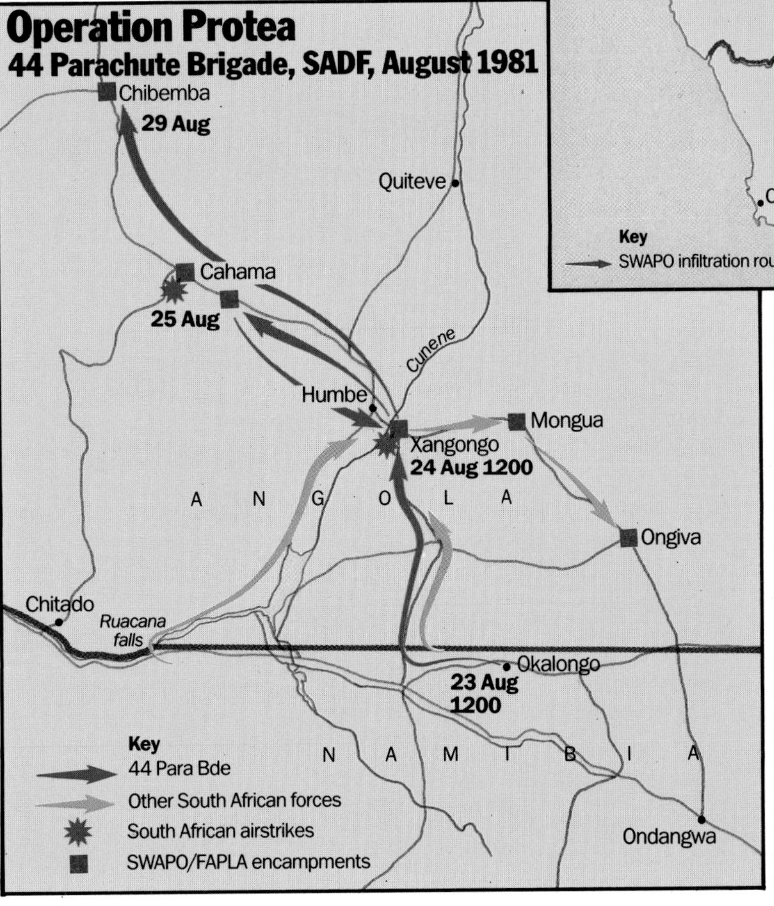

In the early morning of 24 August 1981 the South African Defence Force moved against SWAPO insurgents in one of its largest ever cross-border operations into Angola. While a mechanised force crossed the border at Ruacana falls, a second task force – with the 44 Para Brigade's Pathfinder Company attached – moved on Xangongo. As the force swept forward through southern Angola, a South African Mirage strike went in at Xangongo and at the radar station outside Cahama. The Pathfinder Company penetrated as far as Chibemba and was involved in two sharp engagements with the enemy.

2 PARA, GOOSE GREEN, 28 MAY 1982

British Paras have always proved themselves to be exceptional soldiers. It is part of the Para ethos that the men who wear the maroon beret can go anywhere and do anything. This belief is shared by all ranks of the Parachute Regiment, and so it was no surprise to find them in the Falklands in May 1982.

On 28 May the men of 2 Para were engaged in the assault upon Argentinian forces around Goose Green. The enemy were more numerous and better armed, but these things have never worried the Paras. They were highly trained and motivated, and didn't worry about having to fight at night and conduct an assault 25km from the nearest friendly forces.

'H' Jones is killed

The attack started at 0635 hours, when Major Dair Farrar-Hockley's A Company took Burntside House. They then came under anti-tank and grenade attack soon after. B Company moved forward and charged Argentinian trenches on its left flank. These were soon cleared, the Paras lobbing phosphorus grenades into them.

In the centre, D Company and the Battalion HQ, led by Colonel 'H' Jones, began their move. Enemy resistance was heavy, and the attack began to slow down. Argentinian artillery fire was now raining down on the Paras, though the damp, peaty ground of the battlefield reduced the impact of the shells and lessened the killing power of the splinters. D Company started to take casualties, the men being left where they fell until circumstances allowed them to be relieved (this was not callous – it was the only way a light unit could survive on the battlefield). However, the enemy positions were cleared and A Company was ordered to press on towards Darwin. Enemy artillery fire continued.

Both B and A Companies became pinned down around Boca House and Darwin Hill, the latter containing Argentinians entrenched in well-placed bunkers. Attempts to blow them apart with grenades and anti-tank rockets failed. The Paras were well and truly stuck. Their ammunition was running low and there was no fire support because the weather was too bad for aircraft, and artillery support had ceased to exist. Jones moved forward to assess the situation, and made his own attack round to the right. He was shot and killed. His death inspired A Company to renew its efforts, and it pierced the enemy lines.

At Boca House, meanwhile, B Company brought up some Milan anti-tank weapons to use against the Argentinians. As B Company poured fire into the enemy positions, D Company, which had gone along a slope under the cover of the cliff face, stormed forward, and the Argentinians surrendered. As the entire battalion began to advance towards Goose Green, it came under fire from anti-aircraft guns around the airstrip, but

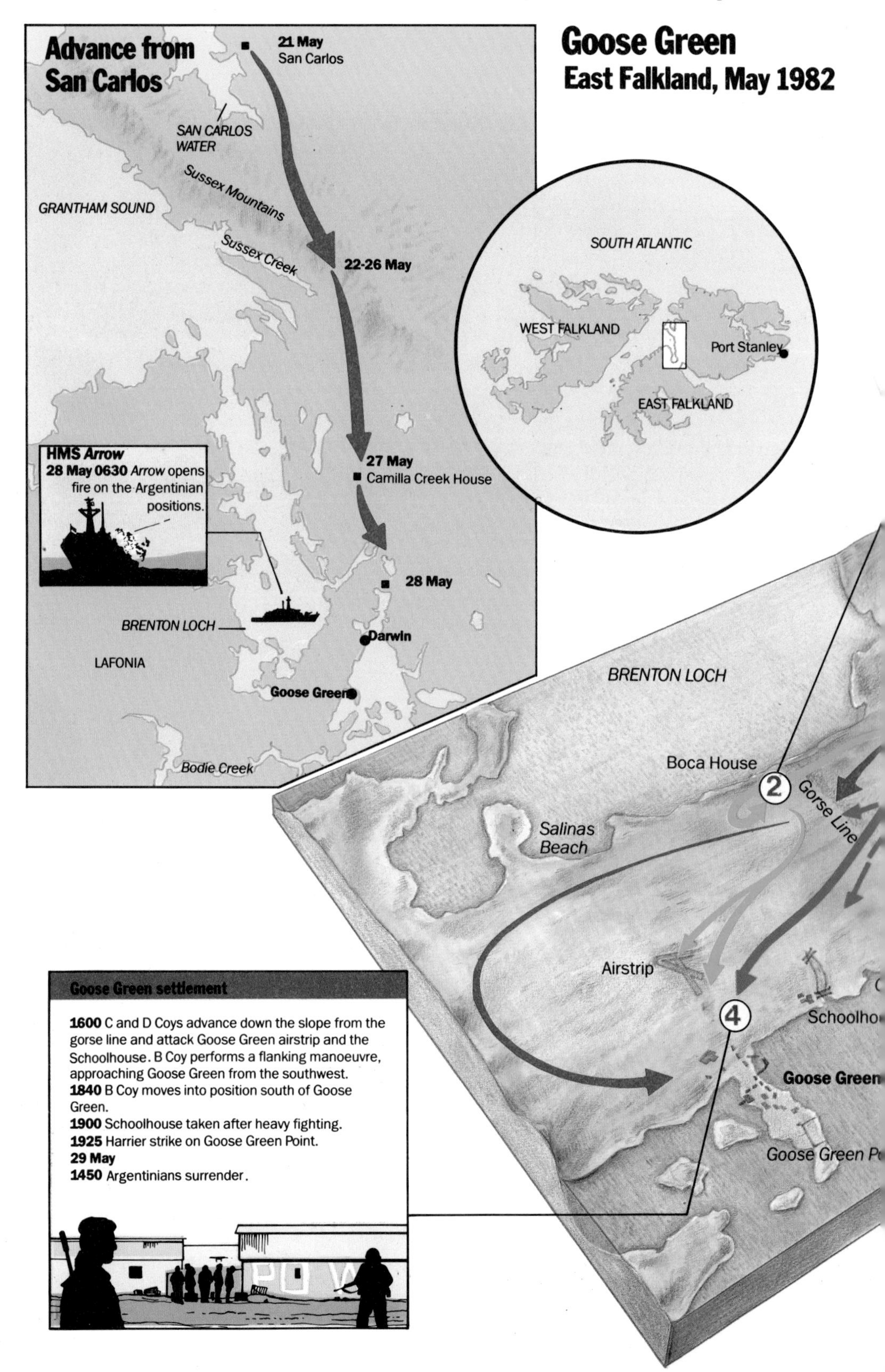

at last a Harrier attack was possible. The aircraft swooped down and dropped cluster bombs on the enemy.

The Argentinians in Goose Green were now besieged, with the Paras dug in around them. The second-in-command of the battalion, Major Chris Keeble, forbade any aggressive patrolling – he wanted the enemy to have time to think about their position. They did. In the morning the Argentinians surrendered. The 2nd Battalion, The Parachute Regiment, had won. For the loss of 15 killed and 30 wounded, they took 1300 prisoners. It had been a victory of courage and tactics over numbers.

BELOW: *Tired but defiant. A Para machine gunner takes a breather while on operations in the Falklands. As usual, the members of the British Parachute Regiment displayed those fighting qualities that have made it the envy of armed forces around the world.*

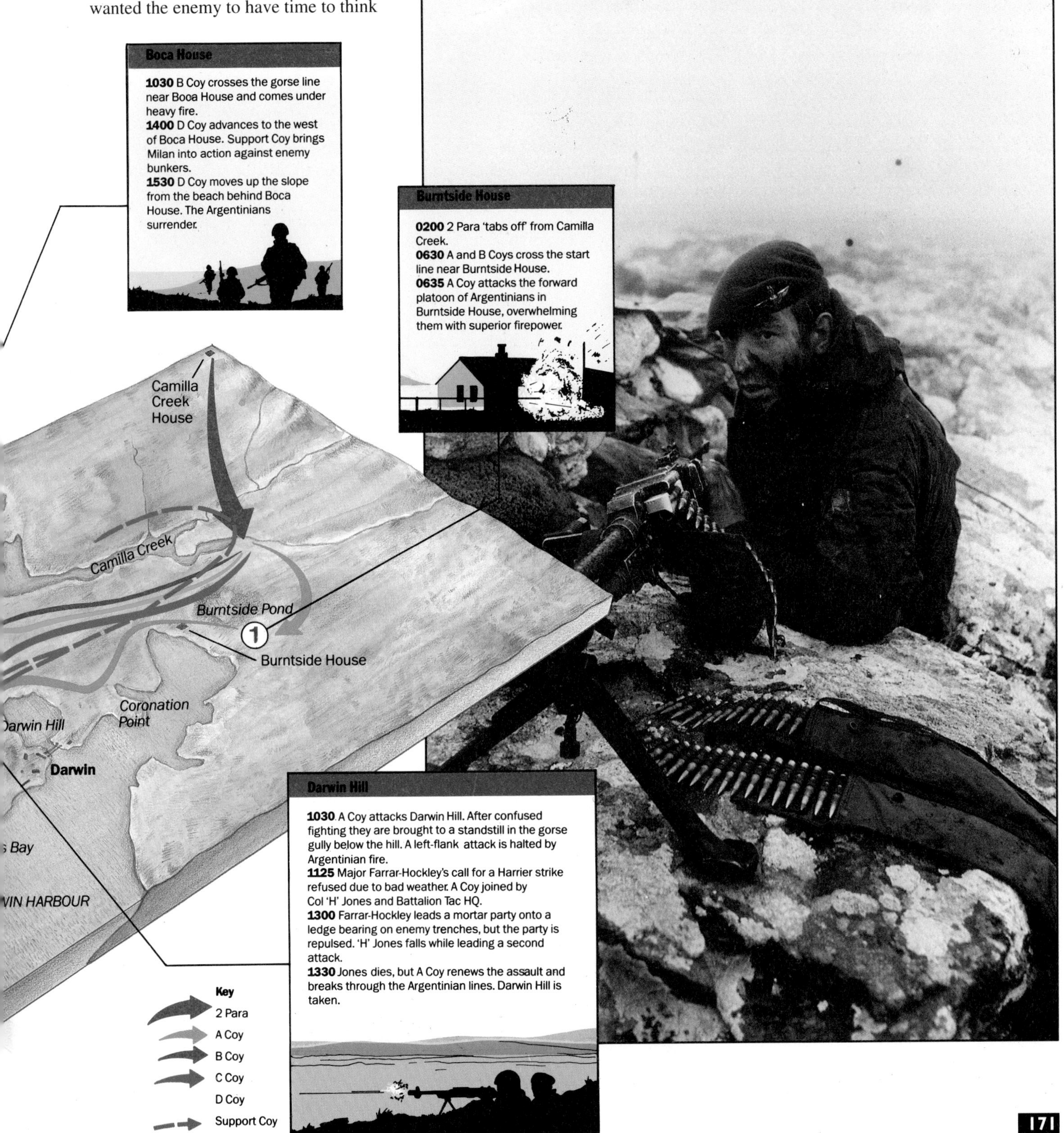

42 COMMANDO, MOUNT HARRIET, 11-12 JUNE 1982

In the spring of 1982, 42 Commando Royal Marines had just completed three months' arctic training in northern Norway. This was fortunate, for when the Argentinians invaded the Falklands it was the ideal unit to spearhead the retaking of the rocky, barren islands.

The unit had been landed at San Carlos on 21 May and had moved inland, engaging the enemy in sporadic actions. However, its most difficult task was the taking of Mount Harriet on 11-12 June. The mountain, codenamed 'Zoya', rises 300m above the plateau skirting Harriet Sound. Along the base of the mountain runs the track between Stanley and Goose Green. The nearby Wall Mountain had been occupied by forward observers, who directed a constant stream of artillery, mortar and naval fire against the Argentinians. The Commando, commanded by Lieutenant-Colonel Nick Vaux, was detailed to take Harriet. Vaux realised that a frontal attack would be suicidal because of mines and enemy machine guns that covered the forward slopes. The ground was very open to the south, and 'right flanking' wasn't really an option. The left offered a covered approach but 45 Commando would be operating there, and so there was a risk of the two units running into each other. Therefore, Vaux decided to conduct an attack from the rear.

A patrol led by Sergeant Collins of K Company tracked a route the Marines could take, though Vaux was still

BELOW: *On the road to Stanley. Tired Royal Marines in the Falklands, a picture that illustrates the miserable conditions the troops of the two sides had to fight in.*

Mount Harriet

42 Commando RM 11-12 June 1982

In the afternoon of 11 June 1982, as 3 Para prepared for its attack on Mount Longdon and 45 Commando readied itself for the assault on Two Sisters, 42 Commando concentrated on the slopes of Mount Challenger before moving off to attack Mount Harriet. Lt-Col Vaux's daring plan involved advancing to a start line southeast of the Argentinian positions. At 0200 the first elements of 42 Cdo crossed the line and the battle for Mount Harriet was on.

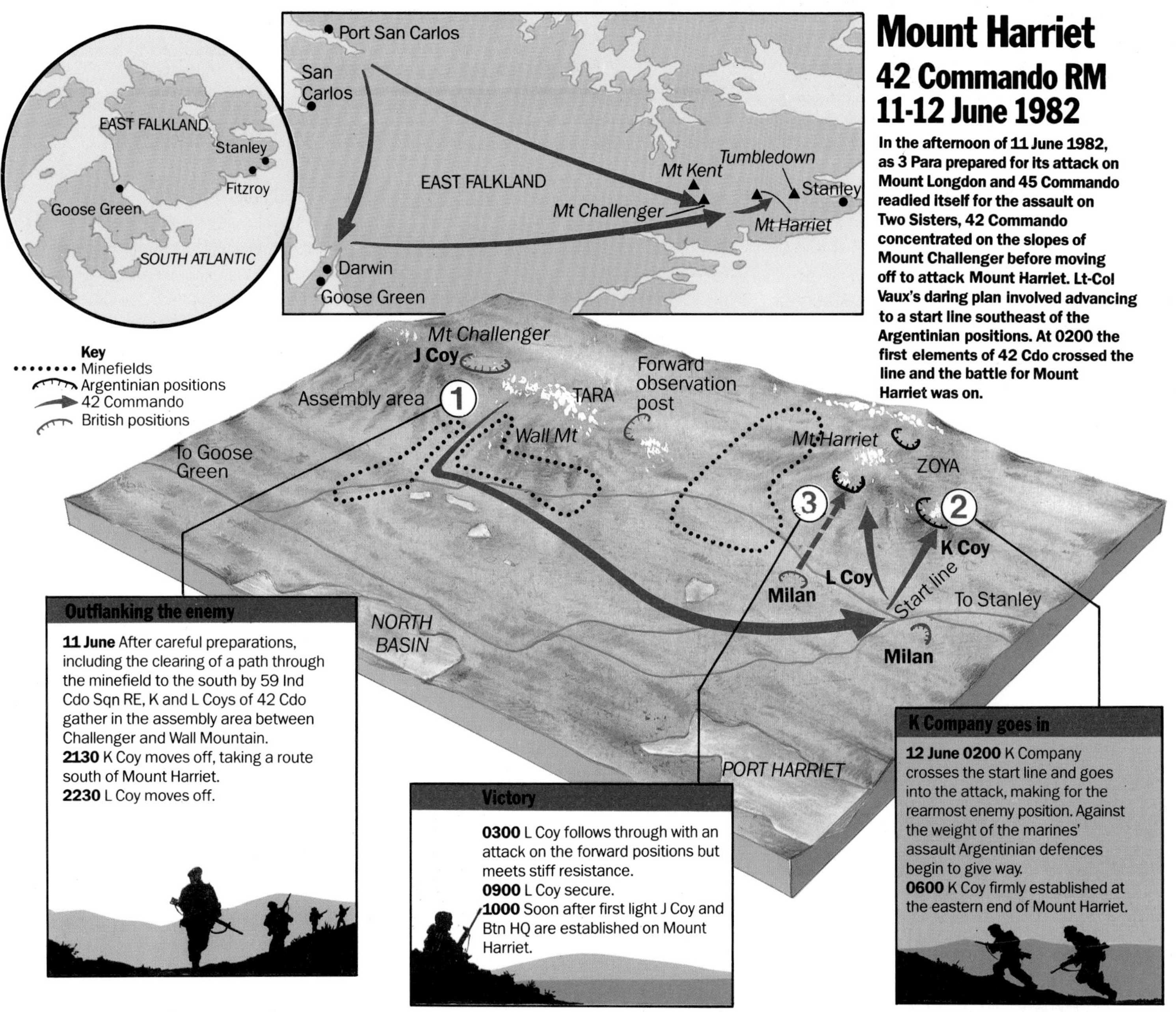

worried about his men trudging across very open ground, which might possibly be illuminated by moonlight. Therefore, artillery and mortar fire was directed at the enemy to distract them. However, the Marines still had to face a night-time march in the face of the enemy – one of the most difficult military manoeuvres.

There were a number of measures Vaux took to ensure his men would be as safe as possible. First, a number of Milans were stationed on Mount Wall to fire on the Argentinian positions when the assault got under way (the Milans didn't have night sights, so the Marines had to lull the enemy into firing on them, thus giving away their positions). Second, there was excellent coordination between two Royal Navy ships, three artillery batteries and 42's own Tac HQ concerning fire support.

The Commando began to move on the afternoon of 11 June, each man camouflaged and weighed down with extra ammunition and equipment. The weather was freezing as hundreds of men tiptoed along a narrow track. They reached the start line, to see 42's mortars illuminate the slope in front of them and the Milans crashing into the enemy machine-gun posts. The attack went in, pressed with vigour by the section commanders. Within minutes K Company had captured an Argentinian command post, several heavy machine guns and four 120mm mortars. L Company, which had been held in reserve, fared less well. It lost the element of surprise and came under heavy fire, which inflicted several casualties. However, the Marines pressed on, their courage and determination winning through.

By dawn the Tac HQ was on the summit of Mount Harriet. The Marines had won a fine victory because of a combination of an excellent assault plan, and, perhaps more importantly, the fighting qualities of the individual Marines themselves.

UNITED NATIONS COALITION FORCES, THE GULF WAR, JANUARY-FEBRUARY 1991

The campaign conducted by the forces of the United Nations against Iraq, following the latter's invasion of Kuwait in August 1990, provides an excellent example of how a modern large-scale military operation should be carried out. Around 600,000 troops of 18 nations took part in the war, with the United States providing the vast majority (some 532,000). The Americans were also given the opportunity of trying out a number of advanced weapons systems in a conventional war situation: F-117A Stealth fighters, Tomahawk cruise missiles, a variety of 'smart' munitions and AWACs aircraft.

A number of elite units were deployed against the Iraqis, among them the US 82nd Airborne Division and 101st Air Assault Division, US Marines, French Foreign Legion units, as well as a host of special forces formations: the US Green Berets, the SAS and the SBS. The Iraqi Army was also large, numbering some 60 divisions which included the elite Republican Guard. The Iraqis built formidable defences on the border between Kuwait and Saudi Arabia, but the air campaign that began in mid-January witnessed the assertion of total air supremacy by the Allies over both

BELOW: *The face of victory. An American soldier photographed during the land assault against Iraqi forces occupying Kuwait, February 1991.*

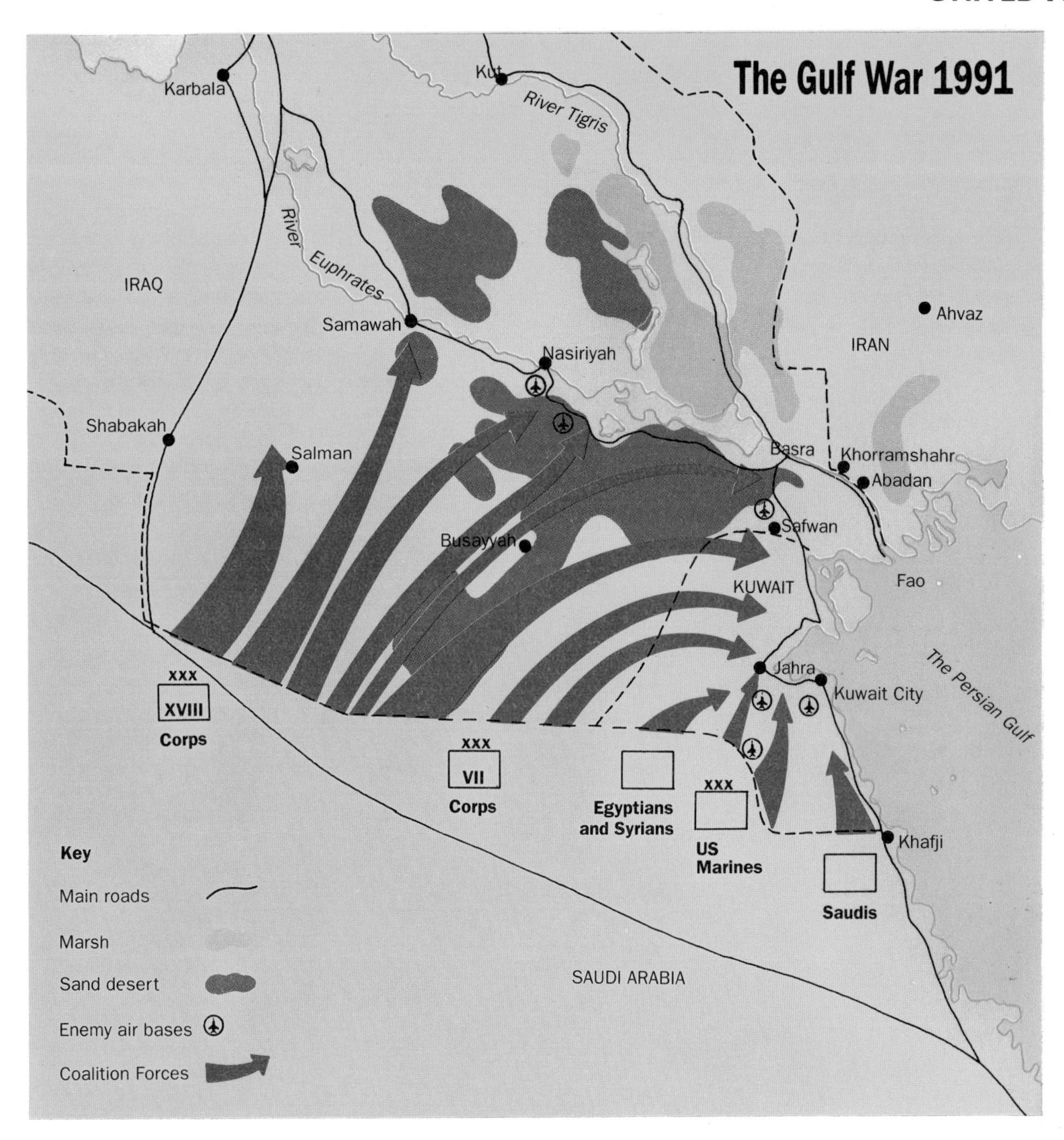

Kuwait and Iraq. Thereafter, an Iraqi defeat was assured. What most concerned Coalition leaders, especially those of the Western forces, was the need to avoid large casualties, a factor that ranked as zero in importance to the Iraqi leader, Saddam Hussein.

Therefore, the main Allied commanders – Generals Powell, Schwarzkopf and de la Billière – devised a plan whereby the main Allied attack would outflank the Iraqi defences and cut them off in a battle characterised by fluidity. In particular, it was important to prevent the Republican Guard units in the Iraqi rear from reinforcing the frontline units. Allied control of the air meant the Iraqis could not move their units at all, thus really sewing up the battle before it started. However, the success of Operation 'Desert Storm' should not be belittled, for it was an example of how an all-arms campaign should be fought.

Special forces units were inserted into Kuwait and Iraq before hostilities began, and they provided much-needed intelligence on enemy dispositions and strength, as well as destroying some of the Iraqi Scud launchers that were bombarding Israel. The only Iraqi attack, at Khafji on 30 January, was easily dealt with by the US Marines and the Saudi 8th National Guard Battalion.

The ground offensive began at 0100 hours on 24 February, the XVIII Corps, 101st Airborne Division and French 6th Daguet Division storming deep into Iraq. Next to XVIII Corps was VII Corps which included the 1st British Armoured Division. In the centre a mixed force of Arabs and US Marines punched a hole through the Iraqi defences, while on the right US Marines and Arab troops pushed on to Kuwait City. The Iraqis, pummelled by weeks of accurate air strikes, never had a chance to make a response.

By 28 February it was all over. For their loss of just over 200 killed, it is estimated that the Allies inflicted up to 100,000 fatalities on the Iraqis. The war had proved yet again that well-trained, well-led forces properly equipped will always overcome poorly trained, poorly led troops. It also illustrated the value of establishing air supremacy over the battlefield, and the contribution that special forces units can make.

Acknowledgements

Shlomo Arad: 144; **Associated Press:** 123; **Brown Packaging:** 162; **Bruce Quarrie:** 33; **ECPA:** 110; **Express Newspapers:** 171; **Robert Hunt Library:** 21, 39, 53, 54, 70; **IDF:** 133, 140; **IWM:** 35, 41, 48, 63, 164; **TRH Pictures:** 8-9, 15, 18, 64, 98-99, 100, 107, 108-109, 128, 130-131, 149, 160-161, 166, 167, 172; **US National Archives:** 126; **US DoD:** 2-3, 6-7, 7, 115, 118, 146-147, 156, 158, 174.
Artworks pages 159 & 175 by Graham Bingham
All other artworks by Becket-Nolan Partnership © Orbis Publishing